NEW HORIZONS AND CHALLENGES
IN ARMS CONTROL AND VERIFICATION

NEW HORIZONS AND CHALLENGES IN ARMS CONTROL AND VERIFICATION

JAMES BROWN
(editor)

VU UNIVERSITY PRESS
AMSTERDAM 1994

A publication of the John Goodwin Tower Center for Political Studies
Southern Methodist University, Dallas, Texas

VU University Press is an imprint of:
VU Boekhandel/Uitgeverij bv
De Boelelaan 1105
1081 HV Amsterdam
The Netherlands

tel. (020) - 644 43 55
fax (020) - 646 27 19

lay-out by Maria Louise Brookman, Amsterdam
typesetting by Mary McComas, Dallas
cover by D PS, Amsterdam
printed by Wilco, Amersfoort

isbn 90-5383-281-5
nugi 667

TABLE OF CONTENTS

PART III: **THE NON-PROLIFERATION TREATY: POLITICAL AND TECHNOLOGICAL ISSUES**

PART IV: **THE CHEMICAL WEAPONS CONVENTION: POLITICAL, TECHNICAL AND ECONOMIC CONSEQUENCES**

PART V: INSPECTIONS AND INSPECTORS: PERSPECTIVES ON VARIOUS TREATIES

PART VI: DISARMAMENT, VERIFICATION, AND ECONOMIC CHOICES

LIST OF ACRONYMS

ABACC	Argentina-Brazil Agency for Accounting and Control of Nuclear Materials
ABC	Atomic, Biological, and Chemical
ABM	Anti-Ballistic Missile
ACDA	Arms Control Defense Agency
ACME	Arms Control in the Middle East
ARPA	Advanced Research Projects Agency
ASEAN	Association of Southeast Asian Nations
AWAC	Airborne Early Warning and Control System
BTWC	Biological and Toxin Weapons Convention
BWC	Biological Weapon Convention
CBM	Continental Ballistic Missiles
CBO	Congressional Budget Office
CD	Conference on Disarmament
CFE	Conventional Forces in Europe Treaty
CIA	Central Intelligence Agency
CIS	Commonwealth of Independent States
CMA	Chemical Manufacturers Association
COCOM	Coordination Committee for Multilateral Export Controls
CSBM	Confidence-and-Security Building Measures
CSCE	Conference on Security and Cooperation in Europe
CTBT	Comprehensive Test Ban Treaty
CW	Chemical Weapons
CWC	Chemical Weapons Convention
DIA	Defense Intelligence Agency
DoD	Department of Defense
DOE	Department of Energy
EC	European Community
EEC	European Economic Community
EMIS	Electromagnetic Isotope Separation
ERM	Exchange Rate Mechanism
EURATOM	European Atomic Energy Community
FUSSR	Former USSR
G-7	Group of Seven (Canada, France, Italy, Japan, Russia, United Kingdom, and United States)
GATT	General Agreement on Trade and Tariffs
GCC	Gulf Cooperation Council
GDP	Gross Domestic Product
GPS	Global Protection System

HEU   Highly Enriched Uranium
IAEA   International Atomic Energy Agency
ICBMs   Intercontinental Ballistic Missiles
IDA   Institute for Defense Analysis
IGY   International Geophysical Year
INF   Intermediate Nuclear Forces Treaty

JCIC   Joint Compliance & Inspection Commission
JTPA   Job Training Partnership Act

KANUPP   Karachi Nuclear Power Plant

LTBT   Limited Test Ban Treaty

MBFR   Mutual & Balanced Force Reduction
MIRV   Multiple Independently Targeted Re-Entry Vehicle
MLRS   Multiple Launch Rocket System
MTCR   Missile Technology Control Regime

NACC   North Atlantic Cooperation Council
NATO   North Atlantic Treaty Organization
NBC   Nuclear, Biological, and Chemical
NIS   Newly Independent States
NNWS   Non-Nuclear Weapons States
NPT   Non-Proliferation Treaty
NRO   National Reconnaissance Office
NSA   National Security Agency
NSG   Nuclear Suppliers Group
NSF   National Science Foundation
NTM   National Technical Means
NWFZ   Nuclear-Weapon-Free Zone
NWS   Nuclear Weapons States

OAS   Organization of American States
OAU   Organization of African Unity
OECD   Organization of Economic Cooperation and Development
OPANAL   Organization for the Prohibition of Nuclear Weapons
OPCW   Organization for the Prohibition of Chemical Weapons

P-5   Permanent Five (China, France, Russia, United Kingdom, United
             States)
PAEC   Pakistan Atomic Energy commission
PD   Prisoners' Dilemma
PNET   Peaceful Nuclear Explosions Treaty
PREPCOM   Preparatory Commission

RDT&E   Research, Development, Test, and Evaluation

SALT	Strategic Arms Limitations Talks
SDI	Strategic Defense Initiative
SLBM	Submarine Launch Ballistic Missiles
SOW	Strategic Offensive Weapons
START	Strategic Arms Reduction Talks
SVC	Special Verification Commission
TOE	Table of Equipment
TRP	Technology Reinvestment Project
TTBT	Threshold Test Ban Treaty
UNSCOM	United Nations Special Commission (Iraq)
UNTAC	United Nations Transitional Authority in Cambodia
WANO	World Association of Nuclear Operators
WMD	Weapons of Mass Destruction

James Brown is Professor of Political Science and Ora Nixon Arnold Research Fellow in American Statesmanship and Diplomacy at Southern Methodist University. His Ph.D. in Political Science is from the State University of New York at Buffalo. He has written extensively on national security policy and civil-military relations, with works having appeared in *Armed Forces and Society, Journal of Political and Military Sociology, Polity, Defense Analysis,* and *Current History.* Professor Brown is a Member of the International Institute for Strategic Studies. He also has served as Special Assistant to Deputy Undersecretary of Defense for Planning and Resources at the Department of Defense and most recently as Foreign Affairs Specialist to the Director of the US Arms Control and Disarmament Agency. His latest books are entitled *Delicately Poised Allies: Greece and Turkey,* and *Challenges in Arms Control for the 1990s* (ed.).

* * * * * *

Alexander Baichorov is the director of the Department of International Security and Disarmament of the Ministry of Foreign Affairs, Republic of Belarus. He holds a Doctor of Science degree in political science from Belarus State University. Prior to joining the foreign ministry, Baichorov served as Political Affairs Officer in the United Nations Secretariat and Chairman of the Political Science Department at Belarus State University.

Kathleen C. Bailey is a Senior Fellow in the Center for Security and Technologies Studies, Lawrence Livermore National Laboratory. Prior to this position, Bailey served as Assistant Director of the US Arms Control and Disarmament Agency and Deputy Assistant Secretary of State in the Bureau of Intelligence and Research. She has a Ph.D. in comparative politics from the University of Illinois.

Thomaz G. Costa is a researcher with Brazil's National Research Council and professor in the Political Science Department of the University of Brasilia. He has also served as a consultant to the Organization of American States. Costa has published on issues affecting Brazil's defense and international security.

Lewis A. Dunn is Vice President and Manager of the Weapons Proliferation and Strategic Planning Department of the Science Applications International Corporation. He is also a former Assistant Director of the US Arms Control and Disarmament Agency. A prolific writer on arms control issues, he holds a Ph.D. in political science from the University of Chicago.

David Fischer has spent most of his professional career in association with the International Atomic Energy Agency (IAEA), having served in the capacity of Director of External Relations, Assistant Director General, and personal advisor to the Director General. Ambassador Fischer has published extensively on the subject of

nuclear proliferation and the proliferation of weapons of mass destruction and is
an authority on the NPT regime.

Ira N. Goldman, a Foreign Affairs Specialist with the US Department of Energy, has
published extensively in the areas of nuclear nonproliferation policy, arms control
and export control matters. Presently, Goldman is responsible for implementing
the US Government's programs in the area of international safeguards, nuclear inspections, and physical protection of nuclear material. He holds a master's degree
in international affairs from the Paul H. Nitze School of Advanced International
Studies, Johns Hopkins University.

Konstyantin Grischenko is presently the head of the Arms Control and Disarmament
Directorate of the Ministry of Foreign Affairs of the Ukraine. Prior to this posi-
tion, he has held a variety of appointments with the former Ministry of Foreign
Affairs of the Soviet Union. Grischenko has a graduate degree from Moscow
State Institute of International Relations.

H. J. van der Graaf is director of the Center for Arms Control and Verification at Eind-
hoven University of Technology. He was a member of the delegation from the
Netherlands to the third CSCE Follow-on Conference in Vienna. General van der
Graaf retired from the Royal Dutch Army in 1988 as a brigadier general. He was
recently appointed as a member of the United Nations Advisory Board on Disarmament Affairs.

Ahmad Kamal has had a distinguished career in the foreign service of Pakistan. He
presently is Ambassador and Permanent Representative of Pakistan to the United
Nations in Geneva. Kamal has studied at the Institut d'Etudes Politique in Paris,
the Fletcher School of Law and Diplomacy in the United States, and the London
School of Economics.

Jack L. Kangas, a professional staff member at the Institute for Defense Analyses, has
also served as a member of the START delegation, and as professor of public and
international affairs at the University of Pittsburgh. He holds a Ph.D. in political
science from Stanford University.

Edward J. Lacey is presently Assistant Vice President at the Pacific-Sierra Research
Corporation. Previously, he was Deputy Assistant Director of the US Arms Con-
trol and Disarmament Agency and also served as Ambassador to the International
Conference on Verification of the Biological Weapons Convention in Geneva.
Lacey holds a Ph.D. in political science from Rutgers University.

Ronald F. Lehman II is assistant to the director of Lawrence Livermore National Laboratory. Previously, he served as director of the US Arms Control and Disarmament Agency, Assistant Secretary of Defense for International Security Policy,
and the US chief negotiator for START. Ambassador Lehman received his Ph.D.
in government from Claremont Graduate School.

Sten Lundbo has had a distinguished career in the foreign service of Norway. He is presently Deputy Director General in the Royal Norwegian Ministry of Foreign Affairs. Lundbo holds a graduate degree from the Norwegian School of Economics and Business Administration in Bergen, Norway.

Evgenii P. Maslin is the director of the Principal Department of the Russian Ministry of Defense. A career officer who graduated from the military academy and the General Staff Military Academy, Maslin presently holds the rank of General-Colonel in the Russian armed forces.

Sean McCormack is an analyst with the Meridian Corporation. He is currently working in the fields of counterproliferation and arms control treaty implementation. A graduate of Colby College, McCormack holds a master's degree from the University of Maryland.

John W. Mentz is a senior analyst with the Meridian Corporation. He has served as a member of several US delegations to the Defense and Space Talks, the Treaty on Conventional Forces Europe, and the Open Skies Treaty.

Victor I. Mizin is a career foreign service officer, having served both in the USSR and Russian foreign ministries. He is presently head of the Department of Non-Proliferation and Export Control of the Russian Federation. He holds a Ph.D. in political science from the USSR Academy of Science Institute of USA and Canadian Studies.

Michael Moodie is president of the Chemical and Biological Arms Control Institute. Previously, he was Assistant Director of Multilateral Affairs of the US Arms Control and Disarmament Agency, and senior fellow and special advisor to the President at the Center for Strategic and International Studies. He has published extensively on issues affecting NATO, arms transfers, and Third World defense industries.

Michael O'Hanlon is weapons and arms control analyst at the Congressional Budget Office of the US Congress. His expertise is in the areas of conventional arms exports, the economics of verification, and the compliance of pending arms control treaties. O'Hanlon received a Ph.D. from the Woodrow Wilson School of Public and International Affairs, Princeton University.

R. Nicholas Palarino is director of the Policy, Security, and Technology Analysis Directorate of Pacific-Sierra Corporation. Prior to this position, Palarino was deputy special advisor to the President of the United States and the Secretary of State for arms control matters. Palarino holds a master's degree in international relations from Kansas State University.

Brad Roberts is the editor of *The Washington Quarterly* and a research fellow at the Center for Strategic and International Studies. His most recent publication, which was written for the International Institute for Strategic Studies in London, is entitled *Chemical Disarmament and International Security*, 1992. He is also the director of a Center for Strategic and International Studies' study group on chemical arms control.

Rachel Schmidt is an analyst with the National Security Division of the Congressional Budget Office of the US Congress, where she works on issues related to defense economics. Schmidt has also held positions as an economist with the US Department of Commerce and the RAND Corporation. She holds a Ph.D. from the RAND Graduate School.

Barbara A. B. Seiders is a defense analyst for Kaman Sciences Corporation. Prior to this present appointment, Seiders served as scientific and technical advisor to Ambassador James Goodby, US Negotiator for the Safe and Secure Dismantlement of Nuclear Weapons. Formerly a chief of research for the US Arms Control and Disarmament Agency, Seiders received her Ph.D. in theoretical quantum chemistry from Duke University.

Mohamed I. Shaker has had a distinguished career in the foreign service, having served in many high-level assignments, for the Arab Republic of Egypt. Presently, he is Ambassador to the United Kingdom. Other posts he has held in the service of his country include assignments at the United Nations in New York and Geneva. Shaker holds a Docteur des Sciences Politiques from the Graduate Institute of International Studies at the University of Geneva.

Donald B. Sole was a career diplomat in the foreign service of South Africa with the rank of Ambassador. He was one of the founders of the International Atomic Energy Agency and served for many years on its Board of Governors. He was also its chairman. Upon his retirement from the diplomatic service, he was appointed to the Board of Directors of the South African Atomic Energy Corporation. Sole is also a fellow of the South African Institute of International Affairs.

Michael O. Wheeler is senior defense analyst at Science Applications International Corporation and also served as special assistant to the Chairman of the Joint Chiefs of Staff as a member of the National Security Staff. He was on the team which negotiated the Missile Technology Control Regime. Wheeler received his Ph.D. in modern analytic philosophy from the University of Arizona.

Maurizio Zifferero is the Action Team Leader for the implementation by the International Atomic Energy Agency of United Nations Security Council Resolution 687 on Iraq. Previously, Zifferero had served as Deputy Director General of the IAEA and director of the Industrial Chemistry Division of the Italian Atomic Energy Commission. He holds a Ph.D. in nuclear and radiochemistry from the University of Rome.

ACKNOWLEDGMENTS

The chapters in this volume are a collection of papers which were commissioned for and presented at the Fourth Annual Conference "New Horizons and Challenges in Arms Control and Verification" held at Southern Methodist University in Dallas, Texas in October 1993, under the auspices of the John G. Tower Center for Political Studies .

I am most grateful and indebted to the conference participants for their thoughtful, well-researched, and stimulating papers which make up this volume. As a result, the decision to publish these symposium papers was an easy one, given the quality of work.

Financial support for this symposium came from the Advanced Research Projects Agency, our principal benefactor, with additional funding from our two corporate sponsors: Aquila Technologies Group, Inc. of Albuquerque, New Mexico, and Pacific-Sierra Research Corporation Center for Counterproliferation of Arlington, Virginia. I am most grateful to each of them for their sustaining interest and maintenance of this conference.

My special appreciation goes to my Administrative Assistant, Mrs. Mary McComas. Her diligent attention to detail in preparing the manuscript was superb, and I am also indebted to her for the valuable comments, commitment, and encouragement which she brought to this project. Without her unfailing support, this conference and this volume would not have come to fruition.

The merits of this work belong to the authors. The views expressed in these papers are not intended and should not be considered to represent the official ideas, views, attitudes, or policies of any agency of the United States Government or any other Government.

The editor is responsible for errors of fact and interpretation.

James Brown
editor

INTRODUCTION

With the demise of the Cold War and the breakup of the Soviet Union, efforts to prevent the proliferation of weapons of mass destruction (as well as conventional arms) into areas of frequent instability and conflict have markedly increased. In addition, the arms control and disarmament agenda has now shifted from its Cold War focus to a much broader and more diffused agenda of non-proliferation.

In this everchanging international environment, arms control and disarmament issues have now taken on a regional dimension. Innovative and creative solutions are necessary by taking the form of multilateral arrangements while at the same time continuing with the traditional focus of global and bilateral restraints. It would appear that multilateral approaches are most appropriate in the context where cooperative security is now fast becoming the norm. As the international community comes to realize the advantages of multilateral arrangements to arms control and disarmament, it can also anticipate that the community of nations will increasingly assign verification, confidence-building measures and peacekeeping roles to the United Nations and to regional security organizations (e.g., CSCE, NATO, OAS, UNSCOM, and WEU). By such actions, multilateral treaties (e.g., NPT, CWC, BWC, and MTCR) will enhance and strengthen the international communities' capabilities in addressing the problem of the proliferation of weapons of mass destruction and the accompanying spread of technological knowledge and information. These new security arrangements will also require innovative, creative, and at times intrusive verification regimes. No doubt national technical means continue to remain the bedrock on which verification regimes are created, but most likely these arrangements will also rest on an interlinking network of cooperative measures. Finally, if a long-term process of arms control reduction is to be actualized, intrusive verification regimes will also become commonplace in the treaties that are negotiated in the future.

The chapters included in this volume explore the several issues that were discussed previously as well as those issues which will be on the arms control and disarmament agenda in the decade to come. The opening remarks by Ambassador Ronald F. Lehman II suggest that a reexamination of our Cold War experiences may assist us in undertaking the arms control challenges which are ahead. He suggests that arms control should be defined broadly to include non-proliferation, defense conversion, confidence- and security-building measures, aspects of preventative diplomacy, and the like, in addition to limitations, restrictions, reductions, and elimination of armaments. This more comprehensive definition, Lehman prefers, more accurately reflects the interaction experienced in the Cold War arena and also more readily addresses the problems that still need to be solved. Much of the Cold War strategy was preoccupied with deterrence theory. Now our attention is focused on the problem of the "undeterrables" -- be they nihilistic terrorists or reckless national leaders. Lehman offers to the reader a list of ten experiences of possible lessons learned from the Cold War. These experiences range from arms control being an integral part of a nation's national security and foreign policy, to avoidance of mirror-imaging, and of arms control involving both competition and cooperation whereby positions change and even reverse to reflect tactical and strategic dynamics and the wider military and political climate. Each of these hypothetical lessons learned looks differently when matched against specific chapters of the negotiating history of the Cold War. Will these rules have significant applications in the world that is before us? Lehman contends that examining these lessons will help determine whether arms control's contributions have been significant in the past and whether they can be significant in the future.

Part I of this collection includes four chapters that examine arms control issues from the perspective of the Commonwealth of Independent States (CIS). The first presentation is by Victor Mizin, who argues that Russia will continue to retain a considerable amount of military power and other countries need to be aware of this, regardless of Russia's obvious socio-economic and political weaknesses. No doubt Russian-US contacts on strategic issues will continue to retain their special character. This special relationship, Mizin argues, will help foster other nuclear powers to enter the post-START nuclear reduction process. Furthermore, Russia is also prepared to explore a Comprehensive Test Ban Treaty. In addition to supporting the NPT extension process, Moscow is also interested in strengthening export control regulations. Mizin argues that it would be unwise for Russia to join the MTCR if COCOM restrictions are not lifted against her. According to the author, there is no doubt that Russia is bound geopolitically to be a great power. It cannot be pushed out of the world political scene because of its present critical domestic situation, but Moscow must continue to seek practical cooperation from the entire world community.

In Chapter Two, General-Colonel Evgenii Maslin argues that there is no single and simple way to avoid the thereat of nuclear weapons proliferation. No country alone can prevent nuclear proliferation; therefore, international cooperation is necessary in order to attain this goal. When discussing the future of nuclear weapons of the former Soviet Union, Maslin contends that with the signing of the Lisbon Protocol, Belarus, Kazakhstan and Ukraine became participants to the START Treaty. By all appearances, all three of these countries are nuclear powers if it were not for their commitment under the Lisbon Protocol to join the NPT as nuclear-free states. This is the case for both Belarus and Kazakhstan. However, Ukraine is, according to the author, a *de facto* nuclear state. The Ukrainian aspirations to possess nuclear weapons is evidenced by the creation of new structures, in particular, the so-called Center of Administrative Control of the Strategic Nuclear Forces of the Ministry of Defense. Maslin also strongly contends that the nuclear weapons possessed by Ukraine are not being adequately inspected nor stored. As a result, it was noted that one nuclear storage area contained more that six to eight times the necessary decommissioned nuclear munitions which could be stored safely; consequently, the temperature and radiation levels of these stored weapons had increased to less-than-safe levels. Such conditions could create a highly explosive situation that threatens first the Ukraine and then its neighbors. The Russian government has attempted to forestall Ukraine's' actions by acceding to the Crimean Agreement in which all of Ukrainian wishes were taken into consideration. Even then, according to Maslin, Kiev evaded the exact date when nuclear munitions would be removed from its territory. Further, Ukraine has raised a claim of indemnity for the cost of the highly-enriched uranium that was contained in its tactical nuclear weapons. The author contends that this demand is illegal. Ultimately, Maslin argues, the way the Ukrainian nuclear weapons issues will be solved will be telling regarding the future of the NPT in 1995 and beyond. Destroying the NPT regime may change the whole view of collective security, whereby many nations will view their national security needs with nuclear weapons.

Konstyantin Grischenko in Chapter Three argues very strongly for the Ukrainian position on nuclear weapons, quite unlike Maslin. It is Grischenko's contention that the Ukrainian situation has been presented in an oversimplified manner based on false assumptions that Ukraine is attempting to renege on its obligations. In reality, Ukraine as an equal successor state to the former USSR has acquired ownership of all nuclear weapons located on its territory, and this is based on international law. Ultimately, Ukraine's decision will depend upon the outcome of the debate in her parliament. The central question to be answered is in what way will Ukraine's security be enhanced or diminished as a result of Kiev's either retaining its nuclear weapons or becoming non-nuclear and relying on other means to guarantee its independence and security. In order for Ukraine to become a non-nuclear power, Grischenko argues, effective guarantees must be given for Ukraine's security by the international community and full compensation accorded for both strategic and tactical nuclear weapons still on its territory. Supporting a strong independent Ukraine is in the best interest of the US, NATO, and the West in general. Ukraine, according to the writer, represents the best guarantee against the recreation of a new neighboring empire which will inevitably endanger the emerging new world democratic order.

The last chapter in Part I is by Alexander Baichorov, who discusses arms control and disarmament issues from the perspective of Belarus. He contends that the most pressing problem for Belarus is the elimination and control of its conventional arms within the CFE requirements and the costs that will be increased in destroying the conventional side of Belarus' security needs. The concern for Belarus is how some of the knotty issues within the CIS will be resolved, namely the status of nuclear weapons in the Ukraine, the Russian-Ukrainian Crimea and Black Sea Fleet, and the menace of ethnic rivalries and Islamic fundamentalism. How Belarus handles its arms control and disarmament issues will depend, according to Baichorov, on the safety and stability of the existing area that surrounds Belarus.

Part II includes six chapters on the topic of regional issues of arms control and verification. The fifth chapter, by Michael Moodie, discusses regional arms control as perhaps being the single most important arms control priority in the years ahead. With the end of the Cold War, instability and conflict arising from regional confrontations is the greatest danger to international security, and arms control represents an important instrument in responding to this challenge. Moodie argues that regional arms control must become a stronger feature of the international security landscape. Perhaps the most severe barrier is a skeptical if not negative attitude that exists among many regional states. In some cases, that attitude is shaped by lack of experience. Beyond the question of experience, however, is the existence of the strong perception that the use of military power is likely to remain a feature of their regional environments for the foreseeable future; therefore, national interest must be protected and advanced with all available policy instruments, including armaments. Moodie contends that, as evidenced by the initiatives taken in the Middle East, there are some hopeful signs on the horizon such as agreements on confidence-building measures between Pakistan and India, the bilateral nuclear inspection agreements between North and South Korea, and a number of developments in Latin America and in the Organization of American States. Arms control must be shown to work in order to overcome suspicions and mistrust, not only of potential adversaries but also of the arms control process itself.

David Fischer's chapter focuses on global and regional efforts to control nuclear proliferation. By increasing the danger of nuclear war, the spread of nuclear weapons puts all nations at risk, but above all the proliferating state itself and its neighbors. Hence in regions of high tension and high technological achievement, regional controls must be joined onto global safeguards. Fischer argues that only a global system can ensure the universal application of uniform standards, and the three decades of IAEA safeguards experience constitute a unique asset; nonetheless, bilateral/regional systems can greatly enhance the NPT safeguards. Such regional arrangements, including adversarial monitoring, may be the only way to coax the determined hold-outs like Israel, but in the more stable or less technologically advanced regime, global safeguards alone are quite sufficient. It is the author's contention that if global safeguards are indispensable, the IAEA should be the appropriate organization to implement this task.

Donald B. Sole's offering in Chapter Seven discusses the case of South Africa, which recently admitted to manufacturing and possessing nuclear weapons and to Pretoria's willingness to destroy them. This chapter surveys the history of the development of South Africa's nuclear energy industry and the decision in the early 1970s to develop the country's own enrichment process, including the question as to whether this was motivated primarily by scientific/industrial needs or by military assistance and cooperation from any other state or states. These issues, Sole contends, must be seen in the context of South Africa's political situation, regional and international, characterized by increasing isolation until 1990. Also examined are the changes that took place after 1990 which ultimately lead to South Africa's dismantling its entire nuclear weapons program.

Ahmad Kamal's presentation focuses on nuclear proliferation in South Asia. The situation, according to the author, is a particularly dangerous mix of deep historical tensions on which a potential nuclear capacity has now been superimposed. Even though nuclear restraint has been exercised by both Pakistan and India, the basic tensions run deep, and the history of three wars is so recent, that international concern about the situation is totally justified. Kamal argues that the incentives toward nuclear proliferation in South Asia appear unstoppable. It is India that has consistently taken the initiative by embarking on its nuclear development program from as early as 1948 and by ceaselessly upgrading its capacity thereafter, as well as developing advanced delivery systems. Pakistan's policy, on the other hand, has been largely reactive, running about 10-20 years behind India's for each of the different stages of the nuclear ladder. Kamal contends that since Pakistan does not have any regional or global ambitions, it has presented a significant number of proposals for the regional reversal of a nuclear race in South Asia. Without exception, all of these proposals have been rejected by India. It is now a growing international realization that the regional approach to disarmament holds the greatest promise in the South Asian nuclear non-proliferation context.

Chapter Nine by Mohamed Shaker discusses the establishment of a nuclear-weapons-free zone and a zone free of weapons of mass destruction in the Middle East. The author argues that the Middle East is still politically unsettled and military conflicts can erupt at any moment because of historically deep-rooted problems. Furthermore, the disintegration of the Soviet Union has led to the availability or potential suppliers of equipment and material which could become components of such weapons. All of these serve as potential sources of instability and do not promote cooperation or enhance confidence among the States of the region. The breakthrough in the peace process between Israel and the Palestine Liberation Organization has engendered hope that one day the negotiators will also be able to come up with a plan which will create and establish the two zones. The Multilateral Working Group on Arms Control and Regional Security of the Madrid process offers the best opportunity to do so. Others have succeeded in Antarctica, Latin America, and the South Pacific; therefore, the Middle East can follow, according to Shaker, even at the expense of meeting this challenge which is fraught with extraordinary difficulties.

Finally, Chapter Ten by Michael O'Hanlon discusses a number of ideas for limiting arms supplies to countries in the Middle East. This region accounts for only 3 percent of the world's population, but in the 1980s it bought an average 30 percent of the world's military goods and services. Given the volatile brew of this region, the world's major powers, no longer fundamentally at odds geopolitically, need a well-defined strategic logic to guide Middle East policy. O'Hanlon proposes a binding cartel arrangement which would focus on the CFE categories of weapons and would limit annual deliveries of arms to each Middle East country. Other proposals that have been made to limit arms supplies to this region are also reversed. Overall, O'Hanlon suggests that a policy that might be appropriate at this time in history is to pressure suppliers not to arm Persian Gulf countries beyond certain relatively modest and common inventory levels. Once those levels are reached, there would be a presumption of denial of future sales unless special circumstances warranted an exemption. Because of its focus on inventories of major weapons systems and the concept of parity between countries on which it would be based, this policy would also share several features with the CFE Treaty. This approach would impose restraints that would have a significant effect upon the scale of regional arms acquisitions. In the end, O'Hanlon believes, the US would be the beneficiary of such a policy. It would reduce the threat to US security and in the end facilitating further defense spending cuts, which would help ensure that the US force structure now planned will be capable of easily countering adversaries which may rise up against American interests in the future.

Part III considers the issues that pertain to the Non-Proliferation Treaty and its renewal in 1995. In Chapter Eleven, Kathleen Bailey discusses four challenges to the nuclear non-proliferation regime and points that they are unlikely to be overcome successfully. If diplomacy and peace efforts fail to prevent the proliferation of nuclear weapons, there will be, according to Bailey, two options left open to the United States. The first is counterproliferation, which includes military action, countermeasures against weapons delivery systems, weapons disablement, and sabotage of weapons capabilities. The author does note that at times counterproliferation measures entail unacceptable risks. The other option noted is deterrence, which may be the easiest response and in many situations may be the most successful. Few proliferant nations are likely to risk annihilation and will therefore be unwilling to threaten other nuclear weapons states. Also deterrence against proliferates is crucial for US non-proliferation policy vis a vis the capable-but-restrained nations like South Korea, Japan, and Germany. Without a strong US extended nuclear deterrent, these nations are likely to seek their own nuclear arsenal. Bailey notes, however, that despite the importance of nuclear deterrence to US national security and dependence of many nations on the US nuclear deterrent, that deterrent is weakening. New weapons need to be tested. Any negotiations of a comprehensive test ban should take into consideration the continuing need for US testing, not only as a means of improving future nuclear designs but also as a way of proving to allies which agree not to proliferate that the US nuclear umbrella over them works.

A companion article to this section is by Ira Goldman, who reviews the NPT regime and its limited verification provisions and essentially non-existent provisions for assessment of compliance and enforcement obligations. The author also points out a chronology of instances in which the NPT compliance questions have been raised, including the cases of Sweden, Romania, Iraq, and North Korea. Goldman also notes several efforts to improve NPT verification, compliance, and enforcement focusing on Articles II and III of the Treaty. The author argues that the NPT remains the cornerstone of international efforts to prevent the further proliferation of nuclear explosives, and the ideas he put forth in the article were offered in the context of strengthening the Treaty's implementation and ensuring its extension in 1995, while recognizing that many of these views require additional analysis and many prove to be politically and technically unfeasible or difficult to implement.

Chapter Thirteen by Jack Kangas delves into Article VI of the NPT regime which established *inter alia* a direct relationship or linkage between non-proliferation of nuclear weapons and the nuclear weapons policies of the then nuclear weapons states -- in other words, between horizontal and vertical proliferation. The author points out that Article VI has been for some twenty-five years a bone of contention between nuclear and non-nuclear states. Kangas revises the historical origins of Article VI and debates over its implementation, the objectives begin both to explain why this article has proven so difficult to operationalize and to probe the relevance of the historical record for the immediate and long-term future. Of central concern to the author is the question of the utility of the concept of linkage between arms control regimes. He suggests that the US government's position leading to the NPT was the correct one: avoid linkage. The discussion of the risks associated with getting on what could be a "slippery slope" and the faulty premises upon which Article VI of the NPT appears to have been formulated was intended to demonstrate that US policymakers should be cautious about linkage, both in a theoretical sense and in the specific case of the NPT.

The last piece in this section is by Lewis Dunn, who explores the problems and prospects for an indefinite extension of the NPT in 1995. Indefinite extension would be most consistent with the key role played by the NPT in supporting global non-proliferation efforts. However, even with intensified US leadership, many difficult problems loom on the horizon and an indefinite extension in 1995 may simply not be attainable. The author argues that single-minded focus on the goal of indefinite extension, moreover, may both intensify the risk of deadlock and make it more difficult to use the 1995 Extension Conference as a means to pursue more limited but achievable steps to strengthen the overall global non-proliferation regime of which the NPT is but one part. To explore these issues Dunn places the NPT in the broader context of global non-proliferation efforts. Some of the challenges to the indefinite extension of the NPT are then examined and assessed. This chapter goes on to establish some guidelines for NPT extension diplomacy of the US and concludes with a discussion of possible ways to use the Extension Conference and the review of the NPT that will accompany it to strengthen the overall US nuclear non-proliferation efforts. Rather than viewing the 1995 Extension Conference simply as a damage control exercise, it should be seen as a valuable forum to enhance non-proliferation overall. To ensure success, Dunn argues that the United States needs to take the lead to shape the terms of the debate in order to rally support among all NPT parties for a renewable long-term, if not necessarily indefinite, extension of the Treaty.

In *Part IV,* the focus is on the Chemical Weapons Convention and the resultant political, technical, and economical consequences. Brad Roberts, in Chapter Fifteen, assesses the prospects for the new CWC at approximately the mid-point between its opening for signature in January 1993 and its intended entry into force in January 1995. The author describes in some detail the work of the international community to put in place the new treaty regime and assesses the likelihood of its entry into force in a timely fashion. The analysis underscores the continuing political challenges confronting the chemical disarmament effort, especially as they derive from a treaty conceived in the Cold War but crafted as a principal instrument on international security in the post-Cold War setting. The widespread disinterest in the CWC in 1993 is not surprising, given the dramatic events around the world. Being outside of the spotlight has in fact facilitated the work of diplomats at The Hague, but if the pattern continues in 1994, we can be certain that deteriorating circumstances will thrust the issue center-stage at a later, more difficult time.

It is Barbara Seider's argument that the Chemical Weapons Convention departs from a trend of stringently verifiable arms control agreements and constitutes more a tool of confidence-building rather than a tool for measuring unacceptable behavior in development and production of chemical weapons. Whatever confidence the CWC might provide is purchased at cost which the United States has weighed and has determined to pay. The compromises necessary for the conclusion of the CWC are costly to the US not just in terms of resources, but also in terms of fundamental principles. Given the potential stakes, the US must be cautious in weighing perceived benefits against costs that can be both extraordinary and subtle. Washington, according to Seiders, must be vigilant that marginal benefits are not purchased at a detriment of undermining the enduring principles of this nation.

Sten Lundbo provides the reader in Chapter Seventeen with a survey of the negotiations on and the implementation of the CWC. The author points out that the CWC is the first disarmament treaty to be agreed upon by the Geneva Conference since the Biological Toxin Weapons Convention in 1971; however, the CWC was much more the result of a truly multilateral process and therefore represents a major achievement for multilateral disarmament. It should also be noted that this is the first global disarmament treaty to which China has been a partner in the negotiation process. Lundbo argues that this Convention is important because it bans an entire category of weapons of mass destruction and because it contains more comprehensive verification mechanisms than any previous disarmament treaty. Furthermore, the principle of short-notice challenge inspections is an innovation in the field of global disarmament. Effective implementation of the CWC demonstrates that it is worthwhile to negotiate multilateral disarmament treaties with such comprehensive verification mechanisms. In this way, Lundbo suggests, the CWC will serve as a guideline for future global disarmament treaties, in particular for the negotiations on a comprehensive nuclear test ban treaty, which will be considered in 1994 at the Conference on Disarmament.

The final piece in this section is by R. Nicholas Palarino, who examines the evolution and the ramifications of the US decision to advocate the CWC challenge inspection regime. The author argues that the Reagan administration's requirements to ensure that the CWC be a verifiable agreement is at odds with the fact that this agreement would need to be verified in the US as well as in other State Parties' territories. The Reagan administration proposed a verification regime that placed substantial and unforeseen burdens on the defense community. Sensitive assets would now be subject to inspection by China, Iran, France and any other State Party that might be on a challenge inspection team. In addition, the author has grave concern that the CWC might be used as a vehicle to collect proprietary business information. Furthermore, Palarino notes that there exists uncertainty of the roles and the requirements for implementation which are compounded by the addition of a non-traditional arms control inter-agency participant, namely the Department of Commerce. The author concludes on a note of caution regarding the safety of US national security assets and the rights of US citizens and industry under the terms of the CWC. Palarino feels that the above concerns were not considered in the negotiation phase but must be dealt with now. The United States must accept the ramifications of these decisions and prepare for implementation.

Part V of this volume discusses the role of inspections and inspectors in implementing arms control agreements. Chapter Nineteen by Sean McCormack and John Mentz identifies three general trends for inspections in the new post-Cold War era. These inspections consist of the dominant role played by multinational inspectorates, the leveling of current trends toward increasingly greater intrusiveness in inspections, and the increased use of inspections as international political tools. The authors note that with the INF Treaty inspections have become an important and integral part of arms control agreements. Regardless of their use, inspections have been driven by, and may be characterized by, the domestic arms control agenda. McCormack notes a shift from bilateral/Euro-centric focus to a multilateral regional focus as a means to stem the flow of the proliferation of weapons of mass destruction. The three trends that were identified are alternatively complementary and antagonistic. Regardless of which trend dominates, it is clear that inspections have entered a new era distinct from the recent Cold War past.

It is Edward Lacey's presentation in Chapter Twenty that examines the little known Antarctica Treaty of 1959 which pioneered the on-site inspection concept as routine inspections, "anytime, anywhere" inspections, and aerial overflight to verify compliance with arms control commitments. Every "inspection" has complete freedom of access at anytime to any or all areas of Antarctica. These on-site inspection provisions are vital in verifying the total ban on all military activities on this continent. They are also valuable for the important precedent they set for on-site inspections in later arms control treaties such as the INF, START, and CWC. Indeed, Lacey notes that the Antarctica Treaty inspections have become an important, if limited, source of practical experience to draw upon for other treaty regimes. This regime plays a major role in assuring the community of nations that the Antarctica continent remains at all times demilitarized and reserved solely for peaceful pursuits. The confidence that these inspections have engendered has led to over three decades of international cooperative effort in the peaceful scientific exploration of the frozen continent. Indeed, Lacey notes that in this new era of global cooperation, the Antarctica treaty inspection regime may well become the model for future cooperative efforts in arms control verification and confidence-building.

Maurizio Zifferero discusses in Chapter Twenty-One the role of the IAEA and the lessons learned in Iraq. The picture that emerged, after over twenty or so inspections, is that of Iraq having a widely-based, well-founded, multi-pronged approach to the production of highly-enriched uranium, combined with a parallel program to assess the requirements and make the necessary preparations for designing and manufacturing a nuclear weapon. It is Zifferero's contention that the essential components of Iraq's nuclear program have been brought to light. However, the events in Iraq have not only highlighted the need to strengthen the IAEA safeguards system but also have heightened the readiness of governments to contribute to these improvements. There is no doubt that the IAEA system has worked well in verifying the non-diversion of declared nuclear material at declared nuclear installations. The system, however, was not geared to provide assurances that no undeclared nuclear installations and consequently nuclear materials existed. According to Zifferero, it was not timidity but the lack of information about undeclared sites meriting inspection that prevented the discovery of Iraq's clandestine program.

Henny van der Graaf's offering in Chapter Twenty-Two examines verification in the context of the Cambodian settlement which was conducted under the auspices of the United Nations Security Council. The concept of monitoring and verifying, in this case, goes far beyond formally negotiated treaty specific verification requirements which were common during the Cold War era. In fact, the author points out that this is not a new phenomenon, having been used in Angola, Namibia, Nicaragua and El Salvador. In the Cambodian case, verification has been used as an instrument in the process of peacemaking and peacekeeping. Van der Graaf contends that this can serve as an example of conflict prevention and conflict resolution including peace operations. Furthermore, the primary function of verification is to verify compliance and deter violations as was in the case. Confidence-building measures should never be the primary purpose of verification. The author notes that the shift in emphasis from treaty specific verifications to verification in a broader context does not mean that the era of formally negotiated arms limitation and disarmament treaties has become obsolete. In fact, verifying the recently concluded agreements of CWC, START, and CFE will be ongoing processes. It is time for the United Nations to explore the lessons learned not only from the Cambodian case, but from other instances, and begin to apply these lessons to the new political realities found today in the international arena.

Chapter Twenty-Three, by Thomaz Costa, contributes to our understanding of how threat perception relates to international inspectors and how this relationship has affected efforts to verify the non-proliferation of weapons of mass destruction in South America. The analysis centers on Brazil's experience with its nuclear policy, particularly its efforts to acquire technological "know-how," and the effect such a policy has on its strategic interactions. This study examines Brazil's efforts in playing two simultaneous strategic "games": one was played with Argentina at the regional level while the other was with the United States in affecting the NPT regime. The author concludes that inspections and mutual confidence-building measures moved hand-in-hand at the regional level. Mistrust, however, continues on the part of Brazil for the IAEA, which it feels serves the interests of the nuclear powers in preserving their technological dominance as well as in controlling the commercial markets for the civilian use of nuclear energy. Costa's paper serves as a warning of how an actor, in this case Brazil, preferred alternative explanations of others' intentions which eventually affected its strategic options, thus bringing about undesired consequences for decisions by policymakers.

The *final section* contains two very important pieces that address arms control and disarmament issues from the perspective of economics and of controlling the proliferation of missiles worldwide. The first piece in this section is written by Rachel Schmidt, who discusses recent US experiences in disarmament and the freeing-up of government resources that could otherwise be used on military purchases. In the case of the United States, these resources are considerable. The author suggests that they be redirected to reduce the federal deficit or to fund public investments which increase productivity, in turn leading ultimately to higher economic growth and a higher standard of living. However, in the near term, she notes that the transition to a less defense-oriented economy would be painful for many workers, communities, and businesses. Schmidt further suggests two approaches for the federal government to follow to ease this transition. The first, as supported by the Clinton Administration, is to consider future industrial production capabilities explicitly in its acquisition decisions today. The second approach involves new spending for defense conversion initiatives. This latter approach will be an issue of contention throughout this decade. Some members of Congress would prefer either that a heavier emphasis be put on federal support to assist workers and communities or that procurement reform be the primary means of promoting civil-military integration.
The last chapter of this volume, by Michael Wheeler, explores the trade in missiles and missile technology and the lessons learned for controlling advanced weapons systems. Specifically, the author examines the Missile Technology Control Regime as a case study from four points of view: the technologies behind modern missiles; the worldwide politics of arms control in the current transitional era; the commercial complications posed by so-called "dual use" systems; and the economics of missile trade and how decisions thereon are taken by different governments. The conclusion that Wheeler reaches is that the MTCR should correctly be seen more as a defensible exercise in balance-of-power politics and less as an attempt to create arms control norms, where norms are understood in terms of internationally-sanctioned bans on trade in nuclear, chemical, and biological weapons.

In conclusion, it is the editor's hope that this volume will stimulate further interest, debate, and analysis at the governmental, industrial, public, and academic levels. Clarification of the strengths and weaknesses of past policies and approaches will ultimately assist in enhancing arms control and verification issues for the international community in the difficult and uncharted waters of the decades ahead.

AMERICAN PERSPECTIVES ON COLD WAR ARMS CONTROL: THE BEGINNING OF THE END OR THE END OF THE BEGINNING?

Ronald F. Lehman II

Ladies and Gentlemen. Friends and Colleagues. I have been asked to open the discussion today by presenting the American perspective on Cold War arms control and the lessons learned from that experience. Other speakers from a number of nations will give contrasting, supplementary, or complementary views. Then we are to sort fact from fiction and derive clear and unanimous guidance for dealing with issues such as Bosnia, North Korea, and the Middle East.

My task is particularly challenging because, in the United States, we do not have a single American perspective on arms control. We must speak in the plural. We must speak of American perspectives. During the Cold War, opinion leaders were often deeply divided on the nature of the Soviet threat and on the role of arms control. Now that the Soviet Union no longer exists, the distinctions of the past have blurred somewhat. Minds have turned to new issues. Memories have become imprecise and in some cases inaccurate. Some disputes have been settled, others have been forgotten or set aside. A tenuous working plurality did emerge in American arms control at the end of the Reagan Administration, and it continued during most of the Bush years. This plurality, however, was never the consensus that is sometimes described in today's rhetoric.

As America approaches contemporary international security issues, new forms of the old divisions are becoming quite evident. Perhaps less polarization exists in current debate, but replays of past disputes and widespread uncertainty about the future in foreign affairs have prevented the emergence of an American consensus on foreign policy or arms control. Who is the threat? Where are our vital interests? What is the purpose of arms control? Should we negotiate further? With whom? And on what?

Are there useful lessons from the recent history of arms control which can help us answer such questions? Yes, but they must be tempered by some lessons which should have been learned many years before. We have entered what is now most often called the "post-Cold War era." That we today name this period by reference to the past rather than the future should not be surprising. No obvious name or phrase has captured what we think is to come. Indeed, we face great uncertainty and numerous alternatives. In speaking of things "post-Cold War," we are recognizing the great impact of that relatively short span of history we called the Cold War. We are recognizing a period of transition. We are also recognizing the important changes now underway. We do not know how long the post-Cold War era will last and to what degree the age which follows will reflect the forces of the Cold War period or the forces which existed before the Cold War or new forces.

As we look at the challenges we face in the years ahead, we can maximize the benefits gained from a re-examination of our Cold War experiences in arms control by defining arms control broadly. Arms control should be understood to include nonproliferation, defense conversion, confidence-and-security-building measures (CSBMs), aspects of preventive diplomacy, and the like, in addition to limitations, restrictions, reductions and eliminations of armaments. This is a broader approach than some popular usage, but this comprehensive definition more accurately reflects the interactions we experienced in the Cold War arena and more readily addresses the problems we still wish to solve.

Some of the problems we confront today are remnants of the Cold War. The end of the Cold War was declared long before all of its by-products were removed from the international sphere. Much work remains if we are to leave the Cold War well behind us. For example, implementing arms control agreements already reached, such as the two START Treaties and the Chemical Weapons Convention, is proving difficult in the midst of the political turmoil created by the breakup of the Soviet Union. Bilateral difficulties are frequently now multinational. And a divided-nation relic of the Cold War poses a particularly dangerous situation as North Korea pursues nuclear weapons.

Tools useful to the solution of problems pre-dating or independent of the Cold War also may emerge as we consider "lessons learned" from the Cold War experience. For example, confidence-building measures (CBMs), which evolved in a complex and often highly formalized way in the East-West context, are being explored in the Arms Control and Regional Security Working Group of the Middle East Peace Process. Measures in the Middle East context may prove very different from those in Europe, but they have become a part of the process nevertheless. Regional approaches to security and cooperation partly modeled on Europe's CSCE have been proposed by Kazakhstan for Eurasia and by others for East Asia and the Pacific. The geostrategic considerations may be quite different, but a number of nations wish to bring greater transparency and certainty to regional interactions. Efforts to develop concepts of preventive diplomacy to deal with regional and ethnic tensions also draw heavily from Cold War arms control developments with their emphasis on the rule of law and the peaceful resolution of disputes.

Still, there is some danger in walking into the future looking backwards. The nearly seventy-five years of the Soviet Union is a very short time compared to the age of many international and ethnic disputes which confront us. The failure of strong, centralized leadership to create a viable "Soviet man" or "Yugoslav" man hopefully reflects a thirst for freedom inherent in everyone, but it may also reflect the sustaining power of culture or tradition. Where those cultural forces reinforce civilized behavior, everyone benefits. Where powerful social divisions lead to repression or violence, everyone is ultimately at risk. The lessons of history become ever more complex the deeper one delves into the past.

Lessons learned from the most recent past are not always easily applicable to the problems of the future, even when we can agree on what those lessons are. Much Cold War strategy was preoccupied with deterrence theory. Now we have turned attention to the problem of the "undeterrables," be they nihilistic terrorists or reckless national leaders. Many of the Cold War CSBMs were advanced based upon an assumption that greater familiarity would bring peace. Today, we watch as peoples most familiar with each other kill each other. We placed nuclear, chemical, and biological weapons at the top of our list of deadly weapons and now watch as mortars, rifles, pistols, and knives take more lives than did those weapons of mass destruction.

We have been pleased to declare the Cold War dead, and we have found it necessary to move on quickly. Thus we have not really taken the time to examine the dynamics of Cold War arms control carefully. Now we have the benefit of some hindsight and leisure. We can see some of the distortions that we, as historians, bring to history. If anything, we have tended to personalize and oversimplify the process of interaction which took place between East and West. We have tended to remember best individuals acting during historic ev ents such as the Cuban missile crisis or at Reykjavik. We have frequently neglected the study of forces, circumstances, and policies which created those often defining moments.

This tendency is reinforced when veterans of the Cold War get together to share memories of what happened. Nevertheless, there is great interest and much value in having actual participants review what they think did happen. Many archives and records in the United States are not yet public, and in the states of the former Soviet Union some initial openness has been reversed. When a more full documentary record is available, it will undoubtedly alter some of what we believe motivated behavior during the Cold War.

Relying solely on the written record, however, would be dangerous. Records may be less selective than some memories, but they are selective nonetheless. Important elements were not always recorded formally or officially or, in some cases, at all. Histories built upon documents made available long after the events took place will tend to be shallow unless combined with accurate and objective recollections of what individuals were doing or thought they were doing.

This is the Fourth Annual Verification Conference at Southern Methodist University. When the late John Tower, former United States Senator and US Chief START Negotiator, helped found the Verification Conference, he and Professor James Brown sought a vehicle to portray the future of arms control more clearly. Each year, the subjects and themes have evolved. But each year we have also listened to a remarkable group of experts describe the past from their experience. Former Soviet SALT and START negotiator Victor Karpov and I were to have opened this year's meeting with a look back from opposite sides of the negotiating table. Unfortunately, Ambassador Karpov has been ill and could not travel. He is a remarkable diplomat who has seen dramatic political events from the "inside of the other side."

Many of the questions you and I still have about events we have lived or studied could probably be answered by Ambassador Karpov. Indeed, imagine if John Tower could have been here once again to engage Victor Karpov. They were counterparts and were central in getting the START talks moving. Senator Tower taught me just about everything I knew about negotiations. He had been prepared for the US-Soviet talks by many years of dealing with the even more formidable challenges presented by the US Congress. Unfortunately, I suspect he didn't teach me everything he knew about negotiating. I fear Victor taught me some of the rest, but then maybe he also learned from my colleagues and me as well.

When former adversaries in the Cold War are brought together, there is a tendency to focus on the common ties, the pleasant moments, or the universal threat of weapons of mass destruction. That would have been easy and interesting for Victor and me to do. And enjoyable. And probably of some use. Overly fond recollections, however, would not have been accurate. I went to Washington, DC, from California's Hoover Institution on War, Revolution and Peace the same year that Aleksandr Solzhenitsyn came to view the Hoover archives. At Hoover, Solzhenitzyn found letters and records of victims of the Gulag Archipelago, human beings who had died believing that no evidence of their existence would survive outside the vaults of Stalin's secret police. The Soviet Union was an evil empire.

Yet, it was with this evil empire that the arms control revolution of the last seven years was negotiated. We should never forget nor entirely forgive some of the posturing at the negotiating table by Soviet negotiators when their government believed the West was vulnerable. The period during the INF deployments is a good case study. Yet, many of the same negotiators joined in the problem solving at the Wyoming Ministerial of 1989, which altered the style of US-Soviet cooperation and also led to the very intrusive Verification Protocol associated with the Threshold Test Ban Treaty and to the Bilateral Chemical Weapons Data Exchange. These important steps toward openness were deeply resented by old thinkers in Moscow. The years that have followed have given us chapter after chapter of that battle over openness and political change which ultimately fractured and then destroyed the Soviet Union.

We are fortunate to have present at the SMU Conference citizens from a number of the new, independent nations that have been formed out of the Union of Soviet Socialist Republics. It is a very distinguished group which will undoubtedly illuminate many areas currently under study. Again, candor is important, both in piecing together more accurate histories and in applying that history to contemporary problems. We have had confrontation in the past; we have somewhat different disputes today. Important political changes, however, now give us a greater capacity to work together.

World events are moving rapidly in the 1990s, and policies are increasingly confused in the turmoil. We sometimes speak as if we have reached the millennium (actually only seven years away), but we often act as if we cannot cope. In arms control, we sometimes act as if the arms control agenda has reached its goals, but we also act as if we cannot hope to succeed in dealing with some of the dangers that arms control was designed to reduce. Are we at the end or the beginning in arms control, or are we perhaps in the midst of a seemingly endless sequence of circles? These are big questions which hang over the more specific questions of lessons learned from the Cold War, but they should be kept in mind.

To facilitate the discussion, let me simply list a number of possible lessons learned from the Cold War arms control experience which can be examined. This is not a complete list, nor does it capture all of the levels of experience from which we can gain. My hope is that the list will provoke useful discussion about both the past and the future. Consider the following:

-- Arms control must be integral to your national security and foreign policy. During the Cold War, both sides stressed that nuclear weapons were a common threat, but negotiations focused on the relative balance of the two sides and the geopolitical impact of deployments, particularly in Europe.
-- Your position is strongest when you have clear principles which are viable because they reflect reality. The theme of effective verification gave the West considerable leverage precisely because it highlighted the closed nature of its totalitarian adversaries.
-- Arms control involves both competition and cooperation; positions change and even reverse to reflect tactical and strategic dynamics and the wider military and political climate. At various times, either the United States or the Soviet Union demonstrated renewed interest in missile defense systems, but it was only at the beginning and at the end of the SALT-START I/II process that such interest was openly expressed on both sides.
-- Grand proposals can alter the debate, change the focus, and have significant strategic impact over time; but they are often more a measure of how far apart you are than how close you are, and they seldom lead to quick progress in formal negotiations.

President Gorbachev's January 1986 proposal to eliminate strategic offensive arms by 1999 captured public attention, but substituted for serious negotiations at the table. Reykjavik had a similar effect. Lost in both was real progress on INF which ultimately led to agreement.

-- Different outcomes can be better or worse for a party, but the negotiation need not be a zero sum game and is unlikely to alter long-term trends radically through its negotiated terms, although its political symbolism and effect may be extremely great. SALT I and SALT II largely codified existing trends, but they gave each side a rationale for following its own political dictates. The Soviet Union modernized its forces while the United States looked to détente to justify relying on the forces it built in the 1960s and canceling its ABM deployments.

-- Timing must often be determined by political or economic developments rather than by military or negotiating developments. Throughout the early INF negotiations, one fact became ever more clear: The Soviet Union had no interest in concluding an agreement until after the Pershing II and ground-launched cruise missiles were deployed. Why make life easy for NATO?

-- Domestic politics and alliance relationships can weigh heavily in calculations of tactics, timing, and substance. Even though no INF Treaty was likely until after deployments, numerous initiatives were taken by both sides to influence US congressional politics and the debates in Germany, the Netherlands, and Belgium.

-- Avoid mirror-imaging, but recognize where we are alike as well as where we are different. In CFE, the United States initially sought to tie the level of some of its forces stationed in Europe to those of the Soviet Union, anticipating that this would bring the superior Soviet numbers down to US levels. As the Warsaw Pact disintegrated, the United States needed to delink quickly to avoid being drawn down to zero, an outcome our allies greatly feared. Our role in Western Europe was different from that of the Soviet Army in Eastern Europe.

-- Prepare for what comes after a breakthrough or agreement, avoid tabling proposals you can't live with, and consider the negotiating and implementing consequences including enforcement and cost. When the United States proposed the zero option in INF, many experts believed that the Soviet Union would never agree to it. This outraged some and pleased others. Moscow did agree to zero, however, and NATO had to adjust to take into account the removal of a large number of expensive systems it had just deployed.

-- Understand the implications of a network of arrangements and whether or not the total is greater than the sum of the parts, or less. The most intrusive negotiated multilateral verification regime is that of the Chemical Weapons Convention. Even with all of its provisions, however, the CWC would have had great difficulty dealing with the threat posed by the Soviet Union if Moscow were to have forces deployed on the Fulda Gap. Instead, we are dealing with independent democracies whose nuclear and conventional forces are subject to extensive constraints and verification, so much so that we are now looking for ways to make the composite regime more affordable.

Each of these hypothetical lessons learned will look different when matched against specific chapters of the Cold War negotiating history. In the discussion today, we must ask whether or not such rules have significant applications in the world we now face. This will help form a more coherent American perspective on the role of arms control. It will also help determine whether arms control's contributions have been significant and whether they can be significant in the future.

PART 1

ARMS CONTROL PERSPECTIVES FROM THE COMMONWEALTH OF INDEPENDENT STATES

Chapter 1

NEW DEMOCRATIC RUSSIAN POLICY IN ARMS CONTROL AND NON-PROLIFERATION

Victor I. Mizin

Dramatic changes in the international environment in the beginning of 1990s have brought about a new framework for national and global security. But one thing is obvious, socialism as a world ideology has inexorably given way to liberal capitalism, meaning democracy, free enterprise, and market economy. The scale and scope of these shifts in world affairs are yet to be assessed. The vision of security is now more and more based on social, economic, and technological factors. The glorious days of arms control, this famous "golden era" of disarmament, seem to have passed away. They are superseded through cooperative demilitarization and the taking of unilateral steps of disarmament by the major military powers, first by Russia and the United States. However, in spite of all of these fundamental changes, military and, consequently, arms control problems are still with us.

The post-Cold War era has proved to be an even more dangerous time than that of the East-West confrontation. A host of regional, religious, ethnic, and other military conflicts overshadow today the commendable achievements that have taken place in disarmament and in the steady pace of arms control agreements' implementation. It is not at all pleasing to admit that along with Yugoslavia, Russia (which is my country) is raising today the majority of concerns in the world media, the general public, and the national security arena. On the other hand, all the fears that were voiced of nuclear proliferation and high-tech weapons deliveries to extremist countries have not come true, at least not for the time being.

Relations between Russia and the other Western countries, at this stage, are an important factor determining the nature and pace of the evolution of international relations. Many in Russia are misinformed regarding the view that the West's declared policy of supporting democratic reforms in Russia has borne no tangible result thus far for the country. Some Russian politicians also allege that the West, above all the United States, sees a weak Russia as its political goal and that the negative processes taking place follow this scenario written by foreign "think tanks" or defense communities. But the majority of Russian experts and government officials think that the West has no alternative on this issue. Preserving and carrying forward the positive aspects of Russian-Western cooperation and integrating the economy of Russia into the world economy will serve as an important guarantee in the foreseeable future toward creating and maintaining the global system of international security. A weak Russia torn by separatist movements, anarchy, and nationalism is the worst nightmare for the whole world. Therefore, the West should be cautious in evolving its new "Russian/CIS" strategy, so as not to humiliate Russian national pride as a world power with its accompanying responsibilities.

Today Russia is engaged in a complex process of defining the objectives and tasks of its foreign and national security policy. Regrettably, this process is sometimes misused to the detriment of the real threat to its national security which is the domestic arena. This results too often in inconsistencies in conducting foreign policy, which sets Moscow apart from the West.

The task of conceptualizing the principles of Russian foreign and national security policy is compounded by the lack of consensus among internal political forces on the nature of the changes that have taken place in the international arena, and Russia's role, place, and goals in this new environment. A further hurdle that must be overcome revolves around the role of this new nation. Is Russia just an "ordinary" country, a regional superpower, or should it continue to pretend to be a global power? Furthermore, there are uniform elements that discount the positive changes that have taken place in the political and military doctrines of NATO and the US and the military cuts in programs and budgets that have resulted. This complicates the framing of any kind of foreign and national security policy which is the objective of the world arena. No doubt Russia is a major player in world affairs, because of its large reservoir of human and mineral resources, geostrategic location, military and cultural potential, and technological capabilities.

The radical changes that occurred in the international arena in the late 1980s and early 1990s resulted in a new level of relations between the superpowers. This created, qualitatively, new opportunities for military interaction between these countries, but it also made possible a fundamental change in the approaches of cutting and eliminating armaments and reducing the dangers of war.

1. National Security Disarmament Rationales

Russia continues to have a considerable amount of military power, which the US and NATO strategic planners inevitably take into account. Strict controls must be established over the arms and equipment of the former Soviet Union, especially its nuclear component. In addition, in-depth reform of the Russian armed forces needs to be carried out. Russia considers itself responsible for ensuring stability and security on the territory of former USSR. This obviously does not mean a new version of the "Brezhnev Doctrine? Moscow has no intention of interfering in the internal affairs of its neighbors which are totally independent and sovereign states. However, Moscow does intend to strengthen stability at its periphery, including protecting its own borders and in participating in peacekeeping operations in accordance with the principles of international law under the auspices of the UN or in joining other peacekeeping efforts with Western partners.

Emerging today are new and promising areas of interaction and cooperation between Russia and the West. These include ensuring the physical safety of the former Soviet Union's nuclear potential, formalizing Russia's status according to the Non-Proliferation Treaty (NPT) as the only legitimate nuclear power, and solving the problem of non-proliferation of weapons of mass destruction (WMD) and missile technology. Russia is already effectively participating in efforts in the world community to reinforce existing non-proliferation regimes by being able to conduct confidential dialogue with traditional "friends" and allies who are wary of US diplomacy.

At present, political relations between Russia and its one-time potential adversaries -- the United States and NATO countries -- have advanced to unprecedented horizons of mutual comprehension. This has prompted Russian President Boris Yeltsin to stress that Russia sees America and other Western countries as "not just partners but allies? However, the military-technological component of Russian policy continues to be defined by this relationship on traditional terms of a nuclear face-off with the United States. This creates, of course, a notable discrepancy between the political declarations of the government and what is voiced by the military-industrial complex.

With democratic reforms proceeding, it is to be expected that harmonizing the political and military technological parameters of the military and incorporating these views into official defense doctrines will constitute, throughout the 1990s and the early twenty-first century, the substance of military political relations. These reforms can be done by gradually restructuring the strategic potentials of each side, increasing the cooperation between military and civilian institutions, increasing transparency, taking the nuclear forces off of alert status, and renouncing the concept of launch on warning.

The mere existence of strategic weapons and the complexities involved in destroying these nuclear weapons along with the protracted nature of this process, relations between Russia and the United States will retain over a considerable period their "special" character in the strategic field. During this same period, Russia and the United States should take a broader view of strategic stability in a multipolar environment and cooperate more extensively in reviewing these issues.

One of the major declared goals of Russian foreign and strategic policy is keeping its military potential at the levels of rational defense sufficiency. This will be enough for deterring foreseen threats, especially those of global proliferation.

As long as nuclear arsenals are present, reducing them in the interest of stabilizing strategic offensive weapons (SOWs) and using these weapons as political instruments are bound to remain a priority theme of the Russian-US dialogue.

2. Future Of Strategic Offensive Weapons

In the postwar decades, the goals of Strategic Offensive Weapons was based on credibility in using these for military purposes. There developed a complex system of co-ordination, that had nothing to do with the existing military-political realities, resulting in SOWs race having its own rules and complex mythology.

Both sides realized the need to play within definite limits and to effect some cosmetic reductions in these weapons by withdrawing obsolete weapons from combat alert. This action codified the existing patterns of nuclear capabilities of the two countries. With the signing of START-II, this may prove to be the final agreement in the Cold War period which provided for large reductions of both Russian and US nuclear arsenals. This treaty is still based on the idea of mutual deterrence and quantitative parity in strategic capabilities. The implementation of START-II will also lead to greater crisis stability. There will be fewer warheads on strategic launchers, which makes these sites less attractive targets for counterforce weapons. Russia will finally be able to abandon the concept of launch on warning, which created an extremely unstable strategic situation. START-II will further provide new opportunities to lend the disarmament process a more multilateral character by first reducing Russian and US warheads to between 3,000 and 3,500. These are deep cuts which may attract other nuclear powers into the disarmament process; therefore, future discussions on cuts in SOWs of or in regulating the development of these may lead to multilateral discussions and afford greater transparency between states in the nuclear sphere.

Another area that requires attention is the non-strategic nuclear forces. The US and Russia should eliminate these weapons without delay. It is clear that in the world today where its evolution is hard to predict, the idea of getting rid of all nuclear weapons is utopian. But spending such money for Russia serves no purpose and time is lost in attempting to find with the United States new common threats and countering them by joint efforts.

The pace of reductions envisaged by START-II can continue and it will not require Russia to take steps to cut unilaterally its nuclear arsenal. With the completion of the reductions as required under START-II by the year 2003, or earlier, Russia can then unilaterally reduce its forces if it can specify its requisite minimum deterrence forces on the basis of consensus from both its political and military experts. France, Britain, and China should then be induced into new multilateral talks on further nuclear reductions. This minimum deterrence force would then meet the need of all for reasonable sufficiency of nuclear weapons. Some experts are discussing a level of 1000-1500 strategic warheads. Smaller quantities are plausible for a countervalue response.

Such reductions require solving some operational and technical problems. The key problem is for Russia not to target the United States with its nuclear weapons and the need to verify this action by Washington. Recurring statements that Russian missiles are not targeted on the United States cannot be checked, nor do these statements provide any assurances. In the more distant future, it may become possible for a group of countries under the aegis of the United Nations Security Council to control jointly the nuclear capabilities of several nations.

In the present multilateral context, it is rather difficult to achieve strategic stability. The existing power asymmetries in overall military strength and the ability to project these forces in different regions of the world now have been replaced by North-South arguments over military high technology procurement and the legitimate accumulation of such weapons. These issues prompt Russia to think afresh its justification of its nuclear arsenal because of the dangers of regional instability.

In this new world turmoil in Yugoslavia and on Russia's southern and southeastern borders, less interest is evidenced by arms control experts over the fate of the Anti-Ballistic Missile (ABM) Treaty and the Strategic Defense Initiative (SDI). Hopefully SDI is a "lame duck," and both Russia and US are united in their adherence to traditional interpretations of the ABM Treaty. Numerous articles and dissertations on the Global Protection System (GPS) have been written which have assisted not only in killing the development of SDI but also in the slowdown of GPS. The fading away of the Iraqi threat further assisted in the positive direction. Because of the collapse of its economy, Russia is not in a position to develop a new generation of exotic weapons such as Brilliant Pebbles or "laser guns."

It is important to mention the negative reaction by several European countries and quite a few Third World countries as well as China who were critical of the GPS idea as infringing upon the third world countries' security interests. In any case, Russia presently is in such a dire socio-economic situation that it can only philosophically review such efforts. It is not in any position to spend billions of rubles to deploy a defensive system against a threat that is not so visible. Before undertaking any further actions on joint antimissile defense systems, Russia, the US, and other possible allies in GPS should undertake an in-depth study to see if there exists the possibility of a global missile threat.

3. Non-Proliferation Of Mass Destruction Weapons

The non-proliferation theme will dominate foreign policy over the next decade. Volumes have already been written on the topic of WMD. Non-proliferation has become a major problem in world political arena, especially WMD that are found on the territory which was the former Soviet Union. Russia is devoted to the task of halting, through a whole series of efforts that include international diplomacy in halting the proliferation of weapons of mass destruction, their delivery vehicles and related dual-use technologies. This problem is nevertheless unresolved. All three of the newly-established republics, Ukraine, Belarus, and Kazakhstan, which, like Russia, have nuclear weapons on their soil have declared their support of the Non-Proliferation Treaty and agreed to accede to it "at the earliest possible date."

The position that the Ukraine has taken gives serious cause for concern. This Republic under the obligation of the NPT has raised a number of reservations. Under pressure from extremist nationalists elements in the Supreme Rada (Parliament) and the Rukh Party, Kiev is becoming more and more intransigent. It appears that Ukraine is out to prolong the presence of SOWs on its soil for as long as it can, or if possible to retain some elements of its nuclear arsenal along with some of the carriers (primarily 46 SS-24s).

At the same time, it is becoming increasingly more difficult for Kiev to provide logical reasons for its position. Russia as well as the other nuclear states are prepared to offer Ukraine, after the withdrawal of the SOWs from its territory, guarantees that nuclear weapons will not be used against Kiev. Russia is also prepared to compensate Ukraine for the nuclear components of its SOWs. This compensation may take the form of either cash or nuclear fuel for Ukraine's nuclear power plants.

The more important issue is to have the Ukraine ratify the START-I Treaty and begin dismantling its nuclear weapons located on its soil. This is the most important issue facing the world community. Let us hope that the Massandra Agreements of September 3, 1993, between Russia and Ukraine, are put into effect, and that all the nuclear warheads that are presently located in the Ukraine are transported back to Russia. Ukraine continues to create roadblocks in implementing this agreement, by arguing that the Massandra Agreement covers only weapons "subject to the START-I Treaty." This suggests that part of the Ukrainian government wants to retain some nuclear weapons on its soil. It is of interest to the international community that Ukraine becomes a non-nuclear state and that the issue of nuclear weapons on its territory be solved in the best political and economic interest of Kiev.

Many of the initiatives undertaken by Moscow in regard to the proliferation of nuclear weapons in the former Soviet Republics are viewed by these republics as an attempt by Russia to re-establish the dictatorship of the "center." However, Moscow is concerned that Kiev cannot maintain its own nuclear forces properly because of economic and technical reasons. Whatever actions Ukraine's parliament decides to take in renouncing its status as a nuclear power depends not on Russia but on the actions of President Clinton and the emphasis that Washington places on the NPT regime.

Russia's stance on Ukraine's nuclear weapons has been criticized by the West as being inflexible. However, in the wake of the Soviet Union's demise, it appears that the United States hurried to recognize the newly-independent states (NIS) without linking diplomatic recognition to the fulfillment of certain conditions. In the case of Ukraine, recognition should have been conditioned on Ukraine adhering to the NPT regime and the completion of the START-I ratification process. Instead of this, Washington quickened the recognition process in order to influence NIS policies, especially on the issue of nuclear weapons. This resulted in the rise of Ukranian politicians who claimed that with Ukranian independence, Kiev was not bound by its non-nuclear status and that it was not in the interest of Ukraine to give up its nuclear weapons especially if it is surrounded by unfriendly regimes. It is evident that Washington's influence over Ukrainian leaders was very limited. In fact, the US reaction has been rather timid and confined only to mild diplomatic declarations.

Washington's behavior is understandable. Initially, the United States believed Ukraine in its desire to be a non-nuclear state. Later, Washington did not want to give Kiev the impression that it was siding with Russia (possessing neo-imperialist tendencies) against the small and independent Ukraine. The Lisbon Protocol might be viewed as a major tactical blunder. Article 5 of this protocol provides that Ukraine, Belarus, and Kazakhstan accede to the NPT regime as non-nuclear states. Furthermore, the Lisbon Protocol does not take into consideration that Ukraine and the other countries were *de facto* possessors of nuclear arsenals which directly contradict the letter and spirit of the NPT regime.

The issue of Ukraine's non-nuclear status is important for Russia not because of the repercussions it might have on its bilateral relations with Kiev. Russia is sincerely concerned about the future of the NPT and the outcome of the 1995 NPT Review Conference. If laxity is shown in the case of Ukraine and its nuclear weapons, then at some point in the future this may give other nations who are at the threshold of becoming nuclear powers the pretext to ignore and undermine the whole NPT regime. It is not outside the realm of possibility that Kiev could cooperate with some Middle and Near East nations to trade nuclear weapons development and maintenance for deliveries of crude oil, especially if Moscow imposes unilateral trade restrictions on Kiev. Further, the whole nuclear issue is aggravated by some influential Ukrainian defense officials who view the possibility of "nuclear rearmament" of Ukraine as the best way-out of their present economic situation. This whole approach may seem provincial or "peasant-like" in considering the disposition of nuclear weapons. It appears that this policy is working.

Nuclear weapons continue to remain on Ukrainian territory and in the custody of Kiev. It appears that Kiev is now procrastinating until the 1995 Review Conference on the NPT takes place, at which time Ukraine believes the NPT regime will cease to exist. The former Soviet Army's 43rd Strategic Missiles Forces and the 46th Army Strategic Aviation with all their combat units and nuclear weapons maintenance squadrons are now a part of the Ukrainian Army. In April 1992, President Kravchuk issued the order stating Kiev was taking over administrative control of these nuclear forces. This takeover was accompanied by a flurry of statements and declarations by Ukrainian politicians justifying this action. Some of these politicians noted that although Ukraine had the personnel, know-how, and industrial facilities to maintain these weapons, it did not possess the economic resources. However, economic resources might be found from, for example Iran, in exchange for participating in a rearmament program. That is why Russia considers this situation very serious requiring a coordinated international effort to bring Ukraine in line with the requirements of the NPT.

How can the non-proliferation regime be improved? Cooperation can be attained by exchanging information on the capabilities of WMD among countries and by joint efforts on countermeasures which should be carried out under the auspices of the United Nations and include diplomatic, economic, and other sanctions that seem appropriate; however, it is more important to reinforce the legal basis of the NPT regime.

4. Some Nuclear Non-Proliferation-Related Issues

The disintegration of the Soviet Union, the division of its armed forces and military assets between the several republics, the building of new statehood, and the crisis in leadership within these republics have made the world community worry, and with reason, about the effective control of the nuclear arsenals and nuclear arms depots in these former Soviet republics. This concern extends to the spread of technologies and material involved in the making of WMD beyond the boundaries of the ex-Soviet Union to Third World countries. Further, the industrial countries of the West need to aid Russia so that Moscow can control and dismantle its nuclear arms. Prompted by this concern, the United States has signed an unprecedented agreement with Russia on the purchase of highly-enriched uranium from disassembled or soon-to-be disassembled nuclear warheads.

Reinforcing safeguards regime and extending the IAEA's inspection regime to all nuclear reactors in the world are the most pragmatic of proposals in providing strict monitoring procedures. It should be evident, however, that monitoring and exchanges of data on the stocks of nuclear materials must be reciprocal and encompass at least all the nuclear facilities of the nuclear powers instead of securing pooling information on only Russia's atomic industry. As the interaction among the nuclear powers grows, it may become feasible to reduce radically the nuclear arsenals to only several hundred warheads per country. This is a quantity that would establish a minimum nuclear deterrence concept that can be agreed upon by all.

Russia and the United States have yet to discuss seriously the scope of a verifiable agreement on halting the production of nuclear fissile materials. Early steps were taken in this direction by statements issued by President Boris Yeltsin on January 29, 1992 and President George Bush on July 13, 1992. Therefore, Russia supports a binding multilateral agreement prohibiting the production of highly-enriched uranium or the separation of plutonium, both of which are outside of the nuclear safeguards. Russia is for creation by the year 2000 of a verifiable and transparent international regime banning the production of these materials.

With a joint moratorium now existing the next stage is a complete cessation and prohibition of nuclear testing on the part of both nuclear superpowers. A real breakthrough toward this above stated goal is to move forward to the next logical stage and that is in limiting explosions to between two and five KILOTONS (the aim of the explosions being to enhance the safety of nuclear warheads), on the understanding that all tests must be ended by the year 1996. An evolving global seismic monitoring system and other techniques of verifying the absence of nuclear tests in the one kiloton range will permit a check on possible violators. It is still however the CTB that remains Russia's preference, and it is the Conference on Disarmament that is the forum to elaborate on the provisions of the CTB.

5. Prospects For Multilateral Efforts For Disarmament And International Security

With the break-up of the Soviet Union, low intensity conflicts have increased along ethnic, religious, and clannish grounds. Many Westerners now speak of a "Balkanization" of world politics and a return to international relations typical of the last century.

The threat of regional instability today suggests that the nuclear threat is acquiring a new quality. There is a danger that WMD may spread and that terrorists may seize nuclear warheads. It is conceivable that WMD may be used in regional conflicts, that separatist groups may resort to nuclear blackmail, and that extremist regimes may seek to procure nuclear weapons.

The task of averting such a development is clearly becoming a key venue for arms control, and perhaps it is even more important than traditional measures to limit the competition in nuclear and conventional arms. Russia therefore considers it important to take multilateral initiatives to strengthen international security, promote disarmament, and adapt the work of the UN and its Security Council to this new world situation. Multilateral disarmament fora will make it possible to bring into the process of disarmament and confidence building other ex-Soviet republics. Such participation will encourage them effectively to join the world political arena and non-proliferation efforts.

Russia has indicated that she favors including on the agenda of the Conference on Disarmament the issue of transparency in arms which is regarded as an important confidence-building measure. All countries, including the CIS states, should provide data to the UN Register on conventional arms as part of a confidence-building effort.

Many developing countries are also convinced that disarmament can no longer take place in a political vacuum and should be coupled with the creation of a non-confrontational system of international relations that is conducive to more extensive economic interaction. This requires that defense industries be converted to civilian production, a priority task for Russia. The optimum way to attain this is to provide the conditions for the privatization of production of these defense industries and to encourage foreign private investment. This approach has nothing to do with "selling out" the national interests and in fact can contribute to Russia's effort to improve the standard of living of its people. The United Nations, too, can assist Russia by establishing an *ad hoc* group on military industrial conversion. Switching Russian enterprises to civilian production ultimately helps reduce Russian arms exports and, indirectly, affects regional tensions.

Special attention must also be devoted to reforming the UN's Conference on Disarmament. The Conference's mechanism should be made more flexible to allow disarmament talks to be carried out in different venues in terms of both participants and objectives (working out not only treaties and agreements but also guidelines, programs of action, etc? In the view of Russia, the Conference on Disarmament (CD) could eventually become an umbrella forum for bilateral as well as multilateral disarmament talks. It could also become a think tank for planning measures for real disarmament. These measures could include regimes for control over compliance measures, creating lower levels of conventional weapons for regional systems, nuclear-free and missile-free zones, areas free from chemical weapons, and devising ecologically safe and financially optimum procedures for re-equipping and eliminating arms.

Another important function for the CD would be to monitor implementation of a number of multilateral agreements on arms control and disarmament. Needless to say, it would be reasonable to begin such radical reforms with modest steps. These could take the form of creating working bodies of the CD that differ in composition from the official composition of its participants and for these working bodies to concentrate on four key items: banning nuclear tests; transparency in armaments; guarantees for the security on non-nuclear countries; and prevention of an arms race in outer space.

The Conference on Disarmament could then become a center for inter-regional debates on disarmament and could also absorb the organizational structures and subject-areas of the US Disarmament Commission and partly those of the First Committee of the UN General Assembly. The CD would become a unique global agency of the world community, addressing the problems of arms regulation, disarmament, and all aspects of military security.

In order to prevent the unauthorized appearance on the world markets of missiles and nuclear technologies from the CIS countries, it is essential to improve the regime on export controls. The same purpose can also be attained if definitive accords within the CIS can be formulated on nuclear non-proliferation between the exporters of nuclear materials.

The Russian Federation has taken steps to ensure compliance with the international obligations undertaken by the former Soviet Union. This includes the creation of an export control regime of which the Commission on Export Control is the regulator. The areas that are regulated include the control of exports of certain types of raw material, equipment, technologies, scientific and technological information or services, including intellectual products and services. These controls apply to the production of military arms and equipment and especially weapons of mass destruction.

To meet the Coordinating Committee for Multilateral Export Controls (COCOM) requirements, Russia has introduced procedures for import certificates, delivery certificates, end-use certificates, and on-site inspections at the request of the exporter. A special commitment letter, as required, has recently been sent to the COCOM. The new international export control organization that is envisaged to succeed COCOM can only be effective with Russia's participation. Presently in Russia we have an effective export control system that eliminates the original concerns of the West and thus eliminates the COCOM restrictions completely.

To show how effective export controls are in Russia today, let me cite one example. Recently, Ukraine approached Russia with the proposal to sign the special agreement, promoting the cooperation between the defense industries of Russia and Ukraine in the field of missiles and missile technologies production. The Foreign Ministry of Russia had to oppose this proposal because of our international obligation to abide by the principals of the Missile Technology Control Regime (MTCR). Ukraine is now being treated by Russia as a foreign state. The political obligations in this case prevailed over the clearly economic benefits.

Russia favors the US position of changing the existing export control regimes, including the MTCR into a universal global mechanism for curbing the spread of weapons and dangerous military-related technologies. There are some experts in both the academic and political community in the United States who propose the amelioration of the MTCR regime whereby it evolves into a type of international IAEA missile non-proliferation body. Such a proposal should assure equal rights for all countries in the area of international scientific and technologic cooperation. It should be understood, however, that any discrimination against Russia in the international high technology markets would be viewed as a relic of the Cold War and unacceptable.

In the recently signed Memorandum of Understanding between Russia and the US, there is a special provision that provides for the continuation of the existing patterns of cooperation between Russia and members of the former Soviet Union with the United States which is intended to contribute to Russia's missile technology programs including the activities related to space and ensuring the safety of strategic missiles. Russia on the other hand refuses to contribute to the MTCR Annex Category I missile programs with other members of the former Soviet Union. Ukraine, for example, does not accept the MTCR regime as it applies to its aerospace industry. Russia and the West should continue to press the NIS members to move toward this noble goal.

Let me conclude by stressing that Russia's desire to move unequivocally toward further arms reductions and non-proliferation enforcement. This is a result of an expanding economy associated with a great industrial power. It is the desire of most of the global community for Russia, in the near future, to develop industrially and to be a politically and socially stable nation.

Chapter 2

THE PROBABILITY OF NUCLEAR WEAPONS PROLIFERATION: INDICATIONS OF MILITARY NUCLEAR ACTIVITIES

Evgenii P. Maslin

The creation of nuclear weapons became an objective factor in the development of science, technology, and the art of war. When nuclear weapons exist in the world and there are states possessing them, the national security policy of non-nuclear countries can be pursued along several guidelines as follows:
-- entering into a military alliance with nuclear states;
-- receiving guarantees from nuclear powers that their nuclear weapons will not be employed against non-nuclear states; and
-- developing, manufacturing, or procuring nuclear weapons of their own.
It is the last guideline that is the subject of our analysis.

The main indication that a state is preparing for nuclear weapons development and production is a corresponding political decision made by its government and, thus, the involvement of a wide spectrum of industrial and scientific complexes. Naturally such a decision is classified, but the fact that it is adopted can be disclosed by direct and indirect signs as described below:

Direct Signs:
-- creating complex industrial enterprises and allowing the procurement materials for nuclear weapons.

Indirect Signs:
-- the non-alignment to the Nuclear Non-Proliferation Treaty (NPT), to the Treaty of Tlatelolco, or the Rarotonga Treaty; the refusal to participate in international negotiations on nuclear non-proliferation problems;
-- nuclear activities and control by the International Atomic Energy Agency (IAEA);
-- the creation of managing structures directly reporting to the National Authority and possessing special powers and functions obviously not corresponding to the announced ones for this organization; and
-- the creation of special structures for foreign economic trade organizations with special rights and with ample financial opportunities to purchase raw materials, equipment, and prototypes from abroad.

A huge role in the development of atomic industry belongs to the experience acquired by non-nuclear countries as a result of the proliferation of nuclear technologies. In this sense the problem of "manpower brain drain" attracts the public attention, and the personnel component becomes a definite factor when a country makes a decision to design nuclear weapons.[1]

Taking into account the global scope of the "brain drain," wide international cooperation and interaction by states can ensure the effective regime only for the peaceful employment of the scientists and experts. As a positive example, we can note the creation of the International Scientific and Technical Center founded by the Russian Federation, the United States, Japan, the European Association on Atomic Energy, and the European Economic Community. One of the main objectives of this Center is to present to scientists and specialists connected with this kind of weaponry, especially those who possess both knowledge and practical skills in the area of weapons of mass destruction and missile delivery complexes, the opportunity to direct their talents toward peaceful means.

1. Nuclear Weapons Non-Proliferation Monitoring

There is no single reliable and simple means to avoid the threat of nuclear weapons proliferation. As complex as the problem is, the solution is just as complicated. No country alone can prevent nuclear weapons proliferation; therefore, international cooperation is of great importance in the sphere of preventing nuclear proliferation. This kind of international cooperation should be fostered, in particular, in the direction of creating certain information as a basis for nuclear non-proliferation monitoring. The criteria and methods to disclose covert nuclear weapons production include the creation of verification and inspection methodologies independent of specific conditions; upgrading the means and techniques for nuclear materials and device detection; and developing the legal norms for international control.

The upgrading of nuclear non-proliferation monitoring at present is one of the most important guidelines for the international community in providing the stability for inter-state relations. Nowadays, such measures for verification and monitoring are accomplished under the auspices of the IAEA. Along with the review of technical documentation on the production and displacement of nuclear materials, the verification, inspections, research, and measurements aimed at actual confirmation of fissionable and nuclear materials' displacement for peaceful purposes represent the primary aims of these measures. The smooth and clear-cut system of the IAEA safeguards provides for the effective control of the presence and displacement of about 95% of the fissionable materials which are produced in the world today.

Currently those states which have not signed the Nuclear Non-Proliferation Treaty and have enterprises capable of carrying out such research fall under the term of "non-declared nuclear activities" and are non-eligible for monitoring; however, nuclear technologies, classified enterprises, and reactors for dual purposes are left unresolved. In this connection it is considered reasonable to develop methodologies and technical means in order to verify the complex of signs which indicate that work is under way to develop nuclear weapons.

2. Capabilities Of Russian Technical Means Of Monitoring

The efficiency of the nuclear non-proliferation monitoring system can be defined primarily by the capability of the technical means to detect and identify products of nuclear activities of a particular state. At first, these would consist of aerosol products' composition which allows the research to define nuclear activities. The capability of aerosol products to spread over large distances allows their sampling from great distances away from the monitored objects and in some cases away from the monitored state territory.

Russia possesses multi-year experience in organizing and carrying out expert work connected with the assessment of these activities, both on internal industrial test sites and test sites of the Ministry of Defense.

The technical means for sampling aerosol products includes airborne filtering and ground-base filtering installations, radioactive noble gas sampling and analysis, and isokinetic sampler plotting boards. Presently registered ranges for detection of particular radio nuclides and heavy metals in samples and the reproductivity of results meet the indices achieved in world analytical practices.

There are a number of complex sampling techniques which allow the researcher to detect aerosol emissions. Among the methods are alpha, beta, and gamma mass spectrometry, atomic emissions, absorption spectrometry, X-ray microanalysis, and radiochemistry, to name a few. These methods allow us to detect with confidence the products connected with the use of nuclear materials (uranium, plutonium, thorium, lithium, tritium) and chemical elements (beryllium and others) and to identify the sources as listed below:

-- installations extracting, enriching, and processing nuclear materials;
-- reactors, atomic power stations, and nuclear energy installations;
-- enterprises for assembling and maintaining nuclear weapons;
-- nuclear munitions being stored or transported;
-- nuclear weapons testing and testing at the initial phase of weapons development; and
-- venting of fissionable products and accidents involving nuclear materials.

It should be noted that by using national technical means such as airborne filtering units, it permits the identification of some of these sources in the atmosphere at a range of 100-1,000 kilometers. The identification of the source and the assessment of some of the parameters of the sample can be implemented no later than the first five days. The Russian AN-30 aircraft is specially equipped for such monitoring purposes. This aircraft is also being used by the United Nations to monitor Iraq's nuclear capabilities.

In May 1994 all the technical and organizational aspects of this aircraft for aerial survey of Iraq were discussed by the UN Special Commission. These flights allowed the United Nations to detect the sources of admixtures formed as a result of military activities in Iraq and to identify the nature of these activities.

It should be noted that the Russian Federation is upgrading its national technical means of radiation monitoring. The creation of a radiation aircraft-laboratory like the AN-72 aircraft is coming to fruition. The aircraft is being upgraded and equipped with the most sophisticated sampling, measuring, navigational, and computer means that will significantly increase the effectiveness of monitoring in comparison with the existing processes.

A comprehensive monitoring system for non-declared nuclear activities might include the following basic elements:

-- a worldwide system of sampling and radiation monitoring based on fixed unmanned (automated) stations (points);
-- mobile processes of sampling and radiation monitoring;
-- establishing a worldwide seismic monitoring system; and
-- on-site inspection as a means to identify suspicious events.

These methods which are found in different countries have different levels of readiness. Developing effective monitoring systems to detect non-declared nuclear activities will require joining efforts on the part of the countries of the world community.

It should be noted that there is close cooperation between the military agencies of the US and Russia in developing a worldwide seismic monitoring network. Presently experiments are taking place on continuous seismic data exchanges between the stations in Albuquerque (US) and Peledui (Russia) using a satellite communication channel. This experiment is now taking place within the framework of the Memorandum on Cooperation between the Seismic Services of the Ministry of Defense of the Russian Federation and ARPA of the US. In the future the number of exchange stations will increase.

3. Nuclear Weapons Elimination In The CIS

The most important measures on nuclear non-proliferation should be those taken by the US and Russia (as the USSR's legal successor) on reduction of nuclear weapons and their withdrawal from the territories of other CIS countries

It should be noted that this is the first time the US and Russia have agreed to eliminate an exact number of nuclear warheads along with their carriers and launchers. The disarmament process today and the development of effective cooperation among the countries in the world has now become irreversible.

In Russia the program for the elimination of tactical nuclear weapons is now in place and operative. This program will eliminate one-third of the sea-launched missile systems by 1995, one-half of the nuclear weapons for tactical aviation by 1996, and all nuclear mines, tactical missiles, and artillery projectiles will be eliminated by the year 2000.

In line with Russian-American cooperation, all of the tactical nuclear weapons have been removed from surface warships and submarines as well from naval ground-launched aviation and have been placed in a central storage facility. In accordance with the agreement between Ukraine and Russia, more than 1,000 tactical nuclear warheads have been withdrawn from Ukraine. Furthermore, the development and production programs of ground-based tactical missiles, artillery projectiles, nuclear mines, short-range missiles, and long-range air and sea-launched cruise missiles have been terminated.

It should be noted that after seven years of START, the level of nuclear weapons must not exceed 5,000 units. Furthermore, in accordance with the agreement of July 17, 1992 between Russia and the US on further reducing strategic offensive arms, the aggregate level of warheads in Russia will be between 3,800 and 4,250 units by 1999 and by the year 2003 all the MIRV intercontinental ballistic missiles will be eliminated.

In addition to the measures undertaken to eliminate nuclear weapons, Russia has also ceased the production of weapons-grade uranium. This fuel is now being converted for nuclear power plants. The 1989 program of halting industrial reactors from producing weapons-grade plutonium is also under way. In particular, two reactors have stopped production in 1993. This is two years ahead of schedule. The remaining three reactors will cease to operate within the years 1995-2000.

4. An Assessment Of The CIS Situation

When the agreements for the formation of the CIS were being signed, no specific decisions which related to the future of nuclear weapons in the former USSR were made. In these agreements the joint nuclear weapons program was only mentioned. The issue of property rights to these weapons was not mentioned. Additional difficulties arose in May 1992 when the Ministers of Foreign Affairs of Russia, Belarus, Kazakhstan, and Ukraine as well as the Secretary of State of the United States signed the Lisbon Protocol to the (Soviet-American) START Treaty. According to the Lisbon Protocol, Belarus, Kazakhstan, and Ukraine became participants to the START Treaty. By all appearances, these are new nuclear powers if it were not for their commitment to join the Nuclear Non-Proliferation Treaty as nuclear-free states.

In the case of both Belarus and Kazakhstan, the strategic offensive arms stationed on their territories are under the jurisdiction and control of the Ministry of Defense of the Russian Federation. Ukraine, on the other hand, is *de facto* nuclear power. It is a known fact that on the territory of Ukraine there is a group of strategic offensive arms, which were earlier part of the Strategic Nuclear Forces of the Soviet Union. This includes fixed strategic missile systems equipped with MIRV-intercontinental ballistic missiles (SS-19 and SS-24) and strategic bombers with low-altitude long-range nuclear-tipped cruise missiles.

In April 1992 the leaders of Ukraine decided to include units and sub-units of the missile forces and the air force in the Table of Equipment (TOE) strength of their armed forces. Then in May 1992 the personnel of two nuclear-technical units of the air force (controlling some 600 nuclear warheads) took the Ukrainian oath, which resulted instantly in the total control of these nuclear weapons by Ukraine. By this action, Ukraine did not proclaim its nuclear status. Joint control that is exercised by Marshal Shaposhnikov, Chief of the Joint Armed Forces of the CIS, has never existed. As yet, Ukraine has not joined the NPT regime, although it has given assurances that it will do so.

The Ukrainian aspiration to possess nuclear weapons is now confirmed by the creation of new structures, in particular, the so-called Center of Administrative Control of the Strategic Nuclear Forces of the Ministry of Defense.

The question is often asked if Ukraine can independently use nuclear weapons. All the missile systems on combat duty on the territory of Ukraine are part of the Russian system of Strategic Nuclear Arms Central Operation Command. Ukraine has no system allowing it to delay centralized missile launchings or to perform autonomous launchings. It is impossible for Ukraine to use nuclear weapons without taking additional measures, but Ukraine does have the necessary base, personnel, and technologies to take such measures in the future. Ukraine has the scientific and technical potential to conduct the required work to unblock the coding devices on the missiles within a short time.

Although in the current state of warming international relations, it is highly unlikely that nuclear weapons will be used; however, the control and maintenance of these weapons in Ukraine creates some anxiety. It is a necessary condition in the maintenance of nuclear weapons that the national nuclear safety system is functioning. The main functions of this systems are the absolute enforcement of the strictly defined measures and rules in nuclear weapons handling; the principal authorities having control over them; complete responsibility for nuclear safety; the systematic inspection and check of the weapons; and the selective periodic inspections of the actual state of the weapons in storage in order to take, if necessary, the proper steps to be able to store them reliably and safely.

The above-mentioned system is in place and being improved in Russia, which is the internationally recognized successor of the USSR in the area of nuclear weapons. The succession of Russia is completely organizationally and technically ensured. To guarantee to the international community the non-proliferation of nuclear weapons and to avoid any nuclear incidents at the same time, Russia is not in a position to guarantee legally nor physically the security of all of the nuclear weapons of the former USSR since many of them are removed from the Russian national nuclear weapons system.

Nuclear munitions and nuclear weapons systems on the whole have always been a source of potential danger. If the standards and rules of handling these weapons are violated because of certain physical and chemical effects occurring during storage and operations, and because of incidental and irregular situations taking place in storage, these conditions could pose a danger.

The risk of reducing nuclear incidents to an acceptably minimum level can be accomplished by proper ammunition design and personnel training, the permanent control by the inspection agencies, the selective check of munitions, and the establishment of proper procedures in case of emergency situations. Suffice it to say, for four years there has not been a single serious nuclear incident such as an explosion, fire, or leak of toxic plutonium in the atmosphere in the USSR.

There are up to several kilograms of plutonium in every nuclear weapon. If dispersed completely because of a fire or a nuclear explosion, the area of dangerous radioactive contamination reaches several hundred square kilometers. In case of a similar incident within a MIRV-missile complex with the presence of a great amount of missile fuel, the danger of contamination from plutonium multiplies several thousand square kilometers. Such an instance would contaminate not only the territory of Russia but her neighbors as well.

The results of the recent 1993 inspection of the nuclear weapons in Ukraine by Russian specialists (when it was still permissible) aroused a lot of anxiety. Presently the systematic inspection and nuclear munitions control by Russian designers and manufacturers have not come to an end. During one of these inspections of a nuclear munitions storage area near Pervomaisk, it was noted that it contained more than six to eight times the necessary decommissioned nuclear munitions which could be stored safely. As a result, the temperature and radiation background (3,000 mCi/hr) had increased to less-than-safe levels. The warranty on many of these nuclear munitions components has already expired, and it is necessary to replace them in order to avoid possible systems damage and the emergence of a highly explosive situations.

The training and retraining of specialists is not being conducted. As a result, the practical skills of the personnel are considerably lost which gives reasons to doubt their abilities to operate efficiently. Systematic investigations, analyses, and assessments of the nuclear munitions in storage beyond the warranty periods are non-existent, while the special rescue teams are actually not qualified in case of emergencies. The inspection commission that worked in Pervomaisk in September 1993 which included the chief designers from Arzamas-16 drew the conclusion that "the current situation is inadmissible and requires urgent action."

Realizing that a crisis situation with nuclear weapons safety exists in Ukraine with possible unpredictable results, it is necessary to emphasize that Ukrainian nuclear weapons are now a threat first to Ukraine and then to her neighbors.

Nevertheless, on July 2 1993, the Suprume Rada of Ukraine came to the decision that Ukraine was the owner of the nuclear weapons which were deployed on its territory. This means that at least till the year 2000 Ukraine is a *de facto* nuclear state. Estimates by Russian scientists confirm that Ukraine has the capability to ensure by the year 2000 the reproduction of several hundred nuclear weapons. At present the nuclear potential of Ukraine is about 1.5 times higher than the potential of Great Britain, France, and China taken all together.

The present situation is such that time is now on the side of Ukraine. There is no need for Kiev to hurry to manufacture its own means of control, maintenance, and monitoring technologies for these nuclear weapons. Finally, creating its own scientific, technical, and industrial base for supporting nuclear weapons' readiness is also unnecessary.

The government of the Russian Federation unambiguously warned the international community against the danger of the unilateral and politically and technically unjustified actions taken by Ukrainian leadership which was aimed at disrupting the agreement of its non-nuclear status. The Russian Government declares, "The efficiency of the nuclear non-proliferation regime is being threatened, making the implementation of the START-1 and START-2 Treaties questionable? A reasonable approach to solving the problem of nuclear weapons on the territory of Ukraine was introduced by the Crimean Agreements, in which practically all of Ukrainian wishes were taken into consideration. Even then the Ukrainian side evaded the exact date when nuclear munitions were being removed from its territory.

There is no doubt that the problem of nuclear weapons proliferation is becoming more critical today. The way that the dilemma will be solved by the international community will affect the future of the NPT regime. Wrecking the Non-Proliferation Treaty may change the conception of collective security, and many countries will connect the ideas of national security with the possession of nuclear weapons.

Today Ukraine raised a claim of indemnity for the cost of the highly-enriched uranium contained in its tactical nuclear weapons which were displaced to Russia in 1992. This demand is illegal for several reasons. First, the main issue regarding the legal succession of Russia to the nuclear weapons of the former USSR is found in the final decision in the documents stated in the limits of the CIS and in the Lisbon Agreement. This was not contested by Ukraine during the time when tactical nuclear weapons were withdrawn from its territory to Russia in accordance with the Russian-Ukrainian Agreement; therefore, the problem concerning tactical weapons having been removed from Ukrainian territory is closed and to return to it anew can only cause damage to the principal legal basis of nuclear non-proliferation regime. This problem does not arise with the other states of the CIS from which tactical nuclear weapons were withdrawn.

Second, if Russia accedes to the Ukrainian claim regarding tactical nuclear weapons, it could only mean a revision of this legal basis of the agreement and the recognition of Ukrainian right to ownership of such weapons. Such action would recognize Ukraine as a nuclear state and would contradict the decision of the CIS made on 6 July 1992 in which the Russian Federation was recognized as the only state possessing nuclear weapons on the territory of the former USSR.

As far as other states of the CIS including Ukraine are concerned, they pledged to join the Nuclear Non-Proliferation Treaty as non-nuclear states. The decision which was taken bears the signature of the President of Ukraine, L. M. Kravchuk. It is worth noting that in a written statement by the Ukrainian government in connection with the signing of the Protocol to the USSR-US START Treaty, it stated, *inter alia,* "The right and burden of possession of nuclear weapons of the former USSR by the directly expressed common consent of Ukraine and all other states, legal successors of the former USSR, was reserved only for the Russian Federation."

The Russian Federation is convinced that any return to this question after the fact not only contradicts the generally accepted norms of international law and practice but is a cause of a dangerous precedent in the struggle for strengthening the nuclear non-proliferation treaty. Thus there is no legal basis for Ukraine to claim indemnity for nuclear weapons withdrawn to Russia.

Third, the statement by Ukraine asking for compensation for the tactical nuclear weapons is just

conjecture. Further, the Russian-Ukrainian Agreement on nuclear weapons displacement from the Ukrainian territory to Russia (18 April 1992) mentions no word about any compensation for the nuclear weapons being displaced.

The fact that Ukraine concluded the above mentioned agreement with Russia without raising the question of indemnity for nuclear weapons and, moreover, the fact that the nuclear weapons withdrawal from Ukraine to Russia is coming to an end, all of this taken as a whole only underlines the legal validity of such a decision in full compliance with the international obligations of Russia and Ukraine and confirms the indissoluble unity of international law and practice in this area.

It is obvious that the problem of nuclear weapons proliferation is a very critical issue, and the way the Ukrainian issue will be solved will be telling regarding the future of the NPT in 1995 and beyond. Destroying the NPT regime may change the whole view of collective security, and there will be many nations which will view their national security needs with nuclear weapons.

5. Conclusion

1. Nuclear weapons are the defining element of nuclear states' armed forces. They remain currently in the arsenal of several countries as the main means for providing strategic stability and in averting war. The possible possessing, development, and manufacture of nuclear weapons and their delivery systems are of great political importance and significantly influence the international arena.
2. At present, there are real conditions internationally for the further proliferation of nuclear weapons. This is fraught with the threat of a reduction in collective security and a growing risk for local, regional, and global nuclear consequences. This is why it is so imperative to search for solutions for preventing nuclear weapons proliferation.
3. Russia's concept in nuclear non-proliferation consists of the following:
    -- firm and constant devotion to the prevention of nuclear weapons proliferation;
    -- securing mutual agreements on nuclear arms reduction throughout the world until there is complete liquidation of nuclear weapons;
    -- developing collective security systems; and
    -- the creation of effective systems and control mechanisms for nuclear weapons non-proliferation and the prevention of violators in international agreements

History has not provided us with the insights to rethink the processes under way and to devise cardinal and mutually acceptable solutions. If the international community does not reach agreement on how to halt the proliferation of nuclear weapons, the NPT regime will be seriously undermined. If this is the case, then the fate of peace on the earth may again be jeopardized.

Notes

1. For nuclear weapons development, approximately 1,300 engineers and 500 scientists are needed, while the portion of atomic experts among them should comprise of no fewer than 10 percent. In other words, in order to solve the problem of nuclear weapons development a country should have about 100 highly-skilled nuclear experts of different professions.

Chapter 3
UKRAINIAN SECURITY AND THE FATE OF NUCLEAR WEAPONS LOCATED ON ITS TERRITORY

Konstyantin Grischenko

Ever since the dissolution of the former USSR, the nuclear weapons that are located in the territory of Ukraine have been a matter of considerable concern, both for Ukraine and for the rest of the world.

A year or so has passed since the five parties to the Treaty on the Reduction and Elimination of Strategic Offensive Arms (START) signed the Lisbon Protocol, which transformed the bilateral Treaty originally signed by the US and the USSR into a multilateral agreement. However, to date the Treaty is not in force, and quite often the Ukraine is blamed for this inaction.

The START Treaty together with the Lisbon Protocol and the Nuclear Non- Proliferation Treaty (NPT) were introduced in the Ukrainian Parliament (Verhovna Rada) for ratification and now are being actively debated in the standing committees and in the *ad hoc* group created for this purpose by the Parliament. The decisions have been heated and all aspects of the nuclear dilemma are being analyzed. Difficult questions are being raised, questions that have no easy answers for a newly independent state which has all the reasons to question seriously the potential threats to its security.

Unfortunately, the rather complex and multifaceted problems related to nuclear weapons which the Ukraine inherited from the former Soviet Union are usually presented in an oversimplified, one-sided manner based on several false assumptions. These include the assumption that Ukraine is attempting to renege on its treaty obligations; that Russia is the sole successor to the Soviet nuclear weapons; and that Ukraine is using nuclear blackmail to secure financial assistance from the West.

The real picture is quite different. In order to see it clearly, it is important to understand the historical, psychological, legal, security, economic, and political dimensions of the nuclear dilemma that is now facing the people of the Ukraine.

1. Historical Dimension

History has taught the Ukrainians that they can rely only on themselves to safeguard their independence and territorial integrity. Our independence was lost for the first time approximately four hundred years ago when an alliance between two equals was unilaterally changed into an uneasy relationship of the Ukraine being subordinate to Russia. Later, this alliance degenerated into unmasked slavery. This experience again repeated itself during the period after the Bolshevik Revolution.

Since the Bolshevik Revolution, some seventy years ago, Ukraine was given the formal trappings of a nominally sovereign state within the Soviet Union. However, life under the Soviet Union for the Ukraine has been harsh and has taken several courses, including artificially-induced famine by Moscow, periodic purges of Ukrainian intelligensia, efforts to eliminate Ukrainian culture and language, the wanton destruction of agriculture, and the persecution and killing of as many Ukrainians by Soviet authorities as was the case under Nazi occupation. For those seventy years, the Ukraine was left alone to cope with these tragedies. Western democracies were too preoccupied with their own problems to be concerned or simply did not care.

Having lived through this historical experience, Ukrainians will never permit their independence to be lost again. They will fight against any threat with whatever means are at their disposal, for the stakes are too high. The opportunity to realize the Ukrainians full potential as a democratic forward-oriented, multiethnic society, striving to become part of modern united Europe is important to our national survival.

2. Present Security Environment

The present security environment around Ukraine is hardly favorable and a period of extreme danger exists. Furthermore, not everyone has been happy to see the emergence of the independent Ukraine. This is especially true of some elements in Russia which view an independent Ukraine as an aberration.

The West was also less then enthusiastic about the emergence of a free Ukraine. One has only to be reminded of the speech President George Bush gave in Kiev on the eve of independence when he preached to the Ukrainians about the dangers of their nationalism. It is true, however, that since this speech was given, attitudes in the West have markedly changed.

Political analysts in the United States who are not naive about the political world and are concerned about American national interests would agree that the mere existence of independent Ukraine is the best guarantee against the rebirth of a new empire within the borders of the former Soviet Union. Such an entity potentially will pose a major threat to the stability and security of Europe and its new emerging democracies.

Unfortunately, there is no evidence of any real commitment to Ukraine by the governments of the US and its allies, be it in the form of adequate political assistance, economic cooperation, or establishing the necessary security arrangements for Ukraine to maintain its independence. In brief, Ukraine interprets these words and action by the West as meaning that the Ukraine is basically on its own for its survival as an independent state.

3. Psychological Dimension

There is also a psychological dimension to Ukraine's nuclear dilemma, stemming from the Chernobyl tragedy. In the aftermath of this catastrophe and up to the period immediately following independence, Ukrainians were not in favor of anything associated with nuclear energy -- even its peaceful use. Public opinion polls today indicate that a substantial majority of Ukraine's population supports the idea of a nuclear option, which is viewed as an indispensable tool necessary to guarantee security and economic self-reliance.

These attitudes are widely shared in Parliament. Nevertheless, the Government, having analyzed all the possible scenarios and alternatives, is firm in its belief that a non-nuclear future is the best option for Ukraine, but it has a very difficult time in trying to convince Parliament and the general public.

4. Legal Dimension

The legal issues regarding nuclear weapons located on Ukrainian territory are unique and unprecedented. It is a fact that in 1990, the Parliament proclaimed that this state would neither possess nor produce nuclear weapons. Subsequently, both in 1991 and 1992 this position has been reiterated.

It is important to note that these documents represent *declarations of intent* and *not legal obligations to the international community*, providing the Executive authority to negotiate and sign international agreements. Nevertheless, the Parliament, under the Constitution, retains the final word on the entry into force of any treaty or obligation undertaken by the Government. In other words, there are no legal obligations which bind the Ukraine to being a non-nuclear weapon state before the final decision of the Parliament is taken to accede to the NPT regime. This is a very important point overlooked by most commentators.

Upon the dissolution of the former Soviet Union, Ukraine did not automatically become a non-nuclear weapon state. The reasons that affect this status follow:

-- Ukraine is an equal successor state to the former Soviet Union and thereby retains the same rights as Russia, or any of the other successor state, to be a nuclear power. The generally-accepted rules of international law provide that the successor state itself decides what rights and obligations of the predecessor state it will continue to assume. As a matter of principle, the Ukraine will never accept the notion that any particular successor state has the right to maintain a continuing status, as claimed by the Russian Federation. The only legal basis for Russian Federation's claim to nuclear status is for the succession states to give such a status to Russia.

It also was agreed by all successor states in Alma-Ata at the end of 1991 that the operational control over nuclear weapons was to be placed with the Joint Command of Strategic Forces of the Commonwealth of Independent States and not with any particular successor state.

These agreements further established a collective operational control of the nuclear weapons of the former Soviet Union, but left open the question of the proprietary rights to those weapons located on the territories of the relevant successor states.

-- According to the laws of Ukraine, which conform to the rules of international law and in particular the Vienna Convention on State Succession, all property of the former USSR that is on the territory of Ukraine (including nuclear weapons) belongs to Ukraine.

-- As the owner of these inherited nuclear arms, Ukraine neither seeks nor has plans to acquire operational control over these weapons within the context of Article II of the NPT regime. It should be noted the NPT does not contain the notion of "ownership" of nuclear weapons.

-- The Ukraine has decided to turn over to Russia half of the tactical nuclear weapons it has in its possession for dismantlement with the other half to be placed under the operational control of the CIS Joint Command. This sends a clear signal to all that Ukraine is not interested in acquiring nuclear capability.

-- The Strategic Nuclear Forces Command has a rather peculiar status. These forces on the territory of the Ukraine are under the operational control of the CIS Joint Command but are supported and maintained by the Ukraine.

In summary, the Ukraine, as the owner of nuclear weapons which it inherited from the USSR, has no operational control over these weapons. This is a unique situation, not fully covered by the definitions of what constitutes a nuclear weapon state, or a non-nuclear weapon state, as provided in the NPT.

5. Economic Dimension

It now appears that Ukraine is expected to shoulder most of the burden of expenses associated with the elimination of the nuclear weapons and their delivery systems, located on its territory. It is obvious because of the state of Ukraine's economy that it is unable now, or in the foreseeable future, to allocate any substantial monies toward the elimination of nuclear weapons based on its territory. That is the reality, and if other states are truly interested in seeing the eventual elimination of nuclear weapons from the Ukraine, they must make an active effort to solve this financial situation.

6. Nuclear Dilemma And The National Interests Of Ukraine

Paramount among Ukraine's national interests is the need as a newly-independent state to maintain its security in an environment that is quite threatening. These threats are those affecting the inviolability of borders and the integrity of the Ukrainian state. Internal instability, which is directly linked to the domestic economic situation, is also threatening. In short, both external security and internal stability concerning the Ukraine depend on the active involvement of the international community and, above all, of the United States in solving both problems.

Such an involvement by Washington to date is sadly lacking. There is a general feeling that the West is only interested in one issue: when will the Ukraine ratify START-I and accede to the Nuclear Non-Proliferation Treaty (NPT)? There is no evidence to suggest that the international community and its established structures (e.g., NATO, the G-7, the World Bank, the European Bank for Reconstruction and Development, etc.) will provide Ukraine with meaningful assistance, either in terms of security or economic aid. This is crucial to the outcome of the debate on the fate of nuclear weapons.

7. Action By The Ukrainian Government

Although the debate on the future of nuclear weapons continues, the commitment by the Executive to a non-nuclear Ukraine remains firm. This is evidenced by practical steps taken by the Government, among which have been the following:
-- the signing of the Lisbon Protocol which transformed the START Treaty from a bilateral are into a multilateral treaty, with the Ukraine as an equal partner;
-- the submission by the President to Parliament of the START-I Treaty and the NPT regime for ratification;
-- the official notification given to the International Atomic Energy Agency (IAEA) that Ukraine was ready to conclude an agreement placing all relevant nuclear facilities under IAEA safeguards.

Other practical steps taken by the Government included negotiations with the Russian Federation, the United States, and other nuclear and non-nuclear states and international organizations, with the view toward concluding agreements that will advance Ukraine's eventual decision to ratify and implement the START and the NPT Treaties.

In the end, the whole nuclear dilemma as it pertains to the Ukraine revolves around this very difficult question: does a country that feels threatened and possesses nuclear weapons, which it neither developed nor produced but inherited as a result of an unexpected twist of history, have the right to exploit its possession of these weapons to guarantee its survival?

Many in the Ukraine believe that all nations have the right to defend their independence and development by either seeking protection through regional or international arrangements or by any other means at their disposal.

The dilemma for Ukraine is quite simple: either effective protection is needed against potential foreign aggressors or, failing that, Kiev will be left with no option but to rely upon its nuclear weapons.

It is rather difficult for Americans and for Western Europeans who have lived under the protection of the US nuclear umbrella for so many years to understand the sense of insecurity that Ukrainians feel, which then enhances their pro-nuclear sentiment. In order for them to overcome these feelings it is important that their national security be guaranteed and international assistance provided to eliminate the nuclear weapons which they possess. Finally, the international community should commit to Ukraine's independence and territorial integrity. More specifically, the minimal guarantees necessary for Ukraine are as follows:

1) In accordance with the principles of the UN Charter and the CSCE Final Act; respect should be given to the independence, sovereignty, and borders of Ukraine.
2) Refrain should be given to the use of political, military, or economic pressures against the Ukraine.
3) Assistance should be rendered if the Ukraine is threatened or is a victim of aggression.

8. START Implementation

Implementing START will create serious economic and ecological issues. Ukraine is in no position economically to afford the cost of eliminating its nuclear arsenal. To do so would inflict serious strains on the economy and might precipitate an economic crisis. Not only is it an obligation of Ukraine, but more importantly it is in the interest of the nuclear powers and the rest of the international community for Kiev to destroy these weapons of mass destruction. Therefore, it is in the interest of all the international community for financing of the dismantlement and elimination be provided as well as the cost to verify these articles. It should be understood that Ukraine is not asking for a handout nor is it attempting to blackmail the international community. It is the belief of Ukraine that this financial support is necessary in order for START to be fully implemented.

The debate that will take place in Parliament will determine if Ukraine will become a non-nuclear state. The basic question that is relevant to these debates is in what way is the Ukraine's security enhanced or diminished if it remains a nuclear state or if it becomes a non-nuclear state relying primarily on other means to guarantee its independence and its security. Presently, Ukraine is faced with a serious external threat to its territorial integrity. It cannot defend itself except by conventional methods. It is, however, the "outside" world that expects the Ukraine to become a non-nuclear power, but this will not happen unless the Kiev is given full compensation for both the strategic and the tactical nuclear weapons found on its soil.

Supporting strong independent Ukraine is in the best national interest of the United States, NATO allies, and the West in general. It also is the best guarantee against the reemergence of a new empire which will endanger the new world order based on shared democratic values.

Chapter 4
CIS: DISARMAMENT AND SECURITY CHALLENGES

Alexander M. Baichorov

Upon the breakup of the Soviet Union, the obligations for non-proliferation fell to the Newly Independent States (NIS) of the former Soviet Union. Up until August 1991 most of the important state security and arms control questions had been decided by the Soviet Union. The newly formed governments of the NIS had no experience or any qualified personnel to deal with these issues. After the dissolution of the Soviet Union and the creation of the Commonwealth of Independent States (CIS) in Viskuly, Belarus, on 8 December 1991, they voluntary assumed these responsibilities.

The problem affecting nuclear weapons was the first major issue that the NIS governments attempted to handle. The agreement on joint measures regarding nuclear weapons was signed in Alma Alta, Kazakhstan, on 21 December 1991, during the second CIS summit. In this agreement Belarus and Ukraine (but not Kazakhstan) took upon themselves the obligation to join the Non-Proliferation Treaty (NPT). At this meeting the CIS members decided that nuclear weapons would become the sole responsibility of the Russian Federation.

The arms control and disarmament arena where the former Soviet Union was a major player, and which rules were more or less known, suddenly became extremely complex and unpredictable. Many old familiar rules were abandoned and no new mutually accepted ones were introduced. Every new player that entered the arms control and disarmament arena had its own perceptions and national habits and, often, with very strange instructions that were cabled from inexperienced government officials. All the major treaties and agreements regarding arms control had to be re-examined and adjusted in light of the new political realities.

1. The Limited Test Ban Treaty, The Biological Convention, The ABM Treaty, And The INF Treaty

It was agreed upon between the members of the CIS that international treaties signed by the USSR automatically became valid for the NIS members unless there was a special decision taken by the highest authorities. Belarus and the other countries of NIS had no difficulties in becoming bound by the provisions of the Limited Test Ban Treaty and the Biological Weapons Convention. The Anti-Ballistic Missile (ABM) Treaty was quite another matter. The installations that were included by this treaty were found in several of the independent states. The provisions of the Treaty had been drawn-up between the US and the USSR and now they did not accommodate the interests of some NIS members. The second reason for concern involved the United States which found it difficult to deal with several countries, as opposed to only USSR.

At the end of September 1993, a five-year review of the ABM Treaty was undertaken. At this meeting it was still unclear if Washington was ready to recognize the CIS states as legitimate parties to the Treaty or if other countries, such as Latvia, should be included in the review process.

In October 1992, in Bishkek, Kyrgystan, the CIS countries agreed among themselves that they should all become parties to the ABM treaty. To date, the implementation of the Treaty is still dependent upon the position of the US.

The negotiating process for the INF treaty was most complicated and time-consuming because of the attention that was paid to every technical detail. Those who negotiated the INF Treaty knew that the extra efforts put into this agreement would assist the START-I Treaty negotiations.

The INF Treaty eliminated the intermediate range missiles. There are, however, inspection provisions to the Treaty which are to be implemented by a number of the former Soviet Republics. Belarus, Kazakhstan, Russian Federation, Turkmenistan, Ukraine and Uzbekistan became parties to the INF Treaty. This created a whole new set of problems for INF implementation. The Special Verification Commission (SVC), established under the INF, was not able to secure all the INF States Parties approval because Turkmenistan and Uzbekistan did not attend the SVC meetings.

Furthermore, there is a debt of $3.8 million accumulated as a result of US inspection activities that have taken place on the territory of the USSR. The Russian Federation claims that because it is the legal successor, the money should go to Moscow. On the other hand, some members of the NIS argue that they must receive the same compensation because a number of the inspections that were conducted by the US were on their territories. Presently, Washington is awaiting word from the CIS as to how these monies will be apportioned.

1.1   The START-I And START-II Treaties

The START-I Treaty that was drafted reflected some of the experiences of the negotiators of the INF Treaty. It was signed by the USSR and the USA on 31 July 1991. The formal dissolution of the USSR and the proclamation creating the CIS did not clarify the situation but rather created a real arms control dilemma for the United States. Washington had difficulty in preserving the vitality of the newly-drafted START-I Treaty. Finally, in May 1992 under the insistence of Washington, Belarus, Kazakhstan and Ukraine signed the Lisbon Protocol and took upon themselves the obligation of ratifying START and acceding to the NPT "in the soonest possible time."

The Joint Compliance and Inspection Commission (JCIC) established under START attempted to implement the USSR-US Treaty to the US, Belarus, Kazakhstan, Russian Federation and Ukraine. The JCIC settled many of the technical problems which hindered the implementation of the Treaty. For example, it managed to establish new points of entry for inspection teams which were obviously not envisaged under START. It further ironed-out many contradictions born by the new political and geostrategic realities. During its six sessions, the JCIC adopted 11 agreements, 10 joint statements and many other mutually binding documents; nevertheless, START-I had not entered into force by the end of 1993.

It is obvious that implementation of the START-I Treaty will contribute greatly to the disarmament process. START-I limits both sides on the number of ICBMs and on the number of nuclear warheads. Moreover, entering into force, the START-I Treaty is the precondition for the implementation of the START-II Treaty which was signed by the Russian Federation and the US in January 1993. START-II halts the operation of a whole class of ground-based multi-warhead ICBMs and cuts heavily into the number of warheads on the SLBMs.

Why has the START-I Treaty not been ratified by all of the negotiating parties? Further, what are the prospects of the Treaty being ratified? The Russian Federation, Kazakhstan, and the Republic of Belarus ratified START-I in February 4, 1993. Belarus did so in spite of the efforts by some political and military circles in Belarus to hold the ratification process captive in order to force the US to provide assistance in keeping the languishing Belarus economy afloat. This was not a foolhardy gesture. At stake were eight mobile SS-25 divisions equipped with 81 ICBMs. Each missile is able to throw its warhead with a staggering accuracy over 10,000 kilometers (6,500 miles). A single warhead's explosive power is equal to 1 million tons of TNT.[1] It is also worth noting that only Belarus ratified the START-I Treaty without reservations. Kazakhstan has ratified START-I but has not acceded to the NPT. Ukraine, on the other hand, is the only party which has partially fulfilled its obligations under the Lisbon Protocol. There are a number of reasons for this.

First, there are influential political and military circles which want to ratify the Treaty at some later day, but they would like to use the ratification process as a possible means of securing foreign aid. These circles are much more powerful in Ukraine than in Belarus. Second, there is a formidable nationalist movement, especially in western Ukraine, which does not want START-I to be ratified. This group would like to see the Ukraine remain a great nuclear power. Further, there are very serious disputes between the Russian Federation and Ukraine over part of the territory known as Crimea as well as the Black Sea Fleet. Some Ukrainian leaders believe that these issues could be easier resolved from a position of strength. Finally, pronouncements have been made by Ukrainian and American leaders which send the wrong signals to the Ukrainian Government. The wrong conclusions are drawn from these pronouncements that suggest that if Ukraine were adament in its position, it might benefit financially.

As we examine the present situation with the START-I Treaty entering into force, we can note a few new developments. Several agreements have been concluded and signed by both Russia and Ukraine concerning the existing problems of the Black Sea Fleet and the status of the city of Sebastopol.

Washington has indicated to the Ukraine that no agreements will be implemented (because of the Nunn-Lugar legislation) which requires Kiev to ratify the NPT. There are indications that Kazakhstan will accede to the NPT, leaving Ukraine the only nuclear state not to have done so. Although START-I was ratified, a series of conditions were attached that are too difficult for Washington to accept. In particular, Ukraine wants compensation for the nuclear materials in any warhead that are destroyed, which also included the tactical weapons already turned over to Russia. Under these circumstances START-II becomes hostage to the START-I entering into force.

1.2 FE And Open Skies Treaties

The CFE Treaty was designed to take into account the military potentials of NATO and the Warsaw Pact, but its ratification and implementation came about after the demise of the latter. The successful implementation of the CFE will become the most significant contribution to building a new European security system and enhancing the confidence among nations in Europe and North America.

It was the Republic of Belarus which prevented the implementation of the CFE in the summer of 1992. A number of reasons were responsible for those actions. The Belorussian Military District contained most of the modern tanks in the Soviet Army. Furthermore, Belarus military commanders could not comprehend why under the CFE Treaty provisions it was necessary to eliminate huge amounts of the most modern military equipment in light of the fact that Belarus does not manufacture battle tanks, armored combat vehicles, combat aircraft or attack helicopters. In addition, strict adherence to the CFE obligations would force Belarus in the future to pay hard currency for the modernization of its armed forces.

When tank divisions were withdrawn from Poland and East Germany, Kiev insisted that some of the elements of the tank division be left in Belarus. This automatically added some 300 battle tanks to the Belarus liquidation liability under provisions of the CFE Treaty. As a result, Belarus must destroy 50 times more battle tanks than France, 10 times more than the United Kingdom, and 1.7 times more than the United States. In spite of having to destroy so many arms and equipment, Belarus will have a very modern arsenal of conventional weapons. After the CFE elimination process is completed, Belarus will retain one battle tank per 5700 inhabitants compared to one per 19,000 in Germany, one per 23,000 in the Russian Federation and one per 44,000 in France. More or less similar ratios will exist for Belarus when compared to other CFE countries in armored combat vehicles, combat aircraft, and attack helicopters.

The amount of money that has been allocated by the Ministry of Defense to meet the CFE Treaty requirements in destroying the several elements is 10 percent of the national budget (56.5 billion rubles). It now appears that the destruction process is falling behind not because of the lack of personnel or technological know-how, but because of the lack of money. Belarus has requested $16 million from the United States and NATO to help underwrite the destruction phase of the CFE Treaty. Kiev feels strongly that the West should help underwrite these costs since Belarus was pressured into ratifying the CFE Treaty and thus forced to expend quickly scarce economic resources that it does not have. Further, by the destruction of the weapons systems, Belarus is of the opinion that proportionately Kiev is contributing far more to lowering the arms race than other CFE signatories and, thus, enhancing the security of Europe. Beyond the financial constraints imposed on Belarus, the timetable to meet the destruction phase of the CFE Treaty also needs to be reconsidered.

The Ukraine supported by the Russian Federation wants to amend the CFE Treaty in order to eliminate the weapons ratios in the Southern Flank. The US and NATO do not support this position, fearing that it will undermine the whole treaty and create a bad precedent. There are, however, some encouraging signs for the CFE implementation phase on the part of the CIS. The Russian Federation and the Ukraine have accelerated their elimination programs and will reach the required levels by the end of the treaty year. On another matter regarding the implementation of the CFE, the CIS countries, for the first time, agreed among themselves on the distribution of the Soviet Union's quota of the financial contributions to the Joint Consultative Commission of the CIS.

In all, the CIS countries consider the CFE Treaty fundamental for establishing a system of security cooperation in the framework of the CSCE. Belarus, the Russian Federation, and the Ukraine have worked hard to make the Treaty effective and to preserve the CFE inspection regime.

The Open Skies Treaty will be another challenge for the CIS arms control process. Belarus has made a firm decision to join the Treaty along with the Russian Federation. There are still many obstacles to be overcome before the Parliaments of Russia and Belarus ratify the Open Skies Treaty. The dissolution of the Parliament of the Russian Federation in September 1993 postponed this ratification process. The Parliament of Belarus might also stand for new elections in spring 1994. All of these events create an air of unpredictability regarding the timeframe that the Open Skies Treaty will enter into force.

2. Arms Control And Security Concerns

Arms control issues in the CIS will be determined to a large extent by the nature of the security concerns in the NIS. These concerns will vary from Islamic fundamentalism to the Russian-Ukranian rivalry over the Crimea and the Black Sea Fleet. How do these two issues affect the arms control processes in the relevant CIS nations? The Russian Federation does not want to deal with strong Islamic states on its southern borders and would like to preserve the safety belt that is created by the Central Asian Republics. The political leaders of these republics need the military and economic support of Russia to cope with the economic, political, cultural, and religious difficulties that might emanate from the South. These joint interests have resulted in the Collective Security Treaty of the CIS signed by Armenia, Kazakhstan, Kyrgyzstan, Russia, and Uzbekistan in Tashkent on 15 May 1992; Tajikistan later also ratified this agreement.

This Collective Security Treaty was formulated along the lines of other security agreements like NATO and the Warsaw Pact. The protocols to this Treaty provide for a unified nuclear and strategic territory which places these countries under the nuclear umbrella of the Russian Federation. Such an arrangement will affect how Kazakhstan reacts in maintaining its nuclear arsenal, especially in light of China having resumed nuclear testing in October 1993.

The dispute between the Russian Federation and the Ukraine over the Black Sea Fleet and the status of the port of Sebastopol has created a whole range of the arms control and disarmament problems. Some Ukrainian leaders tend to consider nuclear weapons as the only deterrence against the military power of the Russian Federation. To counter the Collective Security Treaty, Ukraine has introduced its own initiatives on strengthening regional security in Central and Eastern Europe. This effort has come to naught because of the lack of support from both Central and Eastern Europe's military establishments. There is no doubt that Belarus harbors serious reservations regarding her membership in this Collective Security Treaty.

3. Belarus And The CIS Arms Control And Security Concerns

Belarus, in its Declaration of Independence of July 1990, proclaimed that it would become a neutral and a non-nuclear state. These two principle notions were laid out as foundations for the military doctrine of Belarus armed forces; this doctrine is defensive in nature as indicated by its strategy which forbids using the Belarus military outside of its national borders, with the exception of participating in UN peace-keeping operations.

Furthermore, Defense Minister General-Colonel Pavel Kozlovski announced in his 1993 New Year Speeches that the armed forces would be cut from 180,000 to 100,000 with accompanying cuts in battle tanks, armored combat vehicles, combat aircraft, helicopters, and other weapons systems.[2] Belarus is also taking an actual role in participating in the creation of a new European Security System through the CSCE powers. Finally, Belarus does not exclude participating in some subregional security arrangements, providing that such arrangements do not create a *cordon sanitaire* around the Russian Federation.

4. Conclusion

With the collapse of the security system of the Cold War, the familiar conceptual framework which permitted national security strategists, from both the West and East, to justify various arms control and disarmament requirements are now irrelevant. It is more and more evident that "nuclear explosives are not military weapons and should not be treated as such, either by making plans for their use in battle or by insisting that nuclear arms control agreements be balanced."[3] President Clinton stated in his address to the UN General Assembly in 1993, "Thirty-two years ago President Kennedy warned this chamber that humanity lived under a nuclear sword of Damocles that hung by the slenderest of threads. Now the United States is working with Russia, Ukraine, Belarus, and others to take that sword of annihilation down to lock it away in a secure vault."[4] The CIS countries today are no longer the enemies or military adversaries of the West. This confrontational approach, which permeated the thinking of military strategists and nuclear weapons experts during the Cold War era, still continues to persist. However, it is not these individuals who will determine the national security policies of the CIS states in the near future.

Today there are many spheres in arms control and disarmament where the West and the CIS are natural allies. One such area is the common work that is being done by both sides for the completion of the Comprehensive Test Ban Treaty (CTBT) for the end of 1996. The CIS and the West should work through the Conference on Disarmament to form an alliance to complete the work on the CTBT.

Another sphere where cooperation is necessary is the 1995 NPT Extension Conference. To make this conference a success and to extend the NPT beyond 1995, it is necessary for the East and West to propose additional security guarantees to the non-nuclear participating parties. Additionally, to thwart the proliferation of ballistic missiles capable of carrying chemical, biological, or nuclear weapons cooperation between the CIS and the West is appropriate. The Russian Federation has already joined the Missile Technology Control Regime (MTCR). Other CIS states could follow suit and work together with the West to have the MTCR universally accepted. Other avenues of cooperation might extend from arms transfer of conventional arms to the monitoring of developing new types of weapons of mass destruction. Because of the difficult economic straits that the CIS countries find themselves in today, it does not provide them with the latitude they need to address properly arms control. In fact, in the future they might become more a part of the problem than the solution. That is why it is extremely important for them to receive economic assistance and understanding from the West during this most dangerous period of their economic transformation. The assistance provided under the Nunn-Lugar legislation and the economic package provided by Japan for Belarus, Kazakhstan, Russia, and Ukraine for non-proliferation purposes should also be followed by assistance from other western states to facilitate the creation of a safe and secure international environment.

Notes

1. *Novoye Russopye Slovo,* 4 June 1993.
2. Ibid.
3. Jane M. O. Sharp. "Arms Control and Alliance Commitments," *Political Science Quarterly.* (Winter), 1985-86, p. 666.
4. "US Committed to Making UN Vision a Reality." Speech given by President Bill Clinton to UN General Assembly, 27 September 1993 (*Foreign Policy Speeches,* USIA, September 1993), p. 1.

PART II

REGIONAL ISSUES OF ARMS CONTROL AND VERIFICATION

Chapter 5
REGIONAL ARMS CONTROL: OVERLOOKED NO LONGER?

Michael Moodie

Regional arms control could emerge as the single most important arms control focus in the 1990s. Traditionally, arms control has been pursued either globally, with agreements such as the Nuclear Nonproliferation Treaty (NPT) or the Biological Weapons Convention (BWC) whose goal is universal participation and compliance, or bilaterally, with US-Soviet efforts dominating the process. During the Cold War, important regional agreements were achieved, but generally regional arms control outside Europe was not high on the agenda. One commentator, for example, notes that at the first UN Special Session on Disarmament (SSOD), regional arms control was mentioned barely *en passant*.[1]

The lack of attention to regional arms control was in part a product of the Cold War. The US-Soviet confrontation occupied center stage, and arms control theory was initially developed in response to concerns over how the nuclear dimension of that rivalry could be managed. W. Scott Thompson suggests one outcome of this process was that "social scientists created a virtual cottage industry of arms control literature aimed at the superpowers, whose great size made them the least likely candidates to be persuaded by the literature; little was written in the field of conventional arms control for the more likely candidates in the Third World."[2] Moreover, as Donald Snow points out, the Third World was actually treated as "a place where the Cold War could be fought without the threat of nuclear destruction."[3] Under such circumstances there was little interest in promoting arrangements which might restrict the dynamics of such conflict.

The absence of efforts to constrain arms in regions outside Europe was also the product of the perspectives of developing countries themselves. For a variety of reasons -- some legitimate, some questionable, some downright venal -- developing countries exhibited during much of the Cold War era little interest in arms control that might directly inhibit their military capabilities. During this period, participation of developing countries in arms control was limited largely either to declaratory measures or adherence to global agreements limiting weapons they did not have. Little priority was given to measures constraining the military situation on the ground in their locales.

Geoffrey Kemp argues, however, that "the end of the Cold War accelerated a process that has been underway for some time, namely the regionalization of conflict."[4] In doing so, it has also created new opportunities for regional arms control by highlighting its potential utility to states likely to be caught up in the maelstrom of regional conflict. In addition, economic imperatives are forcing all states of the international community to revisit their choices between guns and butter. In some quarters at least, the sense is growing that if arms control can stabilize the military dimensions of regional relationships in such a way that resources can be redirected to meet economic demands, there may be some value in exploring arms control possibilities.

Regional arms control, therefore, is a feature of the international security environment whose time has come. Whether this opportunity will be exploited remains an open question. This chapter explores the opportunities for and barriers to progress in this increasingly important item on the arms control agenda.

1. The End Of The Cold War And Regional Conflict

With the end of the Cold War, the greatest danger to international security is instability and conflict stemming from regional confrontations. Improved superpower relations will not necessarily lead to less conflict. Indeed, more conflict may be in the offing. How the international community handles Third World conflict will be crucially important to the evolution of the international system. In confronting this challenge, arms control represents a potentially important instrument.

The factors contributing to instability in the developing world are many and varied. Perhaps the most important is a continual presence of a sense of grievance, both within states and in the relationships among them. Ethnicity has emerged as a major factor in this regard, and a primary security challenge of the post-Cold War era will be containing ethnic conflict in the many forms it is likely to assume.[5] This sense of grievance is frequently intensified by a lack of legitimacy and authority of governments that have often failed to deliver basic services.[6] It is also exacerbated by the rise of nationalism, a trend that has reached such proportions in some areas that its has been inflated to "hypernationalism."[7]

The second factor contributing to Third World instability is the inability of governments to ameliorate the conditions giving rise to grievance due to lack of resources. Many governments confront the harsh reality of their physical incapacity to provide for all of their society's members. This inability is worsened by the incessant pressure of numbers as populations rise, debt escalates, and resource consumption accelerates. In commenting on security issues in the Maghreb, for example, Assia Benshalah Alaoui points out that the greatest challenges are perceived to be the socio-economic, political, and cultural demands of fast-growing and overwhelmingly young populations.[8] When these demands cannot be met by the governments of North Africa -- or governments elsewhere for that matter -- the sense of grievance deepens and the prospect for conflict draws nearer.

That conflict has most often taken the form of internal challenges to developing country governments. In the post-Cold War era, however, especially in light of heightened ethnic sensitivity and identification, religious fundamentalism, and hypernationalism, keeping internal conflicts within national borders will be more difficult than ever. The impact of the civil war in Afghanistan on the dynamics between India and Pakistan is one example. Serbian support of their "kinsmen" in Bosnia demonstrates how easy it is for states with a specific agenda to move that agenda forward through involvement in, and sometimes instigation of, disputes of others.

A less well-articulated, if not less well-appreciated, factor fostering Third World conflict is the growing recognition of the absence of constraints on conflict, again in part as a result of the end of the Cold War. The collapse of the US-Soviet confrontation and its projection into the Third World is to likely diminish Washington's and Moscow's willingness to restrain conflict in regions not central to their interests. Despite their competition, perhaps because of it, the United States and the Soviet Union often engaged in Third World conflict management. Their motives were clear: not to jeopardize a major investment in allies, to limit the extent to which Third World conflicts could disrupt the conduct of business more central to managing their bilateral relationship, and, most importantly, to ensure that regional conflicts would not get out of control so that superpower intervention became necessary in a way that produced direct confrontation.[9] US-Soviet competition in the Third World, manifested in their support for different sides in regional rivalries, also had the effect of establishing local balances of power which suppressed the emergence of regional powers with hegemonic ambitions.[10]

With the end of the Cold War, this sense of limits has disappeared. Saddam Hussein was the first challenger to test the "permissiveness of this new era."[11] He is unlikely to be the last.

One impact of this diminished sense of limits of conflict has been to increase the number of potential Third World flashpoints. Ethnicity and nationalism have already been mentioned as potential sources of conflict. A second is the increasingly disparate economic growth rates within the Third World itself. As Chandran Jeshurun describes the situation in southeast Asia, "now the very real danger is that a huge and unbridgeable gap is growing between the [newly industrializing countries] and the stagnant economies of Burma, Vietnam, Laos, Cambodia and the Philippines ... [and that] this socio-economic cleavage will be the cause of new strains in intra-regional relationships."[12] What is true of southeast Asia is true of other regions as well, as tensions between the oil sheikdoms and others in the Persian Gulf demonstrate.

A third potential source of Third World conflict of increasing concern is the environment. The traditional spark in this tinder box has been disputes over resources, including oil and minerals, but, increasingly, over water as well. Growing attention is also being paid to resource management as a source of conflict. There is, for example, a burgeoning literature examining the problem of resource degradation due to bad resource management practices prompting major population movements that lead to conflict.[13] Religious fundamentalism is another source of potential conflict, especially of the virulent variety espoused by Iran and echoed by the government of Sudan, thereby creating tensions with Egypt.

These flashpoints combine with such traditional issues of border disputes, territorial claims, and ideological differences to create a complex and unstable regional mix that does not take much to ignite it.[14]

A diminished sense of limits appears not only to have increased the number of issues which could spark conflict but also to have caused those conflicts that do occur to become much more deadly. The quantity and quality of Third World arsenals are unprecedented; their weapons inventories are larger and more sophisticated than ever. Third World states, however, are not just emphasizing better weapons in larger numbers. They are also pursuing important force structure changes to exploit new and improved technologies. Australian defense analyst Desmond Ball points out, for example, that in southeast Asia, "forces have been restructured from counterinsurgency to modern, high technology forces with increased emphasis on maritime (including land-base air) capabilities."[15] A similar process is underway in many other parts of the Third World.

Potential conflicts can also now be waged over a wider geographic area as a result of new technologies. If Iran, for example, were to acquire North Korea's new Nodong-I missile, as it reportedly is interested in doing, for the first time it would have the capability to strike Israel from its homeland.

North Korea also highlights the problem of new suppliers in the international arms market. The problem is not so much that smaller suppliers will challenge the states who dominate the international arms trade across the board, but that they are capable of producing a few advanced systems which are highly destructive, especially in a Third World context. When that capability is combined with a willingness to sell to anyone with the money to buy, the result is the introduction of capabilities into regions of tension which could both destabilize the regional military balance and increase the destructiveness of war.

Looming over increasing regional tensions is the specter of the proliferation of weapons of mass destruction, the use of which shatters the limitations of conflict. Proliferation is a danger precisely because it creates an explosive combination: a region of great tension and enhanced destructive capabilities. The volatility of this mixture could result in untold devastation and worldwide instability.

Finally, the end of Cold War-era constraints has created opportunities for states interested in asserting their regional influence. A number of states have styled themselves major regional actors, if not hegemonies, in a time of greater pluralism following the demise of the bipolar US-Soviet confrontation. How aggressive these states might become in asserting their regional interests remains to be seen, but, if Saddam Hussein is a harbinger of things to come, their efforts will not always be peaceful.

2. The Need For Regional Arms Control

A growing number of sources of conflict, the absence of restraint, increasingly sophisticated conventional arsenals, the specter of weapons of mass destruction, and muscle-flexing by would-be regional powers combine to create an ever more complex, precarious, and dangerous security environment in many regions of the world. Global approaches to dealing with these problems are important, but they are not enough. Directions of Third World politics and security will more than ever be locally determined, what John Chipman, Director of the International Institute for Strategic Studies, calls the "international relations of parochialism."[16] Regional arms control must now become a part of that process.

A variety of factors must be appreciated in assessing the prospects for regional arms control. These factors contrast with the situation that existed in Europe, where some regional arms control has been successful. The varied sources of conflict have already been mentioned. In addition, states in regions beyond Europe still labor under the shadow of war. Not only have the security perceptions and approaches of many Third World states been shaped by their experience with conflict since the end of World War II -- witness several Arab-Israeli wars and Indo-Pakistani wars -- but they are uncertain at best and certain at worst that such conflicts will be repeated some time in the future. Further, there is no cooperative regional security system similar to the Conference on Security and Cooperation in Europe (CSCE) to provide a framework for the necessary dialogue to resolve security issues. Finally, the shadow of proliferation of weapons of mass destruction has been cast over many regional security environments, and concerns about such weapons have become a major aspect of regional states' security considerations.

In this environment, a number of problems will constitute barriers to successful regional arms control. Perhaps the most severe is a skeptical if not negative attitude toward arms control among many regional states. In some cases, that attitude is shaped by lack of experience. For many developing countries, there is only a small cadre of people with arms control expertise. Many of these experts, however, have had their training and experience in multilateral forums such as the Conference on Disarmament (CD) and the United Nations. In such forums, global regimes are the focus of attention, and while they can do useful work, they provide little opportunity for those involved to gain experience with arms control measures which relate to their actual military situations on the ground.

In terms of one conceptual scheme that categorizes arms control into preventive and curative measures,[17] the experience of most Third World arms control experts is almost exclusively with the former.

Beyond the question of experience, however, is the issue of regional states' perceptions of the utility of arms control. Developing countries view their incentives for acquiring arms and developing military capabilities as no less valid than those of developed states, and in many ways more so. The strong perception exists that the use of military power is likely to remain a feature of their regional environments for a considerable time to come, and national interests must be protected and advanced with all available policy instruments, including armaments. The end of the Cold War has intensified this perception by making it more difficult in the view of developing countries to depend on external support, especially of the superpowers, to buttress their own capacities in meeting their security needs.

W. Scott Thompson argues that the notion that conflict has become unacceptable in the world is a peculiarly Western notion which has not spread to the Third World.[18] The belief persists in many parts of the world in the military solution as the ultimate option of state leaders and the internal and external opponents. The result, according to John Chipman, is that "war has become politics by other means; government is management of conflict; opposition has meant insurgency; and guerrilla activities have become a lifestyle."[19]

Given this perception, it should come as no surprise that regional security analysts have labeled arms control "a Western concept," "alien to the region," or "not a high priority." This view was perhaps best summarized by Chandran Jeshurun in describing attitudes toward arms control in southeast Asia where "governments are disinclined to embark upon confidence building measures that in any way touch upon issues relating to arms transfers, arms control and arms production in the current state of intra-regional and international strategic uncertainty."[20]

Among some countries in the developing world, arms control is also perceived as a policy of developed countries which is hypocritical, selective, and discriminatory.[21] Opposition is especially strong to efforts by developed countries to limit the transfer of technology. The result, as Geoffrey Kemp points out, is "a significant gap between the industrial powers and many regional states that see arms control initiatives as an attempt to interfere with their national security needs at a time when the old collective security umbrellas are being removed."[22]

Although some Third World concerns may be justified, their traditional approaches to arms control have also had a strong self-serving aspect as well. Defense specialist Brad Roberts points out that a few key developing states, which are not necessarily representative of all such countries, have dominated the articulation of the developing countries' security agenda. Throughout the Cold War, these states extended the anti-colonial struggle by using international institutions to press their case for justice and equality. In the security realm, they did so by equating major security problems with actions of the superpowers or European colonizers. The result has been their tendency to take "a primarily ideological view of global and regional security issues."[23]

Moreover, in taking this approach, these Third World security spokesmen accomplished two important national tasks. First, they deflected international attention from their own regional security problems. Second, they were able to legitimize individual decisions -- high defense expenditures, domestic pursuit of particular weapons programs, acquisition of high-prestige systems for which there was little operational need or expertise -- that otherwise may have been deemed unacceptable by domestic constituencies, the international community or both.

Arms control was not immune from this process. In the Third World's post-war rhetoric, arms control basically had to do with controlling the arms of others, primarily of the superpowers and their nuclear weapons in particular. Justice and equality were the developing world' measures of arms control acceptability. Their greatest criticism of the NPT, for example, has been that it is discriminatory by creating one class of countries which could have nuclear weapons and another class that could not. In the post-colonial period, the Third World demanded that Washington and Moscow (and, to a lesser extent, London and Paris) take the necessary steps to reduce their nuclear arsenals as the necessary first step toward "general and complete disarmament." Without that superpower step, however, developing states made it very clear that no one should expect others to do anything.

This approach to security and arms control for much of the last forty-five years has had two deleterious effects on the ability of Third World states to respond to the challenges of the post-Cold War era. First, policymakers in developing countries have little of the room for maneuver they need to make arms control an effective policy instrument in the new environment. Government leaders in both India and Pakistan, for example, argue that they cannot take steps to reverse their nuclear programs because domestic political dynamics would force from power any government that did so. In some countries, constrained policy flexibility is a reflection of weak civil-military relations and the key role of the military in security decisions. In part, however, it is also the result of years of promoting the post-colonial ideological perspective on security questions with a compliant media and an uncritical non-governmental sector, including academia.[24]

Prvovslav Davinic of the United Nations Center for Disarmament Affairs has summarized the second problem for arms control created by the Third World's ideological approach: "Member states are not in a position to deal with all [the new issues] adequately, while, at the same time, remaining 'loyal' to their favorite items from the past."[25] The end of the Cold War has altered the security and arms control agenda. Yet, Third World states, hemmed in by their rhetoric, have been slow to change their focus. Superpower nuclear arsenals remain their preoccupation despite both the massive cuts in US and Russian arsenals entailed in the strategic arms reduction agreements and the eruption of conflict on the doorstep of many of these states. Arms suppliers are still cast as villains forcing unwanted weapons on unsuspecting governments. Technology constraint regimes are still cast as conspiracies of the haves against the have-nots.

These perceptions, however, could change, as a result of a number of factors. One clearly is the ongoing impact of the new agenda close to home. As violence and instability continues to threaten regimes throughout the Eurasian landmass, there should emerge a greater willingness to do something about them. Particularly as the dangers of proliferation become better appreciated and states realize that the stakes of conflict are changing -- indeed, that they likely have more to lose -- measures to reduce the potential dangers should become more appealing. Arms control offers a potentially useful instrument.

A second factor could be the process of democratization, although its impact is the subject of considerable debate. The argument in favor suggests not only that democracies do not fight one another, but that a democratic process could force different choices on national decision makers which shift resources away from the military sphere. Economic realities are yet another factor that could foster new perspectives, as all nations increasingly confront choices between weapons and other national priorities. Even states long thought to enjoy virtually unlimited resources, such as the oil-rich nations of the Persian Gulf, have felt economic pressures so strongly that weapons acquisition plans have been canceled, drawn out, or significantly cut back. More generally, Janne Nolan contends that the "maturation of the international economy ... has helped create a world in which technology and military accommodation with other sovereign states is increasingly less a matter of choice than of necessity and self-interest."[26]

In general, the opportunity exists for development of an appreciation that the military instrument alone cannot guarantee security, and that some form of cooperative approach is needed to meet the security challenges of the post-Cold War era. Here is where arms control becomes a part of the process -- as a tool to assist in the development of that cooperative relationship.

3. Regional Arms Control Challenges

The argument is often posited that there can be regional arms control only if there is movement toward settlement of basic political and geographic disputes among contending parties. As Geoffrey Kemp points out, however, political problems in making progress toward a settlement are sometimes so complex that a decision to postpone major arms control initiatives encourages a continued arms race that has built-in dangers and can lead to war.[27] The argument in favor of delay, therefore, must be rejected. Indeed, the US-Soviet experience demonstrates that a shared interest in arms control can help to maintain a relationship even when tensions run high. In the early 1980s, for example, both sides recognized the value of continuing US-Soviet interaction at the Stockholm talks on confidence building measures when other contacts had virtually ceased. The process of interaction became more important than the product, at least in the short-term. The US-Soviet experience also suggests that arms control can help shape a political relationship in ways which facilitate progress in other areas. States not interested in arms control can always find a reason to delay. In view of the regional arms control agenda, however, such delay is in no one's interest.

3.1 Nonproliferation

The urgency of nonproliferation has intensified because, for the first time in history, the world confronts the potential for a significant number of countries to possess weapons of incalculable destructive potential and the means to deliver them. Although the implications of proliferation are potentially global, its first manifestation will be in regional conflicts, as Saddam Hussein's actions have suggested. Proliferation's first effect would be to redefine regional balances of power and alter the fundamental political dynamics between the proliferant and its rivals. The presence of weapons of mass destruction in a particular region will also complicate the ability of outsiders to intervene in a regional conflict should one erupt. The calculations of the members of the international coalition against Iraq, for example, would have been very different if Iraq had already demonstrated a nuclear capability. In some cases, the presence of weapons of mass destruction may drive a decision that the costs of intervention would be too high to take the risk. For smaller regional states which have a limited ability to defend themselves and watched what happened to Kuwait, such prospects will be most disturbing.

The starting point for nonproliferation efforts should be the international regimes outlawing weapons of mass destruction. Not all key states in various regions are committed to the NPT, the BWC, or the recently signed Chemical Weapons Convention (CWC). Ensuring universal adherence to such agreements is clearly the first priority.

The second is ensuring that all parties are living up to the international obligations they have assumed in adhering to the agreements. Iraq used its membership in the NPT regime as a screen to hide its pursuit of an illicit nuclear weapons program, and a number of other countries appear to be taking the same approach. Regional states, therefore, must position themselves in the forefront of an aggressive effort to strengthen those bodies responsible for implementation of and compliance with international nonproliferation regimes.

Beyond supporting international agreements, is there something that can be done on a regional basis? The answer is clearly yes, as Latin America has demonstrated. The Mendoza Agreement between Brazil and Argentina, to which Chile and Uruguay subsequently adhered, provides one example. In this agreement, signed before the negotiations on the CWC were concluded, the parties committed themselves to a complete ban on chemical weapons. The Treaty of Tlatelolco, making the Western Hemisphere outside the United States a nuclear-free zone, is a second example.

The notion of regional nuclear weapons free zones is another regional approach of long-standing. Recent concerns about proliferation, however, have sparked renewed interest in such measures. African nations, for example, are actively negotiating a nuclear weapons free zone for their continent, a prospect made possible by South Africa's abandonment of its nuclear program and its joining the NPT.

Since 1974, Egypt and Iran have sponsored an initiative at the United Nations calling for a nuclear weapons free zone in the Middle East. Egyptian President Hosni Mubarak, however, has gone beyond this measure, calling in April 1990 for creation in the Middle East of a zone free of all weapons of mass destruction. It is a laudable goal, and one that should be shared not only by regional states but by the entire international community. Indeed, the UN Security Council in essence endorsed this objective in Resolution 687, which elaborated the terms of the cease-fire agreement with Iraq. The resolution noted that the steps to be taken by Iraq "represent steps towards the goal of establishing in the Middle East a zone free from weapons of mass destruction and all missiles for their delivery ..."[28] Translating the objective of a weapons of mass destruction free zone into practical political reality, however, will prove to be extremely difficult.

One of the major problems with the Mubarak initiative, shared by other efforts to stem proliferation, is that it treats the proliferation of weapons of mass destruction as an isolated problem. Proliferation occurs where conflict -- political and military -- rests close to the surface. Nonproliferation, therefore, must be coordinated with other measures designed to promote the resolution of disputes. Proliferation itself, however, can complicate both regional arms control efforts and the search for political solutions. Components of a military arsenal or a particular weapons program can become additional sources of political dispute. This has been the case, for example, in Korea where efforts to advance the North-South dialogue were brought to a standstill by Seoul's concerns over the North's nuclear program. It has also occurred in the Middle East where "the issue of Israeli nuclear weapons will remain the most intractable question facing ... regional arms control negotiators."[29]

There is a second sense in which proliferation is not an isolated issue. Proliferation cannot be defined or analyzed solely in terms of weapons of mass destruction. It must also include conventional weapons as well. Equally important, the two problems cannot be treated as if a firebreak existed between them. Clearly, an important relationship exists between a region's conventional military balance and the calculations which drive some parties to seek an edge through the acquisition of weapons of mass destruction. Israel's nuclear program, for example, was spurred, at least in part, by concern over the combined conventional capabilities of its Arab opponents who had vowed to destroy the state of Israel. Not convinced that it could offset the Arab advantage through conventional forces alone, Israel turned to nuclear weapons to provide the ultimate guarantee of the its survival.

This relationship between conventional balances and weapons of mass destruction tends to be neglected in both policy and analytical circles. Both, however, are dimensions of the complex regional security environments which have begun to emerge in the post-Cold War era, and the relationship between them must be appreciated. In short, nonproliferation -- especially focused on weapons of mass destruction -- cannot become the sole prism through which the challenge of regional security and the objectives of regional arms control should be defined.

3.2   Conventional Arms Control

While nonproliferation must remain an important regional arms control priority, coming to grips with the problems created by conventional weapons is of equal, if not greater importance. Conventional weapons, even those as unsophisticated as the mortars surrounding Sarajevo, have been responsible for more death and tragedy than any weapon of mass destruction. Regional powers spend considerably more of their defense budgets on conventional forces; indeed, prior to the Gulf War, Egypt, India, Israel, Iraq and Syria all had more tanks in their inventories than Britain or France.[30] A number of Asian states are concerned about China's increasing force projection capabilities.[31] India appears to have similar priorities. In general, the world is witnessing a significant trend toward conventional force modernization, and regional states should set their arms control priorities accordingly.

In pursuing conventional arms control in a regional context, priority should not be given to supplier-led restraint regimes. They have not worked in the past, and they are not likely to work in the future. The latest example, the Bush Administration's initiative on Arms Control in the Middle East (ACME), although it had a different cast of players, has had basically the same fate as the Carter Administration's Conventional Arms Transfer talks. The guidelines produced by the five leading arms suppliers in the ACME process are seen as prohibiting nothing the states in question want to do, a perception reinforced by President Bush's decisions during the 1992 election campaign to sell advanced fighter aircraft to Taiwan and Saudi Arabia, decisions supported by then-presidential candidate Bill Clinton.

A process more likely to produce meaningful results is a supplier-recipient dialogue in respective regions in which all parties work to establish their minimal security requirements. Such a dialogue would foster a common understanding of basic requirements and a sense of what would constitute an "excessive accumulation of arms? With such an understanding, states of a region themselves could then agree to forego certain kinds of capabilities mutually considered to be destabilizing rather than have external suppliers attempt to impose restraints. A regional dialogue of this kind would be difficult to initiate and even harder to bring to fruition. Without such an exercise, however, the prospects for unbridled conventional arms races in regions of high tension remain strong.

A second form of conventional regional arms control would be an agreement which regulates the military situation on the ground as the Conventional Forces in Europe Treaty (CFE) does for that area. One should not expect, however, an agreement as far-reaching as CFE to be negotiated immediately. It took the Europeans nearly two decades to reach the point at which such talks could begin, and they were brought to fruition in part by the remarkable political upheavals in the former Soviet Union and Eastern Europe. Other regions with equally thorny security problems must also be given the opportunity to learn how to do arms control business.

For this reason, limited measures should first be required that focus on minimizing the chances for miscalculation, a frequent spark to conflicts that many regional actors consider their most immediate danger. Egyptian General (Ret.) Ahmed Fakhr, for example, argues that many of the military conflicts in Africa are "accidental, unintentional, or inadvertent," and that confidence building measures emphasizing transparency of military matters would help to avoid such disastrous mistakes.[32]

The theme of transparency has become a major focus of efforts to build confidence in many regions. Underlying this focus is the assumption that the more that is known about the armed forces and arms acquisitions of potential adversaries, the less likely a state is to misperceive the actions of its rivals that then lead to miscalculations, which in turn escalate tensions, and eventually erupt in conflict. In short, predictability breeds stability. In various regions, transparency measures have been proposed relating to weapons acquisition, force structures, defense budgets and related military matters. Clearly, states will be more reluctant to share information about some of these elements than about others. Perhaps the starting point should be measures addressing notification and observation of military exercises as well as other forms of military-to-military contacts, which had a major positive impact in the European context. Building on these limited measures, regional states could then move to more ambitious confidence building efforts such as notification of missile test launches or sharing information on weapons acquisitions beyond those to be listed in the United Nations arms transfers register. States might also explore a measure similar to that agreed by the Europeans on "unusual military activities" which provides a state an opportunity to explore the reasons for military actions of neighbors that appear outside their normal pattern, such as a major redeployment of forces.

Although many confidence building measures have been proposed for different regions, little actual negotiation of such measures has actually occurred. In the Middle East, for example, after more than eighteen months of discussion, the multilateral track of the peace process in the form of the Working Group on Arms Control and Regional Security (ACRS) has not yet produced any concrete agreement, although a few limited measures -- relating, for example, to naval forces in the Red Sea -- have been floated informally with some of the participants. In Asia, there has been what is described as an "extraordinary proliferation" of CBMs, yet very few are in place among regional states.[33]

On the Korean peninsula as well, both North and South have suggested a number of CBMs, although of a widely different nature with greatly varying military utility. Little progress was made in securing agreement on any of them, however, before their bilateral talks were, in essence, suspended due to the inability to resolve the dispute over the North's nuclear program. India and Pakistan may have made the most progress in getting CBMs on the books, although even in this case their implementation has not yet been fully realized.[34]

The very limited progress in negotiating CBMs is an indication of how difficult regional arms control is likely to be. There are, however, some reasons not to be totally dismayed at future prospects. Latin America, for example, has produced not only the Mendoza Declaration, but the Organization of American States passed during its 1992 general meeting an unprecedented resolution committing all its members to giving heightened priority to arms control and creating a special working group on the subject. The very existence of the ACRS should probably be seen in the Middle East context as a major step forward despite its lack of formal agreements to date. In a region where tension, suspicion, and animosity have been so high for so long, the fact that the process of exchange has continued over such an extended period is no inconsiderable feat. At some point, however, concrete accomplishments must be forthcoming or disillusionment could set in. Similarly, in southeast Asia, a new forum has been established for continuing dialogue on regional security matters. The Post-Ministerial Conference (PMC) of the Association of Southeast Asian Nations (ASEAN) has come to be universally acknowledged as the occasion for common exploration of regional security problems. The 1993 PMC agreed, for example, to create the ASEAN Regional Forum, whose brief is to examine specific security issues on an ongoing basis.[35]

Common to all of these positive developments is the emergence of regional forums where security problems can be considered on a multilateral basis. In Europe, the CSCE played a similar role, and its existence greatly facilitated arms control progress. In CSCE, the process was often more important than the product, especially when its major actors -- the United States and the Soviet Union -- were at odds. By maintaining the process, however, important habits of cooperation were reinforced. Individual states developed "niche" roles in advancing negotiations, and personal relationships were established that lasted long after negotiators returned to their capitals. Sometimes surprising coalitions were formed. Common stakes in securing agreements were created. Perhaps the emerging regional forums will someday play a similar role for the states in their locales.

Larger, multilateral forums, however, may not always be the most appropriate vehicle for addressing regional security concerns, and flexibility must exist for *ad hoc* arrangements to deal with some problems. The Indonesian-sponsored unofficial workshops supported by ASEAN to address the conflicting claims in the South China Sea, especially over the Spratly and Paracel Islands, is one example.[36] Regional efforts led by Australia to settle the civil war in Cambodia is another. Indian-Pakistani bilateral discussions have probably made more progress than if those talks had been forced into a broader regional forum such as the South Asian Association for Regional Cooperation (SAARC). As regional arms control efforts proceed, states should not become so enamored of region-wide forums that they attempt to resolve all their disputes in that context. Sometimes, large multilateral efforts can become a formula for deadlock which a less formal process might avoid.

4. The US Role

The United States must continue to promote and support regional arms control efforts as it has done in the Middle East, Korea and South Asia. Geoffrey Kemp points out, however, that US policies toward regional conflicts and arms control face a constant dilemma between the desire to limit weapons proliferation and the need to support friends and allies -- ultimately to the point of intervention. Confronting such a dilemma, US policies themselves on issues such as arms transfers and military presence "become a part of the problem of implementing regional arms control arrangements."[37] The US-South Korean Team Spirit military exercise, for example, became a major sticking point in moving forward with the North in dealing with its nuclear program. US military support of Israel also complicates the regional security dialogue in the Middle East since it is the major means by which Israel retains its qualitative military edge over the Arabs.

There is no easy answer to this dilemma for Washington. It is another case of valid, contending interests which must be balanced on an ongoing basis. In part, this continual tension can be managed and regional arms control supported by the United States demonstrating that its support of regional arms control is not for the purpose of advancing the interest of one side over another, as might have been the case during the Cold War. Rather, while it should not shrink from defending the very large interests it has at stake in regions such as the Middle East, the Persian Gulf or East Asia, Washington can also promote its appreciation of the complexity of regional security dynamics in the post-Cold War era. To some extent this can be done by adapting to an arms control situation in which the United States does not necessarily have a seat at the table. It is an unusual position for Washington, but one which it could well face more often in the future. In such a situation, however, the United States can still perform, and may be called upon by regional states to perform, critical functions. These include educating those with little experience and less enthusiasm for the arms control process on its utility, facilitating the process by providing good offices or in other ways bringing contending sides together, monitoring implementation of agreements that may be struck, and guaranteeing the integrity of agreements in the event that compliance falters. They are roles that the US would need some getting used to.

Despite the many challenges, regional arms control must be given a high priority in the years ahead. Many of the most dangerous problems confronting the international community in the post-Cold War era are not global in scope but regionally or even sub-regionally grounded. Europe has demonstrated that arms control can be a useful tool in stabilizing and managing regional security relationships. Although states in other regions are quick to point out that they "are not like Europe," arms control efforts should not be abandoned due to surface dissimilarities, especially when it has not really been tried.

Efforts in regional arms control can build on the limited progress which has been made. Arms control must be shown to work in order to overcome suspicion and mistrust, not only of potential adversaries but of the arms control process itself. Only through such a demonstration will arms control realize its potential as an effective policy instrument in dealing with the dangerous regional hazards which lie ahead.

Notes

1. Jayantha Dhanapala, "Introduction," in *Regional Approaches to Disarmament: Security and Stability*, Jayantha Dhanapala (ed.) (Aldershot: Dartmouth for the UN Institute for Disarmament Research, 1993) p. 3.
2. W. Scott Thompson, "Where History Continues: Conflict Resolution in the Third World," in *Resolving Third World conflict: Challenges for a New Era*, Sheryl J. Brown and Kimber M. Schraub (eds) (Washington DC: US Institute of Peace, 1993), p. 3.
3. Donald M. Snow, *Distant Thunder: Third World Conflict and the New International Order* (New York: St. Martin's Press, 1993), p. 55
4. Geoffrey Kemp, "Regional Security, Arms Control and the End of the cold War," in Brown and Schraub, *Resolving Third World Conflict,* p. 123.
5. For a theoretical examination of many of the problems associated with ethnic conflicts, see Ted Robert Gurr, *Minorities at Risk: A Global View of Ethnopolitical Conflicts* (Washington DC: US Institute of Peace Press, 1993). For a summary of Gurr's approach, see his "Third World Minorities at Risk since 1945," in Brown and Schraub, *Resolving Third World Conflicts,* pp 51-88.
6. James Clad, for example, argues that "from the perspective of loyalty and legitimacy, there is simply not much there." James C. Clad, "Old World Disorders," *Washington Quarterly,* 15, No 4 (Cambridge, MA: MIT Press, 1993), p. 84
7. For an interesting assessment of the impact of nationalism in the post-Cold War era, see James Mayall, "Nationalism and International Security after the Cold War," *Survival,* 34, No. 1 (Spring 1992), pp. 19-35.
8. Asia Bensalah Alaoui, "The Maghreb," in Dhanapala, *Regional Approaches,* p. 157.
9. For more on this point, see Richard Haas, "Regional Order in the 1990s: The Challenge of the Middle East," *Washington Quarterly* 14, No 1 (Winter 1991), p. 183. Donald Snow describes the "implicit rules" of the superpower game as 1) the major interedst of each side was limited to protecting the major investment that it already had in a given government or to currying favor in places where the other side was not dominant; 2) direct challenges in countries where the other side was dominant were avoided; and 3) whenever regional disputes boiled over, both sides had an active interest in avoiding escalation. Snow, *Distant Thunder,* p. 147.
10. Ibid., p. 10.
11. The phrase is W. Scott Thompson's, "Where History Continues," p. 3.
12. Chandran Jeshurun, "Southeast Asia," in Dhanapala, *Regional Approaches,* p. 51
13. For one example, see William H. Durhan, *Security and Survival in Central America: Ecological Origins of the Soccer War* (Stanford, CA: Stanford University Press, 1979).
14. For an example of the potential impact on regional security of these kinds of disputes, see Shahram Chubin and Charles Tripp, "Domestic Politics and Territorial Disputes in the Persian Gulf and Arabian Peninsula," *Survival,* 35, No. 4 (Winter 1993-1994) pp. 3-27.
15. Desmond Ball, "Tasks for Security Cooperation in Asia," in *Security Cooperation in the Asia-Pacific Region,* Desmond Ball, Richard L. Grant and Jusuf Wanandi (Honolulu: Pacific Forum/CSIS, 1993), p. 22.

16. John Chipman, "Third Wold Politics and Security in the 1990s: The World Forget-
    ting, By the World Forgot?", *Washington Quarterly,* 14, No. 1 (Winter 1991),
    reprinted in Roberts, *USSecurity in an Uncertain Era,* p. 128.
17. Trevor Findlay, "The South Pacific," in Dhanapala, *Regional Approaches,* p. 31.
18. W. Scott Thompson, "Where History Continues," p. 2.
19. Chipman, "Third World Politics and Security," p. 122.
20. Jeshurun, "Southeast Asia," p. 65.
21. For a further discussion of these perspectives, see Michal Moodie "Constraining
    Conventional Arms Transfers in the Post-Cold War Era: Problems and Prospects,"
    Annals of the American Political Science Association, forthcoming.
22. Kemp, "Regional Security, Arms Control and the End of the Cold War," p. 127.
23. Brad Roberts, "Arms Control and the End of the Cold War," *Washington Quarterly,*
    15, No. 4 (Autumn 1992), reprinted in Roberts, *US Security in an Uncertain Era,* p.
    273. The discussion in this section draws significantly on the Roberts arguments.
24. Ibid.
25. Prvovslav Davinic, "The New Role of the United Nations in Promoting Arms Limi-
    tation and disarmament," in *Disarmament and Security in Africa,* Disarmament Topi-
    cal Papers 12 (New York: United Nations, 1992), p. 16.
26. Janne Nolan, "Stemming the Proliferation of Ballistic Missiles: An Assessment of
    Arms Control Options," in *Arms Control and Weapons Proliferation in the Middle
    East and South Asia,* Shelley A. Stahl and Geoffrey Kemp (eds.) (New York: St.
    Martin's Press, 1992), p. 172.
27. Kemp, p. 122.
28. Quoted in Mahmoud Karem, "The Middle EAst," in Dhanapala, *Regional Approach-
    es to Disarmament,* p. 133,
29. Ibid., p. 138.
30. Kemp, "Regional Security," p. 128.
31. See, for example, David I. Hitchcock, Jr., "East Asia's New Security Agenda,"
    Washington Quarterly, 17, No. 1 (Winter 1994), pp. 92-93.
32. Ahmed Fakhr, "Transparency in the Military Field as a Means of Building Confi-
    dence," in *Disarmament and Security in Africa,* p. 73.
33. The phrase is Desmond Ball's, *op cit.,* p. 19.
34. For a description of regional confidence measures in South Asia, see "Presentation
    by the Delegation of India," given at the second round of Arms Control and Regional
    Security talks relating to the Middle East, Moscow, September 15, 1992.
35. See Jacquelyn K. Davis and Charles M. Perry, *Security Perspectives and Defense
    Priorities in Northeast Asia* (Washington DC: Institute for Foreign Policy Analysis,
    November 1993), p. 61
36. For background, see Gareth Evans, *Cooperating for Peace: the Global Agenda for
    the 1990s and Beyond* (St. Leonard's: Allen and Unwin, 1993), P. 77.
37. Kemp, "Regional Security," p. 139.

Chapter 6
NUCLEAR ARMS CONTROL: GLOBAL OR REGIONAL?

David Fischer

This analysis examines international and regional controls designed to stop the geographical spread of nuclear weapons (horizontal proliferation) rather than the broader question of reversing the nuclear arms race (vertical proliferation) and reducing existing nuclear arsenals of the avowed nuclear-weapon states. The two issues are interlinked; we cannot expect to have one without the other. But except in this general sense, "downsizing" the nuclear arsenals of the recognized nuclear-weapon states involves the relations between two, or at most a small group of states rather than a global or regional system. This raises a set of issues that are not directly relevant to the subject of this paper (regional versus global approaches to non-proliferation).

1. The Need For A Global Verification System

Since the spread of nuclear weapons increases the danger of nuclear war, it puts at risk the security of all countries. But it obviously does so unevenly. The countries in the "infected" region run the greatest and most direct risk. This was blindingly clear during the first period of proliferation when the US, the USSR, Britain, France and China acquired nuclear weapons and threatened each other with mutually assured destruction. Today, two striking examples of the same mutual concentration of nuclear risk are given by India and Pakistan. Both are able to make nuclear weapons. The other example of proliferation is found on the Korean peninsula. Although Indo-Pakistani and North/South Korean proliferation would threaten other states in the two regions (and elsewhere), the risk of nuclear war would be most acute between the pairs of states themselves. This implies that in the future vigorous and effective regional, as well as global, measures will be needed to contain proliferation in regions where political tensions run high and where there is access to advanced nuclear technology.

1.1 The Limitations Of Regional Agreements

In such cases would not regional efforts alone be sufficient to contain the danger? Would it not be better for the countries in a particular region -- and indeed the rest of the world -- to feel adequately secure if all nuclear activities be reciprocally open at all times to inspection -- for example, if India and Pakistan, the two Koreas, and Israel and the other Middle Eastern states could freely inspect each other? Certainly mutual inspection by hostile or antagonistic countries would normally offer a high degree of credibility, but not high enough.

A few examples will suffice to illustrate the point. Let us look again at the Korean peninsula. What would happen to Korean regional safeguards if the two Koreas were to unite, a prospect that certainly cannot be excluded? What would become of the assurance previously provided by purely bilateral safeguards?

The members of the European Community (EC) have their own regional nuclear safeguards organization, European Atomic Energy Community (EURATOM). The aim of EURATOM is neither to stop the proliferation of nuclear weapons nor to set up a nuclear-weapon-free zone. But if the EC concludes an agreement with a non-EC country or an international organization (e.g., the International Atomic Energy Agency (IAEA) which prohibits military or nuclear explosive use of nuclear material, EURATOM "... must satisfy itself that in the territories of Member States" the prohibition is observed.[1] From the late 1950s to the late 1960s, the US, Canada, South Africa, and Australia deemed that EURATOM safeguards alone were sufficiently effective to permit them to supply nuclear plants and fuel to the EURATOM countries. But the Soviets regarded EURATOM safeguards as deeply suspect, as no more than self-inspection by a small group of NATO countries. When the US and the Soviets were drafting the provisions of the Non-Proliferation Treaty (NPT), the Soviets insisted that *all* non-nuclear-weapon states, including those of the EC (like Germany and Italy), should also accept IAEA safeguards.

Soviet suspicion of the EC has since been transformed into Russian friendship with Western Europe, and the six-nation EC of the 1960s has become the twelve-nation EC of today. Within the next few years, it seems likely to become a fifteen- or sixteen-nation organization. This political transformation has also permitted the IAEA, under the so-called "partnership agreement" of 1992, to reduce substantially the weight of its routine safeguards on the EC non-nuclear-weapon states. *But the IAEA still carries out enough monitoring to verify independently whether the EC non-nuclear-weapon states are complying with their obligation not to divert safeguarded nuclear material to nuclear weapons.*

In other words, despite EURATOM's increasingly multinational character and large and experienced safeguards operation, global safeguards are still needed to provide global assurance of non-diversion. One senses that this meets the wishes of the EC non-nuclear-weapon states themselves which now see their acceptance of IAEA safeguards not only as a political confidence-building measure but also as an indispensable condition for the free flow of nuclear commerce and as an example to other regions of the world.

1.2   The Danger Of Bad Precedents

Excessive reliance on bilateral or regional inspection might also establish some less credible precedents.

EURATOM contains two nuclear-weapon states (France and the United Kingdom, the latter being a depository of the NPT) whose overriding interests are to stop the further spread of nuclear weapons everywhere in the world but especially in Europe. During this century most of EURATOM's members have twice been at war with other EURATOM states, and it is only since the Second World War that they have succeeded in burying ancient hatreds and fears. Thus, all EURATOM states have powerful and, in some cases, unique incentives to ensure that nuclear weapons remain in the hands of only Britain and France, or at least until Europe becomes a single federal state or nuclear weapons are universally prohibited. But to give EURATOM special treatment -- for instance to recognize its safeguards and only *its* safeguards as a substitute for those of the IAEA -- would open the industrialized countries of the North to yet another charge of discrimination on behalf of the "haves" in a system which already carries a heavy burden in this regard.

One means of avoiding such a charge might be to accept the delegation of safeguards to EURATOM as a valid precedent for other regions and to arrange similar delegations elsewhere. But what level of political and technical assurance would be given by a regional safeguards system set up by a group of ostensibly independent states tied by ideology and force of arms to the heels of a superpower or linked together by powerful ties of religion, language, and race? Would the West have been prepared to see a safeguards system operated by the defunct Council for Mutual Economic Assistance (COMECON) (CMEA to give it its correct title) take the place of the safeguards of the IAEA? What international assurance could be offered today by the Arab League or by a Latin American equivalent or by the Organization for African Unity? The assurance would certainly fail to satisfy states outside the region, or even some of those within it, such as Israel in the case of an Arab League safeguards system. As Lawrence Scheinman has put it, "Out of region actors cannot, and will not, count on regional verification arrangements to provide, for example, that states in a region are in full compliance with their undertakings they will want certification from third parties in whose selections they have a say and in whose institutions they are participants."[2]

1.3   The Need For Uniform And Universal Application Of Basic Safeguards

It is also obvious that only a global system can ensure the uniform and universal application of minimum standards of technical efficiency. Such a system can also establish approaches to the highly complex problems of safeguarding various types of nuclear plant and can call upon the resources and help of nations most advanced in nuclear technology. The IAEA has acquired more than thirty years of experience in applying safeguards in a wide variety of political and technical environments. This is a unique and invaluable asset. It is hard to believe that there could be a serious proposal to replace the IAEA with a set of regional arrangements -- or by another international organization.

2. The Role Of Regional Systems

If regional arrangements may be inadequate or suspect in the eyes of non-regional powers, why not dispense with them entirely and rely only on the international safeguards of the IAEA?

2.1   Adversarial Monitoring

There are several good reasons for supplementing global monitoring. The first and most crucial is to gain the confidence of countries that are mutually hostile and have little faith in the effectiveness or impartiality of international organizations. A potent and intrusive regional system is probably a prerequisite for acceptable verification in the politically tense regions of the world. The prime example would be Israel. An Israeli government is more likely in the long run to accept the dismantling of its nuclear arsenal if, as a minimum, Israeli inspectors can freely and directly take part in verifying that no other Middle

Eastern state is clandestinely making nuclear weapons. Saddam Hussein's success in almost developing a nuclear weapon without being detected must have greatly diminished Israel's already low confidence in purely international verification.

While Argentina and Brazil are now prepared to place all their nuclear activities under IAEA safeguards, they are also in the process of setting up what is essentially a bilateral monitoring system. This is probably in response to a legacy of earlier suspicions about each other's nuclear program. It may also offer each partner a means of keeping control of its own sometimes fractious nuclear authorities.

When EURATOM safeguards were negotiated in the late 1950s, the French and Dutch undoubtedly saw them as a means of having their own inspectors in Germany (although this was not publicly acknowledged). Before EURATOM, the Brussels (Western European Union) Treaty, as modified in 1954, was more explicit about the objective of verifying that atomic, biological, and chemical (ABC) weapons were not manufactured by the Federal Republic of Germany.[3]

The same requirement for direct bilateral monitoring was evident in the negotiation of arms reduction treaties between the US and the Soviets -- in the elaborate bilateral safeguards of the INF and START treaties.

2.2   More Effective Sanctions

The present position with regard to sanctions against a breach of non-proliferation undertakings is broadly as follows. Like most other arms control treaties, the NPT makes no specific provision for sanctions; it is tacitly assumed that the parties to each such treaty will individually or collectively coerce into compliance or punish any nation that violates the treaty. In most cases, a breach of the NPT would also constitute a breach of an IAEA safeguards agreement. It would therefore trigger a process in which the IAEA Board of Governors would determine that safeguards had been violated and would report its finding to the United Nations Security Council. On 31 January 1992, the members of the Council, meeting at the level of heads of state or government, proclaimed that they would regard any proliferation of weapons of mass destruction as a threat to international peace and security and would take appropriate action if any violation were reported to the Security Council by the IAEA.[4] In a sense the Council thus declared its intention to serve as the guardian of the NPT and its readiness to act as the supreme authority for ensuring compliance with IAEA safeguards.

In 1993 the IAEA Board promptly informed the Security Council of North Korea's breach of her safeguards agreement and North Korea subsequently announced that she was withdrawing from the NPT. The Council obviously feared that if it sought to take drastic action against North Korea, it would provoke a Chinese veto. It reacted mildly, avoided any direct mention of sanctions, and merely called upon North Korea to reverse her withdrawal from the NPT, and also called for continued negotiations.

It may be argued that although she has violated her safeguards agreement and the NPT, there is still no irrefutable evidence that North Korea has "proliferated" in the sense of actually making a nuclear weapon and that the Security Council's statement of 31 January 1992 cannot yet be invoked. Nonetheless, the course of events showed that the Council is clearly hesitant to enforce North Korean compliance with her non-proliferation undertaking. It is doubtful whether this episode would give a state whose national survival might be endangered by a breach of a treaty, sufficient assurance that it could safely let down its own nuclear guard in the knowledge that the delinquent state would be brought to heel, compelled to reverse course, and adequately punished. Even if the measures now being taken to strengthen the IAEA's ability to detect clandestine nuclear operations are fully effective and even if they are underpinned by a system of adversarial inspections, Israel is unlikely to put her faith in a system that ultimately depends for its authority and enforcement on the United Nations Security Council. It may, however, be possible for a regional treaty to go well beyond the NPT and the IAEA Statute and to provide explicitly for rigorous and reasonably automatic sanctions against any breach of its provisions. One possibility would be a set of individual bilateral undertakings by each of the P-5 nations promptly to come to the aid, by force of arms if necessary, of the injured state -- individual and binding "positive security assurances? Another might be to recognize the injured party's right to take unilateral action against the delinquent state (which Israel would probably do in any case).

Regional arrangements make it possible to agree on considerably more stringent controls than those foreseen in the NPT. For instance, the Korean bilateral arrangement prohibits reprocessing of spent fuel and enrichment of uranium, a prohibition that would be unacceptable under any global system. One reason why such a prohibition could not be universal is that most of the nuclear power plants in Europe, Japan, and North America use (low) enriched uranium for their fuel. They could not possibly agree to a complete ban on enrichment. Moreover, such a prohibition would be hard to defend under Article IV of the NPT, which reaffirms "... the inalienable right of all the Parties to the Treaty to develop research, production and use of nuclear energy for peaceful purposes without discrimination ..."

Another advantage of most regional arrangements is that, unlike the NPT in its present application, they are of indefinite duration. The 1995 conference could extend the NPT for a limited period only, rather than indefinitely. At the time of this writing, the majority of the parties is said to be in favor of the latter option, but a significant number prefers a limited extension. In short, while regional agreements cannot substitute for the international regime, they can strongly reinforce the international system, especially in politically tense regions of the world. In fact, as already suggested, it is likely that it is only in the context of a robust and tested regional settlement that a state such as Israel or India can be brought to accept international monitoring, meshed with regional safeguards.

3. Where Global Monitoring Suffices

Nonetheless, there are many parts of the world (in perhaps 95% of the parties to the NPT) where international safeguards alone suffice -- or must be made to suffice. IAEA safeguards are obviously adequate if the incentive to get the bomb has disappeared or is minimal (e.g., in the non-nuclear-weapon states of the EC, Scandinavia, the Baltic states, Central and most of Eastern Europe, Canada, the South Pacific), or if this adequacy still prevails, the countries concerned are still technologically incapable of making nuclear weapons (e.g., nearly all African and most Latin American countries), or if a system of regional monitoring is still politically out of reach (e.g., most of South East and East Asia, possible excluding the Korean peninsula but including Japan). Recently it has been reported that Japan is reviving a proposal which a Pakistani official made in the mid-1960s for the creation of an "ASIATOM."

4. Existing Regional And Bilateral Systems

From the foregoing analysis, it follows that regional safeguards and non-proliferation or nuclear disarmament treaties, tailored to the specific needs of countries in a particular region and reflecting the political environment in which they were conceived, are likely to differ widely. The following is a brief survey of existing systems.

4.1   EURATOM

EURATOM safeguards, based on the Rome Treaty of 1957, resemble in several respects those set forth in the Statute of the IAEA, which also entered into force in 1957. Both reflect the preponderant influence of the United States at that time. Thus, for instance, the rights of each agency to carry out "any place, any time" inspections are set forth in almost identical terms.[5] In the succeeding years (1957-1975), the detailed safeguards and inspection procedures of the two agencies diverged somewhat, but after the entry into force of the IAEA-EURATOM safeguards agreement in 1975 they became almost identical.

Nonetheless some important conceptual differences persisted. For instance, the Rome Treaty does not prohibit the manufacture of nuclear weapons; its safeguards simply verify that nuclear materials "... are not diverted from their intended uses as declared by the users."[6] EURATOM's safeguards cover all nuclear activities in the EC except those expressly intended for military use. Hence they cover the entire civilian nuclear industry of the EC's two nuclear-weapon states.

The IAEA, like EURATOM, applies its safeguards to all nuclear activities in the EC's non-nuclear-weapon states but, unlike EURATOM, only to one or two selected civilian plants in those nuclear weapons' states.[7] EURATOM deals directly with the managers of nuclear plants and, if necessary, imposes sanctions; EURATOM's sanctions would be directed against the plant, while the IAEA's would hold the government concerned responsible for any breach of a safeguards agreement. The EURATOM system of accounting is more detailed than that of the IAEA and apparently includes verification of the stated end use of every item, perhaps reflecting the fact that EURATOM is nominally the owner of all fissile material in the EC. EURATOM also applies its safeguards to uranium ore; the IAEA does not. With the impending expansion of the EC, the end of Cold War suspicions about the Community, and increasing financial pressure on the IAEA, the latter's inspections in the EC non-nuclear weapon states are likely to become even less frequent in the years ahead.

In some ways the shrinking role of IAEA safeguards in the EC is the opposite of what should have happened. In the atomic euphoria of the mid-1950s, the founders of the EC conceived of nuclear energy and EURATOM as the driving motor of the future European Community. This is unlike the Exchange Rate Mechanism (ERM) and European monetary cooperation as now seen by the Maastricht Treaty as the motor of a European federation. Today, EURATOM's role has shrunk chiefly to that of a safeguarding organization with some safety and related functions. The IAEA could easily carry out EURATOM's safeguards functions in the EC. It is also doing much the same work in Japan,

Sweden and Canada. If the Rome treaties were being negotiated today, it is very doubtful whether they would include the creation of EURATOM. But it is politically inconceivable that EURATOM would now be dismantled or deprived of its safeguards function. The only practicable way to avoid massive duplication between it and the IAEA or the undesirable precedent referred to previously is for the two agencies to share as many tasks as possible and to pool research and development.

4.2   Preventing The Spread Of Nuclear Weapons

The three other functioning regional or bilateral organizations which aim to prevent the spread of nuclear weapons are those created in Latin America by the Tlatelolco Treaty (overseen by the Organization for the Prohibition of Nuclear Weapons -- OPANAL), in the South Pacific by the Rarotonga Treaty and in the agreement between Argentina and Brazil setting up the ABACC.[8]

The Tlatelolco Treaty requires its parties to accept what are, in effect, full-scope IAEA safeguards.[9] Originally the Treaty also made provision for "challenge" inspections (which the Treaty referred to as "special inspections") to be carried out by OPANAL. Any party could require that a special inspection be made anywhere on the territory of any other party (or on its own territory to clear its name of any suspicion about its nuclear activities).[10] During the first twenty-five years of operation of the Tlatelolco Treaty, no party asked for a challenge inspection. When Argentina and Brazil announced their intentions of becoming full parties to the Tlatelolco Treaty, they proposed that the Treaty's provisions relating to these inspections be deleted. Their rationale was presumably that since 1990, and particularly since the discovery of Iraq's large clandestine nuclear weapon program, there had been renewed emphasis on the IAEA's right to carry out "any place, any time" special inspections and that, because of this, the special inspections foreseen by the Tlatelolco Treaty had become redundant.[11]

One of the two protocols to the Tlatelolco Treaty foresees that the five recognize? nuclear-weapon states provide assurances to respect the nuclear-weapon-free status of Latin America and not to use or threaten to use nuclear weapons agains? any party. This is a so-called "negative security assurance."[12]

The Argentina-Brazil agreement sets up a bilateral safeguards and inspection body, the Argentina-Brazil Agency for Accounting and Control of Nuclear Materials (ABACC). A separate four-party agreement between Argentina, Brazil, the ABACC and the IAEA defines the relationship between the safeguards of the ABACC and those of the IAEA. When this agreement enters into force, the IAEA and the ABACC will work together in much the same way a? EURATOM and the IAEA.

It is of interest that Argentina and Brazil found it necessary to supplement IAEA safeguards with such a bilateral system. As noted previously, this is probably a legacy of, and a symbol of the end of, the long-standing nuclear rivalry between the two Latin American countries most advanced in the use of nuclear technology. It is thus a mutual confidence-building measure and, as a result, has paved the way to their renunciation of nuclear weapons.

The only safeguards formally required by the Rarotonga Treaty, which applies to the South Pacific, are those of the IAEA. But the Treaty does establish a control system consisting chiefly of requirements for periodic or special reporting and consultations and procedures for investigating complaints about possible infractions.[13] The Rarotonga Treaty contains protocols similar to those attached to the Tlatelolco Treaty.

Furthermore, good progress is being made in establishing nuclear-weapon-free zones in Africa and South East Asia. Both draft treaties are largely modeled on the Rarotonga Treaty. The African draft[14] also foresees that the only safeguards to be applied in the region are those of the IAEA, but it will also create an African Commission on Nuclear Energy to monitor compliance as well as to promote the peaceful uses of nuclear energy. The draft requires verification of the dismantling and destruction of existing nuclear weapons -- a reference to South Africa's (dismantled) nuclear weapon program.

The South East Asian draft, sponsored by Indonesia, follows the Rarotonga Treaty in stressing the right of innocent passage, of ships of war through the seas which it purports to cover, including warships carrying nuclear weapons (i.e., the US Navy) and the right to use ports in the region as home ports for such vessels.[15]

Under the hastily negotiated and still unimplemented bilateral agreement between the two Koreas, both parties renounce nuclear weapons, but there is no bar to other nations deploying nuclear weapons on their territories nor is there any requirement for "negative security assurances." The Treaty bans the production but not the acquisition of fissile material.

A good case could be made for two additional regional agreements in Europe. The first would be a nuclear-weapon-free zone stretching from the North Cape in Norway to Crete and embracing Scandinavia, Finland, the Baltic states, Poland, Hungary, the Czech and Slovak Republics, Belarus and Ukraine, the Balkans, and Greece. In the 1950s and 1960s, the Polish Foreign Minister Rapacki proposed a forerunner to such an agreement, but the NATO countries saw it as a maneuver to force the West to withdraw its nuclear weapons from Germany and would have nothing to do with this idea.

The second regional agreement would coordinate the nuclear energy policies of the states which have emerged out of the ruins of the Soviet Union, essentially the CIS states but possibly including the Baltic Republics. It would be modeled on EURATOM. For short, let us call it "CISATOM."

Potentially the richest and most powerful non-Russian republic in the Commonwealth of Independent States (CIS) is Ukraine. It is also the only CIS republic which operates a substantial number of nuclear power plants. Ukraine is now desperately short of energy, coal production has declined, and it depends on Russia for its supplies of oil or natural gas, which must now be paid for at world market prices. Ukraine draws some 35% of its electricity from nuclear power. Despite the shadows of the Chernobyl disaster, the Ukrainian parliament recently and reluctantly approved the continued operation of two of the remaining (RBMK type) Chernobyl reactors which were supposed to be shut down at the end of 1993, and the completion of three other "VVER" reactors (i.e., not of the Chernobyl type) on which work had been halted.[16]

All nuclear reactors in Ukraine and other CIS republics as well as one in Lithuania and two in Finland are still totally dependent on Russia for nuclear fuel and nuclear fuel services. All of the reactors' spent fuel goes to Krasnoyarsk for storage or to Chelyabinsk for reprocessing.[17] Almost all reactors in the CIS, Lithuania, and Finland have common safety problems.

Close cooperation among Russia and the other republics which operate Russian reactors seems therefore to be in the common interest. The non-Russian republics also have a direct interest in ensuring that all nuclear plants in *all* republics are operated only

for peaceful purposes and in verifying such exclusively peaceful use by a regional syste?
of inspection.

These factors suggest that there is room for a regional organization of which all
interested republics of the CIS and perhaps Lithuania and Finland would be members.
Other European countries operating VVER reactors might be interested in some form of
association. The organization would give highest priority to enhancing the safety of
nuclear plants. It would be aided in this by the fact that WANO (World Association of
Nuclear Operators) has its headquarters in Moscow and by the extensive programs of the
IAEA and the EC for enhancing the safety of Soviet-designed power reactors. It would
ensure and coordinate nuclear supplies and the disposal of spent nuclear fuel and nuclear
waste and serve as a mechanism for coordinating the use of technical and financial help
promised by the EC countries.

The organization would establish a corps of inspectors and apply safeguards to
ensure that all nuclear plants in its non-nuclear-weapon members were used exclusively
for peaceful purposes. As in the case of EURATOM, these safeguards would be closely
coordinated with those applied by the IAEA and eventually a "partnership" agreement
would evolve, like that between the IAEA and EURATOM. This evolutionary regional
organization might relieve the IAEA of much of the burden of applying routine safeguards. But regional safeguards would also fill a gap in IAEA safeguards since the
regional staff would inspect all civilian plants in the only recognized CIS nuclear weapon
state but not those of the IAEA, which apply to all nuclear plants in France and the UK.

If such a regional agency were set up, it would be crucial to ensure that its staff and
decisionmaking process could not be dominated by any single member.

5. Inherent Limitations On Regional And International Action

It is obvious that only a broad-based international organization such as the IAEA
can undertake the four major verification tasks that are now waiting in the wings:
a)   verifying and possibly taking custody of fissile material released from dismantled
     nuclear warheads;
b)   administering a system for the international management of separated civilian pluto-
     nium (an International Plutonium Management system or IPM);
c)   verifying a cut-off of the production of fissile material for nuclear weapons; and
d)   verification of a comprehensive nuclear test ban.

The IAEA's qualifications for carrying out the first three tasks are plain. The first
three would consist largely of extending current safeguards to cover what were previously military or otherwise unsafeguarded nuclear activities and nuclear stocks. The first
task was implicit in President Eisenhower's proposal in 1953 for creating the IAEA and
the second (administering an IPM) is explicitly foreseen in the IAEA's Statute.[18] President Clinton's proposals in the fall of 1993 for a cut-off and for international verification
of fissile material removed from nuclear warheads and surplus to military needs may at
last bring into life these two long-discussed concepts.

The fourth task, verification of a comprehensive test ban treaty (CTBT), would be
to some extent a step into new territory for the IAEA. But assigning CTBT verification to
the IAEA would have many advantages. It would concentrate in one agency the technical

responsibility for verifying all the principle international components of the nuclear non-proliferation regime. It would be consistent with the IAEA's statutory aim of seeking to prevent the use of atomic energy for military purposes; it would eliminate the need to set up a new international bureaucracy with a separate administrative infrastructure; it would marginally help the IAEA to verify compliance with the NPT and other safeguard? agreements; and it would enhance the IAEA's technical competence in the field of verification. As the most technically oriented agency in the UN family, the IAEA would be well-suited to provide the required services. The direct link that the IAEA has with the United Nations Security Council (which is unique in the UN family) would be a further argument for choosing the IAEA.

CTBT verification would intermesh with the IAEA's other verification activities and they would reinforce each other. For instance, atmospheric sampling designed to detect nuclear tests would complement IAEA sampling of traces of radioisotopes to detect the operation of clandestine reactors or reprocessing plants and might also provide early warning of nuclear accidents. Verification measures, such as satellite observation designed to detect preparations for a nuclear test, would provide early warning of potential breaches of the NPT. Satellite observation could also help detect clandestine facilities such as enrichment plants not easily detected by environmental monitoring. They could thus help the IAEA to establish whether there were any sensitive plants in a non-nuclear weapons state and permit substantial reductions of routine inspection if it could be reasonably well-established that no such plants existed.

The IAEA has had great difficulty in breaking the bonds of zero financial growth. Assigning an important new function to it might release it from this constraint.

The fact that the CTBT will be non-discriminatory (in other words, prohibit testing by *all* parties) while the NPT permits the P-5 to make and keep nuclear weapons might be used as an argument against designating the IAEA as the agent to verify both treaties. The converse can also be argued. Assigning verification responsibility under both global treaties to IAEA points to a future global ban on nuclear weapons as well as on nuclear tests.

The parties to a CTBT are not likely to be identical with the members of the IAEA, and it would probably be necessary to envisage separate intergovernmental arrangements; nonetheless, the present composition of the IAEA Board is reasonably appropriate for the verification of a CTBT. The five nuclear-weapon states are *de facto* permanent members of the Board as are the leaders in nuclear energy in other parts of the world (Latin America, Africa, the Middle East and South Asia, the Far East, and South East Asia and the Pacific Rim). Twenty-two additional elected members ensure equitable geographical distribution. Assigning CTBT verification to the IAEA could have a profound effect on its role, scope, and structure. There might be some concern that extending the IAEA's responsibilities would detract from the IAEA's principal verification function -- nuclear safeguards.

6. Verification Responsibilities That Are Likely To Remain National Or Possibly Bilateral

Dismantling the nuclear weapons themselves is likely to remain beyond the reach of international or regional verification. The technologists who made the weapon and the plant where it was made are best equipped to take it to pieces. Any outsider who takes part in the dismantling process may learn many of the secrets of nuclear weapon manufacture. To introduce outsiders into the process is therefore to run the risk of nuclear proliferation.

Ingenious ideas have been put forward about the use of black boxes and instruments that would permit an international inspector to verify that nuclear specific weapons have been dismantled without acquiring any classified information. So far, however, each of the two leading nuclear-weapon states has shown great reluctance to allow experts from the other, let alone international inspectors, to verify its own dismantling operations.

7. Conclusions

The NPT contemplated a single universal nuclear safeguards regime although it did recognize in Article VII "... the right of any group of States to conclude regional treaties in order to assure the total absence of nuclear weapons in their respective territories."

In the more stable and pacific or technologically undeveloped regions of the world, the global safeguards of the NPT and the IAEA are sufficient. In all parts of the world they provide the indispensable basis for monitoring non-proliferation; however, in regions which are torn by acute political tension or in which the memory of mutual distrust is still strongly present, global safeguards may not provide the assurance needed to persuade nations to renounce nuclear weapons. It has proved necessary to supplement the global regime by more intrusive, far-reaching regional arrangements which permit bilateral inspection by antagonists that may prohibit certain nuclear activities permissible under the NPT and that may also provide for draconian challenge inspections and swift, certain, and severe sanctions for any breach of the regime.

Notes

1. *Treaty Setting up the European Atomic Energy Community (EURATOM)*, Article 77(b), Her Majesty's Stationery Office, London, 1967, S. O. Code No. 59-113-0-67, p. 27.
2. Lawrence Scheinman, *The Changed International Poliotico/Military Environment* Paper presented at PPNN International Workshop, "South Asia, Nuclear Energy and Nuclear Non-Proliferation," Kandy, Sri Lanka, 4-7 November 1993, PPNN Paper Number CG14/2.
3. Jozef Goldblat, *Agreements for Arms Control*, Taylor and Francis Ltd., London, 1982, pp. 145-148.
4. This declaration by the Council's members cannot, of course, prevent any permanent member of the Council from using its veto to prevent collective Council action.
5. *Treaty Setting up the European Atomic Energy Community*, Article 81, *Statute of the International Atomic Energy Agency*, Article XII.A.6.
6. *Treaty Setting up the European Atomic Energy Community (EURATOM)* Article 77(a)

7. The UK made available for IAEA safeguards all its civilian nuclear plants and France offered a more limited selection, but financial constraints on the IAEA permit only a very limited exploitation of these offers. In fact, at present, no plants in nuclear weapon states are being safeguarded by the IAEA.

8. The similarities and differences between the NPT and the Tlatelolco and Rarotonga treaties are summarized in David Fischer, *Towards 1995: The Prospects of Ending the Spread of Nuclear Weapons* (London: Routledge, 1993).

9. Tlatelolco Treaty, Article 13.

10. Tlatelolco Treaty, Article 16.

11. In fact, the special inspections foreseen by the Tlatelolco Treaty are more rigorous and less open to dispute than the special inspections authorized by paragraphs 73 and 77 of the standard IAEA full-scope safeguards.

12. The other protocol requires extra-regional states to apply the Treaty to their possessions in Latin America. Both protocols have been ratified by all the states concerned.

13. Rarotonga Treaty, Articles 8-10 and Annexes 3 and 4.

14. The latest draft is contained in UN General Assembly document A/48/371 of 18 October 1993.

15. Despite this deference to the US Navy's sensibilities, neither the US, nor France, nor Britain has ratified the protocols to the Rarotonga Treaty.

16. According to Vladimir Fuks, the head of the nuclear utility, *Ukratomenergoprom*, Ukraine will build three new VVER nuclear stations. (Clive Cookson, Scientific Editor, *Financial Times*, 10 September 1992)

17. "Understanding the CIS: Lord Marshall's View," *Nuclear Engineering International*, September 1992, pp. 5-6.

18. IAEA Statute Article XII.A.5.

Chapter 7

THE SOUTH AFRICAN NUCLEAR CASE IN THE LIGHT OF RECENT REVELATIONS

Donald B. Sole

The beginning of South Africa's (SA) interest in nuclear energy can be traced back to war time London when South Africa's Prime Minister and Minister of Defense, General J.C. Smuts, for the first time came to learn of the attempt to harness the power of the atom. I myself had a small role in this insofar as I arranged for him to meet Niels Bohr, the Danish nuclear physicist, who had been spirited out of occupied Denmark to ensure that his talents would not be available to the Nazis.[1] After seeing a paper dealing with aspects of the Manhattan Project, Smuts had discussions with Sir John Anderson, Lord President of the Council, whose responsibilities included nuclear energy. Back in South Africa, Smuts received a request from Anderson, arising out of their discussion, to arrange an investigation into reported deposits of radium and pitchblende in South Africa and Namibia. This derived, as A.R. Newby-Fraser relates in his book "Chain Reaction," from references to the presence of radioactive minerals in South Africa contained in geological papers dated 1915 and 1923 and to the presence, as geological adviser on the Manhattan Project, of Professor G.W. Bain of Amherst College, who after a visit to the Witwatersrand in 1941 had taken back to the United States various specimens of reefs being mined. He tested a specimen for radioactivity, and this then led to a joint visit to South Africa by Professor Bain and Dr. Charles Davidson of Great Britain. Their visit provided the justification for the large-scale sampling and subsequent confirmation of South Africa's uranium potential. In 1948 the South African Parliament passed the Atomic Energy Act in terms of which an Atomic Energy Board was established whose functions were *inter alia* "to undertake the production of atomic energy" and to stipulate the conditions for "prospecting and mining for prescribed materials" (mainly uranium and thorium). From 1950 onwards successive contracts were concluded by the SA mining industry ; the uranium purchasing organization was set up by the United States and British governments and was known as the Combined Development Agency.

In terms of these contracts, South Africa provided the United States and Britain from 1953 until 1967 with huge amounts of uranium for employment in various military programs, much of it at a time when major deposits of uranium ore in the United States, Canada, and elsewhere had still to be discovered. There is little doubt that at this early juncture the South African uranium supplies were vital to the United States' military program.

1. Relations With The Western Nuclear Powers

In this early period, close relations existed in the nuclear field between SA and the US. In 1957 a formal Cooperation Agreement was concluded covering the peaceful uses of atomic energy this Agreement was later amended to enable it to run until the year 2000 Many South Africans were trained in various aspects of nuclear engineering in the US (88, for example, between 1958 and 1974). In 1965 it was the US which supplied SA with its first research reactor (SAFARI 1) using 90% enriched fuel (also supplied from the US).

The pattern of SA nuclear relations with the United Kingdom was also very similar. As a member of the Combined Development Agency, Great Britain played a major role in financing the development of South Africa's uranium potential. Britain thereafter purchased thousands of tons of SA uranium, processed to uranium oxide (U308) before delivery, for both military and civil purposes. Facilities were furnished for the training of SA nuclear scientists and information was supplied on nuclear plant safety and health aspects. A collaboration agreement was concluded with the South African Atomic Energy Board in 1957. The Chairman of the United Kingdom Atomic Energy Authority, Sir John Hill, visited South Africa. Close contact was maintained with the Atomic Energy Research Establishment at Harwell, which was presided over for a time by a South African, Sir Basil Schonland. The rapport between South African and British scientists in the nuclear field was even better than was the case with the United States. The same was true of nuclear relations between Britain and South Africa in the diplomatic field. At international nuclear conferences and discussions, London regarded South Africa as one of its most dependable allies.

South African nuclear collaboration with the Federal Republic of Germany (FRG) in these early years probably took its origins from the contact made between the South African and German delegations at the First International Conference on Peaceful Uses of Atomic Energy held in Geneva in August 195? The South African delegation included, in the persons of Dr. Meiring Naude, President of the Council for Scientific and Industrial Research, and Dr. H.J. van Eck, head of the Industrial Development Corporation, two powerful and influential dignitaries possessing particularly close ties with Germany. At that time German nuclear activities were only in their initial stages; their nuclear links had been mainly with the Americans and the British. Quite clearly they welcomed contacts with the South Africans who were, of course, at the time very much *personae gratae*, also with the Americans and the British. In the following years there was a considerable expansion of relations between South Africa and the Federal Republic in the nuclear field. South African nuclear scientists regularly visited German nuclear research centers at Julich and Karlsruhe. Dr. Ampie Roux, head of the South African Atomic Energy Board, was a frequent visitor to the FRG. Other highly-placed German officials, in turn, visited South Africa. Professor Becker of Karlsruhe, inventor of the German jet nozzle enrichment process, made one visit to the South African Atomic Energy Board headquarters at Pelindaba, as did other leading German nuclear scientists. These contacts led to the elaboration of proposals between the German firm of Steag and the South African authorities designed to facilitate a comparative study of the German enrichment technology developed at Karlsruhe; but, as a result of publicity, nothing came of these proposals.

South Africa's nuclear relations with France initially were never in the same warm category as those with the United States, Great Britain, and the Federal Republic. The language barrier as well as the traditional aloofness of France *vis-a-vis* South Africa played a role in this. But France, despite being a uranium producer itself, soon became an important buyer of South African uranium. As a nuclear weapons power, France claimed the right to purchase its uranium free of safeguards, as did the United States and the United Kingdom. France accordingly took it amiss when the other major producer of uranium (Canada) refused to supply it on this basis. South Africa, in this respect, thus acquired a psychological advantage in the French market. In the 1960s and the 1970s,

France was actively pushing ahead with its nuclear power program designed to make nuclear energy, percentage wise, the largest source of the country's electric power. South Africa accordingly looked to France as an important market for its uranium and as a possible supplier of South Africa's first nuclear power station.

2. South Africa In The International Nuclear Community

In the 1950s and the 1960s, South Africa was also riding high in terms of its international, as opposed to its bilateral, relations in the field of nuclear energy. Under President Dwight D. Eisenhower's Atoms for Peace Program, SA was one of only six other Western countries invited by the US to participate in the exploratory discussions which ultimately led to the establishment of the International Atomic Energy Agency (IAEA) in Vienna. SA played an important role in the Drafting Conference in Washington, which drew up the IAEA's Statute, and was encouraged by the United States to push through a draft clause which, it was assumed, would assure a permanent seat for South Africa on the Board of Governors of the IAEA, provided that SA continued to be "the member most advanced in the technology of atomic energy including the production of source material" in the region of Africa. When the IAEA was set up in Vienna in 1957, South Africa played an active and highly respected role in the Agency's affairs. In 1959-1960 SA was the first member of the Board of Governors to be elected to the chairmanship of that body on a free vote by its membership.[2] South Africa was similarly active at international conferences on nuclear matters and played an important role in the work of the Nuclear Suppliers Group based in London.

3. South Africa's Indigenous Enrichment Process

In South Africa itself, there was considerable euphoria deriving from the achievement in this field both of the mining industry and even more so on the part of South African scientists who were engaged in developing an indigenous process of uranium enrichment. The scientists concerned had at one time considered the possibility of collaborating with the mining industry in developing a peaceful nuclear explosive technology which conceivably might have been successful in promoting the development of new mines. This never got under way. Another nuclear research program which came under consideration was the development of a locally designed power reactor, but this approach too was abandoned at an early stage in favor of greater concentration on the development of an indigenous enrichment proces?

As a major producer of uranium, it made sense that the limited resources of manpower and funds should be devoted to the beneficiation of a domestic product, uranium. The team which worked on uranium enrichment was led by Dr. Wally Grant and succeeded in developing an indigenous isotope separation technology called "the stationary walled centrifuge." This process was uniquely South African in origin although the anti-South African lobby overseas alleged that it had, in fact, been developed from Professor Becker's jet nozzle process at Karlsruh? These allegations were devoid of substance, as the German scientists themselves readily acknowledged in private. On July 20, 1970, Prime Minister John Vorster formally announced the development of the new process for uranium enrichment and the building of a pilot enrichment plant based on this process. Vorster emphasized that the research and development program was directed toward peaceful purposes and he invited "any non-Communist countries desiring to do so" to collaborate in the further development of the process. He also emphasized South Africa's willingness to place its nuclear activities under a safeguards system including inspections subject to three conditions which he defined as follows:

a)   South Africa will in no way be limited in the promotion of the peaceful application of nuclear energy;
b)   South Africa will not run the risk of details of the new process leaking out as a result of the safeguards inspection system; and
c)   the safeguards system, while efficient, is to be implemented on such a reasonable basis as to avoid interference with the normal efficient operation of the particular industries.

It will be noted that none of these conditions was incompatible with the IAEA safeguards system.

In 1968 the US, in close collaboration with the USSR, had promoted the conclusion of the Non-Proliferation Treaty (NPT) designed to combat the dangers of nuclear proliferation. South Africa signed the Final Act, but in common with a number of other countries had not yet come to any conclusions about adhering to the Treaty. With the United States so concerned about the dangers of nuclear proliferation, the announcement by South Africa of the building of a pilot enrichment plant was not at all welcome to the Americans. They themselves were understandably not interested in Vorster's offer to collaborate with friendly countries in developing SA's enrichment process, and they actively discouraged other countries from responding positively to South African overtures. The only *public* expression of foreign interest in this offer of which I am aware was a statement by Count Lambsdorf, the economic expert of the German Free Democratic Party, in the course of a debate on energy in the Bundestag in April 1975, stating that the Federal Republic should consider participation in South Africa's enrichment project. This statement was made following a visit by Count Lambsdorf to SA at a time when the West German Nuclear Power Construction Consortium, Kraftwerk Union, was active in tendering for South Africa's first nuclear power project at Koeberg.

Ironically, had any Western country been prepared to cooperate in response to Mr. Vorster's invitation, South Africa's enrichment plant would inevitably have been subjected to IAEA safeguards and no nuclear weapons program would have been feasible.

4. South Africa's Decision To Develop A Limited Nuclear Deterrent

In 1974 a decision was taken by Prime Minister Vorster to develop a limited nuclear deterrent capability and to construct a suitable test site. This deterrent capability was to consist of seven nuclear devices (of which six had been completed when the program was terminated) in the form of a large "gun-type" projectile weighing about 1 ton, measuring 685mm in diameter and about 1.8m in length. The device was fundamentally designed to be exploded underground with a zero risk of contamination. It could not have been used in South Africa's well-known G5 artillery system but could conceivably have been dropped from one of South Africa's Buccaneer aircraft. The estimated explosive force was 10-18 kilotons TNT equivalent. The first device was completed in 1980. The principal components of each device were stored separately in steel vaults and a stockpile of fully assembled devices never existed.

What was the motivation for the decision, first to construct the nuclear device and then to proceed toward completion of the total of seven which had been envisaged?

In his statement to Parliament on March 24, 1993, President F.W. de Klerk described the motivation as follows:

> The decision to develop this limited capability was taken against the background of a Soviet expansionist threat in Southern Africa, as well as prevailing uncertainty concerning the designs of the Warsaw Pact members. The build-up of the Cuban forces in Angola from 1975 onwards reinforced the perception that a deterrent was necessary -- as did South Africa's relative international isolation and the fact that it could not rely on outside assistance, should it be attacked.
>
> No advance nuclear explosives, such as thermo-nuclear explosives, were manufactured.
>
> The program was under the direct control of the head of government. Knowledge of the existence of the program was limited to a number of ministers on a "need-to-know" basis.
>
> The strategy was that, if the situation in Southern Africa was to deteriorate seriously, a confidential indication of the deterrent capability, would be given to one or more of the major powers, for example the United States, in an attempt to persuade them to intervene.
>
> It was never the intention to use the devices and from the outset the emphasis was on deterrence.

To the above official analysis, some additional supplementary comments are necessary.

In April 1974, a Communist government took power in Portugal paving the way for the loss of the Portuguese empire in Africa. Portugal's rule in Angola and Mozambique had always been viewed by successive South African Prime Ministers as constituting major guarantees for South Africa's own security. In addition, the situation in Rhodesia (Zimbabwe) was seen to be deteriorating. Domestically the concept of a "total onslaught" by Communist forces, controlled by the Soviet Union, was increasingly being promoted, partly for party political purposes. Indeed the propaganda to this effect was introducing a degree of paranoia among senior military officers and other government personnel, although not in the Department of Foreign Affairs. Another factor in the situation was the enthusiasm on the part of the scientists for working toward the completion of the nuclear cycle. It was the scientists who originally persuaded the Prime Ministe? to authorize the funding required to enable them to develop their own uranium enrichment process. Having achieved notable advances in this field, the further step of constructing a nuclear weapon could be regarded as the ultimate scientific challenge. It was this combination of scientific enthusiasm and the Prime Minister's reading of the South African security situation, in a world where South Africa was fast losing its remaining friends, which triggered the decision to authorize the funds required for the development of a nuclear deterrent. Furthermore, it was the situation in Angola which provided the final and crucial incentive to press ahead with a nuclear deterrent program once the initial decision had been taken.

Cuban troops, with Soviet backing, were pouring into Angola and were seen as constituting a *major* threat to South West Africa. Had the Cubans crossed the border, South Africa would have been compelled to intervene. A major conflict could have developed in what is now Namibia with the Cubans being presented to the world as the liberators of the Namibian people and the South Africans as the heartless oppressors opposing liberation. South Africa would have been placed in a "no win" situation, unless the United States could be persuaded to intervene (e.g., by applying pressure to the Soviet Union and its Cuban satellite).

What leverage could South Africa bring to bear on the United States? South Africa in normal circumstances has no leverage whatsoever vis-a-vis the United States. But a threat to use a nuclear device as a weapon of last resort could conceivably provide some leverage. South Africa would have to be in a position, if necessary, to demonstrate its capability, using a nuclear test as evidence. I am convinced that, as President de Klerk stated, there was never any intention to use a nuclear device other than as a form of political leverage. South Africa's top nuclear scientists would have argued that control over the nuclear device should not be entrusted to the military whose political judgment many of them distrusted. Nor would the head of government have any illusions about the disastrous consequences for South Africa should he authorize the use of a nuclear device for any military purpose.

According to Dr. Waldo Stumpf, Chief Executive Officer of the Atomic Energy Corporation, in an address in Washington on July 23, 1993, the strategy had a three-phase character. This strategy was confirmed again by the South African government in 1981 and remained unchanged up to the termination of the deterrent program.

Phase 1: Maintain uncertainty about the capability. In other words, neither confirm nor deny that this capability does exist.
Phase 2: Should an invasion by the Cubans be threatened, make this capability known on a confidential basis to say, the US, to induce them to intervene as necessary.
Phase 3: If this tactic is unsuccessful, then demonstrate to the world that SA has this capability by carrying out an underground test.

This was the sole reason for the authorization given for the construction of the test site at "Vastrap" in the Kalahari, the existence of which was first revealed in 1977 by a Soviet reconnaissance satellite and confirmed by a US surveillance satellite. As a result of this revelation, the proposed use of the site for possible underground tests was abandoned. In 1987 the shafts at the Kalahari test site were once again inspected as a precautionary measure since the overall strategy was then still in place.

What had happened between 1974 and 1987 to justify this contingency planning? South Africa had become the best known pariah state in the international community. Th? United Nations Security Council had imposed a mandatory arms embargo. An oil embargo was in place, albeit not very successfully. Economic and financial sanctions were being enforced by the countries of North America, the EC, the Commonwealth, the Soviet Bloc, most of Asia and most of Latin America, not to speak of Africa itself. Practically all forms of nuclear cooperation had been terminated. South Africa was almost completely isolated. The Cubans were still in Angola and no one dreamed that the break-up of the Soviet Union was imminent. In the event, however, the strategy never moved past Phase 1 and the program was terminated before the contingency envisaged in Stage 2 ever arose.

5. Motivation For Terminating The Nuclear Deterrent Project

Mr. de Klerk, in his statement to Parliament on March 24, 1993, advanced the following reasons:

> On my assumption of office as State President it was already evident to me, and also to my colleagues who were also informed, that it was in our national interest that a total reverse -- also in respect of our nuclear policy -- was called for.
>
> A cease-fire in Angola was agreed. On December 22, 1988 a tripartite agreement was signed at the United Nations with Cuba and Angola which provided for the independence of Namibia and the withdrawal of 50,000 Cuban troops from Angola.
>
> The Cold War had now become to an end and developments leading to the destruction of the Berlin Wall and the break-up of the Soviet bloc had become the order of the day. Furthermore, the prospects of moving away from a confrontational relationship with the international community in general, and with our neighbors in Africa in particular, to one of cooperation and development, were good.
>
> In these circumstances a nuclear deterrent had become, not only superfluous, but in fact, an obstacle to the development of South Africa's international relations.
>
> World opinion had also become increasingly opposed to nuclear weapons, and significant advantages for South Africa could be forthcoming should it accede to the NPT. Although it already had an advanced nuclear technology base and nuclear industry, accession would facilitate the international exchanges of the new technology for its future development. It could also be of benefit to our neighboring states and in due course to Africa as a whole.

Other factors which were probably relevant but which were not specifically mentioned by President de Klerk were that the bi-polar world had given way to a situation where there is only one super power. It was imperative that South Africa improve its relationship with the US.

Furthermore, South Africa's uranium enrichment process had proved far more expensive than expected and in the long run it was important that South Africa have access to cheaper sources of enriched uranium, which would not be feasible without adherence to the NPT.

The domestic reform program, initiated by President de Klerk on February 2, 1990, would sooner or later lead to the establishment of a black majority government, probably headed by the African National Congress which had close links with proclaimed terrorists organizations such as the PLO and the Governments of Colonel Ghadaffi

(Libya) and Fidel Castro (Cuba). Inevitably, if that black majority government was thought to have access to nuclear weapons, it would be viewed with profound distrust and suspicion by the western powers.

The benefits deriving from President de Klerk's reversal of previous policies are undisputed. In the international nuclear context this reversal was warmly welcomed. The South African Government was further praised for the promptness with which it concluded the safeguards agreement following its accession to the NPT in July 1991. South Africa's action was linked to the decision of Argentina and Brazil to place all their nuclear material under safeguards. Steps taken by SA on the one hand and Argentina and Brazil on the other were also seen as intensifying pressure for moves toward the establishment of nuclear-free zones in the Middle East and South Asia. In the African context the way is now open for the conclusion of a Convention for the Denuclearization of Africa, a goal which South Africa would like to see achieved before the convening of the NPT Review Conference in April 1995. South Africa's relations with the IAEA have been normalized, but this normalization has not yet led to the return of its seat on the IAEA Board of Governors. It is expected that SA will soon resume its membership of the Nuclear Suppliers Group.

6. Questions Answered And Unanswered

Following President de Klerk's statement, a number of issues were raised by members of the international nuclear community. Most of these have since been answered; some remain unresolved. A few examples follow:

Question: Why were the existence and the termination of the nuclear deterrent program not announced at the time of accession to the NPT?

Answer: Politically this might have been more correct but the announcement was delayed for two reasons: complex negotiations were being conducted at the time regarding the reform of the domestic political system. Internationally, the timing would not have been appropriate as it would have coincided with the world attention to the Iraqi situation. There was a real danger that South Africa would have been regarded as a second Iraq.

Question: Did South Africa receive outside assistance in developing the nuclear deterrent?

Answer: It has been known for decades that any industrial state with access to the raw material required and possessing sophisticated scientific and engineering skills can construct a nuclear device. SA easily fulfilled these criteria. It had no help from anybody either on enrichment technology or on nuclear weapons technology. Only SA born citizens were permitted to work on the program; even citizens by naturalization were excluded.

Question: How correct is the figure of highly enriched uranium (HEU) reported by SA to the IAEA? Is there not an "apparent discrepancy" or "material imbalance" in relation to the capacity of the enrichment plant?

Answer: Criticisms in some US circles of the manner in which SA terminated its nuclear weapons program ignore the very relevant fact that the NPT makes no provision for procedures where *a state with nuclear weapons but not a* *party to the Treaty* may become a non-nuclear weapons state with a view to accession to the Treaty. The Treaty indeed never envisaged that nuclear weapon states should become non-nuclear weapon states unless and until complete nuclear disarmament was achieved. South Africa had therefore no guidelines to follow in the disposal of its nuclear devices. Also in the nature of things South Africa could not request the international community to provide analysis standards, bearing in mind that it had been debarred from the UN General Assembly, had been evicted from the IAEA Board of Governors, and had been unseated from the General Conference of that Agency. South Africa's position was unique and completely without precedent.

Details of the reason for the material imbalance have been provided both to the IAEA and to the interested public, and the IAEA has been invited to make whatever further checks it feels necessary. The current situation is that the IAEA inspectors have satisfied themselves in full.

Question: What quantity of HEU has SA accumulated and what is to be done with it?

Answer: As is standard IAEA practice, the precise quantities are confidential and are not disclosed either by the IAEA or the reporting countries. HEU was at one stage offered to the UK and subsequently to the US. Neither was interested at the time. The current position is that SA's stockpiles of HEU will continue to be used for large scale isotope production in terms of existing and future commercial contracts, all of which are under full IAEA safeguards.

Question: What steps has SA taken to prohibit the dissemination of its nuclear weapons technology by those who developed or acquired it?

Answer: Not more than 1000 individuals were involved in the development of the program and not more than 400 at any one time. Work was strictly compartmentalized and knowledge of the total program was limited to a very minimum, probably less than ten people. In terms of new legislation on the subject of "The Non-Proliferation of Weapons of Mass Destruction," it is illegal for any South African to assist in any program related to the construction of any such weapons.

Question: Was SA responsible, as alleged by the Central Intelligence Agency, for the occurrence on September 22, 1979, when a US Vela satellite detected a double flash of light in the Southern Ocean of the kind normally associated with a nuclear explosion?

Answer: The CIA report was an assumption rather than an allegation and no evidence has been adduced to connect either South Africa or Israel with the incident. According to a report by a White House panel of experts released on July 17, 1980, the flash was probably the result of a tiny meteoroid striking the satellite causing the light burst recorded by the spacecraft's instruments. Dr. Walter Stumpf has since disclosed that in 1979 SA had only achieved "very impure" HEU of "reasonably low enrichment, about 80%? It would have been impossible to explode a nuclear device in the atmosphere, with its then existing dirty uranium and low enrichment, that did not produce any fall-out?

Question: What are some of the non-proliferation lessons to be drawn from the South African experience?

Answer:

a. Undoubtedly it has provided a boost for the extension and renewal of the NPT. At the same time it has revealed deficiencies in the IAEA safeguards system in as much as the current system, *inter alia*, applies only to declared facilities and material. How these weaknesses can be remedied without at the same time creating disincentives for any "threshold" state to adhere to the NPT, presents a real challenge.

b. South Africa was the first state, not party to the NPT but possessing nuclear explosive devices, to accede to the Treaty. The precedents set in South Africa's case may possibly prove a guide to how the denuclearization of the Ukraine and Kazakhstan should be handled.

c. The South African case emphasizes the extent to which resorting to nuclear weapons is linked with national conceptions of security and underlines how the most important counter to nuclear proliferation is the provision of *effective* security guarantees for the state concerned.

d. The South African experience also shows that the institution of embargoes, the application of boycotts, and the cancellation of contracts can be completely counter-productive, thereby depriving the international community, or a particular state, of the ability to apply leverage and pressure through the promotion of continuing dependence on outside supply. In retrospect, it was a major error on the part of the US to renege on its contracts for the supply of HEU for South Africa's research reactor and for the enrichment of uranium supplied from SA with the view to subsequent manufacture into fuel elements for South Africa's power reactors. The attitude adopted toward Vorster's 1970 invitation to cooperate in the development of South Africa's enrichment process was similarly mistaken. All this should have lessons for the Nuclear Suppliers Group in deciding on policy *vis-a-vis* any state with a nuclear potential.

Notes

1. I was serving on the staff of the SA High Commissioner in London at the time.
2. By agreement between the two super powers, USA and the USSR, each had respectively nominated the countries to be voted into the chairmanship for the first two years of the IAEA's existence.

Chapter 8

NUCLEAR NON-PROLIFERATION ISSUES IN SOUTH ASIA

Ahmad Kamal

The events of the last four years have been marked by the steady transformation of the bipolar world which emerged from the ashes of the Second World War into a unipolar system with the United States as the indisputable and sole surviving Superpower. While this major shift in the world's power structure has been achieved rather peacefully, it has not created an environment where conflicts have ceased to exist or where peace is universal. The Iraqi invasion of Kuwait and the Gulf War that followed, ethnic strife in the territories of the former Soviet Union, aggression and genocide in the Balkan peninsula, raging civil wars in Africa, the violent suppression in many parts of the world of the struggle for the self-determination of peoples, and many other simmering conflicts are stark reminders that we are far from achieving a new and happier world order.

Even so, the sudden collapse of the Soviet Union and the end of the Cold War have created new opportunities for pursuing arms control initiatives which were mere pipe dreams until very recently. There is an increased possibility of a Comprehensive Test Ban Treaty (CTBT), perhaps even before the 1995 Non-Proliferation Treaty (NPT) extension conference. Joint moves toward this end are a testament to the desire of the former adversaries to lead the way in creating a basis for peaceful international relations.

Having set the pace for their relationship with Russia, the United States and its allies have now focused their attention on the proliferation of weapons of mass destruction and their delivery systems in the developing countries. This is on the assumption that the primary threat to international peace and security now emanates from the acquisition of nuclear weapons by countries in regions of tension. Both in the Conference on Disarmament in Geneva and elsewhere, elaborate efforts are being made to create new arms control measures and mechanisms which are designed to meet the challenges perceived as arising out of such proliferation.

The traditional focus of nuclear non-proliferation concerns has been directed toward five regions, namely, the Korean Peninsula, South Asia, the Middle East, South Africa, and Latin America. By a sheer quirk of history, Ukraine and Kazakhstan have now been added to this list, but their cases are totally dissimilar to the first five.

With the signature of the Non-Proliferation Treaty by South Africa and the bilateral non-proliferation agreement in South America between Brazil and Argentina, these two regions no longer figure on the list of areas of concern. That leaves three regions, the Middle East, South Asia, and the Korean Peninsula, as the regions of non-proliferation concern today. The political dynamics in each of these three regions is significantly different, and, consequentially, developments are also noticeably dissimilar in each one of them, as are possible solutions.

1. South Asia

In South Asia the situation is a particularly dangerous mix of deep historical tensions on which a potential nuclear capability has now been superimposed. Even though commendable nuclear restraint has been exercised by both India and Pakistan, the basic tensions run so deep, and the history of three wars is so recent that international concern about the situation is totally justified.

The basic causes of tension between India and Pakistan lie essentially in (a) the deep misgivings between Hindus and Muslims, each of whom fears being submerged by the other; (b) the unwillingness of a Hindu-dominated India to accept the reality of the 1947 Partition which resulted in a Muslim homeland of Pakistan, and the consequential Indian belief that Pakistan is just a passing aberration which will ultimately coalesce with Mother India; (c) the core problem of the disputed territory of Kashmir, which is essentially an unfinished chapter of Partition and has led to three onerous wars between the two countries, but which India constantly seeks to sweep under the carpet as if it were a non-existent dispute; (d) India's conviction that, because of its size and resources, it has to be recognized as the dominant regional power, on the same level as China; and (e) Pakistan's own conviction that the most acute, and perhaps the only, threat to its security comes from India and its hegemonic ambitions, as witnessed by all its neighbors.

As a result, the nuclear compulsions of both countries differ enormously in substance and content. This is most visible in their respective approach to regional disarmament. India has constantly sought to project its nuclear policies within the context of what it perceives as Chinese nuclear pressures, even though there is no evidence to-date of China ever having threatened India in this area. In a like manner, the Indian development of intermediate range ballistic missile delivery systems and of a blue-water navy are projected as a reaction to a perceived Chinese threat. The net result is a refusal by India to see South Asia as a self-contained region.

Pakistan, on the other hand, perceives its only security threat as coming from India, and has therefore reacted with a security policy aimed at (a) maintaining a minimum deterrence level in conventional armaments; (b) a loose alliance either with the United States or with China in order to give its defense preparedness some additional degree of depth; and (c) a constant espousal of regional disarmament in the South Asian context, encompassing both conventional and nonconventional arms. Should this line of Pakistani thought and action achieve a certain degree of implementation, undiminished security would be achieved at the minimum level of armaments, and many of the concerns about nuclear proliferation in South Asia would automatically subside.

2. India's Nuclear Program

In the face of a deep psychological and intellectual divide between India and Pakistan, the incentives toward nuclear proliferation in South Asia appear unstoppable. Noticeably, it is India which has consistently taken the initiative by embarking on its nuclear development program from as early as 1948, by exploding its own atomic device in 1974, and by ceaselessly upgrading its capacity thereafter, not only through a significant and worrisome level of plutonium reprocessing and stockpiling, but also through the development of advanced delivery systems.

Within one year after gaining independence from Britain, India had initiated its nuclear program with the establishment of its Atomic Energy Commission. In 1955 India signed nuclear cooperation agreements with the United States, United Kingdom and Canada, and in 1956 its first uranium research reactor became fully operational. India continued to develop its capabilities in the nuclear field, but following the Sino-Indian border war in 1962, the nuclear weapons option became a reality which until then Indian defense planners had been pursuing clandestinely to avoid going against a public posture of using nuclear energy only for peaceful purposes.

India's pursuit of the nuclear option was, therefore, the reason why it did not sign the NPT regime. Furthermore, it did not want to be excluded from the highly prestigious club that nuclear status conferred on a nation. Its declared objections to the discriminatory nature of the NPT, though justified, were only a smokescreen for its nuclear ambitions.

Another significant milestone in the Indian drift toward the so-called peaceful nuclear explosion in 1974 was the alleged US tilt toward Pakistan during the 1971 war, which prevented India from launching a full scale attack against what was then West Pakistan. Having been cheated out of its desire to eliminate Pakistan completely by the show of strength of a nuclear superpower, India became convinced that in order to establish itself as a major power in the region, it would have to assert itself in a manner which others would respect. The drift toward the Pokhran nuclear test become inevitable. To India watchers, its test of a 12 kiloton "peaceful nuclear explosion" in 1974 came as no surprise and conclusively established India's ability to manufacture nuclear weapons.

2.1 Nuclear Power Generation Capacity

India's present nuclear power generation capacity is over 1500 megawatts. Additional power plants are under construction and India's nuclear power generation target is 10,000 megawatts by the turn of the century.

Except for the Tarapur plant, which has two light water reactors, all of India's nuclear plants, operating and under construction, are heavy water plants, which can be operated to produce high quality plutonium. One of these, the 100 megawatts Dhruva reactor, which began operations in 1985, is reportedly capable of producing 25 kilograms of plutonium a year. This is enough for about three nuclear weapons annually, assuming it was operated solely to produce plutonium.

Despite five small plants to manufacture heavy water for its reactors and two more under construction, India has become increasingly dependent on imports of heavy water. Between 1983 and 1987, India engaged in extensive clandestine purchases of heavy water to enable it to operate its nuclear facilities without having to place them under International Atomic Energy Agency (IAEA) safeguards.

India has a significant reprocessing capability at Trombay and Tarapur. The Trombay plant can reprocess 30 metric tons of spent fuel per year, the Tarapur plant 100 metric tons. These plants are open to international inspection only when they are reprocessing fuel from India's four safeguarded power reactors.

India has also followed the plutonium route for bomb-making. Western generosity has enabled it to generate a tremendous nuclear capability, mostly unsafeguarded. Only four of India's nuclear power reactors (two each supplied by US and Canada) are under safeguards. Its powerful research reactor at Dhruva is not safeguarded, nor are its reprocessing plants and numerous other nuclear facilities, operational or under construction. In fact, India has a complete nuclear fuel cycle not open to IAEA inspection. Four unsafeguarded nuclear reactors, the Madras I and II nuclear power plants and the Cirus and Dhruva research reactors, together with two plutonium extraction plants at Tarapur and at the Bhabha Atomic Research Center, form the backbone of India's nuclear weapons capability by permitting the production of plutonium totally free of international non-proliferation controls.

As early as 1984, a Carnegie Endowment Task Force study rated India's bomb-producing capacity as considerable. It concluded that (a) even with its unsafeguarded plutonium stocks, India would appear to be capable of manufacturing at least two or three dozen nuclear weapons; (b) India's research reactors alone could provide an annual production rate for nuclear warheads of over ten a year, giving India more than 200 by this means alone at the turn of the century; (c) by 1990, the potential size of an Indian nuclear force would be impressive, almost certainly over 100 warheads and possibly several hundreds; and (d) if India were to pursue a vigorous program, it could make a thermonuclear device within three years from 1984.

2.2   Nuclear Delivery Systems

In parallel with this nuclear program, India has also been acquiring a capability to deliver nuclear weapons with precision over long distances. In addition to a large fleet of supersonic aircraft (MiG-23s, MiG-27s, Mirage 2000s) which could serve as delivery vehicles, India has developed a ballistic missile capability disproportionate to its genuine defense requirements.

India stepped into the guided missile arena in the early 1960s. In 1983, an Integrated Guided Missile Development Program was sanctioned by then Indian Prime Minister, Mrs. Indira Gandhi, with an allocation of Rs. 7.8 billion for the acquisition of missile technology over the next ten years. As a consequence of these efforts, India has been able to develop advanced guided missile systems, including surface-to-surface, surface-to-air, and anti-tank missiles. Notwithstanding the 1987 Missile Technology Control Regime (MTCR), India has developed its capability through clandestine purchases abroad and through the reverse engineering of missiles obtained from both Western and former Communist block suppliers.

India's most prestigious intermediate-range nuclear weapon capable surface-to-surface missile, the Agni, was first test fired in 1989 and is reported to have hit its target 1000 km away with desirable accuracy. Efforts to increase its potential range from 2500 km to 5000 km are being made, even though at 2500 km it can engage targets as far as Kazakhstan, major areas of China, in the Association of Southeast Asian Nations (ASEAN) countries to the East, and in the West as far as Iran, the Persian Gulf and Saudi Arabia. Once the missile range is extended to 5000 km; it will be able to hit targets in the whole of China and Kazakhstan, to the West as far as Turkey, Egypt and the Horn of Africa and Japan, the ASEAN countries, and in some parts of Australia depending upon the location from which it is fired. In addition, India has also developed a nuclear weapons capable shorter range (250 km) surface-to-surface missile, Prithvi, which compares favorably in accuracy and destructive ability with similar missiles in the arsenals of the US, China and Russia.

India's acquisition, by leasing a Charlie class nuclear powered submarine from the Soviet Union in 1988, ostensibly for training purposes, introduced a new dimension in the nuclear equation in South Asia as well as in the surrounding region. Even though the submarine was not armed with nuclear missiles, its presence in the area was enough to disturb the equilibrium in the sub-continent. The return of the submarine to Russia after three years has done very little to soothe the anxieties that its arrival generated.

3. Pakistan's Nuclear Program

Pakistan's nuclear policy has been largely reactive, running about 10-20 years behind India for each of the different stages of the nuclear ladder. Even so, Pakistan has not reached the stage of having or exploding a nuclear device, though it has acknowledged having developed a certain capacity.

Pakistan's nuclear program began in 1956 with the creation of the Pakistan Atomic Energy Commission (PAEC). In the early 1970s, the IAEA itself conducted a study of Pakistan's energy requirements and recommended the adoption of an ambitious program envisaging the construction of about 20 nuclear power plants by the end of the century. This recommendation by the IAEA was duly adopted by the Government of Pakistan. At that stage in the 1960s, the government possessed only two nuclear facilities, a small (5 mw) research reactor (PINSTECH) and the Karachi Nuclear Power Plant (KANUPP), which was constructed under a bilateral cooperation agreement with Canada under IAEA safeguards.

The decision to accord priority to nuclear power generation was based on a number of objective factors. Pakistan possessed low oil reserves, depleting gas fields, and poor coal deposits. Meanwhile, the price of imported fuel had quadrupled, and, with growing consumption, the bill for oil imports had jumped from $60 million a year in the 1960s to almost $500 million in the mid-1970s. It remained at a high level of $1.5 billion in the 1980s and has continued to rise constantly due to increased demand. At the same time, the potential for hydroelectric power, after the construction of the Mangla and Tarbela Dams and the problems over the construction of Kalabagh Dam became very limited. With energy demand growing at the rate of more than 500 megawatts annually, it was obvious that the only viable option for Pakistan was the installation of nuclear power plants.

Thus, Pakistan had more reason than most countries to aim for nuclear energy self-sufficiency because of its poor natural energy resource base. Its peaceful nuclear program envisaged the establishment both of heavy water reactors of the Canadian (CANDU) type which use natural uranium fuel, and light water reactors which utilize enriched uranium. The acquisition of an enrichment facility was an integral part of the program. To ensure optimum utilization of fuel, the program also contemplated the establishment of a reprocessing plant which was to be purchased from France. This and all other nuclear facilities were to be acquired from one or the other of the industrialized countries, under the normal safeguards of the IAEA. However, external circumstances determined a different course of events.

Pakistan's peaceful nuclear program was the primary victim of India's nuclear explosion in 1974. As a reaction to India's misuse of Canadian supplied technology and equipment for its 1974 nuclear explosion, Canada halted fuel supplies for KANUPP in Pakistan. It then recoiled from a commitment to supply a fuel fabrication plant and, finally, terminated all nuclear cooperation with Pakistan. Meanwhile, a campaign was launched by the US to prevent additional countries from acquiring enrichment or reprocessing facilities. France then reneged, under US pressure, to honor its signature on the contractual commitment for the supply of a reprocessing plant under IAEA safeguards to Pakistan although work had already begun at Chashma.

In the wake of the termination of Canadian cooperation, Pakistani engineers and scientists were able, through their own indigenous efforts, to keep the KANUPP power plant operational at a less than optimum level. Pakistan also succeeded in constructing a fuel fabrication plant. Following the imposition of restrictions under the London Club, efforts were also initiated to master the technology of uranium enrichment. For this purpose, an experimental facility was constructed at Kahuta.

Pakistan has confronted continuing difficulties in securing a response from Western suppliers to its invitation for bids for the construction of a 600 megawatt reactor at Chashma. It has only been recently that an agreement has been signed with China for the supply of this facility.

Furthermore, IAEA inspectors have carried out dozens of inspections of KANUPP. They have certified on each occasion that no diversion of nuclear material from this or any other facility under IAEA safeguards has taken place in Pakistan. At the same time, however, Pakistan has refused to accept the imposition, as a precondition for the supply of nuclear equipment and technology on a commercial basis, of full-scope safeguards over all its facilities, especially those which have been indigenously constructed. Full-scope safeguards would be discriminatory, especially *vis-a-vis* India.

Meanwhile, Pakistan has had to purchase some components abroad for its indigenous facilities. In view of the general presumption that Pakistan would follow India's example, such purchases have been dramatized and distorted to reinforce the theory that it is fully engaged in a nuclear weapons program. Despite the economic justification for its nuclear program, Pakistan's efforts to obtain technology and equipment from external sources have been thwarted, leaving it with no option but to develop its capabilities from its own resources, which it has accomplished with a reasonable degree of success.

India's attempt in the dismemberment of Pakistan in 1971 and its nuclear test in 1974 provided the spark for Pakistan's decision to upgrade its nuclear program so that, if necessary, it could counter Indian designs on its territorial integrity. As such, Pakistan's nuclear program is primarily a response to its conflicts with India since its independence. The primary reason for this hostility is the core dispute over Kashmir, which the United Nations duly recognizes as a "disputed territory" whose future should be settled through a plebiscite.

Unlike India, Pakistan has been careful not to cross the threshold by carrying out a nuclear test or by acknowledging its nuclear weapons status. This policy is based on Pakistan's genuine commitment to nuclear non-proliferation. In addition, Pakistan realizes that once the nuclear arms race is launched in the sub-continent, she would not be able to keep up with India's program, given the basic asymmetry in power and resources between the two countries.

4. Nuclear Ambiguity

The policy of nuclear ambiguity - neither confirming nor denying the possession of nuclear weapons - has been pursued by both countries, although subtle differences exist. Since its nuclear test in 1974, India has been affirming the peaceful nature of its nuclear program. At the same time, it has failed to respond to the numerous Pakistani initiatives which would expunge, for all time, the nuclear genie from South Asia. Its concern with China's nuclear arsenal has failed to convince anyone of this need, especially since there has been no attempt on the part of Peking at nuclear blackmail.

Pakistan's approach, though less ambiguous, still leaves some doubts about its present status. After denying for years that it was engaged in a nuclear weapons program, Pakistan finally admitted in early 1992 that it had attained the capability to produce a nuclear device but had, through a conscious decision, chosen not to do so.

5. Regional Non-Proliferation

Despite doubts about India's ability to accept the notion of a nuclear equation between the two countries, Pakistan has taken at face value India's pronouncements that its nuclear program is peaceful. Pakistan does not have any known global or regional ambitions. It has further presented a significant number of proposals for the regional reversal of the nuclear arms race in South Asia. These proposals have included (a) a nuclear-weapons-free-zone in South Asia, in 1974; (b) a joint declaration renouncing the acquisition or manufacture of nuclear weapons, in 1978; (c) the simultaneous accession to the Non-Proliferation Treaty, in 1979; (d) mutual inspections of each other's nuclear facilities, in 1979; (e) the joint and reciprocal acceptance of IAEA safeguards, in 1979; (f) a bilateral or regional nuclear test ban treaty, in 1987; and (g) a Five Power Conference, under United Nations' auspices, on a nuclear non-proliferation regime in South Asia, in 1991.

Without exception, all of these recommendations have been rejected by India, on the conceptual grounds that nuclear non-proliferation is both vertical and horizontal, and therefore not a regional but a global problem. The net result has been that India's nuclear program has proceeded unabated. Likewise, Pakistan's own reactive thinking and policy ha? advanced.

6. United States Actions

Despite Pakistan's consistent and long-standing attempts at the denuclearization of South Asia, it has been at the receiving end of US pressures to abandon its nuclear option without a satisfactory *quid pro quo*. The US policy of coercing Pakistan by threatening and then cutting off US economic and military assistance has, however, failed to produce its desired effect and might even have accelerated nuclear proliferation in South Asia.

The United States being the third major actor and arbiter in South Asia was expected to exercise even-handed pressure on both India and Pakistan to reverse the potentially dangerous nuclear spiral in the sub-continent. Pressure fell upon Pakistan as a result of the Pressler Amendment, and the result was a cut-off in aid. By and large, this line of action has been self-defeating because it creates no incentives for India to be responsive to the United States' and global concerns regarding non-proliferation. Pakistan, for its part, does not understand why it is being penalized, even though it is India which has a far more advanced nuclear program and which is the very cause of Pakistan's own reactions.

US opposition can, in any case, delay but not indefinitely prevent a nation with a sound technical base from developing nuclear capability. It can, and perhaps has, also resulted in some loss of US influence and strengthened the nuclear lobbies. Mere opposition cannot halt proliferation by itself. The decision to exercise a nuclear option is based on politico-military and security considerations. A more productive way of pursuing this matter is to address the causes of tension between the two countries and to ensure some kind of solution to the core dispute over Kashmir. This result might lead to a peaceful de-escalation of the nuclear rivalry between the two countries.

7. NPT and South Asia

The NPT is the cornerstone of the non-proliferation regime. As the 1995 Extension Conference draws near, there will be increasing pressure on the states which have still not signed to accede so that the treaties objectives are strengthened.

No amount of raw pressure on India and Pakistan will force these two countries to change their attitudes toward the NPT. India's reservation against the discriminatory nature and unequal obligations of the Treaty still remain to be addressed. The NPT's greatest flaw is that the nuclear weapon states have failed to fulfill their legally binding commitment to pursue nuclear disarmament, including a comprehensive nuclear test ban. In addition, the nuclear weapon states have failed to provide unconditional assurances against the use or threat of use of nuclear weapons to non-nuclear weapon states, thus contributing to the weakening of the NPT regime itself.

Pakistan shares India's perception on the discriminatory nature of the NPT; however, its commitment to nuclear non-proliferation in South Asia is a determining factor, which is why it has repeatedly offered to the sign the NPT simultaneously with India.

Furthermore, the global approach to non-proliferation is based on a rather curious paradox: weapons of mass destruction when possessed by the developed states further deter and create stability, but these very same weapons are considered destabilizing when they are acquired by developing states. East-West deterrence is said to have preserved world peace for 40 years, but that rationale is not always considered safe for other confrontations. Despite this mind-set, the case of India and Pakistan (two nations sharing a common and disputed border and a history of armed conflict) has shown that deterrence is applicable universally and that it has proved to be effective when all other options have failed to prevent a conflict.

8. Future Prospects

Pakistan has made a number of proposals, which are still on the table, to prevent a nuclear arms race in South Asia. These proposals can produce the desired result only if there is a genuine shift in India's perception of its own role in the region and in the world. While a roll-back is neither desirable nor realistically achievable, a verifiable nuclear freeze is an alternative worth pursuing; nevertheless, such efforts would have to be preceded by an amicable and satisfactory solution of the outstanding disputes between the two countries, particularly the question of Kashmir.

Despite stubborn Indian objections, there is a growing international realization that the regional approach to disarmament holds the greatest promise in the South Asian nuclear non-proliferation context. Useful solutions could emerge as a result of the proposal for a Five Nation Conference between the United States, China, Russia, India, and Pakistan, or even by a later idea of a more restricted tripartite conference just between the United States, India and Pakistan.

Other possibilities also exist. A nuclear freeze should be considered on the production and stockpiling of fissile materials, accompanied by a credible verification mechanism. Even though this type of freeze would not, by itself, answer all proliferation concerns in South Asia, it could be viewed as a confidence-building measure and perhaps mark the beginning of a downward spiral in nuclear tensions and ambitions.

Meanwhile, as current moves toward a Comprehensive Test Ban Treaty take place in the Conference on Disarmament in Geneva, a new window of opportunity is opening in which India may not be able to resist international pressures to cap or reverse its nuclear programs and policies. If this should happen, it is conceivable that Pakistan could be expected to follow suit, and nuclear non-proliferation in South Asia will become a reality.

One reason for this new possibility is that both countries believe in the general principle of non-discrimination, under which exists the best chance for controlling both vertical and horizontal proliferation. If there is movement toward controlling vertical proliferation and this movement appears to be discernible, it also becomes increasingly difficult to resist action to prevent horizontal proliferation.

Nuclear proliferation concerns in South Asia have, therefore, to be addressed through a correct mix of global and regional approaches, with a decided emphasis on the latter.

On the global front, an early conclusion of a comprehensive test ban treaty, universally negotiated and adhered to with an adequate verification mechanism, will automatically pull horizontal proliferation in its wake.

Finally, on the regional front, non-discriminatory and equal pressure on both countries to address root causes would also produce the same results, with the additional advantage of releasing enormous resources to be diverted toward the economic well being of both nations' population masses.

Chapter 9

THE ESTABLISHMENT OF A NUCLEAR-WEAPON-FREE ZONE AND A ZONE FREE OF WEAPONS OF MASS DESTRUCTION IN THE MIDDLE EAST

Mohamed I. Shaker

The establishment of a nuclear-weapon-free zone (NWFZ) and a zone free of weapons of mass destruction (WMD) in the Middle East is of the utmost importance for several reasons. The Middle East is still politically unsettled and military conflicts can erupt at any moment because of historically deep-rooted problems. Furthermore, the disintegration of the Soviet Union has led to the availability of potential suppliers of equipment and material which could become components of such weapons. In addition, the countries of the Middle East can also enhance their existing capabilities in weapon technology with the assistance of other developing countries. All of these serve as a potential source of instability and do not promote cooperation or enhance confidence among the States of the region. The United States, as well as other Western States, are deeply involved in the Middle East and are concerned with its stability. This region is important to the West since it is a great source of energy potential and possesses a unique strategic location accessible to Africa, West Asia, the Mediterranean and the Red Sea area.

The renewed peace process in the Middle East since the Madrid Conference in 1991 and the recent agreement signed by Israel and the Palestine Liberation Organization (PLO) in September 1993 have triggered hope for the establishment of the two zones free of nuclear weapons and free of weapons of mass destruction. With regard to the latter, the Chemical Weapons Convention (CWC) signed in Paris in January 1993 constitutes an important source to draw upon in reducing weapons of mass destruction on a regional level.

This paper will draw an overview of the ideas necessary to establish the two zones. This will be followed by a brief discussion of the basic elements required in creating such zones, namely the scope of prohibition, geographic delimitation, and modalities. Special emphasis will be placed on verification.

1. An Overview

The idea of establishing nuclear-weapon-free zones has captured the imagination of disarmament negotiators for many years. The first step in this direction was the Antarctica Treaty of 1959;[1] however, the first densely populated area to be declared a non-nuclear zone was Latin America. In 1967 the Latin American countries with the leadership of Mexico signed an agreement establishing a nuclear-weapon-free zone in Latin America called the Treaty of Tlatelolco.[2]

The establishment of such a zone prompted Mexico at the Conference on Disarmament (CD) to introduce a draft text of what has become Article VII of the 1968 Treaty on Nuclear Non-Proliferation (NPT)[3] Article VII states "Nothing in this Treaty affects the right of any group of States to conclude regional treaties in order to assure the total absence of nuclear weapons in their respective territories."

The conclusion of the Treaty of Tlatelolco, followed by the NPT, inspired many countries to work on the establishment of similar zones in different parts of the world such as Southeast Asia, the South Pacific and the Middle East. This is not to say that no similar efforts had taken place before the 1967-1968 period. The declaration of Africa as a zone free of nuclear weapons and European schemes such as the "Rapacki Plan" for Central Europe are prominent examples.

With regard to the Middle East, it must be stated that in 1974 Egypt and Iran took the initiative before the United Nations General Assembly for the establishment of a nuclear-weapon-free zone in this region; subsequently, Egypt undertook, on its own, the pursuance of this initiative at the UN General Assembly.[4]

At the beginning, Israel abstained in the vote on the Egyptian initiative but since 1980 it has joined in adopting the annual UN General Assembly resolution on this matter. In this respect it differs from a similar initiative by Pakistan for the establishment of a nuclear-weapon-free zone in Southeast Asia, which has failed so far to generate a consensus at the UN mainly because of India's opposition to it.

The resolutions of the UN General Assembly concerning the establishment of nuclear-weapon-free zones in the Middle East have evolved over the years. The essential elements of the resolutions are as follows:

-- The establishment of a nuclear-weapon-free zone will supplement the NPT regime.

-- Until the establishment of such a zone, all the countries concerned must in good faith make serious declarations that they will abstain on a reciprocal basis from producing, storing, or possessing (in whatever form) nuclear weapons and the means to deliver them and will further abstain from permitting third parties to keep nuclear weapons in their territories.

-- The IAEA will play a major role in safeguarding the nuclear activities of the countries concerned.

-- The declaration that the countries make in the creation of this zone is to be deposited with the UN Security Council.

-- The nuclear-weapon States must abstain from any activity that would be in conflict with the goal of establishing such a nuclear-weapon-free zone and must co-operate fully in sustaining such a zone.

-- The role of the UN Secretary General is to continue to examine ways to establish such a zone.

In 1988 the UN General Assembly took an important step forward in adopting a resolution requesting the UN Secretary General to prepare a study on effective and verifiable measures which would facilitate the establishment of a nuclear-weapon-free zone in the Middle East.[5] Three consultants were appointed by the Secretary General to assist in the preparation of this study. By mid August 1990 the study was completed, and by October it was made available to the members of the United Nations.[6] The 1990 study reached the conclusion that it was feasible to establish a nuclear-weapon-free zone.[7] This study would serve as the basis for initiating further talks in establishing such a zone.

In 1990, a few months prior to the Persian Gulf crisis and before issuing the United Nations study, President Mubarak of Egypt proposed the establishment of a zone free of weapons of mass destruction in the Middle East. He sensed the dangers menacing the stability of the Middle East from the proliferation of WMD. Apart from the nuclear capabilities of Israel, which have been a great source of worry for the whole region, the revelations regarding Iraqi planning and producing nuclear, chemical, and biological weapons proved that Egypt's worries were not unfounded.

President Mubarak's proposal was comprised of two components:[8]

-- All weapons of mass destruction without exception should be prohibited in the Middle East and all States of the region should make equal and reciprocal commitments in this regard.

-- Verification measures and modalities should be established to ascertain full compliance by these States.

Furthermore, Egypt underscored that certain terms had to be taken into account which included qualitative and quantitative symmetry existing within the military capabilities of the region. Precarious asymmetries could not continue to prevail, for they undermined a just and comprehensive peace. Also increased security for the region could be established if lower levels of armament could be attained. This would be acquired through political deliberations and disarmament arrangements rather than the force of arms. Finally, arms limitation and disarmament agreements should consider the equal rights and responsibilities of the States concerned and be legally binding commitments in the field of disarmament.

At the beginning Mubarak's idea received lukewarm support from the major Western powers. Later, the five major countries which are suppliers of arms (France, Great Britain, People's Republic of China, Russia, and the United States), which also happen to be the five permanent members of the UN Security Council, supported the idea in their meeting in Paris in July 1991. They even went on record by voting to implement fully the UN Security Council Resolution 687 on Iraq. This resolution clearly expresses concern over the threat which all weapons of mass destruction pose to the peace and security of the Middle East.

In this respect the implementation of Security Council Resolution 687 against Iraq suggests a nuclear-weapon-free Iraq or an Iraq free of weapons of mass destruction. This could be a dramatic beginning of creating the two zones.

Moreover, on 29 May 1991 US President George Bush presented a proposal affecting arms control issues in the Middle East. This proposal stressed the necessity of States in this area adhering to the NPT and called upon all major weapon-exporting countries to cease the supply of weapons of mass destruction into this region.

With the advent of the peace process and the establishment of a Multilateral Working Group on Arms Control and Regional Security of the Madrid Process, there is hope that this forum will constitute a practical and pragmatic way to negotiate, in more detail, the establishment of a nuclear-weapon-free zone and a zone free of weapons of mass destruction. The Multilateral Working Group has had four meetings thus far alternating between Washington and Moscow, but no progress has been made on this issue. However, some marginal progress has been made with regard to creating confidence-building measures, such as the participation of representatives of the countries of the Multilateral Working Group in an exercise of the CSCE which took place in the United Kingdom in March 1993. Moreover, in July 1993 Egypt hosted an intercessional workshop on the issue of verification and confidence-building measures.

In the last meeting of the Multilateral Working Group in Moscow, the Israelis seemed reluctant to enter more deeply into the modalities of a nuclear-weapon-free zone although the Israelis have on many occasions fully supported this idea. They have even joined the consensus of the UN on the importance of creating such a zone since 1980. It is presumed that the two co-sponsors of the Middle East Peace Conference, Russia and the United States, will exert their influence to push ahead with furthering these discussions. It is anticipated that if there is progress on the bilateral negotiating track, then more progress will come about in the Working Group. One of the encouraging features in the latter effort is the IAEA's participation since May 1993.

The two zones proposals are now on the table. Any progress achieved on one of these proposals will naturally have a positive effect on the other. It should be pointed out that a number of Arab countries have refused to sign the Chemical Weapons Convention for the simple reason that Israel has not yet acceded to the NPT regime or accepted the application of full scope safeguards on all its nuclear activities. Although these Arab nations, in particular Egypt, are fully convinced of the merits of the Chemical Weapons Convention and have fully participated in the negotiations leading to the conclusion of this Convention, it is difficult for them to sign the CWC. Israel continues to possess unsafeguarded nuclear activities which are a real threat to the region and its security. This position of the Arab States is not a new one and has been made clear since the convening of the Paris Conference on Chemical Weapons in 1989.

There is also an apparent link between the establishment of a nuclear-weapon-free zone in the Middle East and the one proposed in Africa. Some African States, specifically those in North Africa, will also be involved in the establishment of both zones. This link has been recognized by the United Nations and the Organization of African Unity, a working group entrusted with creating the modalities of the African nuclear-weapon-free zone.

2. The Scope Of Prohibition

It should be noted that the definition of what constitutes nuclear weapons has not been defined in the NPT. A definition was provided, however, in Article 5 of the Treaty of Tlatelolco which reads as follows:

> For the purpose of this Treaty, a nuclear weapon is any device which is capable of releasing nuclear energy in an uncontrolled manner and which has a group of characteristics that are appropriate for warlike purposes. An instrument that may be used for the transport or propulsion of the device is not included in this definition if it is separable from the device and not an indivisible part thereof.[9]

The term "nuclear weapons" in the NPT regime was understood to mean nuclear bombs and warheads. The negotiators for a nuclear-weapons-free zone in the Middle East may wish to follow the example of the Treaty of Tlatelolco in defining nuclear weapons. It should also be pointed out that the NPT prohibit "other nuclear explosive devices" as well. This term was introduced in the Treaty to take into consideration the potential use of nuclear explosive devices for peaceful purposes. This technology has not proven to be feasible, and the whole issue of peaceful nuclear explosions has been left unanswered; therefore, in the context of a nuclear-weapon-free zone in the Middle East, this term is not expected to re-emerge.

Regarding weapons of mass destruction, the chemical weapons prohibited would be all chemical warfare agents, gaseous, liquid, or solid which are banned because of their toxic effect on man, animal, and plant. Chemical weapons have much in common with biological weapons, but a greater degree of control can be exerted on their effects.

Recall that the 1925 Geneva Protocol is the principal international instrument against the use of Chemical Weapons.[10] However, experience of recent years has shown that it falls short of coping with the developments which took place in the areas of acquisition, production, use, and stockpiling. Needless to say, the Geneva Protocol of 1925 only bans the use of Chemical Weapons but not their production or their possession.[11]

The negotiators of a zone free of weapon of mass destruction in the Middle East will have to rely on both the Geneva Protocol and the 1993 Chemical Weapons Convention. Likewise, they will have to rely on the Biological Weapons Convention (BWC), which was concluded in 1972, prohibiting development, production, stockpiling, and acquisition of biological weapons. It is quite significant that while some Arab States have not signed the CWC, only 10 Middle Eastern countries have ratified the BWC.

3. The Geographic Delimitations

The 1975 UN study on nuclear-weapon-free zones presupposed a zone in the Middle East which would include 15 States extending from Libya to Iran including the Gulf States and Israel. This study was abiding by legal definition of the United Nations as to what countries constitute the geographic region known as the Middle East. It did not include the Northern African States: Mauritania, Morocco, Algeria, and Tunisia, nor did it include the Sudan. It should be noted that the Arab League in 1974 went on record in stating that a nuclear-weapon-free zone in the Middle East should include all the Arab States plus Iran and Israel.

The 1990 UN study took a different course than that of the 1974 study. It further benefited from a study undertaken by the IAEA which included a definition similar to that of the 1975 study.[12] The new study spoke of core countries and peripheral countries. Core countries meant the Middle Eastern countries involved in the Arab-Israeli conflict plus Iran. The peripheral countries are those existing in the area that can be involved in the establishment of the zone but not necessarily from its inception.

The 1990 UN study also includes the bodies of water such as the Red Sea and the Persian Gulf as well as the international waters such as the Suez Canal. The nations of the Middle East may also wish to learn from the experiences of the parties to the Treaty of Tlatelolco. For example, this treaty permits the transit of nuclear weapons through the Panama Canal and has triggered serious reservations on the part of the parties to the Treaty. In the Middle East this issues should also be seriously considered, for it has very delicate and intricate ramifications.

4. Modalities With Special Emphasis On Verification

A nuclear-weapon-free zone in the Middle East presupposes that the parties may have already adhered to the NPT regime. All Arab States are parties to the NPT except

Algeria, Oman, and the United Arab Emirates. Iran is a signator, and Israel would be expected to adhere to the NPT if it joins a nuclear-weapon-free zone in this region. The main obligations which the parties have to such a zone are similar to those undertaken in the NPT plus the additional obligation to guarantee that there is a complete absence of nuclear weapons in the established zone. The zone should also benefit from negative guarantees similar to those secured by the signatories to the Treaty of Tlatelolco (e.g., the non-use or the threat of use of nuclear weapons against the States in the zone). In creating the different provisions of this nuclear-free zone, the negotiators may wish to benefit from the experiences gained in negotiating the Treaty of Tlatelolco and the Treaty of Roratonga. The latter established a nuclear-weapon-free zone in the South Pacific.

One of the most difficult and delicate issues is that of verification. As in the case of the Treaty of Tlatelolco, IAEA safeguards should be applicable in the Middle East.[13] In its last report to its General Conference in 1993, the IAEA reported the responses and comments of some states of the region regarding the safeguards issue.[14] The common denominator in all of the responses so far received by the Agency is the central role which is expected to be played by the IAEA. One suggestion recommends that a regional inspectorate be created to work jointly with the IAEA after the successful conclusion of a peaceful settlement in the Middle East. Meanwhile the IAEA has incorporated additional features to strengthen its safeguards system. It has introduced regional or mutual inspection by affected parties. This latter verification procedure has been adopted by Argentina and Brazil and is one which could be adopted by other nations in order to enhance confidence-building measures.

The Chemical Weapons Convention can be used as an example of a verification system. It provides some interesting features which could be easily adopted, such as prompt access by inspectors and challenge inspections. Another concept which could be of great advantage is the use of soil, air, and water sampling to enhance confidence in the absence of undeclared nuclear activities .

The IAEA organized a workshop in Vienna in May 1993 on the modalities and the methods of application of safeguards in a future nuclear-weapon-free zone in the Middle East.[15] The objective was to assist Middle East experts in learning the different modes of verification.

Israel's adherence to such a zone or to the NPT regime would naturally be a special case in verification. An inventory of nuclear material accumulated over the years under no international review will be necessary and should be carefully undertaken to guarantee that all nuclear materials are accounted for. The adherence of South Africa to the NPT and to the signing of the safeguards agreement with the IAEA should be noted and should serve as an example to be applied to Israel when adhering to the NPT regime or to a nuclear-weapon-free zone in the Middle East.

As for chemical weapons, the modalities and the verification procedures adopted should be greatly guided by the CWC regime. As noted previously, the CWC has introduced new verification techniques including prompt access by inspectors and challenge inspections. Furthermore, the modalities of the Biological Weapons Convention of 1972 would be of great interest in affecting the modalities of a zone free of weapons of mass destruction in the Middle East. However it must be noted that the verification system of the BWC is still quite primitive. This is why in 1991, during the third review conference of the BWC, an *ad hoc* group of experts was created to report on verification procedures by the end of 1993. One of the ideas being entertained is that of drafting a special protocol dealing with BWC verification and compliance procedures.

5. Conclusions

The objective of establishing a nuclear-weapon-free zone and a zone free of weapons of mass destruction in the Middle East is not now and has never been in the realm of reality, however bleak and desperate the situation seemed to be. The breakthrough in the peace process, however meager it may seem, engenders hope that one day the negotiators will also be able to come up with a plan which will create and establish the two zones. The Multilateral Working Group on Arms Control and Regional Security of the Madrid process offers the best opportunity to do so. It might be difficult to expect this without a political settlement of the Arab-Israeli conflict. However, time should not be wasted. Profound work is needed and time is of the essence.

The reservoir of knowledge and experience existing in this field and the studies undertaken by the UN and the IAEA and other non-governmental groups should all be drawn upon by governments and negotiators involved in the peace process.

The road toward the establishment of the two zones is bumpy, but with political will this objective will be reached. Others have succeeded in Antarctica, Latin America, and the South Pacific. The Middle East can follow, even at the expense of meeting this challenge which is fraught with extraordinary difficulties.

Notes

1. See *Status of Multilateral Arms Regulation and Disarmament Agreements* Vol. 1 (New York: United Nations, 1993), pp. 22-32.
2. Ibid., pp. 72-109.
3. Ibid. pp. 110-159.
4. For a full account of the initiative and its examination by successive sessions of the UN General Assembly, see Mahmoud Karem, *A Nuclear-Weapon-Free Zone in the Middle East. Problems and Prospects* (New York: Greenwood Press, 1988).
5. UN General Assembly Resolution 43/65, 7 December 1988, paragraph 8.
6. UN Doc. A/45/435, 10 October 1990.
7. In 1974 the United Nations undertook an in-depth study on creating a nuclear-weapon-free zone. See UN Doc. A/10027/ADD. 1.
8. Conference of Disarmament Doc. CD/989, 20 April 1990.
9. *Status of Multilateral Arms Regulation, op. cit.*, p. 76.
10. Ibid. pp. 5-21.
11. Moataz M. Zahran, "Towards Establishing a Mass-Destruction-Weapon-Free Zone in the Middle East," Institute for Diplomatic Studies, Ministry of Foreign Affairs of the Arab Republic of Egypt, October 1992, p. 26.
12. *Technical Study on Different Modalities of Application of Safeguards in the Middle East*. IAEA-GC (XXXIII)/887, 29 August 1989.
13. Ibid.

14. *Application of IAEA Safeguards in the Middle East.* IAEA GC (XXXVII)/1072, 6 September 1993.
15. *Modalities for the Application of Safeguards in a Future Nuclear-Weapon-Free Zone in the Middle East.* An International Atomic Energy Agency workshop, 4-7 May 1993.

Chapter 10
LIMITING CONVENTIONAL ARMS SALES TO THE PERSIAN GULF

Michael O'Hanlon[1]

For perhaps the first time in its history, the United States is determining the size of its military forces largely in reference to the size and capabilities of the military forces of developing countries. Yet the United States and other major industrialized powers are also the main sources of modern weapon systems for those countries.

Arms sales often serve important foreign policy goals for countries such as the United States, allowing the supplying country to help important friends and allies strengthen their own defenses as sanctioned by the United Nations Charter. Conventional arms transfers therefore enjoy a certain legitimacy in the eyes of the international community, in contrast to trade in nuclear, chemical, and biological weapons. For the specific interests of the United States, often characterized as the only superpower, the case for certain types of arms sales is even stronger. In some situations they can contribute to a fairer sharing of the defense burden, reducing the chances that the United States will feel it needs to play the role of world policeman on its own. In other cases they can facilitate US military operations by effectively prepositioning certain equipment, supplies, and facilities that the United States itself might make use of in the event of conflict.

But the Middle East -- and today, particularly the Persian Gulf -- presents problems. The Middle East accounts for only about 3 percent of the world's population, but in the 1980s it bought on average some 30 percent of the world's military goods and services transferred internationally. At the end of the 1980s it dedicated more than twice as much of its annual output to military spending as any other region,[2] and it continues spending at a very sizable if somewhat reduced clip today (see Tables 1 and 2). Weapons and military establishments do not tend to sit idly in the Middle East; war has been a prominent feature of the region throughout the post-World War II era. Not only the frequency, but also the nature of war in this area causes concern, often threatening the very existence of individual leaders and even their countries. Mideast conflicts tend to occur within confined geographic bounds and on rapid time scales, exacerbating pressures to escalate to the most dangerous types of weaponry.

Despite a recent decline in the volume of the arms trade with the Middle East, ongoing tension and conflict in the region could spark a new arms race there, especially when coupled with excess weapons inventories and production facilities in the chief supplier countries. The end of Soviet aid to Syria and Libya and progress in peace talks have brightened the outlook considerably along the front line of the Arab-Israeli conflict.[3] But risks in the Persian Gulf region remain acute. Oil continues to provide the wherewithal for military forces that are disproportionate to the sizes of the region's countries and economies.[4] Iran and Iraq remain virulently anti-western, and Iraq may in the near future be able to achieve a lifting of UN sanctions against it.

The United States is fortunate to have a number of allies in the Mideast region. But while US allies in the Persian Gulf region have worked cooperatively with the United States in recent years, and avoided initiating wars on their own, they remain monarchies with much different perspectives on human, social, and political rights than the West. Under these circumstances, political and military alliances have their limits.

Table 1   **Mideast Military Spending In Perspective**

1989 (ACDA)		1992 (IMF)	
Region	Military Budget/GDP	Region	Military Budget/GDP
Middle East	12	Middle East *	7.2
North America	5.5	United States	5.3
Africa	4.5	Africa	2.3
South Asia	3.5	Asia	2.4
European NATO	3.5	EC	2.4
Neutral Europe	2	Other Industrial	
East Asia	2	Countries	2.0
Latin America	1.5	Latin Am./Carib.	1.1
Warsaw Pact	11	Countries in	
		Transition, not	
		Including FSU	3.8

* This category includes the developing countries of Europe. According to the IMF, these are Turkey, Cyprus, and Malta.

Source: Arms Control and Disarmament Agency, *World Military Expenditures and Arms Transfers, 1990* (1991), p. 18; International Monetary Fund, *Worl Economic Outlook, October 1993* (Washington, DC International Monetary Fund, 1993), p. 106.

Given this volatile brew, the world's major powers, no longer fundamentally at odds geopolitically, need a well-defined strategic logic to guide Mideast policy. There is a certain urgency to their efforts. The Perm-5 process is in serious trouble, major arms producers differ considerably in their views about which countries are pariahs and which weapons are destabilizing, and global economic troubles make the Persian Gulf especially tempting for all arms suppliers. The region could again enter an arms race, and supplier countries could find themselves antagonizing each other repeatedly, unless some common strategic logic guides the rearming of the region.

A cartel arrangement among the major suppliers was proposed in 1991 and this was the subject of a 1992 CBO study, *Limiting Conventional Arms Exports to the Middle East*, from which this paper is derived. But a cartel, while probably not impossible in the abstract, no longer seems a practical option. It would be sufficiently difficult to devise and implement. A strong political consensus would be necessary to make it work. Such a consensus probably would be possible only after a defining moment in the region's history, like a major war. It probably is not possible now, especially in the current environment where Russia, China, and the United States have become suspicious of each other's intentions and sincerity. But a more informal approach, guided by some of the same principles that might shape a cartel arrangement, may prove useful. This paper proposes one possible approach.

Table 2 **Major Importers And Exporters Involved In Sales To Developing Countries, 1992**
(Agreements, Measured In Billions Of US Dollars)

| IMPORTERS | | EXPORTERS | |
Country	Amount	Country	Amount
1. Taiwan	10.0	US	13.5
2. Saudi	4.5	France	3.8
3. Indonesia	1.4	U.K.	2.4
4. Kuwait	1.1	Russia	1.3
5. Malaysia	1.0	Germany	0.7
6. Egypt	0.8	Spain	0.5
7. Israel	0.7	Italy	0.4
8. Singapore	0.6	Israel	0.3
9. Thailand	0.5	Iran	0.2
10. UAE	0.5	China	0.1

Source: Richard F. Grimmett, "Conventional Arms Transfers to the Third World, 1985-1992," *Congressional Research Service,* Washington, DC, 1993, pp. 56, 59.

1. What Might Limits Look Like?

The frameworks for supplier-imposed limits that appear in the CBO study, mentioned herein, focus on the CFE categories of weapons -- tanks, armored combat vehicles, artillery, combat aircraft, and helicopters, plus missile systems and major naval vessels.

In their simplest form, limits would apply directly to numbers of weapons in the inventories of Mideast countries. A different approach, and the one emphasized in the CBO study, would limit annual deliveries of arms to each Mideast country. One particular variant of this approach would weight equipment by quality or dollar value, and then place limits on the annual trade as measured in these units. The limit might be set at around $700 million a year on each Mideast country's aggregate imports of major weapons systems (from all suppliers combined).

The value assigned to each type of weapon might be known as a "shadow price.? There undoubtedly would be some contention over proper shadow prices, but historical transaction data as well as scoring systems like the TASCFORM method could provide benchmarks.

The study's $700 million limit on major weapons would be consistent with a regional allocation for defense of around 5 percent of aggregate GDP. This is in contrast to levels of over 10 percent in the recent past. The 5 percent level would be high enough to permit US allies to continue most of their current defense programs. It also would not be so severe as to force the major arms suppliers from their preeminent positions in the market. As such, there would be less likelihood that a rogue supplier could find a major market position and sabotage the cartel effort.

Limits could be phased in to allow the honoring of existing contracts, as well as an opportunity for Saudi Arabia and other fairly weak countries of the region to catch up with Iraq while UN sanctions remained in place against the latter country.

Limits on CFE categories of equipment, as well as other large combat systems, probably could be monitored fairly well by national technical means and facilitated by database exchanges on the times, nature, and means of equipment deliveries. This assertion is based on the fact that the intelligence community reports arms transactions with a reasonable degree of confidence and precision, especially in regard to large weapons platforms. Monitoring these accords would be harder than monitoring CFE in some ways, since on-site inspections presumably would not be available to supplement overhead intelligence systems. In addition, since sales of weapons components such as tank engines would be counted against the limits, there might be some imprecisions from trying to count the traffic in smaller types of equipment. But exchanges of detailed databases, combined with the fact that nearly all shipments to the Middle East would entail ships leaving from major ports in various parts of Eurasia, would provide verification advantages.

The limits could well serve the interests of chief US friends and allies in the region -- Israel, Egypt, Saudi Arabia, other Gulf Cooperation Council (GCC) countries, and Jordan. Israel tends not to import as much weaponry as its neighbors and possesses the region's best defense industrial base as well as its best military. (See Table 3 for one measure of its superiority that does not even take into account what may be its single greatest asset, the quality of the personnel comprising its forces? The $700 million ceiling would allow it to continue future military programs at rates comparable to those of the recent past. Egypt also has a good defense industrial base and is militarily stronger than all of its immediate neighbors with the exception of Israel. Jordan would not be affected, since it imports considerably less than this framework would allow.

The CBO limits would require a revamping in western arms sales practices towards the GCC. Under this approach, the United States would not be able to make major sales of M1 tanks, F-15 aircraft, Patriot air defenses, MLRS artillery systems, Apache helicopters, and other offensive systems on the scale of recent years. Sales of equipment such as AWACs, air-to-air missiles, spare parts, communications gear, runway infrastructure, and the like would not, however, be affected by this approach. The United States might have to find more innovative and cheaper ways to buttress regional defenses in the future by selling more used aircraft such as A-10s. (Perhaps somewhat surprisingly, Iran's imports of major weapons platforms have not been blatantly in excess of the benchmark of $700 million per year per country. Israel, Egypt, Syria, and Libya also remain near or below the ceiling. Only the GCC countries, and most notably Saudi Arabia, are considerably above it.)

However, the military programs of Iran and Iraq -- the major potential adversaries of the GCC countries -- would also be subject to significant constraints. The manpower-poor countries of the GCC might be better able to counter Iran or Iraq if regional force levels were kept to lower levels. Although they still would depend on western help if attacked, parity at lower levels of forces would save them money and make it easier for the United States to play the role of security guarantor should that prove necessary.

It is often argued that the sheer number of arms suppliers precludes any possibility of supplier-led restraint in today's world. For certain types of weapons systems, this argument probably is true, but for high-performance major combat platforms it is not. In recent years, the Perm-5 countries have produced about 85 percent of all major weapons traded internationally, measured in dollar value. If most of the rest of the NATO allies were also to join an effort to limit sales, over 90 percent of the world's supply of major weapons platforms -- combat aircraft and helicopters, main battle tanks, armored combat vehicles, and artillery -- could be controlled even if China decided not to participate.[5] And virtually all of the high-technology models would be subject to limits. This is not an unimportant result for the Mideast region, where decisive victories generally have gone to modern, well-equipped forces.

Table 3   **Mideast Military Powers Today (Rough Ranking)**

Country	Norm. Div's	Wings	Tank	APCs	Arty	ACs	Helos
Israel	4.5	3.7	4,000	5,000	1,500	750	90
Syria	3.3	2.9	4,500	3,800	2,500	640	115
Egypt	2.5	2.0	3,000	3,500	1,500	500	90
Libya	1.9	2.5	2,300	2,000	1,500	400	75
Iraq	2.1	2.0	2,300	3,000	1,500	320	125
Iran	1.3	1.3	800	800	1,500	200	10
Saudi Arabia	0.2	1.6	800	2,300	500	300	20
Jordan	1.2	0.4	1,300	1,000	500	115	25
Rest of GCC	0.3	1.0	500	900	400	300	70
Pre-War Iraq	5.7	2.9					
US, 1991	24.8	61.3					
Base Force	20.9	53.7					
"Bottom-Up" Forces	17.0	45.0					

Notes: Normalized Divisions and Wings correspond to the TASCFORM scores for a US armored division equipped with M1 tanks and associated equipment, and an air wing equipped with F-16 combat aircraft, respectively.

APCs   - Armored Personnel Carriers   ACs   - Fixed-Wing Combat Aircraft
Arty   - Artillery   Helos - Helicopters

Source: CBO, *Limiting Conventional Arms Exports to the Middle East* (1992), p. 82; International Institute for Strategic Studies, *The Military Balance 1993-1994* (London: Brassey's, 1993); personal estimates.

2. Other Ideas For Limiting Arms Sales To The Region

A number of other studies and approaches to limiting the arms trade, besides the CBO effort of 1992, have been put forth in the last two years or so and merit consideration. These studies are summarized below.

2.1   Reinforce Positive Trends In Present Policy

Some observers remain confident that putting pressure on the radical states of the region, notably Iran and Iraq, and emphasizing restraint on missile technology as well as technologies related to weapons of mass destruction remain the most hopeful avenues for the future. This was essentially the policy of the Bush Administration and has effectively been adopted by the Clinton administration as well.[6]

Some recent trends in geopolitics may bode well for such an approach. The cutting off of Soviet aid and concessional sales to the likes of Syria, Libya, and Iraq; the Gulf War; and the global decline in oil prices have weakened virtually all of the region's radical states and made it difficult for them to rearm. But the Persian Gulf region remains nettlesome. The Director of the Central Intelligence Agency has made this very point in 1992 and 1993, indicating serious concern about the potential for both Iran and Iraq to rebuild conventional forces and to acquire weapons of mass destruction over the next 5 to 10 years.[7]

Moreover, the ability of the United States to pressure other suppliers into limiting sales to Iran and, ultimately, Iraq may be compromised by its own avidity to sell arms (see Table 2). Many of the world's other suppliers have begun to see US policy, which has allowed the United States to capture over half the global arms market and to make very substantial sales to the GCC monarchies, as at least somewhat hypocritical.

2.2   Place A Moratorium On Sales

Some individuals have argued for a moratorium on arms sales to the Middle East. Such a policy would have the advantage of preserving, at least on paper, a set of Mideast force balances that tend to favor US allies.

However, preserving a balance on paper is easier than doing so in practice. Modernization and maintenance plans in countries like Israel, Egypt, and Saudi Arabia could be thrown into considerable upheaval, with military forces eventually suffering significant consequences. Consequently, the defense forces of these countries might become less able to fend off attack even if aggressors themselves were weaker and, in short, war would become less predictable and its outcome potentially more subject to chance. Moreover, this region's countries undoubtedly would make efforts to find alternative sources of weaponry at home and abroad, were the major arms suppliers to turn off all spigots.

Such a framework also could prove impossible to negotiate. Most suppliers probably would consider it too drastic, especially since all see the Middle East as an important arms market. Indeed, in fairness, this idea was proposed immediately after the Gulf War and probably was intended more as a bold way to initiate arms export limits than as a long-term solution. But at this point it probably has become unrealistic altogether.

2.3   Freeze The Sizes Of Inventories

The notion of freezing equipment inventories at present levels was advocated in a major report conducted under the auspices of the Henry Stimson Center in Washington.[8]

It would require destruction of an old piece of equipment for each new version of the same category of weaponry that was to be imported.

While not an unreasonable first step to regional arms control, this approach would permit a very significant amount of modernization. Without more specific guidelines, there would be little to prevent MiG-21 aircraft from being replaced on a one-for-one basis by MiG-29's, F-4s by F-16s, T-55s by T-80s, and so forth. As measured by the TASCFORM scoring system -- a way of evaluating combat capability through static measures of equipment quality -- military capability could increase by factors of 2 to 5 without inventories increasing numerically at all.

In addition to this general problem, an inventory freeze would give an advantage to those countries currently possessing large arsenals. For the cases of Israel and Egypt, two of the better-armed Mideast powers, the consequences of such a development might be acceptable to the United States. But this approach also would favor Syria. Even more to the point it could lock in Iraqi superiority in the Persian Gulf region. Finally, this approach would allow the Mideast countries to continue spending inordinate fractions of their wealth on the military.

2.4   *Sell Only To Certain Types Of Regimes*

A recent legislative proposal by Senator Mark Hatfield and Congresswoman Cynthia McKinney would establish obstacles to selling arms to countries that are undemocratic, that are systematically abusive of human rights, or that fail to comply with the reporting requirements for the newly-fashioned UN registry of international arms transactions.[9]

Such an approach, while perhaps not reliable for all eras and all situations, seems generally reasonable for today's world. It is not inconsistent with the CBO study's focus on the non-democratic Persian Gulf region. Casting a particularly skeptical eye on sales to this region may be appropriate, especially because countries of the GCC are probably not capable of providing for their own self-defense.[10]

But this approach taken to the extreme could deny arms to certain governments that need and deserve help, and that can play the role of useful military allies to the United States. To take Cold War examples, aid to countries such as Taiwan and South Korea (even at times when their governments were not truly democratic) served US interests, and was in a sense the lesser of two possible evils.

Even today, there would be problems associated with applying this approach rigorously. It leaves unanswered very nettlesome issues about how one defines democracy. Is the existence of Kuwait's or Jordan's parliament sufficient proof that their peoples have a voice? What about a country like Mexico, or one of several Southeast Asian states, where some of the trappings of elections are present but where irregularities may continue to cloud the processes of popular rule? If one does not apply this approach rigorously, it no longer is clear what guidance it truly provides.

2.5   Limit "Destabilizing" Weapons?

Another set of ideas would focus explicitly on so-called offensive or destabilizing weapons. The United States itself has adopted such an approach in its efforts to limit ground-to-ground ballistic missile systems, as discussed elsewhere in this paper. Others might extend the concept to attack aircraft and possibly to tanks and attack helicopters.[11]

However, the key US ally in the region, Israel, relies extensively on mobile systems such as aircraft for its defenses. These weapons also provide a credible ability to retake territory if it is captured in an initially successful invasion. Such tactically offensive operations might have strategically defensive or deterrent purposes, yet require "offensive" weapons to conduct.

Moreover, the United States is not proving entirely successful at convincing other countries that missiles are bad but F-15s are good and legitimate. Absent a more compelling definition of destabilizing weapon, this type of approach is likely to be sufficiently fuzzy that prospective sellers will see their own wares as legitimate but the wares of others as dangerous.

3. Conceptualizing A Policy For 1994 And Beyond

A policy that might be appropriate at this point in post-Cold War and post-Gulf War history might pressure suppliers not to arm Persian Gulf countries beyond certain relatively modest and common inventory levels. Once those levels were reached or exceeded, there would be a general presumption of denial of future sales unless special circumstances warranted an exemption. Because of its focus on inventories of major weapons systems, and the concept of parity between countries on which it would be based, it would share several features with the Conventional Forces in Europe (CFE) Treaty. For this reason, it could be thought of as a "CFPG" framework, for Conventional Forces in the Persian Gulf region.

This type of framework would draw on many of the features of other recent proposals for limiting the arms trade. Like existing US policy, it would identify Iran and Iraq as the major threats to US and regional interests. Like the Hatfield/McKinney approaches, it would focus on the most nondemocratic of the world's major arms consumers. The Stimson Center report focuses on inventory levels and institutes a presumption of denial for sales to countries exceeding specified levels. But like the earlier CBO effort, it would impose restraints that would have a significant effect upon the scale of regional arms acquisitions.

What weapons levels might be appropriate for each country? In keeping with the goal of restraining regional military spending to perhaps only half its prior value, limits on the order of 1,000 to 1,250 tanks; 1,500 to 2,000 armored combat vehicles; 1,000 to 1,250 pieces of artillery; 250 to 300 combat aircraft; and 75 to 100 combat helicopters might be appropriate. Such limits would allow some additional room for strengthening GCC forces, but would not allow Iraq to exceed its current arsenal. They also would be consistent with the $700 million per year limits at the heart of one of the CBO options, and as such should be consistent with the goal of reducing Mideast military spending to 5 percent of average GDP.

Were inventories kept to these levels, Iran or Iraq might offer only half as strong a foe to US forces as anticipated in the Bottom-Up Review (see Table 4). The chief threats to US security that now concern policymakers would therefore be reduced, perhaps facilitating further defense spending cuts, or at least helping ensure that the US force structure now planned will be capable of easily countering adversaries which may rise up against American interests in the future.

Table 4   **Major Regional Conflicts And US Force Planning**

TYPE OF EQUIPMENT	EXPECTED FORCES OF FOE
Tanks	2,000 - 4,000
APCs	3,000 - 5,000
Large-Bore Artillery	2,000 - 3,000
Combat Aircraft	500 - 1,000
Naval Vessels	100 - 200
SCUD-Class Missiles	100 - 1,000

Source: Les Aspin, Secretary of Defense, "The Bottom-Up Review? Forces for a New Era," Department of Defense, Washington, DC, 1993, p. 5.

4. Appendix: Economic Implications Of Ideas In The CBO Study

There would be both good and bad economic news associated with any successful effort to restrain the Mideast arms race. But the bottom line is that military spending is a non-productive investment which should be minimized in favor of more beneficial expenditures -- where this is consistent with states' security needs.[12]

Under the main approach laid out in the CBO study, sales of major weapons to the Middle East would be reduced by about 50 percent relative to levels typical of the 1980s. Even if the United States absorbed half of these cutbacks, US exports probably would fall by no more than some $3 billion a year -- 20 percent of the country's total annual arms exports and about 5 percent of its annual defense production. As sales to the Middle East fell, US gross domestic product would be reduced by just 0.02 percent, and even this very slight loss in GDP would be only temporary.

If US exports were reduced by $3 billion a year, up to 75,000 defense jobs could be lost out of a private-sector defense industrial base of about 2.5 million individuals. Forgone sales would represent 2 percent or more of current output levels in only a few of the 420 major US industrial sectors. In certain specific sectors, however -- such as the tank industry -- effects could be considerably more severe, since foreign arms sales represent a major source of business at this particular point in time. Should defense industrial base considerations argue in favor of keeping lines open, the beneficial effects of arms sales generally could be supplanted by low-rate production for the Department of Defense, with annual costs in the hundreds of millions of dollars range.

The effects of lost exports would be slightly more noticeable in some other western supplier countries. But in all cases macroeconomic conditions would not be significantly affected. However, the former Soviet republics -- and especially Russia -- could feel more significant effects because their arms sales are principal sources of hard currency.

There is a good deal of positive economic news as well, however. If limits on the arms trade could maintain or improve Mideast security while also reducing defense expenditures, the countries of that region could obtain significant economic benefits. Mideast countries typically have been spending almost 5 percent of their wealth on arms imports, and over 10 percent on their militaries in general. If major arms imports were reduced by one-half and all arms imports in aggregate by one-third, as might be expected under the CBO approach, a significant amount of hard currency would become available for more productive purchases. Many of these would be made from western countries, largely neutralizing the effects of lost exports from the arms trade. Moreover, these investments -- if made wisely -- eventually could increase the average level of real GDP in major Mideast countries by 2.5 percent or more. These effects clearly would benefit the Mideast countries themselves, and also would result in larger markets for the United States in the future.

Notes

1. The author is an analyst in the National Security Division of the Congressional Budget Office. Views expressed in this paper, however, are his own and not attributable to CBO.
2. Congressional Budget Office, Washington, DC, *Limiting Conventional Arms Exports to the Middle East* (1992), pp. 1-17; Arms Control and Disarmament Agency, Washington, DC, *World Military Expenditures and Arms Transfers, 1990* (1991).
3. See for example, Yahya M. Sadowski, *Scuds or Butter?: The Political Economy of Arms control in the Middle East* (Washington DC: The Brookings Institution, 1993), p. 22
4. See for example, Edward R. Fried and Phillip H. Trezise, *Oil Security: Retrospect and Prospect* (Washington DC: The Brookings Institution, 1993), p. 25.
5. *Limiting Conventional Arms Exports to the Middle East,* p. 13
6. For a defense of this type of approach, see Geoffrey Kemp, *The Control of the Middle East Arms Race* (Washington DC: Carnegie Endowment for Internatinal Peace, 1991), pp. 177-183.
7. Statement of Robert Gates, Director of Central Intelligence, before the Defense Policy Panel of the House Committee on Armed Services, March 27, 1992, pp. 4, 8, 11-16; and Statement of R. James Woolsey, Director of Central Intelligence, before the Senate Governmental Affairs Committee, February 24, 1993, pp. 8-14.
8. Alan Platt, ed., "Report of the Study Group on Multilateral Arms Transfer Guidelines for the Middle East," Henry L. Stimson Center, Washington DC, 1992, p. 43.
9. See for example, "Legislation to Block Foreign Arms Sales Introduced Today," *Inside the Pentagon,* November 18, 1993, p. 14.
10. Secretary of Defense Cheney, while favoring arms sales to the GCC countries to help provide a front-line defense against Iraqi or Iranian aggression, made the point that these countries would require US help in the event of major war even if arms were sold to them. See statement of Secretary of Defense Richard Cheney before the House Committee on Foreign Affairs, March 19, 1991.
11. See Carl Conetta, Charles Knight, and Lutz Unterseher, *Toward Defensive Restructuring in the Middle East* (Cambridge MA: Commonwealth Institute, 1991); Center

for International Security and Arms Control, *Assessing Ballistic Missile Proliferation and Its Control* (Stanford, CA: Stanford University Press, 1991).
12. For support for this position, also see International Monetary Fund, *World Economic Outlook, October 1993* (Washington, DC: International Monetary Fund, 1993), pp. 104-109.

PART III

THE NON-PROLIFERATION TREATY: POLITICAL AND TECHNOLOGICAL ISSUES

Chapter 11

CHALLENGES TO THE NUCLEAR NON-PROLIFERATION REGIME

Kathleen C. Bailey

While there have been recent events which strengthen the nuclear non-proliferation regime -- such as the adherence to the Nuclear Non-proliferation Treaty (NPT) by France, China, and South Africa -- there are also some challenges which seriously weaken the prospects for stemming the spread of nuclear weapons. This paper focuses on five of the most serious challenges and posits that they are unlikely to be overcome successfully. The United States must be prepared to take strong measures, including counterproliferation tactics and reorientation of its nuclear deterrent.

1. Cheating And Detecting With Surety

Iraq and North Korea signed the NPT, then violated it by pursuing nuclear weapons capability. Both used their NPT status to help mask their clandestine nuclear programs. Iraq declared its publicly known nuclear facilities and placed them under safeguards by the International Atomic Energy Agency. Meanwhile, it built secret, undeclared nuclear facilities which were well-hidden, effectively preventing their discovery by national technical means. They were discovered subsequent to Desert Storm, primarily as a result of information from a defector.

North Korea undertook secret plutonium reprocessing in violation of its NPT commitments. It was able to do so, in part, because it continually delayed the completion of a safeguards agreement with the IAEA -- an agreement required by the NPT. The illicit activity was conclusively determined only after sample collection and analysis conducted in conjunction with routine and *ad hoc* inspections by IAEA officials.[1]

It is noteworthy that the secret nuclear programs of Iraq and North Korea may be more extensive than is presently known, even after "anytime-anywhere" special inspections conducted by the United Nations and best efforts of US and other intelligence gatherers. For example, Iraq may have an underground reactor capable of producing plutonium. Although experts have searched for such a reactor and none has been found, suspicions still remain among some UN inspectors and Western government officials. Furthermore, UN inspectors have stated their belief that Iraq continues to hide nuclear-weapons-related data, drawings, equipment, and other resources that will be applicable in renewing the program in the future. Likewise, North Korea may have more plutonium than it has now admitted to having, or may have made significant advances in nuclear weaponization.

The cases of Iraq and North Korea reveal two important problems with relying on the NPT, or any treaty verification regime, to prevent nuclear proliferation. First, Iraq demonstrates the limitations of detection technology. Without good intelligence from a human source, it will be difficult if not impossible to discover secret facilities, materials, or weapons which are well-hidden or have no unique observable features.[2] No matter how well safeguards inspections are bolstered in the future, they are unlikely to match the intrusiveness and close scrutiny of the UN inspections in Iraq -- inspections which probably still have not fully revealed the nuclear weapons program.

Second, the case of North Korea demonstrates that, regardless of how much the capabilities of inspectors to ferret out weapons activities are improved, national sovereignty can be an obstacle. Despite insistence by the international community that North Korea allow IAEA special inspections, Pyongyang has stonewalled. North Korea has even thwarted the relatively non-intrusive routine inspections of the IAEA to change film or batteries in observation cameras.[3] The country has argued that its non-compliance is justified because the inspections are a "Western conspiracy."

The NPT has no provisions which would deter a nation from using it as a smoke-screen; it has no sanctions or other punishment for violators. As of this writing, North Korea has been in noncompliance with its NPT obligations for well over a year but has suffered no serious repercussions.

If Iraq resuscitates its nuclear weapons program in the future, or if North Korea remains in the NPT while violating it, other parties could conclude that having their own nuclear deterrent offers more security than a treaty that can be broken by its parties.

2. Acquiring Nuclear Weapons And Delivery Systems

The problem of missile proliferation is integrally related to the threat posed by nuclear proliferation. Obviously, a weapon that is deliverable is a much greater threat than one that is not. In the past, countries which pursued nuclear weapons capability generally did not have delivery systems other than aircraft.[4] The spread of ballistic and cruise missiles has changed this. Nuclear-capable missiles have been developed by Israel, India, and North Korea; Ukraine, Kazakhstan, and Belarus inherited them from the former Soviet Union. Others are trying to develop or buy such missiles.

"Crude" cruise missiles -- those which are not supersonic or do not have sophisticated capabilities such a terrain-mapping guidance -- can be produced by many nations. Commercially available Global Positioning System[5] receivers can be used for guidance. Any country with a technical infrastructure which can support avionics and aircraft industries can design and build a workable cruise missile.[6] It is even possible to imagine a scenario in which propeller-driven aircraft could be used to deliver nuclear or other weapons of mass destruction.

Existing air defense technologies and capabilities currently are not highly effective against attacks from airplanes or cruise missiles. These systems also are extremely expensive to build, operate, and keep technologically up-to-date. Thus, existing air defense capabilities are not widely deployed.

Even the former Soviet Union and the United States have had serious difficulties defending against air-attack scenarios. Recall that Mathias Rust landed his Cessna airplane in Moscow's Red Square. Also, the United States has not succeeded in stymieing the flow of aircraft delivering illegal drugs despite substantial use of sophisticated surveillance and intercept capabilities.

Defenses against ballistic missiles are equally if not more deficient. The famed Patriot anti-ballistic missile system, originally credited with intercepting most of the SCUDS launched by Iraq during the 1991 Gulf War, may actually have had limited success.[7] Nations now under threat from nuclear proliferants -- such as Japan and South

Korea -- are attempting to acquire upgraded Patriots, but even the improved defensive system may be inadequate in the face of enemy ballistic missiles. In the future, nations such as North Korea are likely to try to incorporate countermeasures into their offensive missiles to negate the effectiveness of missile defenses.

The increasing availability of delivery vehicles exacerbates the threat posed by nuclear weapons to the potential victim, who must deter or defend against the nuclear enemy in absence of effective missile and air defenses. In the future, unless technological advances allow for affordable defense against delivery systems, nations which ordinarily would not want nuclear weapons will seek them anyway as a deterrent against nuclear threats.

3. Nuclear Weapons As Bargaining Chips

Meeting the demands of proliferant states that their weapons be exchanged for political or financial capital is akin to dealing with terrorists or extortionists. And it will have the same effect: states will note that nuclear weapons are excellent bargaining chips. Two cases -- that of North Korea and of Ukraine -- make this apparent.

North Korea established a nuclear weapons program and perhaps produced nuclear weapons. The program came under suspicion when North Korea failed to complete its safeguards agreement with the IAEA,[8] as required by the NPT, and when Western intelligence agencies gathered information on probable plutonium production and reprocessing. During 1992, IAEA inspectors conducted six inspections and visits to North Korea. Samples of plutonium which North Korea declared were analyzed, as were samples taken from a nuclear reprocessing waste storage site. North Korea had declared that the waste at that site was from a single reprocessing campaign. The results of the IAEA's analysis revealed inconsistencies. Specifically, the IAEA reported:

-- The characteristics of the declared and presented plutonium product are not consistent with the irradiation history of the fuel declared by [North Korea] to have been processed during the single reprocessing campaign; and

-- The characteristics of the presented plutonium product and waste and the declared irradiation history of the reprocessed fuel are mutually inconsistent and inconsistent with the declaration that they resulted from the single campaign.[9]

Although North Korea permitted additional brief visits by the IAEA on September 11 and 14, 1992, it did not allow close inspection of a building, under military control, which probably had underground waste storage. Subsequent meetings between North Korea and the IAEA failed to resolve the inconsistencies, and in January 1993, the IAEA stated that it could not preclude that grams or kilograms of plutonium had been reprocessed by North Korea. On February 26, 1993, the IAEA formally asked for a special inspection of two key sites. North Korea, stung by the request, announced on March 12, 1993 its withdrawal from the NPT, but later suspended that withdrawal in the face of political pressures and promises of negotiations.

The nuclear weapons program, refusal to allow inspections, and the threat to withdraw from the NPT placed North Korea in a position to bargain for economic, military, and political advantages. To entice North Korea, the United States agreed to cancel military exercises with South Korea. Furthermore, it extended security assurances to

Pyongyang that no nuclear weapons were in South Korea and offered North Korea inspection rights to US military bases in South Korea, as well as the discussion of simultaneous inspections of nuclear facilities in both Koreas.[10]

Ukraine is also using nuclear weapons to negotiate for political, security, and financial advantage. In May 1992, Ukraine signed the Lisbon Protocol stating that it would give up nuclear weapons and sign the NPT "in the shortest possible time," but it failed to live up to the promise. Instead, the Ukraine Rada (parliament) declared ownership of the nuclear weapons on its soil on July 2, 1993. Ukraine has ordered personnel associated with the nuclear weapons to take a loyalty oath to Ukraine[11] and is reportedly attempting to gain "positive control" of these weapons -- the ability to target and launch the missiles.[12]

Although Ukraine's leaders still pay lip service to the idea of becoming a non-nuclear-weapons state, the demands to be met before its doing so are increasing. Even though the United States signed an agreement with Ukraine to provide $175 million in assistance for warhead dismantlement and an additional $20 million for retraining of personnel, Ukraine continues to insist that it must receive at least $3 billion. It also demands security assurances from Europe and the United States. In September 1993, Ukraine further increased its demands. It said that compensation would also be required for the tactical nuclear weapons which were removed from Ukraine by Russia immediately following the breakup of the USSR.[13] Russian officials claim that Ukraine will never be satisfied; as soon as one demand is met, another will take its place, and the bargaining will continue as long as Ukraine is allowed to keep the nuclear weapons.

On November 18, 1993, the Ukraine Rada finally ratified START I and the Lisbon Protocol, but with reservations that nullify the effects of ratification,[14] including:

-- The requirement to join the NPT as a non-nuclear weapons state (Article V of the Lisbon Protocol) is considered to be non-binding and Ukraine will not yet adhere to the treaty;
-- Disarmament commitments will be met only if "sufficient international financial and technical assistance is provided;" and,
- Only 36% of the launchers and 42% of the strategic warheads on its territory will be dismantled until other demands are met.

Other nations cannot help but notice that North Korea and Ukraine have, in very different ways, used nuclear weapons as bargaining chips. Allowing the negotiations to occur and meeting the demands of the two nations simply reinforce to other nations that nuclear weapons can be very useful politically and economically.

4. Nuclear Weapons And Their Use

There are at least three primary reasons why the risk of nuclear war between or among new nuclear weapons states[15] is higher than was the risk of war between the United States and the Soviet Union. First, *direct* armed conflict between new nuclear weapons states is more likely today. Any conventional conflict between them could escalate into a nuclear exchange. Although the United States and Soviet Union were locked in ideological battle and, often, in armed conflict through surrogates, they did not directly engage one another. In South Asia and Northeast Asia -- two regions suffering from conflict and confrontation, as well as nuclear build-up -- the combatants border one another and have fought wars against one another in recent history.

Second, new nuclear weapons states have invested less time, money, and expertise in technologies and procedures for safety and security of nuclear weapons. It is very unlikely, for example, that India, Pakistan, or North Korea has developed permissive action linkage devices to assure a high level of control over nuclear weapons use.

Third, new nuclear weapons states are likely to have fewer bureaucratic and behavioral "strings" that limit the potential use or threat of use of nuclear weapons. The five declared nuclear weapons states have spent much time and effort understanding the implications of nuclear weapons use and "reading" one another's intentions in order to avoid nuclear war. From these experiences have come the Washington-Moscow "hot line" and a host of other measures to minimize the risk of nuclear exchange. Development of these procedures and attitudes regarding nuclear weapons is not only a function of time but of public and governmental discussion. Generally, new nuclear weapons states do not even admit they have nuclear weapons, which precludes such discussion.

5. Countering Or Deterring Proliferation

If diplomacy and peace efforts fail to prevent the proliferation of nuclear weapons (or, it can be argued, other weapons of mass destruction), there will be essentially two options left open to the United States. The first is counterproliferation, i.e., those actions which can be taken to eliminate or neutralize proliferation once it has occurred. Counterproliferation measures include military action against weapons or weapons development capabilities (preferably before they culminate in deployed weapons); countermeasures against weapons delivery systems (including effective defenses); weapons disablement and render-safe technology development; and sabotage of weapons capabilities.

In some cases, counterproliferation measures entail unacceptable risks. For example, if the United States or a coalition were to attempt to destroy North Korea's nuclear facilities or to forcefully remove its weapons-usable nuclear materials, the results might be the spread of nuclear contamination on a wide scale and/or massive conventional war between the North and South. Also, success is far from guaranteed. For example, North Korea might hide its weapons materials in a deep tunnel or some other unreachable, indeterminable location. Success of counterproliferation is most likely when the program in question is not fully developed or when the proliferant nation is unable to retaliate. The Israeli attack on Iraq's nuclear reactors was an example of an act of counterproliferation, but it only delayed Iraq's quest.

Deterrence may be the easiest response and in many situations may be the most successful. Few proliferant nations are likely to risk annihilation and will therefore be unwilling to threaten other nuclear weapons states. Some defense analysts may argue that rogue nations are undeterrable because they do not fear -- or else do not believe the threat of -- severe retaliation. There is evidence to the contrary, however. Iraq, a nation that might be categorized as "rogue," is in fact deterrable. This was proven when Iraq did not use its chemical or biological weapons against Israel. It was deterred by something, perhaps the veiled threat of Israeli retaliation with nuclear or chemical weapons.

Deterrence against proliferants is also crucial for US non-proliferation policy vis-a-vis the capable-but-restrained nations like South Korea, Japan, and Germany. Without a strong US extended nuclear deterrent, these nations are likely to seek their own nuclear arsenals.

On July 28, 1993, former Japanese Foreign Minister Kabun Muto told Japanese reporters:

> There is a clause in the NPT allowing withdrawal from the treaty. If North Korea develops nuclear weapons and that becomes a threat to Japan, first, there is the nuclear umbrella of the United States upon which we can rely. But if it comes down to a crunch, possessing the will that 'we can do it' is important.[16]

Although German officials have not publicly said the same, it is true that the US nuclear umbrella over NATO countries has been crucial to preventing nuclear proliferation in Europe.

Despite the importance of nuclear deterrence to US national security and the dependence of many nations on the US nuclear deterrent, that deterrent is weakening. The drawdown in numbers of nuclear weapons under the START agreements is not the issue. Extended deterrence results from both the adversary and the protected country believing that the United States not only has a weapon that can inflict unacceptable damage, but also has the will to use that weapon. There are fundamental problems with the US nuclear deterrent to twenty-first century threats from proliferants:

- The stockpile composition is probably inappropriate to deter some future threats. It is largely composed of strategic weapons with high yield, designed to incapacitate hardened targets. Their use would create considerable collateral damage, which limits their usability in small attack options.
-- The stockpile is no longer being tested, so its reliability will become increasingly uncertain and any problems that are found cannot be corrected with high certainty. This may signal to nations protected by the US umbrella, as well as those nations' adversaries, that the US is not serious about maintaining a strong deterrent.

To correct these deficiencies, the United States should reconfigure its nuclear arsenal to match better the likely threat scenarios of the future. The objective is not to use nuclear weapons, but to ensure that they are usable so that they will not have to be used. This sounds like contorted logic, but it is imperative that the promise of US retaliation against proliferant weapons be credible. Only then will nations be fearful of exercising their own potential to pose a nuclear threat to others.

New weapons should be tested. Any negotiation of a comprehensive test ban should take into consideration the continuing need for US testing not only as a means of proving future nuclear designs, but also as a way of proving to allies which agree not to proliferate that the US nuclear umbrella over them works.

Notes

1. North Korea probably would not have allowed sample collection had it been aware of the nuclear analysis capabilities of the IAEA. North Korea apparently was un-

    aware that telltale signatures of nuclear activity could remain even after glove boxes and other equipment had been decontaminated, and that analysis of waste from reprocessing could reveal how many reprocessing campaigns had occurred.

2. This problem will be exacerbated in countries which have civil nuclear programs with uranium enrichment or plutonium reprocessing that could be used to obscure weapons activities.

3. R. Jeffrey Smith, "North Korea Said to Harm UN Ability to Verify Nuclear Compliance," *The Washington Post*, October 28, 1993, p. A13.

4. Aircraft certainly can be used for nuclear weapons delivery. Unmanned missiles might be preferable, however, because they can be much faster (and therefore difficult to intercept or defend against), are not subject to pilot control or error (missiles can be extremely accurate), do not endanger the lives of highly trained pilots, and may be cheaper (particularly considering maintenance and pilot training costs).

5. The Global Positioning System is a constellation of satellites whose signal can be intercepted and used to calculate position with high accuracy.

6. See W. Seth Carus, *Cruise Missile Proliferation in the 1990s* (Westport, CT: Praeger Publishing Co., 1992) for a thorough description of the ease with which less-developed countries may acquire cruise missile technology capable of delivering weapons of mass destruction.

7. Moshe Arens, Israel's Defense Minister during Desert Storm, has said that very few Patriots actually intercepted incoming SCUDS. The US Army has stated that this depends on the definition of interception, which it defines as knocking SCUDS off course. Using the Army's criterion, sixty percent of the SCUDS were successfully intercepted. See Tim Weiner, "Patriot Missile's Success a Myth, Israeli Aides Say," *The New York Times International*, November 21, 1993, p. 13.

8. North Korea acceded to the NPT in December 1985, but did not finalize a safeguards agreement with the IAEA until April 1992.

9. International Atomic Energy Agency, Information Circular 419, April 8, 1993, p. 3.

10. R. Jeffrey Smith, "US Outlines Compromise in Korea Talks," *The Washington Post*, May 27, 1993, p. A 43.

11. Chrystia Freeland, "Ukraine Seeks Control of Nuclear Missiles," *The Washington Post*, April 11, 1993, p. A 24.

12. This was publicly reported (see Bill Gertz, "Ukraine Pursues Missile Control," *The Washington Times*, June 10, 1993, p. A7). It was also independently confirmed in the author's conversations with Russian General Colonel Evgenii P. Maslin.

13. Speech by General Colonel Evgenii P. Maslin before a conference on Arms Control and Verification at Southern Methodist University on October 16, 1993.

14. Translation provided by the Embassy of Ukraine dated November 19, 1993 of the "Resolution of the Supreme Rada of Ukraine" dated November 18, 1993.

15. New nuclear weapons states refers to those other than the declared five nuclear weapons states (United States, Russia, United Kingdom, France, and China).

16. Sam Jameson, "Foreign Minister Says Japan Will Need Nuclear Arms if N. Korea Threatens," *The Los Angeles Times* (Washington edition), July 29, 1993, p. 3.

Chapter 12

NPT VERIFICATION AND ENFORCEMENT: PROBLEMS AND PROSPECTS

Ira N. Goldman[1]

The Non-Proliferation of Nuclear Weapons Treaty (NPT) is similar to other multilateral arms control treaties of the 1960s and early 1970s (e.g., Limited Test Ban Treaty, Biological Weapons Convention, Seabeds Treaty, Environmental Modification Convention) in that it has limited verification provisions and essentially non-existent provisions for assessment of compliance and enforcement of obligations (including a lack of sanctions for non-compliance). This reflects a number of factors, including the difficulty at that time of establishing either practical or non-intrusive verification arrangements, as well as the fact that these agreements were viewed by many as being primarily confidence-building measures. In fact, out of all the agreements of that period, the NPT broke new ground by establishing the principle of on-site inspections by an independent, international inspectorate, the International Atomic Energy Agency (IAEA).

The lack of strong verification and compliance provisions in such multilateral treaties was in marked contrast to US/USSR arms control agreements that were painstakingly concluded beginning in the early 1970s. These treaties contained increasingly detailed and elaborate provisions and institutional arrangements for verification and compliance.

This verification and compliance obsession began to affect the multilateral arms control arena, as reflected in the negotiations and conclusion of the Chemical Weapons Convention (CWC). Despite strong doubts that a chemical weapons ban could be effectively verified, years of negotiations resulted in more detailed verification provisions than in any previous multilateral arms control treaty. As a result, concepts such as "challenge inspections," "managed access," and other features of the CWC are now being cited as possible measures to be utilized for other multilateral agreements, either existing or proposed. The efforts of the IAEA to strengthen the NPT safeguards system in the wake of the discovery of Iraq's nuclear weapons program have included studies of the CWC's provisions, and even the Biological Weapons Convention, which for years was considered to be unverifiable. It is now being examined for possible verification strengthening measures.

A review of NPT verification, compliance, and enforcement is particularly opportune considering both recent and upcoming events. These include the discovery of Iraq's NPT violations through United Nations Special Commission (UNSCOM) and IAEA inspections pursuant to UN Security Council Resolution 687 and resultant IAEA efforts to strengthen NPT safeguards; North Korea's non-compliance with its IAEA, full-scope, NPT safeguards agreement and its "suspended" withdrawal from the NPT; and the upcoming conference in 1995 to review and extend the NPT.

1. NPT: Basic Obligations And Verification Provisions

The NPT's principle non-proliferation obligations[2] are contained in its first three articles, which can be summarized as follows:

- *Article I* - Nuclear weapon states (NWS) undertake not to transfer to any recipient, and not to assist *in any way* encourage or induce any non-nuclear weapon state (NNWS) to manufacture or acquire nuclear weapons or other nuclear explosive devices, or control over such weapons or devices.
- *Article II* - NNWS undertake not to receive the transfer, or manufacture or acquire nuclear weapons/nuclear explosive devices, or *seek* or *receive any* assistance in the manufacture of nuclear weapons or nuclear explosive devices.
- *Article III* - Each NNWS undertakes to accept safeguards, in an agreement to be concluded with the IAEA within 180 days from becoming a party to the Treaty; safeguards shall be applied on all nuclear material in all peaceful nuclear activities; exports of nuclear material and specially designed or prepared equipment to NNWS must be subject to safeguards.

In addition, Article VI of the NPT contains what is often termed its "arms control and disarmament" obligation, that is, the undertaking of each party to pursue negotiations in good faith on effective measures relating to cessation of the nuclear arms race at an early date and to nuclear disarmament, and on a treaty on general and complete disarmament under strict and effective international control.

The purpose here is not to analyze in detail the nature of the undertakings stated in these three articles, which have been reviewed in exhaustive detail by many other authors,[3] but rather to reiterate and emphasize several points that have been made elsewhere. First, the precise bounds of the commitments in Articles I and II are subject to debate. While the negotiating history of the Treaty available to the public, including the US Senate's ratification record, provide a guide to interpreting the obligations, there has (purposely) never been an attempt by the parties to describe specifically the activities which would constitute violations of Articles I and II.

At the same time, it is self-evident that the nature of the undertakings in Articles I and II are inherently difficult to verify. They incorporate such a wide range of potential activities that it is impossible to imagine any type of practical routine verification or inspection procedure which could realistically expect to detect the proscribed activities. At the same time, the Treaty, due to the accepted standards of the time, did not include any type of challenge or suspect activity inspection procedure to be used to investigate allegations of non-compliance with the commitments in Articles I and II.

In fact, the obligations undertaken in Article II are verified only indirectly and incompletely, that is, through the application of Article III. Often referred to as the NPT's "verification" provision, this is a mischaracterization. Article III contains several basic obligations (e.g., each NNWS shall accept safeguards, in an agreement to be negotiated with the IAEA; such safeguards shall be applied to all nuclear material), but the actual verification arrangements are only specified in the safeguards agreement itself. Both the IAEA "model" NPT safeguards agreement[4] and the specific agreements for each NNWS party were determined well after the negotiation and entry into force of the NPT.

Article III states that acceptance of safeguards will be for "... the exclusive purpose of verification of the fulfillment of the obligations under the Treaty with a view to preventing diversion of nuclear energy from peaceful uses to nuclear weapons of other nuclear explosive devices." While this formulation could be interpreted either broadly or narrowly, the IAEA has in fact carried out its verification activities in a fairly narrow manner (certainly as directed by its member states), focusing almost solely on accounting for declared nuclear materials in NNWS. Safeguards do not apply to the transfer or receipt of nuclear weapons or devices, which would be a means for verifying Article I, or to verify that a NNWS is not making preparations for developing a nuclear explosive device (Article II).[5] Furthermore, as exposed by Iraq, IAEA safeguards have not had the objective of detecting clandestine, undeclared nuclear activities.

The IAEA Secretariat is responsible for implementing NPT safeguards agreements, in accordance with the IAEA Statute and relevant policies, with defined procedures for reviewing states' implementation of their safeguards obligations. The IAEA Board of Governors is responsible for drawing conclusions as to whether member states have in fact complied with their safeguards agreements, and specifically for making judgments of non-compliance with these obligations. The Board itself, however, does not conclude that a country is in violation of its obligations under Article III of the NPT. Such a conclusion is implicit in any judgment by the Board that a state is in non-compliance with its NPT safeguards agreement.

Beyond Article III, the only other provision of the Treaty relating to verification and compliance is Article VIII 3, which notes that every five years a conference may be held (at the request of the parties), "... with a view to ensuring that the purposes of the Preamble and the provisions of the Treaty are being realized." The four Review Conferences that have been held conducted wide-ranging reviews of all aspects of the Treaty, but have not proven to be an effective means for judging "compliance," even though some parties have raised allegations of "violations" of various provisions of the Treaty. This is because there has been an attempt to agree on consensus final documents at the conferences. Finger-pointing at individual parties is a certain means to ensure non-consensus. The final document of the 1985 NPT Review Conference[6] contained the following text in regards to implementation of Articles I and II:

> The Conference acknowledged the declarations by nuclear weapon states Party to the Treaty that they had fulfilled their obligations under Article I. The Conference further acknowledged the declarations that non-nuclear weapons states Party to the Treaty had fulfilled their obligations under Article II. The Conference was of the view therefore that one of the primary objectives of the Treaty had been achieved in the period under review.

The draft 1990 NPT Review Conference final document contained somewhat stronger language on Article II, as there were already concerns about both Iraq's and North Korea's compliance with the Treaty. Article VI has usually been at the center of such debate over "compliance," and disagreements over implementation of Article VI have resulted in two conferences not being able to agree on a final declaration.

Concerning "enforcement" or sanctions, there are no provisions in the Treaty specifying remedial or punitive actions for parties in violation of their obligations.

2. Examples Of NPT Compliance Issues

The following is a brief and by no means exhaustive chronology of a number of instances in which NPT compliance questions have been raised. This chronology provides an interesting comparison of the broader political context in which such compliance questions have been viewed, as well as an evolution of the approach with which the international community has dealt with NPT compliance concerns. These examples may also be drawn upon for ideas to strengthen verification, compliance, and enforcement aspects of the NPT without the need for change to the Treaty text itself.

2.1   Sweden

In April 1985, a Swedish technical weekly newspaper, *Ny Teknik,* claimed that the Swedish National Defense Research Institute (FOA) had performed a variety of physics experiments, some involving gram quantities of plutonium, which were related to nuclear weapons research and development after the date of Sweden's adherence to the NPT.[7] This article, as well as subsequent reporting in both the Swedish and US media, raised questions as to whether Sweden had violated its NPT obligations. US newspaper reports at the time indicated that the US Nuclear Regulatory Commission had delayed approvals of a number of nuclear export licenses for Sweden pending information and clarification of the Swedish activities.

Aside from the media speculation, the issue was never raised further, including at the 1985 NPT Review Conference during review of implementation of Article II of the Treaty. The amount of plutonium allegedly involved was within exemption limits of the IAEA safeguards, and consequently there was no violation of Sweden's safeguards agreement with the IAEA. The IAEA took no actions and made no statements in regard to the allegations.

The relative lack of international attention and concern was certainly a reflection of the time which had lapsed since the activities had taken place. The ambiguous nature of the Swedish activities as they pertained to the NPT's obligations, as well as the fact that Sweden had established impeccable non-proliferation credentials in the years that have followed and was viewed as an international leader in non-proliferation efforts helped lessen attention to these activities. In essence, Sweden was "excused" from its minor misbehavior, without so much as an explanation from either national or international authorities.

2.2   Romania

At the IAEA Board of Governors meeting in June 1992, Director General Blix told the Board that the Government of Romania had informed the IAEA that the regime of former Romanian dictator Ceaucescu had separated 100 milligrams of plutonium in December 1985 in a hot laboratory from an indigenously produced fuel rod irradiated in a US-supplied Triga research reactor at the Pitesti Nuclear Research Institute.[8] The new Romanian government discovered evidence of the past activities in April 1992 and immediately informed the IAEA, which conducted an extraordinary inspection of the materials.

The activities should have been reported at the time and thus constituted a violation of Romania's NPT safeguards agreement. However, the IAEA did not hold the new government responsible for the past violation and consequently the Board merely took note of Blix's report. No further action was taken.

2.3   Iraq

Following the conclusion of the Gulf War, the UN Security Council passed Resolution 687 which contained the conditions for a permanent cessation of hostilities. Section C of this resolution required Iraq to accept unconditionally immediate on-site inspection of Iraq's nuclear facilities based on Iraq's declarations and the designation of any additional locations found by the UN Special Commission (formed for the purpose of carrying out this part of the resolution). Furthermore, UNSCR 687 required the destruction, removal, or rendering harmless of all nuclear weapons or nuclear weapons usable material or any subsystems or components or any research, development, support or manufacturing facilities related thereto, and to place all of Iraq's nuclear weapons usable material under the exclusive control, for custody and removal, of the IAEA. The resolution called upon the IAEA and the Special Commission to develop a plan for the future monitoring and verification of Iraq's compliance. The resolution also called upon Iraq to reaffirm its obligations under the NPT, and noted that the long-term monitoring plan would take into account Iraq's rights and obligations under the NPT.

In the course of ensuing inspections, the IAEA and the UN Special Commission uncovered clear evidence that Iraq had pursued a large-scale program aimed at the development of nuclear explosives, including the parallel development of a number of uranium isotope separation technologies. These activities, which had not been declared to the IAEA, were conducted both at sites co-located with safeguarded nuclear activities and at separate independent locations. The inspections indicated that Iraq had produced small quantities of enriched uranium, and had also carried out clandestine, undeclared irradiation and plutonium separation experiments at a safeguarded reactor.

On July 18, 1991, as a result of the information produced by the inspections, the IAEA Board of Governors found that Iraq had failed to comply with its safeguards agreement pursuant to the NPT. In keeping with the requirements of the IAEA Statute, the Board promptly reported this matter to the United Nations Security Council. This fact, along with continued Iraqi obstruction in carrying out the terms of UNSCR 687, led the Security Council to pass Resolution 707, which condemned Iraq's non-compliance with its obligations under its safeguards agreement with the IAEA, "... which constitutes a violation of its commitments as a party to the NPT." The resolution demanded that Iraq "halt all nuclear activities of any kind, except for use of isotopes for medical, agricultural or industrial purposes" until the Security Council determined that Iraq was in full compliance with the two resolutions "and the IAEA determines that Iraq is in full compliance with its safeguards agreement." Finally, the resolution required that Iraq "... comply fully and without delay with all its international obligations" including those in resolutions 687 and 707, "and in the NPT and Iraq's safeguards agreement with the IAEA."

With these events, in less than six months the system of NPT verification, compliance, and enforcement had been transformed. Never had such intrusive on-site nuclear inspections been carried out; never had the IAEA Board of Governors found a party to be in violation of its safeguards agreement; and never had any party been found to be in violation of its NPT obligations. Further, the Security Council, under its Chapter VI authority related to maintaining international peace and security had effectively sanctioned Iraq's violation of the NPT by restricting its right to pursue almost all avenues of nuclear development. By doing so, the Council had essentially suspended Iraq's rights under Article IV of the NPT.

Almost as significant is what did not happen. The Security Council's finding of NPT violation was based upon Iraq's non-compliance with its safeguards agreement; hence, the Council found Iraq in violation of Article III of the NPT. Despite substantial evidence both at that time, and especially several months later, that Iraq was engaged in a nuclear weapons development effort, the Council never made an explicit finding that Iraq was in violation of Article II of the NPT. In addition, neither Iraq's violations nor the Council's actions have been cited by NPT parties.

Depending upon one's view, either the NPT parties abdicated any responsibility they may have had for judging and disciplining Iraq or they rightfully let the IAEA and the Special Commission take action on a matter of highest importance to international security. The fact that the nuclear situation was inextricably bound up in the complex of issues with the Gulf War made it inevitable that this matter would continue to be pursued by the Security Council. At the same time, it established a clear precedent for future instances of NPT compliance and enforcement matters.

2.4   North Korea

While it took over twenty-one years after the entry into force of the NPT for the Security Council to consider its first NPT case, only two years later another NPT party was "in the dock." The Democratic People's Republic of Korea acceded to the NPT in December 1985 and found a variety of excuses over the next six years not to complete negotiations on its NPT safeguards agreement with the IAEA. While this put North Korea in technical violation of Article III, many other states had also not fulfilled the requirement to negotiate the required safeguards agreement within the eighteen months specified in the Treaty. However, in North Korea's case the stakes seemed much higher, as it became an open secret that North Korea was operating a nuclear reactor and constructing what appeared to be a nuclear reprocessing plant and other associated fuel cycle facilities in direct violation of its NPT obligation to have safeguards on all its nuclear activities.

In April 1992, after concluding a bilateral denuclearization agreement with South Korea (which included a renunciation of the production of fissile materials on the Korean Peninsula) and facing increased international pressure, North Korea finally brought into force its NPT safeguards agreement. North Korea declared the various nuclear facilities at Yongbyon and IAEA *ad hoc* inspections commenced. After six IAEA inspections in 1992, evidence acquired by the IAEA and information made available to it led the Agency to conclude that North Korean declarations concerning reactor operations and reprocessed nuclear material were inconsistent. The IAEA concluded that there were additional sites that could contain evidence of additional North Korean reprocessing campaigns beyond the single campaign that had been declared. After extensive discussions with North Korean authorities failed to resolve the discrepancies, Director General Blix of the IAEA formally requested a "special inspection" of the two suspected waste sites on February 9, 1993, which was refused by the North Koreans on February 16. Consequently, on February 25, 1993, the Board of Governors adopted a resolution formally requesting access to the sites and gave North Korea one month to comply (GOV/2636).[9] On March 12, 1993, North Korea declared that it was exercising its right of withdrawal under the NPT, and on March 18 North Korea again formally refused the request for a special inspection. On April 1, 1993, the Board of Governors adopted resolution stating that North Korea was in non-compliance with its NPT safeguards agreement and that the IAEA was unable to verify non-diversion of nuclear material and so notified the UN Security Council.[10]

Prior to Security Council consideration of the issue, the NPT Depositories (US, UK, and Russia) issued a statement expressing regret at North Korea's actions. On May 11, 1993, the Security Council adopted Resolution 825, with China and Pakistan abstaining, calling on North Korea to reconsider its withdrawal from the NPT, and to honor its obligations under the Treaty and its safeguards agreements. The resolution called upon the IAEA to continue consultations with North Korea in order to resolve the issues and urged member states to encourage North Korea to respond positively to the resolution. The Security Council's action was much less decisive, due largely to China's insistence that North Korea not be sanctioned and that further dialogue be encouraged with North Korea.

Following the Security Council's action, the US initiated a direct bilateral dialogue with North Korea in order to resolve the complex of issues, with primary US objectives being full North Korean compliance with the NPT and with its IAEA safeguards agreement. The outcome of this matter remains very much in question, as North Korea has continued to refuse IAEA access to any locations in order to perform routine maintenance on safeguards equipment in order to ensure the continuity of safeguards. The possibility of renewed Security Council action on this issue appears high.

3. Strengthening NPT Verification, Compliance, and Enforcement

Iraq and North Korea present vivid examples of both ways to strengthen implementation of the NPT as well as the limitations that any set of measures may face. Even with virtually unlimited access for inspections, and the full support of the UN Security Council and the international community, doubts persist whether Iraq's full nuclear capabilities have been revealed and neutralized. Similarly, North Korean compliance with the NPT remains elusive, despite its complete international isolation on this matter.

Efforts to improve NPT verification, compliance, and enforcement should focus on Articles II and III of the Treaty. However, current discussions concerning international verification related to a fissile material cut-off, nuclear material removed from nuclear weapons, a Comprehensive Test Ban Treaty (CTBT), and other initiatives could result in direct and indirect means to verify aspects of both Article I and Article VI.

3.1 Verification

3.1.1 Strengthen IAEA Safeguards

One means to strengthen NPT verification, without the need to change the Treaty, is afforded by the fact that the existing verification arrangements are specified in the safeguards agreements and not in the Treaty itself. Thus, strengthening the IAEA safeguards system, both through reinterpreting and fully utilizing the rights specified in the IAEA's Statute and safeguards agreements and through the introduction of new techniques and technology, is a principle way for improving verification of the Treaty. A primary objective of the IAEA's post-Iraq safeguards strengthening efforts has been to develop means to detect undeclared nuclear activities. The IAEA has indicated that it intends to use information, such as intelligence information, provided by member states in such efforts.

3.1.2 Inspection Activities Related To Articles I and II

In the course of UNSCR 687 inspections in Iraq, the IAEA/UNSCOM inspections uncovered evidence of Iraqi activities related not only to production of fissile materials for nuclear explosives, but also to nuclear weapons design and development activities. Information developed through these inspections almost certainly indicated that Iraq was in non-compliance with Article II of the NPT, although as previously noted, no such determination was ever made by the Security Council.

A potential means to strengthen NPT verification would be to develop formal procedures for investigating allegations of Article I and II non-compliance. Such activities are beyond the mandate and scope of current IAEA inspections under the NPT, which focus solely on nuclear material. However, a protocol could be negotiated by parties to the NPT to establish procedures for IAEA inspections in regard to these two articles. However, both the implementation and effectiveness of such verification measures would seem questionable. In Article I, inspections would be for the objective of determining whether some form of technical expertise or assistance had been provided by a nuclear weapon state to a non-nuclear weapon state, something almost impossible to accomplish.

In the case of Article II, the effort would focus on challenge inspections of sites suspected of being involved in weaponization activities, such as high explosive test sites or possible weapon design centers. For both Article I and II inspections, a potentially serious problem would involve the exposure of inspectors to weapons information, thus itself posing proliferation risks. This risk could be mitigated by utilizing inspectors only from nuclear weapon states.

An alternative to the IAEA would be to establish a United Nations body to investigate Article I and II compliance issues. This could be an extension of the Special Commission which has been established for Iraq, and which has developed substantial nuclear-related expertise. An advantage of such a body is that it would be responsible directly to the Security Council, of which all five permanent members are now parties to the NPT. United Nations responsibility for Articles I and II would enable the IAEA to focus on nuclear material inspections (both declared and undeclared). However, the disadvantages would include the fact that the subservience of such a body to the Security Council could create serious questions about its vigilance in pursuing Article I compliance concerns. Also splitting the responsibilities between two separate bodies (the IAEA and the Special Commission) could weaken the overall effort to detect violations of Article II and III, which are interrelated.

3.2   Compliance

3.2.1 Formalize Role Of Security Council

The events surrounding both Iraq and North Korea have vividly demonstrated the critical role of the Security Council in NPT compliance and enforcement. IAEA Director General Blix has repeatedly noted that access to the Security Council is a vital element of efforts to strengthen the safeguards system.

The Security Council has in essence become the unofficial institution of NPT compliance and enforcement. This has occurred in an *ad hoc* manner, pursuant to the Council's general responsibilities for preserving international peace and security, and on the provision in the IAEA Statute calling for the Board of Governors to report safeguards compliance matters to the Council. One could argue that this is a sufficient basis for the Council to continue to serve the function it has informally taken up. However, it may be useful to establish a more formal role, without impinging upon the Council's broad rights.

This could be accomplished through a number of means including passage of a Security Council resolution in which the Council would *de facto* designate itself as the NPT compliance and enforcement body, as part of its broader responsibilities; or the five permanent members of the Council could adopt an agreed statement with similar effects. However, either step could be resented by non-nuclear weapons states party to the NPT, who may see it as a usurpation of responsibilities of the parties, as well as an effort to make the Treaty a tool of the nuclear weapon states. Alternatively, the parties to the Treaty (for instance at the 1995 NPT extension and review conference) could agree upon procedures for review of compliance decisions by the parties themselves with referral to the Security Council as an ultimate step.

3.2.2 *Strengthen Role Of Parties*

The US has often made the point that the NPT benefits the security of all the parties to the Treaty, and consequently the maintenance and strengthening of the Treaty is in the interest of all parties. Consequently, efforts to involve the parties themselves in issues of compliance and enforcement could be seen as a logical means to strengthen the Treaty and its implementation. Possible options for strengthening the role of the parties include:

a. a formal mechanism at review conferences (e.g., a committee or sub-committee) to review compliance matters;
b. *ad hoc* meetings of parties (in between review conferences) to address compliance issues;
c. means for referring compliance issues through specific means to the UN Security Council; and
d. communications for the parties to raise compliance issues, such as depositories letters or statements co-signed by individual parties.

Any compliance review arrangements that rely upon consensus decision-making will be less likely to be effective in addressing difficult compliance issues. Further, it should be noted that non-aligned parties would seek to include reviews of Article VI (and perhaps Article IV) in any such effort to further define compliance review procedures. However, if the NPT is indefinitely extended in 1995, or achieves a lengthy extension, such inclusion of Article VI may not seem as threatening as has traditionally been perceived.

3.3 *Enforcement*

Multilateral treaty "enforcement" contains a number of possible tools, including international political pressure; selected, targeted sanctions or broad economic sanctions;

and the threat or use of military action.

US nuclear non-proliferation policy has attempted to isolate those countries that have refused to undertake binding international legal commitments not to acquire nuclear explosives, such as adherence to the NPT or full-scope safeguards agreements. US law provides preferential treatment in a number of areas (approval of exports; nuclear cooperation, etc.) with countries with good non-proliferation credentials. In addition, in cases of US concern with countries compliance with the NPT, Washington has undertaken international diplomatic efforts to bring pressure upon or to isolate such countries (e.g., North Korea, Iran).

Further, US law contains a variety of sanctions related to nuclear, chemical/biological, and missile proliferation, particularly actions by countries that violate their international obligations. The Atomic Energy Act, the Nuclear Nonproliferation Act, the Foreign Assistance Act, the Export-Import Bank Act and other legislation contain sanctions. These acts include the cessation of US nuclear cooperation and exports and US foreign military or economic assistance if a recipient country carries out certain acts (e.g., violation of the NPT or an IAEA full-scope safeguards agreement; detonation of a nuclear explosive device; transfer of reprocessing and enrichment equipment or technology).

These sanctions are completely unilateral; few if any other countries have such sanctions. The only current means for imposing international sanctions for NPT-related violations are through the Security Council. Consequently, a possible avenue for strengthening NPT enforcement lies in defining and putting in place multilateral sanctions related to violations of the NPT, including violations of NPT safeguards agreements. In this way violators would know they face a predictable set of punishments if found to be in violation of such obligations. Sanctions could range in intensity from initially a withdrawal of certain privileges (limited to the nuclear field and more broad-based), to suspension of various forms of cooperation and assistance (e.g., participation in IAEA assistance programs, suspension of NPT Article IV rights), and finally to a complete economic embargo. A number of possible options exist, including:

a. the US could approach other countries, particularly nuclear exporters and countries with substantial foreign assistance programs, to adopt similar nuclear-related sanctions as already exist in US law;

b. Washington proposing a multilateral initiative with the objective of a "harmonization" of NPT-related sanctions, similar to what has been accomplished in the nuclear export control arena under the NPT Exporters Committee and the Nuclear Suppliers Group.

Enforcement actions related to potential use of force would remain under the authority of the United Nations Security Council.

4.   Conclusion

The NPT remains the cornerstone of international efforts to prevent the further proliferation of nuclear explosives. The ideas presented here have been offered in the context of strengthening the Treaty's implementation and ensuring its extension in 1995, while recognizing that many of these views require additional analysis and may prove to be politically or technically unfeasible or difficult to implement. However, as the subject of

NPT verification, compliance, and enforcement is likely to be raised in the context of the 1995 NPT discussions, it behooves the US to consider such ideas and perhaps to prepare proposals or initiatives in this area designed to support overall US objectives in regard to the NPT, nuclear non-proliferation, and other arms control and non-proliferation areas.

Notes

1. The views and opinions presented here are solely the author's and do not reflect positions of the US Department of Energy or the US Government.
2. Treaty on the Non-Proliferation of Nuclear Weapons, 1968.
3. See, for example, Mohammed Ibrahim Shaker, *The Nuclear Non-Proliferation Treaty: Original Implementation 1959-1979.* (London: Oceana Publications, 1980).
4. The Structure and Content of Agreements between the Agency and States required in Connection with the Treaty on the Non-Proliferation of Nuclear Weapons. (Structure and Content Document). INF/CIRC/153, corrected by the International Atomic Energy Agency, 1972.
5. Lawrence Scheinman, *The International Atomic Energy Agency and World Nuclear Order.* (Washington, DC: Resources for the Future, 1989), p. 168, footnote 2.
6. Final Document, 1985 Non-Proliferation Treaty Review Conference, NPT/CONF III/64/I (Geneva: UN, 1985).
7. Mitchell Reis,*Without the Bomb: The Politics of Nuclear Proliferation.*(New York: Columbia University Press, 1988), pp. 73-77.
8. Ann MacLachlan, "Romania Produced Unsafeguarded Plutonium, Blix Tells IAEA Boards of Governors", *Nuclear Fuel,* June 22, 1992, pp. 16-17 and Ann MacLachlan, "Romania Separated Tiny Amount of Plutonium in Secret in 1985", *Nucleonics Week,* June 25, 1992, p. 16.
9. IAEA Board of Governors Document, GOV/2636, Feb. 25, 1993.
10. IAEA Board of Governors Document, GOV/2645, April 1, 1993.

Chapter 13

THE NPT AND LINKAGE ARMS CONTROL: THE PAST, PRESENT, AND FUTURE OF ARTICLE VI

Jack L. Kangas

Article VI of the Non-Proliferation Treaty (NPT) states "Each of the Parties to the Treaty undertakes to pursue negotiations in good faith on effective measures relating to cessation of the nuclear arms race at an early date and to nuclear disarmament under strict and effective international control."[1] The language of Article VI is generalized in that it obligates *all* Parties to the Treaty, but because of the primary association of the "nuclear arms race" and "nuclear disarmament" with the nuclear powers, it is clear that the intent was to address their responsibilities in the context of the non-nuclear nations' willingness to forgo nuclear weapons. As noted in a detailed history of the events leading up to the signing of the NPT, Article VI was drafted to reflect the responsibilities of the nuclear powers as a "*quid pro quo*" for the non-nuclear states' "renunciation" of nuclear weapons.[2] A direct relationship or linkage between the non-proliferation of nuclear weapons and the nuclear weapon policies of the nuclear weapon states, between what is called horizontal and vertical proliferation, was thereby established in the text of the NPT.

Controversy over Article VI has surfaced at each of the 5-year reviews of the NPT. A pattern has developed where certain non-nuclear nations attempt to enforce the *quid pro quo* by placing demands on the nuclear powers to do more in the execution of their responsibilities with respect to the language of Article VI. For these non-nuclear nations the concept of linkage has been viewed as a useful tool in the effort to block the spread of nuclear weapons. For its part, the United States has from the beginning resisted the idea of coupling the NPT with other arms control regimes, believing that even before the NPT was signed: "Linking the conclusion of the NPT with other measures would ... hamper the conclusion of the former without reaching agreements on the latter."[3] The language of Article VI can be read as a compromise among several nations with respect to the issue of how direct or specific the linkage between the NPT and other regimes should be stated. At one point in the negotiations, India's position was that the NPT had to include an article that would actually obligate the nuclear-weapon states to negotiate a program of reduction of existing weapons and their delivery vehicles.[4] This form of rigid coupling was avoided in the end, but the residue of this kind of thinking continued to surface for years to come, particularly at the five-year reviews.

At the Fourth Review conference in 1990, some informed observers noted a distinct movement by the United States in the direction of compromising its resistance to linkage over the issue of the relationship of the NPT to a comprehensive test ban treaty (CTBT). In an informal paper circulated at that review, the US delegates circulated a paper which included the following sentence: "The Conference recognizes the significant importance placed upon both negotiations towards a comprehensive nuclear test ban treaty during the next five years and the relationship between the discontinuance of all nuclear explosions in all environments and the long term viability of the Treaty."[5] In doing so, "The USA was thus ready to recognize the existence of a widespread perception of a long-term 'linkage', but would not agree that the fate of the NPT must or should depend on the conclusion of a CTBT before 1995."[6] Supporters of linkage "had wrung from the USA a surprisingly frank admission of 'linkage.'"[7]

Article VI will almost certainly be an important topic of discussion at the important 1995 Review conference where decisions will be made regarding the extension of the treaty. A representative of the Indonesian government, for example, noted in October 1993:

> [T]he success of the 1995 Conference will ultimately depend upon an objective reappraisal of the commitments undertaken by the nuclear-weapon states and by the endeavors to transform the NPT into a truly universal non-discriminating regime,' and an unidentified UN consultant familiar with preparations for the 1995 conference was recently quoted to the effect that "... most NPT members were unwilling to vote for indefinite extension because they would then lose what they perceived to be their only measure of influence to maintain pressure on the NWS [nuclear weapon states] to meet their Article VI treaty obligations: 'general and complete disarmament.'[8]

Article VI therefore remains an important issue in the continuing effort to block the spread of nuclear weapons.

This paper is concerned with the possibility that the United States could come to accept the argument that linkage between arms control regimes is in principle a worthwhile arms control goal. One can read into the history of the Fourth Review conference the beginning of a "slippery slope" slide for the United States; therefore, the next section of this paper will examine in a theoretical way some of the potential risks or consequences of getting on that slope.

1. The Slippery Slope

What are the possible consequences of moving in the direction of tight linkage? Earlier in this paper one of the potential results was referred to: progress on the regime of immediate concern could be hampered while at the same time nothing materialized in the other regimes. This is in effect the hostage argument which says that regime A should not be held hostage to regime B, considered by proponents of regime A to be a different regime or decision area which is best addressed on its own terms. The argument here is that regime A is already sufficiently problematic and controversial in itself without complicating it further by hindering it with another layer or layers of complexity. To burden regime A in this manner would lead to delays of one sort or another and postpone prospects for the realization of regime A's objectives. The analogy to a hostage situation suggests coercive intent on the part of those pressing for tight linkage and an aversion on the part of those being coerced to dealing with hostage-takers on grounds that it will only exacerbate the problem further.

Another possible consequence could be that once a commitment is made to concede or agree to linkage between regimes A and B, pressure can build to do the same for A and C, the latter being yet another problematic regime. We might refer to this kind of development as the "Nth linkage problem" where, like the Nth country problem, the linkages are proliferated to a point where A gets linked to B, C, D, etc. This situation can develop because there may not be any consensus on the part of those advocating linkage as to what the most critical linkages are. Once the first linkage is established, regime A could be besieged with so many multiple linkages that progress in any one of them is frustrated and the entire process paralyzed.

A further risk associated with the "slippery slope" is similar to but analytically distinct from the one described immediately above. It stems from the consideration that regime A is unlikely to be the only regime in the universe of arms control regimes where pressure may be building to develop linkage. Pressure could exist, for example, to couple regimes C and D or E and F. Agreeing to linkage between A and B may lead not only to pressure to accept linkage between A and C or D, etc., as in the previous case, but also between C and D or E and F, regimes that may be only remotely related in content to regime A but nevertheless of serious concern within the context of a more comprehensive arms control agenda. This kind of development holds the potential for opening up as great a Pandora's Box of issues as in the previous case.

A variant of the latter two cases is the situation where, once linkage between regimes A and B is acknowledged and a commitment made to work A and B in tandem, additional pressure develops to couple B with C as part of a larger package designed to move all three regimes forward. Three rather than two regimes then become the object of attention and run the risk of becoming inextricably linked to each other.

Yet another possible consequence of getting on the "slippery slope" of linkage is that negotiating constraints may be imposed, forcing negotiators for example to work under the pressure of deadlines, thus compromising the quality of the end product. The result of this can be badly drafted language or a failure to have considered adequately the implications of a certain course of action. It can also lead to the "kick the can" syndrome in arms control negotiations where resolution of different but very important issues is indefinitely deferred, the responsibility being passed off to implementing bodies not chartered to make what are in the final analysis policy decisions. High-confidence verification regimes can be prime casualties of this kind of approach to negotiations.

In addition, another consequence could be simply that a commitment to deliver on the promise of linkage cannot be met. That is, regime B turns out to be impossible to move forward despite the best intentions and hardest "good faith" efforts. It moves beyond the control of the negotiators. There is no arms control regime that is not subject to change and even transformation through time. As regimes evolve they can assume a new or different identity which brings with it an altered set of issues to resolve. A regime that appears manageable at one point in time can become quite unmanageable over the course of even several weeks or months. Regime theorists argue that regimes are seldom pronounced dead but there are in arms negotiations, as in life itself, cases where movement and functions have stopped even though official certification of status has yet to be issued.

Finally, a further risk of moving toward linkage is that the participants can become locked into a pattern of negotiating behavior where almost every issue is dealt with in the context of a *quid pro quo* framework where the game is zero-sum. Everything negotiated is weighed on the scale of linkage rather than on the merits of its own terms and every proposed measure must satisfy some external criteria and meet some often fuzzy and ill-defined standards. No matter what the measure, it runs the risk of being interpreted as part of an effort to mask the true agenda, to gain an unfair advantage, to discriminate further against those who profess to be the only ones genuinely interested in the control of nuclear weapons.

2. Flawed Premises

Against the background of this theoretical discussion of the potential risks associated with the "slippery slope" of linkage, the next section will examine some of the more specific inadequacies of the specific linkage implied in Article VI. This will be done by attempting to show that the various premises upon which Article VI was formulated were flawed not only in light of subsequent events but even at the time the article was put into the treaty.

One premise underlying Article VI appears to be that all the nations supporting the Treaty shared the view that all nuclear weapons were to be uniformly stigmatized as being bad for international security. They were to be forsworn by those who did not yet have them and given up by those who had already acquired them. The difficulty with this premise was that at the time Article VI was being formulated nuclear weapons were viewed even by some staunch supporters of the NPT as being critical to their national security. Nuclear weapons were the centerpiece of the flexible response doctrine of NATO adopted in 1967 at the very same time the NPT was being negotiated. Also in those same years long-range nuclear weapons were being developed and deployed to support the strategic doctrines of the major nuclear powers.

Already prior to the signing of the NPT, there was a school of thought within the international arms control community which argued that nuclear weapons could, in the final analysis, have a stabilizing rather than destabilizing effect on international security. Many prominent arms control experts and theorists of the period were either of this persuasion or took an agnostic position on the question.[9] There was not, in other words, any consensus within the expert arms control community of the time regarding the valuation of nuclear weapons (nor is there today any consensus).

A further premise which can be read into the language of Article VI is that the dynamics of nuclear proliferation on a global scale could somehow be governed by the behaviors of two sets of nations, the haves and the have-nots. This was an over-simplified two-sided game approach to the problem of proliferation, which failed to take into account its formidable complexity. The strong supporters of linkage would pit the non-nuclear nations against the nuclear powers in a struggle of competing agendas where the success of non-proliferation would be dependent on the extent to which the nuclear powers disengaged from the race of armaments and pursued the path of disarmament. In the process of working out this representation of how to solve the problem of proliferation, critical elements of the real dynamics were neglected. For example, while from the perspective of the non-nuclear nations the nuclear powers might be viewed in coherent terms (they all had nuclear weapons), in reality each nuclear power was so beset with a set of issues *vis-à-vis* other nuclear powers that it was extremely unlikely that they would all pull themselves together in the interest of stopping nuclear proliferation. For the United States and the Soviet Union, the main event was their bilateral relationship, and maintaining a nuclear weapon capability had a greater priority than satisfying the demands of those arguing for cessation of the arms race and disarmament. Two other nuclear powers, France and China, chose for many years to remain outside the NPT because they had other, more important nuclear agendas to pursue. The point here is that much more than a two-sided simplified game was being played by each of the nuclear powers, and to the extent it was being played it was not at all clear that this particular model dominated the behavior of the players.

The thinking behind Article VI in this connection appears to be that the nuclear powers by demonstrating their commitment or lack of commitment to stopping the nuclear arms race and nuclear disarmament have a direct, if not decisive, impact on the decisions of would-be proliferators with respect to their proclivity for exercising the nuclear option. The premise seems to be that their calculus of decision is based heavily on what the nuclear powers do or do not do. This premise needs to be challenged on the grounds that it may be accurate in some cases but runs the risk of slighting other possible motives for going nuclear, having to do for example with such considerations as regional arms balances and geopolitics, international prestige, etc. The art and science of uncovering the motivation behind the nuclear ambitions of proliferators remains to this day in a largely undeveloped stage.[10]

One consequence of suggesting that the decision making of potential proliferators is geared to the policies of the nuclear powers without addressing other possible motivating factors can be that a ready means is provided for rationalizing a pursuit of the bomb or a refusal to forgo the nuclear option. The case of India may be appropriate to cite in this connection in that the proponents of a nuclear capability for that country have probably spent more time blaming the state of proliferation on the West, particularly the United States, rather than doing the work of trying to develop a coherent and persuasive strategic rationale for India's nuclear weapons program.[11]

A further premise of Article VI seems to be that the objective of bringing the arms race to a close could be effected within a very short period of time, "at an early date." Nowhere in the NPT was "arms race" defined but, according to one account of the negotiations on the NPT, the general understanding at the time was that the term referred to "the quantitative increase in nuclear weapons and their delivery vehicles, and their qualitative improvement." In 1969 the United States and the Soviet Union began negotiations on strategic weapons against the background of the NPT but progress was slow, and after 25 years the lasting effect of the negotiations on the stockpiles of the two countries remains uncertain in view of the problematic status of the START agreements. The reference in Article VI to the "arms race" and its association with quantities of weapons led many to ignore the importance of strategic stability and the insight that under certain scenarios levels of weapons may not be particularly relevant. The association with qualitative improvements in weapons greatly underestimated the ability even for parties negotiating in good faith to control such technical developments as the improved accuracies of weapons. The expectation that the nuclear powers would or even could close down their nuclear weapon programs "at an early date" (within 5 years?) was an extraordinarily heroic one.

A final premise which can be read into Article VI is that nuclear disarmament could be brought under "strict and effective international control." The framers of Article VI were well aware of the failed effort embodied in the Baruch Plan of the late 1940s to bring nuclear weapons under some kind of international control authority.[12] At the time the NPT was being negotiated, there was not much of an historical basis for any of the parties involved to believe that a control authority could in fact be established to oversee the dismantlement of all nuclear weapons. Within the framework of the NPT the International Atomic Energy Agency (IAEA) was designated to play an integral role regarding safeguards, but it was not part of any monitoring and verification system designed to police disarmament. How exactly a "strict and effective" control regime was to materialize was apparently not given much attention at the time.

3. The NPT-CTBT Linkage

The foregoing discussion of the "slippery slope" and the flawed premises upon which Article VI seems to have been based provides a context for examining the current argument for linking the NPT to a CTB Treaty.

A prominent US arms control group has recently argued: "If the US government comes to understand and accept that *the single action it can take which will most dramatically strengthen the non-proliferation regime and the NPT itself is to move seriously toward a CTB*, then the conference of 1995 will become not merely a success but a triumph."[13] This is a particularly strong expression of the belief in the power of linkage and endorsement of policies to ensure that linkage is realized.

This kind of thinking with its roots in early linkage theory may very well be behind the decision of the US Congress to mandate a unilateral ban on all US testing beginning September 1996 unless other countries start to test; in the meantime the United States is to begin negotiations for a CTBT which would take effect prior to 1996. Earlier, the Clinton Administration had committed itself to the same approach. The Congressional formulation does not specify that US long-term testing policies are dependent on the conclusion of a CTBT, but it clearly puts pressure on the nuclear powers to get an agreement signed. To the extent that the Congressional mandate was driven essentially by concerns about the NPT, some might argue that the linkage is weak because it does not necessitate the conclusion of a CTBT; however, the likelihood that the United States would be able to follow through on its unilateral commitment to end testing in the aftermath of a failed attempt to conclude the comprehensive treaty appears somewhat remote. By this interpretation one can arguably conclude that a relatively tight conception of linkage between the NPT and a CTB is at the basis of the Congressional mandate. If this is in fact the case, one can ask what the prospects are for concluding a CTB before 1996 and while trying to answer the question be attentive to the potential risks involved in this particular case of linkage and to the kind of flawed premises that might be at work.

In what follows it will not be possible to consider the full range of political and technical issues which would need to be addressed in a more comprehensive study. For the purpose at hand, it may be adequate to focus on just a few key issues. In the political category is the question of the universality of the CTB, specifically whether two of the current nuclear powers, China and France, are prepared to join and cooperate in a CTBT.

On the same day that China conducted its underground nuclear test of 5 October 1993, it issued a statement which included the following passage:

> China fully understands the sincere desire of the non-nuclear states for an
> early conclusion of a comprehensive test ban treaty through negotiations

and believes that such a treaty has its positive significance. While supporting its early conclusion, China will take an active part in the negotiating
process and work together with other countries to conclude this treaty no
later that 1996. At the same time, China believes that a pledge by all
nuclear-weapon states not to use nuclear weapons at all is of even greater
significance as it is a more effective step towards the non-proliferation goal
underscored by the Treaty on the Non-Proliferation of Nuclear Weapons.
To this end, China strongly calls for a parallel negotiation by all nuclear
weapon states aimed at concluding an international convention on unconditional non-first use of nuclear weapons against non-nuclear states and
nuclear-free zones.[14]

With this statement the Chinese put the arms control community on notice that in
their view the success of non-proliferation was more dependent on the signing of a no
first use convention than on a CTBT. The argument is that it will be "a more effective
step" and therefore, by implication, a more important course of action to follow. It has
priority over a CTB as far as the Chinese are concerned.

Here the Chinese are extending the concept of linkage by agreeing to the coupling
of regime A (NPT) not only to regime B (CTBT) but also to regime C (no first use convention). The sense of priorities they have established suggests that at some point in
the future they may come to argue that a no first use convention is in fact indispensable
to the success of the NPT and that a CTB is not worth very much, and therefore not
deserving of support, unless the convention on first use is worked out concurrently or
beforehand. What the Chinese have done in effect is to create a three-way linkage
among the NPT, a CTBT and a no first use convention on nuclear arms. In order to
move the NPT forward, it will be necessary to move two other regimes forward as well.

In the case of France, the French Defense Minister said in the fall of 1993 with
respect to French participation in a CTB negotiation, "We have some scientific and
technological catching up to do ... There is no reason whatsoever to let others secure a
technological and scientific supremacy while we do not have it ourselves."[15] There is
reflected in this statement the long-time French concern, dating back to the time when
France was pursuing the nuclear option, that it would be locked into a position of technological and scientific inferiority as a result of constraints imposed by an arms control
agreement. Earlier the French concern was with the effects of an NPT and now with
the effects of a CTBT. It is not clear what "supremacy" means to the French in this
context, but it clearly has something to do with the comparative quality of French
nuclear weapons when contrasted with those of Russia and the United States, and perhaps with the weapons of other nuclear powers as well. Later in the same year the
French Defense Minister said that France would not take part in CTB negotiations until
it acquired a simulation capacity which could take as many at 10 years to achieve.[16]
Whether the French come to base their CTB decisions on the way they eventually
choose to read their S&T status or on the successful acquisition of a technical simulation capability, the result is the postponement well beyond 1996 of a French commitment to an CTB treaty.

The French are engaged here in a form of linkage behavior which does not couple
arms control regimes but rather links a particular regime, in this case a CTBT, to a set
of important considerations that in the French view cannot be separated from a concern

with a CTB. Perhaps the most important consideration is that the French appear to continue to greatly value nuclear weapons. Nuclear weapons, i.e., French nuclear weapons, are not stigmatized but are assigned a significant value in French deterrent doctrine and defense policy. To ban the testing of weapons implies the devaluation of nuclear weapons in terms of quality and the willingness to use them, and the French appear not to be prepared to accept this trade-off, at least for the foreseeable future.

Could a CTBT be concluded without China and France being signatories to the agreement? In a theoretical sense the answer to this question is yes (just as they were not members of the NPT for more than two decades), but realistically it is very difficult to accept the argument that the other nuclear powers would be prepared to tolerate a ban while China and France would be free to pursue possibly extensive nuclear weapon testing programs. (Current thinking in the US government is of course to drop a commitment not to test after 1996 in the event any other country tests even one weapon in that period.) Some may believe that China and France would not be prepared to violate the norms of a CTB even though they were not official parties to a CTB Treaty, but this belief needs to be challenged on the grounds that in the past both China and France have been quite prepared to go against the collective grain in matters of international security. Relying on a kind of "moral suasion" by "setting a good example" would not appear to be a realistic policy decision.

One of the most important issues surrounding the current technical debate on the CTB is the question of how to define a "ban." If a ban is defined as one which would prohibit all tests of nuclear explosives, there arises the question of whether "... very low-yield tests of inertial confinement approaches to controlled fusion, with or without tests using gram quantities of plutonium," are included.[17] If nuclear explosives are defined in terms of the magnitude of the nuclear yield compared to what it would be if a quantity of high explosives were detonated, having the same weight as the detonating device, the definition "would clearly not include inertial confinement fusion tests related to controlled fusion power plants, reactor tests, or 'zero yield' tests of implosion systems" but "it is much less clear what would be forbidden under such a definition." Finally, a definition that would rule out explosions producing observable fission chain or thermonuclear reactions might have some positive advantages but "... would also make it possible to cheat at yields below the threshold for long-range detection of explosions." All of this is to say that the way "nuclear explosives" is defined for purposes of a CTBT will have a critical bearing on the viability of the agreement because the definition could be exploited by those interested in cheating and is related in a more general sense to the question of adequate monitoring and verification of the provisions of a CTBT.[18] This is not to say that this important definitional issue cannot eventually be worked out to a point where all positions are confident about putting their signatures to an agreement, but the complexity of the issue does raise questions about trying to resolve it satisfactorily under some kind of near-term deadline.

Another related technical issue has been raised by a researcher at the Interdisciplinary Research Group Science, Technology and Security in Darmstadt, Germany. The researcher has concluded that "underground nuclear weapon tests have lost their unique significance for vertical proliferation," and that potential proliferators could believe that the nuclear powers having access to sophisticated technologies were continuing to develop their weapons without actually testing them. To ensure an effective CTB regime, according to this researcher, the following technologies had to be restricted: contained

hydronuclear tests; particle beam fusion accelerators; "Trailmaster," an X-ray genera-
tor; inertial confinement fusion; and supercomputers.[19] If this assessment is accurate, it
is not at all clear how it would be possible to restrict this group of technologies effectively when one considers past and current difficulties associated with the various
export control regimes related to nuclear technologies.

4. Final Thoughts On Linkage

This paper has attempted to argue the case for avoiding tight linkage between
arms control regimes. The discussion of the risks associated with getting on what could
be a "slippery slope" and the faulty premises upon which Article VI of the NPT in particular appears to have been formulated was intended to demonstrate that US policymakers should be cautious about linkage, both in a theoretical sense and in the specific
case of the NPT. The discussion of the relationship of the NPT to a CTBT was intended
to draw attention to some of the difficult political and technical issues associated with
that particular linkage. The prospects for resolving such issues in tandem with meeting
US objectives at the 1995 Review conference do not appear to be particularly promising.

As suggested, the position of the US government early on in the negotiations
leading to the NPT was the correct one: avoid linkage. It is a fair question to ask, of
course, what risks and penalties might be associated with a principled stand against
linkage. There is no doubt that some non-nuclear countries will choose to interpret this
stand as evidence of a lack of US commitment to a comprehensive international
security. Whether such an interpretation would be the decisive factor in a particular
non-nuclear nation's decision to go nuclear, however, is very much open to question.
One would hope that responsible non-nuclear nations would carefully consider US
efforts taken in each of the arms control regimes and not base their policies on the US
attitude toward linkage.

One must also recognize that there may be times when linkage cannot realistically
be avoided or when the stakes are such that linkage is judged to be in the US interest.
With respect to these circumstances, this presentation is simply a friendly reminder that
the perils of getting on any high slope should not be underestimated, as even the most
experienced skier will tell you. The terrain should be carefully examined well in advance of the main event.

Notes

1. Coit D. Blacker and Gloria Duffy (eds.), *International Arms Control: Issues and
    Agreements,* (2nd ed.)by the Stanford Arms Control Group (Stanford: Stanford
    University Press, 1984), p. 395.
2. Mohamed I. Shaker, *The Nuclear Non-Proliferation Treaty,* Vol. II (New York:
    Oceana Publications, 1980), p. 564.
3. Ibid., p. 566.
4. Ibid., p. 569.
5. David Fischer and Harald Muller, "The Fourth Review of the Non-Proliferation
    Treaty," in *Sipri Yearbook 1991,* World Armaments and Disarmament (New York:

Oxford University Press, 1991), p. 578.

6. Ibid.

7. Ibid., p. 583.

8. Both quotations in this paragraph can be found in *The Arms Control Reporter*, Vol. 12:12, December 1993, p. 602.B.255.

9. The reader is referred to Pierre Gallois, *The Balance of Terror: Strategy for the Nuclear Age* (Boston: Houghton Mifflin, 1961) and the essays by Alastair Buchan and Stanley Hoffman in Alastair Buchan (ed.), *A World of Nuclear Powers?* (Englewood Cliffs: Prentice-Hall, Inc., 1966). The argument for a stabilizing effect was later given wide currency in Kenneth Waltz, *The Spread of Nuclear Weapons: More May Be Better*, Adelphi Paper No. 171. International Institute of Strategic Studies, London, Autumn 1981.

10. Two sources worth consulting on this point are Stephen Meyer, *The Dynamics of Nuclear Proliferation* (Chicago: University of Chicago Press, 1984) and A.A. Masrui, "The Political Culture of War and Nuclear Proliferation: A Third World Perspective," in H. Dyer and L. Mangasarian (eds.), *The Study of International Relations* (London: MacMillan and Co., 1989).

11. For example, refer to the approach adopted in K. Subrahmanyam (ed.), *Nuclear Proliferation and International Security* (New Delhi: Lancer International, 1985).

12. Still worth reading in this connection is Joseph I. Lieberman, *The Scorpion and the Tarantula: The Struggle to Control Atomic Weapons, 1945–1949* (Boston: Houghton Mifflin, 1970).

13. James F. Leonard, *Strengthening the Non-Proliferation Treaty in the Post-Cold WarWorld*, Washington Council on Non-Proliferation Working Paper Number One, Washington, DC, October 1992.

14. *The Arms Control Reporter*, Volume 12:11, November 1993, p. 608.D.9.

15. Ibid., p. 608.B.277.

16. Ibid., p. 608.B.280.

17. The quotations in this entire paragraph are taken from Theodore B. Taylor, "Nuclear Tests and Nuclear Weapons," in Benjamin Frankel (ed.), *Opaque Nuclear Proliferation: Methodological and Policy Implications* (London: Frank Cass, 1991), pp. 188–189.

18. One suggestion is to leave imprecise the definition as to what constitutes a nuclear explosion. See George Bunn and Roland Timerbaef, "Avoiding the 'Definition" Pitfall to a Comprehensive Test Ban," *Arms Control Today*, Vol. 23, No. 4, May 1993, pp. 15–18. This approach, of course, runs an equal and perhaps even greater risk of being "designed around" by those who would seek to exploit the way the provisions of an agreement are written.

19. *The Arms Control Reporter*, Vol. 12:8–9, August-September 1993, p. 608.C.9.

Chapter 14

NPT EXTENSION: PROBLEMS AND PROSPECTS[1]

Lewis A. Dunn

In April 1995, the parties to the Non-Proliferation of Nuclear Weapons Treaty (NPT) will gather to determine its fate. The United States and the other Group of Seven countries have called for an indefinite extension of the Treaty in 1995. Indefinite extension would be most consistent with the key role played by the NPT in supporting global non-proliferation efforts. However, even with intensified US leadership, many difficult problems loom on the horizon and indefinite extension in 1995 may simply not be attainable. Single-minded focus on the goal of indefinite extension, moreover, may both intensify the risks of deadlock and make it more difficult to use the 1995 Extension Conference as a means to pursue more limited but achievable steps to strengthen the overall global non-proliferation regime of which the NPT is but one part.

To explore these issues, this chapter first seeks to place the NPT in the broader context of global non-proliferation efforts. Some of the challenges to the indefinite extension of the NPT are then examined and assessed. The chapter sets out some guidelines for US NPT extension diplomacy and concludes with a discussion of possible ways to use the Extension Conference and the review of the NPT that will accompany it to strengthen overall US nuclear non-proliferation efforts.

1. The NPT And Non-Proliferation

For the past several decades, the United States has led global efforts to prevent the further spread of nuclear weapons. These efforts seek respectively to make it technically more difficult for countries to acquire nuclear weapons, to lessen incentives to do so, to build international norms and institutions, and to consider briefly how the NPT supports and extends many of these measures.

1.1 The Non-Proliferation Spectrum

Nuclear export controls and multilateral supplier controls, making it technically more difficult for proliferation problem countries to acquire nuclear weapons, are an essential pillar of those efforts. In recent years, significant steps have been taken to strengthen these measures. These range from the revival of the Nuclear Suppliers Group, as a forum for consultations and action against proliferation, to the strengthening of national controls in key countries, not the least of which is Germany.

International inspections of non-proliferation commitments by the International Atomic Energy Agency (IAEA) also can play an important role. Such inspections can build confidence by providing a means for countries to demonstrate their compliance with their non-proliferation undertakings. Conversely, rigorous IAEA inspections can help deter cheating, or at least increase the difficulties, costs, and possibility of detection by other means of such violations. Since the revelations about Iraq's clandestine nuclear weapons program came to light after the 1991 Gulf War, the IAEA has taken significant steps to enhance its inspections processes.

Measures to reduce the incentives for countries to acquire nuclear weapons must be at the heart of any non-proliferation strategy. Throughout the Cold War period, strong US alliances with European countries, Japan, and South Korea made a critical non-proliferation contribution. Those alliances still have a non-proliferation role to play. Still elsewhere, reducing incentives may call for new regional confidence-building measures, as occurred between Argentina and Brazil in the 1980s or which may yet take place with the two Koreas. These steps are aimed at lessening insecurity that drives proliferation. More fundamental efforts to alleviate or resolve underlying political disputes are also essential, not the least for containing proliferation in the Middle East.

Wider global nuclear arms control initiatives provide an essential context for more specific US and global non-proliferation efforts. Nuclear arms reductions, typified by the prospect of deep reductions of the US and Russian nuclear arsenals, can create a climate in which it is more difficult for other countries to pursue nuclear weapons. Such reductions also legitimize an activist US non-proliferation posture. In turn, tighter global controls on plutonium and highly-enriched uranium, as proposed in President Clinton's new non-proliferation policy, offer a means to constrain the pursuit of nuclear weapons and lessen the risk of nuclear diversion. Similarly, successful pursuit of a Comprehensive Nuclear Test Ban Treaty (CTBT) would help to strengthen further a global anti-proliferation climate, which in some countries could help tip the balance against seeking nuclear weaponry.

1.2   The NPT Dimension

The role of the NPT in supporting a global strategy of non-proliferation, however, is frequently overlooked, underestimated, or forgotten in the stress of dealing with more immediate non-proliferation problems or pursuing regional or global initiatives. Since its entry into force in 1970, the NPT has been at the center of these global non-proliferation efforts. Many of these more specific measures rest in part upon the foundation provided by the Nuclear Non-Proliferation Treaty. Faced with the many political, military, and economic uncertainties of the post-Cold War world, a robust and credible NPT is even more essential.

Under Article I of the NPT, all five acknowledged nuclear weapons states have pledged not to assist other countries to manufacture or otherwise acquire nuclear weapons or nuclear explosive devices. With the collapse of a nuclear superpower, the former Soviet Union's commitment has taken on new significance. It provides a continuing prod on Russia to put in place needed controls on nuclear materials and nuclear exports. Now that China has joined the NPT, this obligation serves as an important new restraint on that country's nuclear cooperation with other countries. Should political upheaval and succession crisis follow Deng Xiaoping's death, this obligation to ensure nuclear control will grow in importance.

Equally important are the nearly 160 countries which have made a legally-binding commitment under Article II of the NPT not to acquire nuclear weapons or explosive devices. With isolated exceptions, all of these countries are honoring this pledge. Near-universal good-faith adherence to this Treaty sends the signal that a world of many nuclear powers is avoidable, thereby influencing decision-makers and helping create a norm of non-proliferation. In turn, this NPT obligation provided a ready-made vehicle to roll back successfully South Africa's possession of nuclear weapons. The Treaty may yet play a comparable role for Ukraine and Kazakhstan. Without North Korea's NPT membership, the international community would be on far weaker grounds in pressing Pyongyang to give up its possible nuclear ambitions. Looking ahead for a number of countries, like Japan in Asia, Germany and Turkey in Europe, and Egypt and Saudi Arabia in the Middle East, NPT membership is a critical sea-anchor on their possible responses to future regional political and military uncertainties.

The NPT's nuclear supply obligations under Article III are an essential legal, political, and normative foundation for multilateral and national nuclear export controls. More broadly, US nuclear diplomatic efforts to convince these suppliers not to export specific items to countries of proliferation concern have traditionally been able to point to other suppliers' NPT membership to encourage their nuclear restraint. In the greatest number of non-nuclear weapon states, adherence to the NPT provides the legal basis for International Atomic Energy Agency safeguards to detect misuse of peaceful nuclear cooperation. Should the NPT collapse in 1995, a new basis would be needed for these inspections. Similarly, peaceful nuclear cooperation among countries would undoubtedly shrink in a period of greater concern regarding the consequences of such cooperation.

Not the least, Article VI of the NPT sets out a vision of a world in which nuclear weapons have eventually been eliminated while, in the interim, committing all parties to "good faith" negotiations on effective measures toward that goal. In so doing, the Treaty establishes a legal and moral imperative for the United States and Russia to seek to roll back four decades of nuclear competition, but the obligations of Article VI apply as well to China, France, and the United Kingdom. This offers the necessary means to encourage these countries to join future multilateral bans on nuclear testing and the production of plutonium and highly-enriched uranium for weapons as well as a continuing process of nuclear reductions. However, without the reassurance provided by the NPT that increasingly widespread proliferation can be avoided, all of these nuclear powers would be far less prepared to undertake new and far-reaching nuclear arms control and disarmament commitments.

Non-proliferation policy must work on many levels and in many mutually reinforcing ways. As the preceding brief summary suggests, the NPT cuts across virtually all of those levels and clearly deserves its much-touted status as a pillar of US non-proliferation policies. The task ahead will be to preserve and strengthen it.

2. NPT Extension: The Preparatory Phase

During negotiation of the NPT in the mid-1960s, a number of countries, including Germany, Italy, and Japan, opposed making the Treaty of indefinite duration. Instead, as reflected in Article X, it was agreed that after twenty-five years the parties to the Treaty would meet to determine by an absolute majority of all the parties "whether the Treaty shall be extended indefinitely or for an additional fixed period or periods."

International preparations for the 1995 Extension Conference have been underway since late 1991. As part of this preparatory process, 128 parties to the NPT met in May 1992 and again in January 1994 in New York. Additional meetings of this Preparatory

Committee will occur September 12-16, 1994, in Geneva and January 23-27, 1995, again in New York. The Extension Conference itself will be held from April 17-May 12, 1995, in New York. The parties to the NPT have also agreed that as part of the process of extension in 1995 a review of the Treaty will occur. This is consistent with the past practice of holding a Review Conference every five years since the NPT's entry into force in 1970.

During this preparatory process, a wide range of procedural and organizational issues will be discussed. Matters include whether the decision to extend the Treaty should be taken by consensus or by vote; how to determine and in what order to take specific proposals on its extension; and how to structure the debate, the overall agenda, and the rules of procedure. It also will be necessary to choose a president for the Extension Conference. Two candidates have been put forward. The East European states have endorsed the candidacy of Poland. The Non-Aligned Movement countries have proposed Ambassador Jayantha Dhanapala of Sri Lanka, who had been a key player in working out a compromise final document at the 1985 NPT Review Conference.

In thinking about these and still other procedural questions, the procedural issues that matter need to be distinguished from those on which little is at stake. Winning agreement to the right rules of procedure for the Extension Conference, for example, clearly is critical. Depending on the specifics, these rules either could help or impede a successful extension, (e.g., by making it more difficult to attach conditions to the extension decision, influencing the order in which proposals are considered, and shaping the overall pacing of debate and decision).

How an ultimate extension decision is taken will also be important. The Treaty provides that the extension decision is to be made by a majority of all of the NPT parties, not simply by those parties present at the Extension Conference. With over 160 signatories, this will call for a vote of at least 80 plus countries for whatever extension decision is taken. However, an extension decision taken by consensus not by vote, if attainable, would best demonstrate continued support for the Treaty. By contrast, a narrow majority vote even for indefinite extension would likely generate questions about the extent of support for the NPT, while quite possibly leading some countries which had voted against that result to withdraw from the Treaty.

Getting the right Conference President is another key matter. In 1990, a weak President, who clashed personally with other key players, contributed to the inability of the Review Conference to reach agreement on a final document. By contrast, the presence of a well-liked and respected president in 1985 helped to smooth out differences and made it easier for countries to compromise their differences in a group of "Friends of the President." By contrast, other procedural issues matter far less. For instance, debates over background documents or permitting observers at the Preparatory Committee hearings will be of little, if any, lasting import.

3.   Debate And Decision: Old Issues And New Concerns

Turning to the substantive issues which will dominate the debate -- and the decision -- at the 1995 NPT Extension Conference, many of these issues are all but certain to consist in part of the traditional debates about NPT implementation at past Review Conferences. But several other broader issues can be discerned, such as the post-Cold War uncertainties and discrimination taking place under the NPT. "Wild card" countries also stand out. These could significantly shape the outcome, but their likelihood or views are uncertain. Viewing all of these elements together, there is every reason to be concerned that the Extension Conference could be characterized by considerable controversy and serious difficulties in winning consensus support for indefinite and unconditional NPT extension.

3.1   Meeting The NPT's Goals

The NPT has three goals: to enhance all countries' security by preventing further spread of nuclear weapons; to foster the peaceful uses of nuclear energy under effective international safeguards; and to encourage a process of nuclear arms control and global disarmament. Countries' positions on NPT extension will be shaped first by perceptions of how well these NPT goals are being met. The overall record is very good and getting better, but it is not untarnished.

If past Review Conferences are a guide, the vast majority of the parties to the NPT can be expected to acknowledge that the Treaty has helped to head off runaway proliferation and added to their own security. In particular, most developing countries now agree that the NPT is an important instrument of international security. At the same time, questions about the NPT's effectiveness are certain to be raised. If ambiguity persists about North Korea, South Korea, Japan, and other countries in Asia, this could give the NPT a less than wholehearted endorsement. Troublesome questions also will likely be posed regarding Iraq's ability to pursue an undetected clandestine nuclear weapons program in violation of its NPT obligations and despite IAEA safeguards. Elsewhere within the Middle East, Israel's possession of nuclear weapons will shape Arab countries' attitudes toward NPT extension, though success in the present Peace Process may mute the tone of debate.

Actions by the nuclear weapon states in fulfilling their obligations not to assist other countries to acquire nuclear explosives will not go unscrutinized. In this regard, allegations of Chinese assistance to Pakistan's nuclear weapons program may result in questions about whether the nuclear powers have met their obligations under the NPT. Further, though nuclear weapons cooperation among weapon states is not precluded by the Treaty's ban on non-assistance, rumored Russian aid to China's nuclear weapons program --whether true or not -- could prove another contentious issue.

For many developing countries which are parties to the NPT, both positive and negative security assurances from the nuclear powers continue to be seen as one of their *quid pro quos* for renouncing the right to acquire nuclear weapons or explosive devices. Positive security assurances are commitments by the nuclear powers to assist non-nuclear NPT parties threatened with nuclear attack. Negative security assurances are commitments by the nuclear weapons states not to attack non-nuclear weapons states.

With regard to such assurances, several steps have been taken over the past decades. In parallel statements, endorsed by the United Nations Security Council in UNSC Resolution 255, the United States, the former Soviet Union, and the United Kingdom all signaled their readiness in 1968 in the event of nuclear aggression or the threat of nuclear aggression "to act immediately in accordance with their obligations under the United Nations Charter." So far, neither China nor France (now that they are NPT parties) have associated themselves with this earlier positive security assurance. Nor has Russia explicitly reaffirmed the 1968 Soviet pledge. Since the NPT's entry into force in 1970, all five nuclear powers have also pledged not to use nuclear weapons against non-nuclear weapon states party to the NPT but only China's statement is unconditional. Calls for more encompassing, legally binding, and less conditional security assurances will undoubtedly be part of the debate over the security benefits of the NPT.

Over the past decade, the contribution of the NPT in supporting the peaceful uses of nuclear energy has not been a major issue at past NPT Review Conferences. This may change at the NPT Extension Conference. The peaceful uses issues could well turn out to be a matter of considerable debate and division among the parties. At the least, Iran can be expected to argue that continuing US efforts to gain other countries' support for a *de facto* embargo on any nuclear-related trade with Tehran will violate the NPT's promise of the fullest possible access to peaceful nuclear cooperation and technology. Other developing countries may also challenge recent multilateral efforts to tighten still further nuclear-related exports controls, in particular the 1992 agreement among the Nuclear Suppliers Group to introduce a new system of controls on dual-use exports. For the developing countries, such controls may even be seen as part of a broader Western attempt to deny advanced technology to the developing world and impede its industrialization.

The heart of this more traditional debate about the value of the NPT, however, will revolve around how well the nuclear weapon states are meeting their arms control and disarmament obligations under Article VI of the Treaty. To recall, Article VI calls for good faith negotiations to end the nuclear arms race for nuclear disarmament and for general and complete disarmament. Debates over implementation of these nuclear disarmament obligations have always been the most controversial and difficult at the NPT Review Conferences. There is no reason to expect differently at the Extension Conference.

Dismantlement not production and modernization of nuclear weapons, if current agreements are fully implemented, will be the major task of the next decade and beyond for the United States and Russia. Under the Strategic Arms Reduction Treaties (START I and II), the two nuclear superpowers have agreed to reduce sharply their strategic offensive nuclear forces to between 3,000 to 3,500 nuclear warheads by 2003, if not the year 2000. Both countries have already taken parallel unilateral steps to eliminate ground-launched tactical nuclear weapons as well as to withdraw virtually all other tactical nuclear weapons from deployments outside of either Russian or US territory. Multilateral negotiations on a comprehensive nuclear test ban are to begin in January 1994, in the Geneva Conference on Disarmament (CD). President Clinton has also proposed new multilateral negotiations on an international convention to ban the production of plutonium and highly-enriched uranium for nuclear explosives. Closely related, he has made clear US readiness to submit fissile material no longer needed for inspection by the IAEA. Implementation of these agreements and new initiatives should suffice to convince all but the most doctrinaire that the nuclear arms race has ended and a process of global nuclear roll-back is well underway.

There are many obstacles and pitfalls still to be overcome in this nuclear arms control and disarmament process. At best, successful implementation of existing agreements and the negotiation of new ones will be technically complex and politically difficult. Consequently, support for indefinite extension could prove hard to muster; acrimonious debates or even deadlock cannot be precluded.

Specifically, Ukraine's continuing reluctance to adhere to the NPT threatens to slow the process of US-Russian nuclear reductions. Further Chinese nuclear weapon tests could yet undermine political support for a test ban elsewhere. Conversely, CTBT negotiations will raise many complex issues and could bog down in rancorous debates over the scope, duration, verification, and other details of an eventual treaty. Similarly, future multilateral negotiations to ban production of plutonium and highly-enriched uranium for weapons or outside international safeguards also pose potential risks as well as benefits for NPT extension. This is especially so if any ultimate agreement is perceived to add new discrimination in favor of the nuclear weapon states, for instance, continuing the practice of requiring less stringent verification of their commitments than now is required of non-nuclear weapon states under the NPT.

Further, by the time of the 1995 NPT Extension Conference, the process of nuclear reductions, assuming it remains on track, will have only begun. Even assuming full implementation of the START reductions, the numbers of nuclear weapons possessed by the United States and Russia would still be greater than when the NPT was signed in 1968. Though desirable, rapid conclusion of nuclear testing and production agreements by 1995 seems unlikely, in light of the multilateral character of the negotiations and the complexity of the issues. In response, parties could prove very reluctant to go forward with an indefinite extension. Alternatively, there could be a movement among some countries to hold NPT extension hostage to agreement in these areas. Many possibilities for hostage-taking exist. These include simply seeking legally binding commitments from the nuclear power to conclude negotiations by a certain date, possibly to deferring an extension decision and instead adjourning for a period of five years until negotiations had concluded.

3.2   Uncertainties And Discrimination

The Cold War world has ended but a new international political order has yet to take shape to replace it. The 1995 NPT extension debate and decision will be shaped, as well, by countries' responses to the unprecedented uncertainties of this post-Cold War world. These uncertainties abound across the world's most volatile regions.

In Europe, Russia's national integrity remains in question and its future political make-up has yet to be determined. Ukraine appears increasingly wedded to a new form of nuclear ambiguity, repeatedly affirming its intention to give up former Soviet nuclear weapons but taking as few steps as possible in that direction.

Within the Middle East, recent agreement between the Palestine Liberation Organization (PLO) and Israel may lead toward an eventual regional settlement, or it could yet break down in intensified violence and wider regional conflict. How long the United Nations will stay the course in Iraq is a matter of great concern among that country's neighbors, including both Turkey and Iran. In turn, Iran's own apparent nuclear weapon ambitions, if they lead toward attempted clandestine violation of that country's NPT obligations and an eventual nuclear capability, could have a ripple effect within that area. The collapse of the Soviet Union has brought with it a new danger in the loss of nuclear weapons materials, if not weapons, into this region, posing the danger of instant proliferation.

Within India and Pakistan, pro-bomb forces are putting pressure on the leaderships of both countries to take the last step across the threshold to open deployments of nuclear weapons. Though neither country is a signatory of the NPT, open deployments would shake global non-proliferation efforts. In particular, wider perceptions that the prospects are good for avoiding runaway proliferation would be shaken. For its part, China shows all signs of becoming an economic giant early in the next century. What is less clear is whether internal political upheaval will yet again thwart that process, possibly leading to regional separatism. Conversely, if political upheaval is avoided, questions remain about whether China will take advantage of its growing economic strength to build up its nuclear capabilities and assert a preeminent political-military role in Northeast Asia. Either outcome would further unsettle Japan, already made uneasy by the prospect of a nuclear-armed North Korea.

From another perspective, these uncertainties strengthen the case for long-term NPT extension in 1995. Without a robust and credible NPT, these uncertainties would be far greater. Many countries would likely reassess their own nuclear abstinence and quite possibly take steps to move closer to a nuclear option. Moreover, the NPT's specific obligations, as already noted, can make an important contribution to dealing with some of the more pressing proliferation problems that exacerbate today's uncertainty.

At the same time, the very uncertainties of the post-Cold War world very likely will make some non-nuclear countries more reluctant to sign an indefinite extension of the Treaty in 1995. For them, indefinite extension could well be regarded as too constricting, as entailing a loss of national freedom of action for a period of uncertainty. Japan is a good example. At repeated meetings of the Western Group of Seven nations over the past two years, Japan has consistently been the most reluctant to endorse the goal of indefinite extension. Each endorsement, moreover, has been followed by backtracking. Most recently, the new Japanese Prime Minister, Morihiro Hosokawa, stated his support for indefinite NPT extension in his maiden speech to the Japanese Diet in August 1993. Soon thereafter, however, Japanese officials let it be known informally that this was his personal view, that he had not been fully briefed on the complexities of the issue, and that the ultimate position of the new coalition government still had to be determined.[1]

NPT extension debate and decision also will be shaped by certain other "sleeper" issues which have been present but not prominent in the deliberations of the Review Conferences. In that regard, controversies over the discriminatory nature of the Treaty pose the greatest threat to success. Already, there is growing interest in quite a few non-nuclear countries in seeking to redress this discrimination, particularly if they are to be asked to renounce nuclear weapons indefinitely. Proposals have surfaced to make agreement by the nuclear weapon states to a timetable for eliminating nuclear weapons a condition for indefinite extension.

At the least, the nuclear powers, especially the United States and Russia, should be prepared for sharp challenges to their right to possess nuclear weapons indefinitely. In this regard, the Extension Conference certainly comes too soon. For the first time in many decades, the possibility exists of a fundamental reorientation of how the United States, Russia, and the other acknowledged nuclear powers think about nuclear weapons. Across a fairly wide political spectrum within the United States, for example, questions are being asked about how low the process of nuclear reductions can go, what steps can be taken to stand-down US and Russian nuclear forces while reductions proceed, what should be the future role of nuclear weapons in the post-Cold War world, whether nuclear deterrence is still relevant, and whether it is possible that the international community can take custody or control of residual nuclear arsenals. But this process of rethinking the nuclear future will take time. Attempts to force the pace at the NPT Extension Conference will more likely than not backfire.

3.3 Wild Cards

A number of wild cards also could significantly affect NPT extension. Consider only a few examples.

China's eventual position on new initiatives banning nuclear testing and materials production for weapons will go far to determine whether those negotiations succeed. At the Extension Conference, its stance could either exacerbate or contribute to resolving disputes on key issues. However, very little is known about Chinese thinking, not the least since the start of a more routine arms control and non-proliferation dialogue was put on hold after the Tiananmen Square uprising.

France's positions and strategies are somewhat better known, and established channels of communication exist to clarify issues. But like China, France is a new participant in NPT diplomacy. France's position on future nuclear arms control matters, and on more fundamental issues of the long-term future of nuclear weapons, will be critical. Here, too, what stands out is the fact that unlike past Review Conferences, an American readiness to compromise may not suffice in order to avoid divisive votes or even deadlock.

Furthermore, Ukraine's retention of nuclear weapons could affect thinking in Central Europe, Central Asia, and beyond. Israel is publicly assumed now to possess a significant nuclear arsenal; how much attention its Arab neighbors will place on this issue at the Extension Conference and whether they will make Israeli NPT adherence a condition for indefinite extension remain open questions. North Korea's ultimate intentions remain difficult to discern. Will Pyongyang cut the best bargain possible to give up its pursuit of nuclear weapons or to string the international community along while building the bomb? As already suggested, open nuclear deployments by India and Pakistan would send shock waves through the NPT community.

4. A Strategy For Success In 1995

The NPT Extension Conference will take place in April 1995. A number of guidelines stand out for achieving success. These guidelines include defining success successfully; taking the case for NPT Extension "on the road," by including appointment of an NPT Ambassador to carry-out widening circles of consultations; continuing attempts to contain proliferation in Northeast Asia and South Asia; and energetic pursuit of the Clinton Administration's new testing and fissile materials initiatives. Further efforts to be taken for achieving success include keeping the START reductions process on track; readiness to take further steps to lessen the sense of perceived discrimination between NPT non-nuclear and nuclear weapon states; and finally, thinking seriously about practical steps which must be implemented to use the combined NPT extension and review process to strengthen wider global non-proliferation norms, institutions, and undertakings.

4.1   Defining Success Successfully

For the many reasons already discussed, the odds are low that the United States will be able to win agreement to an indefinite NPT extension. Defining success as an indefinite extension also unnecessarily puts the United States (and its NPT supporters) on the defensive by encouraging countries to hold the NPT hostage for the purpose of agreements to particular undertakings. Even if the United States were ultimately prepared to compromise on disarmament issues, any one of the four other nuclear powers could upset a potential deal.

Furthermore, it is wrong to assume that the United States and its Western supporters can easily and with low costs back away from this goal of indefinite extension during the Extension Conference. Having defined success in this manner, an "eleventh hour" retreat will likely be viewed as a defeat. Questions will be raised about parties' support for the Treaty. Once having encouraged a process of bargaining over how much the United States and the other nuclear powers are prepared to negotiate for NPT extension, positions may harden, divisiveness overwhelm cooperation, and reluctance to appear weak by compromising take hold. The result could be an unintended deadlock -- or a shorter NPT extension than might otherwise have been possible.

Despite these risks, redefining success successfully during the period leading up to the Extension Conference will take considerable diplomatic finesse, now that the United States has committed itself to the goal of indefinite extension. However, should extensive and continuing consultations indicate that the prospects are indeed gloomy for indefinite extension, this would provide the opportunity to revisit the issue before the closing stages of the preparatory process. Specifically, US officials could indicate at the third or fourth Preparatory Committee meeting that while the United States believes that indefinite extension would be preferable, it is fully prepared to support unconditional renewal of the Treaty for another twenty-five years with provision for further periodic extensions (or an indefinite extension, should a majority of the parties so decide at that time). In explaining this shift, US officials could emphasize the importance of avoiding divisive debates, let alone deadlock, that could undermine the Treaty's credibility and its contribution to global stability. Washington's NPT diplomacy could also state in a quite straightforward manner that while the future of nuclear weapons must be addressed in the years ahead, the time is not ripe to go beyond the basic nuclear disarmament obligations already part of the NPT. In effect, US strategy would be to turn the NPT Extension Conference from a negotiation over the period to a rallying of the parties behind the notion that another renewable twenty-five year term for the NPT is the obvious and logical course to adopt.

Some legal scholars and analysts may argue that the preceding approach is precluded by the language of Article X (2) of the NPT.[2] In their view, only three choices are said to exist: indefinite extension; extension for an additional fixed period, after which the Treaty dies; or extension for an indefinite series of additional fixed periods. But this position has not been universally accepted, not the least by the developing country which is a party to the NPT. It is also hard to imagine that should a consensus of the parties decide not to follow explicitly one of these three options, this would be questioned by the United States or other NPT supporters. At that point, both *realpolitik,* as well as the traditional international legal maxim, that the parties of a treaty, by agreement, can in effect make clear how they understand their obligations will govern countries' views on the extension options which can be crafted.

4.2 Getting Out on the Road

Extensive and continuing consultations with other governments will be absolutely essential for success, whether or not success is defined as indefinite NPT extension. Such consultations have already begun among the NPT depositories (United States, Russia, and the United Kingdom) as well as at the level of the G-7 summits. In addition, several circles of bilateral consultations need to be initiated or extended with Western countries, countries of Eastern Europe, China, and the developing world. Bilateral consultations could then be supplemented by consultations among groups of countries. In this regard, a group of "Friends of the NPT" might be established to bring together both developed and developing countries, non-nuclear and nuclear weapon states.

Further deliberations would provide a means to ask critical questions and determine other countries' positions. These discussions offer a means to help shape the terms of the extension debate, both making the case for the NPT and cautioning against imprudent or untimely demands. Consultations also could prove invaluable as a means of early warning of possible problems. Not the least, widening circles of consultation will help to build up habits of frankness and cooperation among individuals, thereby making success more likely in 1995.

Given the importance of this process, implementing extensive consultations will be a nearly full-time job. The Clinton Administration, therefore, should give serious consideration to the appointment of a special NPT Ambassador. This individual also could take the lead in crafting Washington's responses to the many procedural and substantive issues ahead as well as serve as a focal point for implementing US' NPT extension strategy.

4.3 Containing Regional Proliferation Problems

US efforts to contain proliferation on the Korean Peninsula and in South Asia remain essential. Space precludes a full discussion here. With regard to North Korea, measures need to be taken to step-up the pressure. These include national sanctions to seeking China's agreement to international isolation of North Korea, as a last resort. Even if unsuccessful, such steps would help to demonstrate the seriousness of resolve and help contain spillovers on the Asian continent. More direct actions to reassure Japan must include a reaffirmation of Washington's security ties and the possible cooperation in missile defenses, which continue to grow in importance.

The establishment of a more routine dialogue on nuclear issues with China might pay off not only in better understanding of Chinese positions on NPT extension but also in greater Chinese readiness to support Pyongyang's isolation if that becomes necessary. China's actions also are likely to be crucial in helping to dampen proliferation pressures in South Asia, since India continues to view China as its main security threat. Here, multilateral nuclear testing and production bans could offer the best vehicle to constrain the nuclear weapons activities of all three members, China, India, and Pakistan. Continued diplomacy is needed also to ensure international support for long-term monitoring in Iraq by the IAEA.

4.4 Coming To Closure On CTBT, Cutoff, And START Implementation

With an eye on April 1995, energetic pursuit of both a CTBT and a convention banning production of plutonium and highly-enriched uranium for weapons or other nuclear explosives clearly is in order. Negotiators should seek to achieve substantial progress on both fronts before the Extension Conference, thereby putting the negotiations on a fast track rather than conducting business as usual. Possible interim steps in testing might be explored. One possibility would be a politically binding moratorium agreement among the five nuclear powers to go into effect in January 1995 for a period of three years or until conclusion of a CTBT, whichever comes first. Other nuclear powers besides the United States, which has already done so unilaterally, might be encouraged to cease production of nuclear weapons materials. In turn, Russia might be urged to follow the US's example to place materials from surplus warheads under IAEA safeguards. Such actions would help to symbolize the end of the nuclear arms race and the transition to nuclear rollback.

Ukraine's position will remain critical for successful START implementation. But neither limited economic payoffs nor warnings that retaining former Soviet nuclear weapons would result in worsened relations with the West have so far sufficed to convince that country to honor its prior commitments. Wider Western efforts to put in place a new network of political, military, and economic ties with Ukraine may offer somewhat more hope of eventually tipping the balance against keeping former Soviet weapons.

4.5 Toward A Global Nuclear Taboo

New actions are now in order to meet long-standing calls by NPT non-nuclear weapon states for positive security assurances. A first step would be the passage of a new United Nations Security Council Resolution committing all five nuclear weapon states to take action in accordance with their UN Charter obligations to assist NPT parties threatened with nuclear aggression or which are subject to nuclear attack. The United Nations Secretary General might also be given explicit responsibility to track possible nuclear crises and report to the Security Council. This could help strengthen the presumption of action in the event of a proliferation-triggered nuclear threat or crisis. The possibility also warrants consideration of reviving and revamping the UN's Military Staff Committee as a means to coordinate responses to future instances of nuclear blackmail or attack against NPT parties.

Closely related, the time has come for the United States, after consultations with NATO, to adopt a posture of no-first-use nuclear weapons. Parallel commitments should be sought from Russia, France, and the United Kingdom as well as a reaffirmation of China's earlier pledge not to use nuclear weapons first. With the collapse of Soviet power in Europe and the shifting conventional balance on the Korean Peninsula, the threat to use nuclear weapons first no longer is necessary to deter aggression. Maintaining a robust US conventional military presence in Asia should offset any possible misinterpretation of Washington's shift in its nuclear posture.

Adoption of no-first-use postures would end the two decades' debate over negative security assurances. Agreement by all the NPT nuclear powers to give up the option to use nuclear weapons first would also be an important step to eliminate the perceived political or military discrimination of the NPT. Further, a US commitment to no-first-use could help provide a normative foundation for longer-term efforts to contain proliferation and its consequences.

4.6 Strengthening The NPT Regime

The process of reviewing and extending the NPT in 1995 also offers a major opportunity to buttress overall non-proliferation efforts. This could take the form either of endorsement of key non-proliferation principles by the parties in a final declaration or calls for follow-on initiatives in appropriate implementing or negotiating forums. For instance, final document endorsement could be sought for any or all of the following: agreement by all suppliers, including China, to require full-scope safeguards; acceptance by all parties of an obligation not to assist other countries to acquire nuclear explosives; and the vigorous use of special inspections right by the IAEA as well as of new safeguards techniques (e.g., use of environmental monitoring; recourse to the United Nations Security Council to backup NPT compliance; and greater transparency in nuclear supply matters).

Follow-on initiatives could also be proposed and endorsed with a call made for their pursuit in new or established forums. Discussions could be encouraged, for example, between the IAEA and other international monitoring bodies to be established under the Chemical Weapons Convention (CWC) as well as future agreements to determine whether important synergies exist that buttress overall non-proliferation monitoring. Consideration might be given to endorsing an international convention banning nuclear smuggling, thus extending the Convention on the Physical Protection of Nuclear Materials. A nuclear smuggling convention could help to ensure effective materials and weapons controls and require its parties to cooperate in apprehending and/or extraditing individuals involved in nuclear smuggling against international and nationals laws.[3] Still another possibility would be the creation of an NPT-Secretariat to track implementation of the NPT and to help the parties focus on compliance issues as well as to craft common responses. In the past, US opposition to such an idea would have been assured. Now, such an organization might be more acceptable.[4]

The specific details, however, are less important than the basic idea. Rather than viewing the 1995 Extension Conference simply as a damage limiting exercise, it should be seen as a valuable forum to enhance non-proliferation overall.

5. On The Road To 1995

Since the pursuit of a non-proliferation treaty first began in earnest in the early 1960s, the United States has always played a vital NPT leadership role. US officials have been at the center of negotiating, then in successfully implementing, preserving, and strengthening the Nuclear Non-Proliferation Treaty. With the 1995 Extension Conference looming on the horizon, Washington's leadership is now vitally needed. To ensure success, the United States needs to take the lead to shape the terms of the extension debate, to defuse potentially divisive if not destructive issues, to pursue vigorously President

Clinton's newly proposed nuclear arms control initiatives, and ultimately to rally support among all NPT parties for a renewable long-term, if not necessarily indefinite, extension of the Treaty. The agenda is large, the stakes are high, and time is of the essence.

Notes

1. This is based on personal conversations of the author at a recent meeting of Americans and Japanese on nuclear proliferation issues.
2. George Bunn, Charles van Doren, and David Fischer, for example, have taken this position.
3. This idea was first suggested by two of my colleagues, Burros Carnahan and Jaci Smith.
4. My colleague Blair Murray first suggested this idea to me.

PART IV

THE CHEMICAL WEAPONS CONVENTION: POLITICAL, TECHNICAL, AND ECONOMIC CONSEQUENCES

Chapter 15

THE CHEMICAL WEAPONS CONVENTION: NAVIGATING THE PASSAGE FROM OPENING-FOR-SIGNATURE TO ENTRY-INTO-FORCE

Brad Roberts

It is a truism of arms control that the negotiation of treaties generates more interest than does their implementation. Once the spotlight passes from the high politics of the negotiating endgame, new issues attract the headlines and the attention of policymakers. What was politically stimulating begins to look bureaucratic and mundane. There is a tendency to assume that everything will fall into place and work as originally intended. Nowhere are these tendencies and assumptions more in evidence than in the chemical weapons domain. Nowhere are the risks of complacency as great.

This chapter offers an assessment of the prospects for the new Chemical Weapons Convention (CWC) at approximately the mid-point between its opening for signature in January 1993 and its intended entry into force in January 1995. It describes the work of the international community to put in place the new treaty regime and assesses the likelihood of its entry into force in a timely fashion. The analysis underscores the continuing political challenges confronting the chemical disarmament effort, especially as they derive from a treaty conceived in the Cold War but being crafted as a principal instrument of international security in the post-cold war setting.

1. The Preparatory Commission

The CWC was opened for signature at a ceremony in Paris on January 13, 1993, after nearly two decades of negotiation in the Conference on Disarmament (CD), a multilateral arms control forum associated with the United Nations in Geneva. The treaty is slated to enter into force six months after 65 states have deposited their instruments of ratification with the depository states but not before two years after opening for signature. The number 65 was chosen in an effort to promote broad adherence to the treaty before its entry into force, and contrasts with the much lower number of 20 in the case of the Biological and Toxin Weapons Convention. The two year period was agreed in order to give a preparatory commission (the PrepCom, composed of representatives of all signatory states) the time to build up the Organization for the Prohibition of Chemical Weapons (OPCW). The OPCW will oversee the functioning of the treaty regime by receiving declarations by states parties, monitoring the destruction of weapons and their production facilities, and investigating allegations of non-compliance. The six month delay was created in order to know when to begin the task of hiring and training the OPCW staff and purchasing the necessary support equipment. The OPCW will be headquartered in The Hague, The Netherlands, the location also of the work of the PrepCom.

The OPCW will be an institution similar in function to the parallel entity created to monitor compliance with the Nuclear Non-Proliferation Treaty and its associated safeguards, the International Atomic Energy Agency (IAEA). The similarities are many: it will be internationally staffed and directed, it will look to its members and to the UN Security Council to deal with serious non-compliance, and it will be funded according to an allocation of obligations that puts a hefty burden on the US treasury. But the differences are also numerous. The OPCW is functionally equivalent to only that part of the IAEA that deals with compliance issues; it has no parallel function to promote civilian uses of relevant technologies. It will enjoy a right to challenge inspections and access to undeclared facilities beyond that historically enjoyed by the IAEA. Once the period of weapons destruction has ended (a decade after entry into force) it will scale down significantly and operate largely on the basis of challenge inspections. Moreover, the chemical problem being different from the nuclear one, the OPCW is likely to be an instrument of first resort rather than last resort, as the IAEA has tended to be in the past for states concerned about monitoring non-compliance by treaty members.

The PrepCom began its work in February 1993 with an ambitious mandate -- to complete its work in time for the earliest possible entry into force -- but without so much as a gavel or plan of work. During 1993 it got off to a solid start, completing an impressive array of plans for the structure and functioning of the OPCW and its various bodies, including an executive council and a technical secretariat. Working groups on various specific topics were created and their work has been reviewed and where necessary revised and endorsed in plenary meetings of the PrepCom. The group has overcome the early inertia generated by the shift of venue from Geneva to The Hague. Its work has grown more focused over time on the more difficult challenges. A business-like tone, in contrast to the often polemical tenor of the CD, has been achieved.

A primary goal of the PrepCom process has been to deepen and sustain the engagement of the countries outside of Western Europe and North America. Such countries are well represented in the PrepCom and the provisional technical secretariat and in the working group process. The CD provided a basis for this process, as a multilateral body involving approximately 40 countries, though for most of the chemical weapons negotiations it was organized into blocs drawn along Cold War lines. To a certain extent, regional groupings in the PrepCom threaten to supplant the old blocs as organizing entities; such tendencies have been in evidence in debates on subjects such as the number of official languages adopted by the PrepCom. In contrast to the CD, where many non-Western countries used the negotiating process to advance political agendas sometimes quite removed from the chemical weapons issue, the nonideological character of the dialogue in The Hague is striking. To illustrate this point one need only note the fact that the United States found itself working in close partnership at the autumn 1993 plenary session with Iran, whose representative chaired the meeting, and China -- just a short few weeks after the United States navy had sought to disrupt an alleged Chinese shipment of chemical warfare precursors to Iran.

With more than 150 states having signed the treaty at the mid-way point between 1993 and 1995, and with more than half generally turning up for the plenary meetings of the PrepCom, the developing world would appear to be as closely involved in the ongoing work of building the new regime as it was in its negotiation. The PrepCom has proven especially useful as a learning experience for those many countries that did not participate in the CD negotiations but are signatories, such as Israel, for example.

But the West remains the principal driving force in the ongoing intellectual work associated with crafting the regime. Of the 83 states participating in the autumn 1993 plenary meeting, only approximately 20 percent actually spoke up.

The fact that the work of the PrepCom has gotten off to such a solid start has generated in national capitals and the interested public a general optimism that the process of putting together the chemical disarmament regime is going smoothly and that once the treaty enters into force it will be near global in its scope and fully effective in its implementation. This year, 1994, may well prove these assumptions misplaced.

The challenge is two-fold. First, the PrepCom has, in some sense, dealt with the easiest tasks first, hoping to generate a spirit and habit of pragmatism and compromise that will be necessary to finalize the provisions for challenge inspections, industry supervision, and the exercise of OPCW authority. Second, the PrepCom can only look after the mechanics of the new treaty; the real work of creating the regime relates to the politics of getting states to sign the treaty, ratify it in timely fashion, implement the CWC nationally, and ultimately participate cooperatively in the task of managing noncompliance. This political agenda is beyond the purview of diplomats working in The Hague. More precisely, it is properly the task of policymakers in key interested states who, so far at least, have shown little evidence of carrying through on that national interest.

2. The Year 1994

The basic question in 1994 is whether the number of states parties (i.e., states that have deposited their instruments of ratification with the designated depository states) will have climbed from the total of 4 at the end of 1993 to the necessary 65 by July 16, 1994 (six months before the earliest possible entry into force date in January 1995) in order to trigger the entry into force -- and if not, what the fallback plan will be. The key implicit requirement is that not just any 65 but the right 65 states are parties -- those with chemical weapons, related military research and development programs, chemical industries producing precursors for chemical warfare agents, and those in regions in conflict. The treaty makes no provision for a specific set of states, but politically it is inconceivable that a large set of nations would ratify their signatures without the "right 65" being firmly engaged.

The largest obstacles are in Russia, but it is far from being the only problem country in the ratification phase of CWC implementation.

3. The Russian Federation

In Moscow, the chemical disarmament issue has been caught up in the general paralysis of policymaking caused by the collapse of the Soviet Union, the disintegration of existing political institutions, and the changing civil-military relationship. Early in his tenure as Russian president, Boris Yeltsin appointed a presidential commission on issues related to Russia's compliance with its chemical and biological weapons treaty commitments, for the explicit purpose of advising the president and parliament on new policies and for the implicit purpose of securing domestic political support for the dismantlement of existing weapons. The commission has disappointed many who note how little it has to show after three years of work -- to say nothing of the expenditure of some US funds from the Nunn-Lugar bill for the safe and secure dismantlement of Soviet unconventional weapons. To be sure, it faces an uphill task in promoting weapons destruction programs in an era when the central government has little or no credibility on environmental protection. Moreover, it has been unable to forge consensus among the disparate forces evident in the political life of Russia today. The Soviet Union first promised to put in place a chemical munitions destruction program at the Wyoming summit of 1989, and Russia's continued failure to create a viable destruction program is a serious roadblock on the path to global CWC implementation.

Ideally, the new Russian parliament elected in December 1993 will make ratification of the CWC an early priority and will approve at the same time the necessary implementing legislation, including a weapons destruction program. This is a reasonable scenario, especially if one assumes that the new team will want to get on with new business as quickly as possible in order to show that it can govern. On the other hand, ratification may be held hostage to continued political paralysis or the parliament may ratify without approving a destruction program, raising many questions internationally about both Russia's ability and its will to honor its new treaty commitments.

It is conceivable that the treaty might enter into force without Russian participation, though this is politically unlikely as Russia has declared its possession of a large chemical munitions stockpile (about 40,000 tons of chemical warfare agent) and doubts continue to persist about the actual status of its ostensibly now defunct offensive program. If the treaty does enter into force without Russia but with the United States, there would be serious implications for the inspection of US facilities and munitions destruction, given the current assumption that a separate, bilateral US-Russian agreement will manage -- and fund -- this task.

4. The United States

In the United States, ratification of the CWC has been delayed by the larger problems caused by the political transition from George Bush to Bill Clinton. Those problems include the normal ones associated with a period of transition in US presidential politics, including the slow pace of personnel appointments and a review of national policy. But they have been compounded by a deep debate within the new administration about the significance and place of arms control in national strategy and by the crisis-driven process of foreign policymaking in its first year. Thus only on November 23, 1993 did the new administration submit to the Senate the CWC signed by outgoing Secretary of State Lawrence Eagleburger 11 months earlier.

Over the many years of negotiating the chemical disarmament treaty and the year since its opening for signature, the executive branch has done little to communicate with its legislative partner about the CWC. The Clinton administration is likely to reap the consequences in mid-1994 as the Congress struggles to understand a treaty that is neither short nor simple and whose many weaknesses and short-comings make sense only after much study and in a larger context that will not be easily defined. Both houses of Congress will have a role to play: the Senate in its constitutional role of offering advice and consent to ratification, and the House because implementing legislation will require its joint approval. For their review, they will require not only the convention itself but also an article-by-article analysis of its provisions, a draft of the implementing legislation, an assessment of the treaty's verifiability, a viable munitions destruction program, and -- if they can be finalized -- the Wyoming memorandum of understanding and the protocols to the bilateral US-Russian agreement. The speed with which these items reach the Congress is being treated as symbolic of the administration's commitment to the CWC.

That speed is best described as a slow trickle.

As in Russia, the destruction program is proving difficult to finalize and fund, as US policymakers face a long list of technical, fiscal, environmental, and political problems, especially in those eight locations where chemical weapons are stored in the United States. Under the CWC, weapons destruction must begin one year after entry into force and proceed over a 10-year period. A five-year extension may be granted by the OPCW executive council in extreme circumstances. Noteworthy is the fact that the destruction of the vast majority of the US chemical weapons stockpile was mandated by the Congress in 1985 as a *quid pro quo* for the short-lived binary weapons production program of the Reagan administration -- and this has yet to get on track.

It is difficult to imagine that the Senate will support ratification without firm Russian support for the treaty in the form of both treaty ratification and a credible program for stockpile destruction. Between them, the United States and Russia possess roughly 95 percent of the world's declared chemical weapons stockpiles (Iraq is the only other state to acknowledge its possession of chemical weapons, although more may follow with declarations of possession once the treaty enters into force). It is equally difficult to imagine that the United States would choose to abandon the new regime, for which it labored so long in Geneva, whatever the opposition of Congress on specific points so long as Russia is on board.

5. Other States Parties

Even if both Russia and the United States should somehow manage to deposit instruments of ratification by early summer 1994, significant doubts remain about other key states.

In Europe, for example, ratification appears to be receding further into the future and looks increasingly likely sometime in the first half of 1994. The delay stems in part from a decision by the European Community to proceed in unison toward ratification as a part of the experiment in political cooperation and the effort to forge a common foreign policy. This has the effect of tying the Community to its slowest partner. In many West European states, ruling parties find themselves governing with declining mandates, which translates into diminished room for parliamentary maneuver and less willingness among party leaders to use scant political capital for non-essential priorities. In Britain, for example, the agency charged with carrying out the CWC ratification process is the Ministry of Trade and Industry that, under a weak Conservative Party government, has an agenda on domestic reform quite remote from the disarmament agenda. In Germany, federal elections threaten to delay and defer the ratification process. Nowhere in Europe does the CWC appear deeply unpopular. But the implementing legislation is certain to touch on the interests of broad sections of industry and on property rights, and thus may move less smoothly.

In a more basic sense in Europe, chemical disarmament appears to have lost some of its importance for political leaders with the passing of the Cold War. In years past, the CWC would have generated intense support in the general fervor for arms control and as a tool for managing the Soviet threat. Today, its benefits for international security are less immediate and less likely to generate deep support in industrially developed and generally peaceful societies.

Elsewhere in the world, prospects for CWC ratification will be driven largely by regional security perceptions. It appears unlikely that all states in the Middle East will be party to the treaty upon its entry into force (Egypt and Syria probably will not; Saudi Arabia, some other Arab states, and Israel probably will), as the chemical weapons issue has grown increasingly intertwined with the regional security and peace dynamic. In South Asia, both India and Pakistan have signed the treaty but here too regional diplomacy may determine the timing of such accession as the chemical issue is considered in the larger context of evolving security relations. Elsewhere, many states are likely to await the outcome of events in Washington and Moscow, not wanting to be party to a convention that offers no prospect of bringing effective disarmament.

6.   Future Scenarios

In late 1993, only four countries have deposited instruments of ratification, of which Sweden is the most prominent. The first half of 1994 will witness either a flood of new ratifications or continued logjam. Looking to the future, there are three basic possibilities.

6.1   Entry Into Force On Target

Everything may indeed work as planned with the 65 state-threshold being crossed in mid-1994, with Russia and the United States and the other developed countries among those 65, and with entry into force on target in January 1995.

If this happens, states that have only begun to think about their national obligations to implement the treaty will have to move quickly to put programs in place. The fact that so few states have worked through, at the bureaucratic level, the implications of implementation points to the likelihood of a bumpy first year as incomplete or inaccurate declarations are filed and discovered, as destruction programs are rushed into work, and as the OPCW begins to function.

The odds in favor of this first scenario are of less than 50/50 and, in late 1993, are declining.

6.2   Delay Into 1995

This assumes that there will be no flood of ratifications in early 1994 but that matters will come together well enough to permit most of the important states to deposit instruments of ratification during 1994, delaying entry into force until mid-1995.

Such a delay might not pose much of a problem and might actually be useful in providing the time to put together implementation programs. But there are a number of wildcards deriving from the uncertain politics of national elections in many key states and the 1995 review conferences for the Nuclear Non-Proliferation Treaty and, probably, for the Biological and Toxin Weapons Convention. Failure in one or both of those conferences could have serious negative consequences for the CWC.

The odds of this second scenario are better than 50/50, and increasing.

A less likely variation on this theme is that the other states parties will proceed with ratification and entry into force without US and Russian participation. This is a legal possibility but politically unlikely. One result of such an outcome would be to shift the focus of the treaty from disarmament of the chemical weapons powers to the monitoring of chemical industries. This is a shift that would generate a political backlash.

6.3 Delay Beyond 1995

If the CWC does not enter into force at all in 1995, its momentum will have dissipated significantly, raising doubts about its future viability. The CD negotiations were given a major fillip by perestroika in the Soviet Union, George Bush's election as US president, and the Persian Gulf War. These events energized the process, but they have also receded quickly from the scene, having been supplanted by a more crisis-oriented international agenda, leaders more focused on domestic issues, and by an accelerating diffusion of power and authority internationally. The work of the PrepCom having been completed, the cadre of chemical disarmament experts would be shifted to assignments more productive than sitting idly in a headquarters building in The Hague while their foreign ministry bosses lobby national decisionmakers at home.

The odds of this scenario are small. But the outcome is by no means impossible. Russia is in a time of deep turmoil. Europe appears gripped by ennui. The United States is tepid in its international engagements. New challengers to the global status quo are appearing on the world scene, some of them emboldened by their possession of weapons of mass destruction.

The longer the delay, the larger the consequences. Any significant delay would begin to raise larger questions about the capacity of the international community to formulate and implement a cooperative security agenda transcending traditional East-West and North-South divides and about the will and capacity of the nations that took an active role in negotiating this regime to articulate a security agenda for the post-cold war world. Failure to implement the treaty in timely fashion would arise from -- and reflect -- a Russia tending toward anarchy, a Europe devoid of leadership, a United States increasingly isolationist in outlook, and aggressive new hegemons in regions in conflict. In this sense, the fate of the CWC is both hostage to -- and a measure of -- the historical watershed of the 1990s. The arms control framework crafted with such care and energy in the Cold War may not survive the emergence of a more fluid international environment.

7. Conclusion

Timely entry into force of the chemical disarmament regime will not result only from the skillful work of diplomats currently toiling in The Hague to build the new OPCW. Policymakers in national capitals must take on their important tasks if the CWC is to realize the ambitions of those who created it. These include prompt ratification of the treaty, creation of national authorities to oversee national implementation, work with industry to prepare early declarations and subsequent monitoring, diplomatic pressure on hold-out countries, and engagement with Russia.

This work should prove cathartic to diplomats, parliamentarians, arms controllers, and senior policymakers. After all, they grew up on the Cold War. By confronting the political realities of chemical weapons proliferation and control, they will be compelled to grapple with the realities of the new era: the salience of multilateral over bilateral or unilateral measures, the essentiality of consensual responses to the proliferation of militarily-relevant technologies, the importance of the views of states in the developing world on the global security agenda, and the sense of drift in Western capitals about national purpose and interest. Above all, the effort will help to bring into focus the stakes involved in the first post-cold war decade when successful cooperative measures will bring new security, or their failure will bring new conflicts.

The widespread disinterest in the CWC in 1993 is not surprising given the dramatic events and important political changes around the world. Being outside of the spotlight has in fact facilitated the work of diplomats in The Hague, who have needed to come to grips with a pragmatic agenda and to create new ways of working together. But if the pattern continues in 1994, we can be certain that deteriorating circumstances will thrust the issue center-stage at a later, more difficult time.

Chapter 16

CHEMICAL WEAPONS CONVENTION: THE COSTS OF CONFIDENCE

Barbara A. B. Seiders

Negotiations toward a treaty banning chemical weapons began in August 1968 when the issue was first placed on the agenda of the Conference of the Committee on Disarmament in Geneva. Those negotiations were concluded nearly 25 years later when the Chemical Weapons Convention (CWC) was signed in Paris on January 13, 1993. The CW negotiations began in an era in which arms control was viewed more as a risk to national security than as a contribution. In the intervening 25 years, other agreements were concluded [e.g., Intermediate Nuclear Forces Treaty (INF), nuclear testing verification protocols, Strategic Arms Reduction Treaty (START), Conventional Forces in Europe Treaty (CFE), etc.) Relative to arms control treaties of the earlier era, these agreements reflected an evolutionary trend toward greater intrusiveness, higher degrees of verifiability, greater technical detail and specificity in implementation provisions. Concurrent with this evolutionary process was the increasing recognition of arms control as a rational constituent of prudent national security policymaking. In addition, the arms control process took on value as a means to define norms of acceptable behavior in the security relations among nations.

The Chemical Weapons Convention, which is expected to enter into force in January 1995, departs from a trend of stringently verifiable control arms agreements and constitutes more a tool of confidence building and a tool for measuring unacceptable behavior in development and production of chemical weapons. Whatever confidence the CWC might provide is purchased at cost, a cost which the United States has weighed and has determined to pay.

1. Intrusiveness Vs. Constitutional Right To Privacy

In evaluating the inspection provisions for the Convention, the unprecedented degree of intrusiveness to be imposed on the chemical industry was justified in part within the US on the basis of that industry being a "heavily regulated industry." Such a "heavily regulated industry," already subject to government licensing, might have a lessened expectation of privacy.[1] Within the United States, it was expected that CWC reporting requirements could be met by existing requirements of the regulatory agencies with oversight of the chemical industry. Following a thorough review of existing reporting requirements, the Arms Control and Disarmament Agency (ACDA) determined that the nature and scope of information required was not already available by way of other regulatory mechanisms. In all likelihood, to preclude the possibility of a conflict between the exercise of Constitutional protections and international treaty, the US Congress will be obliged to impose, as an element of implementing legislation, a body of fundamentally new -- and undoubtedly heavy -- regulation on the US chemical industry to ensure compliance with the Convention. In their briefing to the chemical industry, ACDA made clear the following:

-- "there will be new regulatory requirements for much of the chemical industry";
-- in declarations and reporting, there will be "unprecedented coverage of specific chemicals and associated facilities"; and
-- the Convention requires "reporting from companies that do no reporting
now" of "details not required by existing regulations," and "compliance in a
very short timeframe."

The chemical industry will likely pay a double cost: they will be subjected to highly intrusive inspections erroneously justified on the basis of "heavy regulation," as well as suffer additional, unprecedented regulatory burden.

In addition to examining the feasibility of obtaining relief from the Fourth Amendment's constitutional protections of industry by exerting the argument of lessened expectation of privacy of a pervasively regulated industry, legal experts have identified other means of ensuring that the US not be in a position of potential treaty violation over the legitimate exercise of Fourth Amendment protections. Many of the possibilities proposed proceed from the basis that the Convention is "essential to our national security," and that it is therefore "imperative that Congress take steps to prevent the pursuit of [protection of constitutional rights] from interfering with enforcement of the Convention except for clear and bright-line transgressions of the Fourth Amendment."[2]

A particular example is the recommendation of prohibiting facility owners from seeking injunctive relief from a warrantless inspection under the Convention, where injunctive relief is acknowledged as "an accepted remedy to protect constitutional rights." If the CWC is truly essential to US national security interests, such efforts to set aside constitutional rights and protections might be warranted. If the Convention provides only marginal potential benefit to our national security undermining those rights and protections would be to sell short those principles that have so well stood the test of time.

2.   Openness Vs. Compromise Of Confidential Business Information

In his tenure as Director of ACDA, Ambassador Ronald F. Lehman frequently sought to level the playing field among international treaty parties by bringing other states through arms control treaty to conditions already existing within the US. Openness, inherently stabilizing, was a favorite focus. Lehman sought to develop arms control proposals which would provide the United States with a degree of access to the territories and societies of other states equivalent to the access that those states already had in the United States.

The Lehman approach was well founded. This approach had also been tested in court. In a suit brought by Dow Chemical against the Environmental Protection Agency over whether the outdoor portion of a Dow plant site was entitled to Fourth Amendment protection from government surveillance, the court ruled against Dow, citing "what is observable by the public is observable without a warrant by a Government inspector as well."[3]

As proposals for inspections extend beyond current US practices, however, the value of additional openness contributing to US security is counterbalanced by the increased potential for infringement on right to privacy on the part of US industry, and loss of protection of confidential business information. Quoting Olson,[4] Carnahan notes

> In the chemical industry, the loss of trade secrets 'can cripple even a giant company, and can be fatal to a smaller enterprise;' under the convention, there may well be a 'multimillion dollar price tag attached to potential trade secret losses.'[5]

Increased openness is a worthy objective for enhancing national security, and the chemical industry is to be applauded for their support of the efforts of government to magnify security by way of the Convention. In evaluating the balance between the opposing principles of openness and privacy in the elaboration of arms control provisions, industry (or society at large) should not be asked to suffer the risk unless the advantage to national security is commensurate with the potential cost.

3. Agreement In Principle Vs. Agreement In Detail

The Intermediate Nuclear Forces Treaty, the Strategic Arms Reduction Treaty, the verification protocols to the Threshold Test Ban Treaty (TTBT), and the Peaceful Nuclear Explosions Treaty (PNET) were negotiated to exquisite detail. In every case, US negotiating teams first secured agreement on the right to obtain verification information, and then proceeded to secure agreement on the detailed means by which that information would be obtained.

For example, in the TTBT verification protocol, both Soviet and American negotiating teams knew basically (at least in scientific terms) what constituted the "hydrodynamic yield measurement zone," what its role was in yield verification, and why its precise definition was necessary as an element of the protocol. Furthermore, both sides were motivated to conclude the verification protocol. Nonetheless, agreement on the definition of the hydrodynamic yield measurement zone, as well as "standard" and "nonstandard" test configurations, took months of discussions at the negotiating table.

Despite the extraordinary level of detail agreed in these treaties, issues of interpretation and compliance (some of them significant) have still arisen between the parties, to be resolved in joint compliance and implementation bodies.

In the Chemical Weapons Convention, the provisions "in conducting perimeter activities, the inspection team shall have the right to use monitoring instruments; take wipes, air, soil, or effluent samples; and conduct any additional activities which may be agreed between the inspection team and the party."[6]

None of the details implied in the above provision are further elaborated: what type of monitoring instruments there are, how those instruments are to be used, what type of "additional activities" are envisioned. This is representative of the Convention overall: negotiators succeeded in obtaining agreement in principle, but not in detail. Elaboration of the necessary detail has been left to the Preparatory Commission,to be completed before the CWC entry into force, which is anticipated in 1995. Furthermore, the critical requirements for verification of the obligations of the Convention may ultimately be left to negotiations between inspection team leaders and the challenged party at the time of inspection. These discussions will take place under tremendous pressure of time and political expediency. The complexity of the CWC, both in the scope of its provisions and the diversity of its signatories, lacks a badly wrought compromise between the negotiability of the detailed provisions and the soundness of their contribution to the effective verification of the treaty's obligations.

4.   Effect On Civilian And Defense Industry

Nuclear weapons, delivery systems, and the other military services are federal assets, the equity of society at large. Arms control treaties, undertaken on behalf of a society, constitute management of those federal assets. Examples of treaties that constitute legitimate management of federal assets on behalf of a society include INF and START. The objective of these treaties is the elimination of elements of the nuclear stockpiles of the US and its key adversary. While their implementation will negatively affect some sectors of private industry, the sectors affected are overwhelmingly associated with the maintenance of these federal assets.

The CWC is very different in that it imposes unprecedented federal management of private assets in the interest of national security. In addition, management of these private assets will be not only federal but international as well. Weighing the balance, governments sacrifice degrees of sovereignty in the name of enhanced security from arms control. The cost of that sacrifice of sovereignty is solemnly borne as loss of freedom by society.

The preponderance of private assets covered by the provisions of the CWC, described previously, are understood to have no involvement in war fighting preparations. International oversight of activities not prohibited by the treaty, as a means to enforce prohibitions of the treaty, is a peculiar method of enforcement under international law.

A variation on this theme, controlling prohibited arms by regulation of what is not prohibited, is proposed in the implementation of Resolution 687 on Iraq. Under this resolution, some attention has been given to tagging conventional weapons (not restricted under Resolution 687) as a way to verify that they are not prohibited nuclear, chemical, or biological weapons. This is a questionable approach which is justified in the aftermath of unprovoked aggression by Saddam Hussein. Action taken under this resolution needs to be scrutinized as a general principle of arms control.

5.   Sovereignty Vs. Legitimized International Coercion

One aspect of the CWC is the imposition of trade sanctions against nonparticipants. This requirement will limit chemical trade. These sanctions are to be applied independent of whether the country is believed to aspire to chemical weapons possession. The provision of sanctions is a responsive approach which could be especially helpful in controlling acknowledged miscreants; however, it is also a form of internationally legitimized coercion exercised against states which have no intention of manufacturing chemical weapons. This provision of the CWC is contrary to the spirit of American jurisprudence of a presumption of innocence until proven guilty.

6.   Cost Of National Implementation

Whether or not the US chemical industry will suffer heavier regulation as a result of the implementation of the CWC, it is evident that the US economy has sufficient flexibility and robustness to accommodate the additional requirements. The over-and-above reporting burden will tax individual chemical companies, but it certainly will not threaten the overall industry. The regulatory environment in which many US companies operate was established over a period of years, allowing the infrastructure to be well established without undue stress on the industry at any one time. However, the industrial sectors of many developing countries have neither the extensive existing regulatory infrastructure nor the economic flexibility or robustness which developing countries possess. Absent also are the many industry regulatory functions which will be necessary to ensure national compliance.

A tenuous economy and the absence of regulatory infrastructure may result in two types of costs. First is the direct cost to the country associated with national implementation in order to comply with the CWC. If a country cannot meet this cost, it will likely pay a political cost associated with losing face. The second type is the cost of asymmetrical compliance that accrues to those who do comply. In both cases, confidence in the objectives of the Convention may be undermined, and not strengthened.

7.   Conclusions

In signing the Chemical Weapons Convention, the US weighed the numerous compromises presented and what follows are the detrimental effects:

-- imposition on industry of highly intrusive inspections which could jeopardize confidential business information;
-- imposition on industry of additional and unprecedented regulatory reporting burdens;
-- the comprising of protections under the Constitution for the sake of a treaty whose contribution to national security may be marginal at best;
-- implementation of treaty provisions which have been formulated with undue haste or left to on-site inspection negotiations;
-- the exercise of international oversight on a significant sector of private assets with the loss by degree of sovereignty by the nation and of freedom by society;
-- the imposition of verification provisions on an industry the overwhelming preponderance of which is recognized to be innocent of the prohibited activities that are the object of the Convention;
-- the acceptance of coercion by sanctions, directed at the innocent as well as those presumed guilty, as a legitimate tool of international relations;
-- the cost of asymmetrical compliance and commensurate loss of confidence in the regime if states are unable to afford the national measures to ensure implementation of the provisions of the Convention; and
-- the direct cost to parties to establish national implementation mechanisms, or loss of face in the failure to do so.

On balance, the United States has determined that these and other detriments outweighed the benefits of the CWC. As the US continues to seek new means to establish enhanced security relations through arms control and confidence building, it should also remember that the benefits that might accrue from such arrangements came with some cost. The compromises necessary for the conclusion of such agreements can be costly not just in terms of resources, but also in terms of fundamental principles. Given the potential stakes, in each instance, the US must be cautious in weighing perceived benefits against costs that can be both extraordinary and subtle. Washington must be especially vigilant that marginal benefits are not purchased at the detriment of undermining the enduring principles of this nation which will carry this country -- and the world -- into the new century.

Notes

1. B.M. Carnahan, "Chemical Arms Control, Trade Secrets, and the Constitution: Facing the Unresolved Issues," *International Lawyer*, Spring 1991, pp. 167-186; E.A. Tanzman and B. Kellman, "Legal Implications of the Multilateral Chemical Weapons Convention: Integrating International Security with the Constitution," *New York University Journal of International Law and Politics*, (1990), Vol. 22, Nr. 3, p. 475; E.A. Tanzman, "Constitutionality of Warrantless On-Site Arms Control Inspection in the United States," *Yale Journal of International Law*, (1988), Vol. 13, Nr.1, p. 21.
2. E.A. Tanzman and B. Kellman, *op. cit.*
3. K. Olson, "The U.S. Chemical Industry Can Live With a Chemical Weapons Convention," *Arms Control Today*, Vol. 21 (November 1989).
4. Ibid.
5. B.M. Carnahan, *op. cit.*, pp. 167-186.
6. Article 36, Annex 2 of the Draft Convention on the Prohibition of the Development, Production, Stockpiling and Use of Chemical Weapons and On Their Destruction.

Chapter 17

THE NEGOTIATIONS ON AND THE IMPLEMENTATION OF THE CHEMICAL WEAPONS CONVENTION - POLITICAL AND ECONOMIC CONSIDERATIONS

Sten Lundbo

As the sole negotiating forum for global disarmament questions, the Geneva disarmament conference was responsible for elaborating a comprehensive prohibition on chemical weapons. Chemical weapons were placed on the agenda of the conference in 1969, but it was not until 23 years later that the Conference on Disarmament (CD) finalized this task.

This happened on 3 September 1992 when the Conference on Disarmament adopted the report of its *ad hoc* Committee on Chemical Weapons containing the text of the Convention on the Prohibition of the Development, Production, Stockpiling and Use of Chemical Weapons and on Their Destruction (hereafter referred to as the Chemical Weapons Convention or CWC).

On 30 November 1992 the 47th Session of the United Nations General Assembly adopted without a vote Resolution 47/39, which commended the Convention and called upon all States to sign and become parties to the Convention at the earliest possible date. It further called upon all States to ensure effective implementation of what was described as "this unprecedented, global, comprehensive and verifiable multilateral disarmament agreement."[1] The draft resolution had a record number of co-sponsors.

1. A Result Of Truly Multilateral Negotiations

This was the first disarmament treaty which the Geneva Conference on Disarmament had finalized since it elaborated the Convention on the Prohibition of the Development, Production and Stockpiling of Bacteriological (Biological) and Toxin Weapons and on Their Destruction, hereafter referred to as the Biological and Toxin Weapons Convention in 1971 (BWC). The Chemical Weapons Convention was, however, much more the result of a truly multilateral process than the Biological and Toxin Weapons Convention.

The latter convention was finalized when the co-chairmen of the Conference of the Committee on Disarmament -- the United States and the Soviet Union -- drew up an agreed draft in 1971 and subsequently submitted separate but identical texts to the Conference.[2]

In the 1970s the Soviet Union and the United States conducted bilateral negotiations on chemical weapons; thus in 1974 the two countries announced to the CD that they had agreed in principle to consider a joint initiative with respect to the conclusion of an international convention dealing with the most dangerous lethal means of chemical warfare. The Soviet Union and the United States held a total of 12 bilateral negotiating sessions between 1974 and 1980 and submitted two joint reports to the Conference on the progress of their negotiations in 1980.[3]

The new series of bilateral talks which began after the US-Soviet summit in Geneva in November 1985 served as a problem-solving exercise with a view toward speeding up the negotiations in the Conference on Disarmament. They were not intended to replace the multilateral negotiations. This change in the nature of the bilateral talks from the 1970s to the 1980s confirmed that the CD was responsible for pursuing the negotiations on the finalization of the Chemical Weapons Convention.[4]

Nevertheless, the bilateral talks held by the United States and the Soviet Union on chemical weapons between the Geneva Summit in 1985 and the completion of text of the CWC in 1992 had a positive effect on the progress of the work of the Conference on Disarmament.

The Conference established a separate subsidiary body for chemical weapons in 1980. Four years later, this body was given a full negotiating mandate; however, the mandate did not authorize the Committee on Chemical Weapons to undertake the final drafting of the Convention. The Committee was not given this authority until 1990.

The First Special Session devoted to Disarmament, which was held in New York from 23 May to 30 June 1978, decided to abandon the co-chairmanship of the Conference on Disarmament and to introduce a system whereby the chairmanship is rotated among all the members on a monthly basis.[5] In this way, all members of the Conference acquired a more direct responsibility for the negotiations.

In 1982 seven countries participated as observers in the negotiations. This number rose considerably during the 1980s, and in 1992 when the negotiations were completed, a total of 46 states were observers in the Committee on Chemical Weapons. Some of these countries made substantial contributions to the work of the Conference.

2. A Long History Of Negotiations

At the International Peace Conference which met at The Hague in 1899, declarations were signed prohibiting the use of dumdum bullets and asphyxiating gases, and the launching of projectiles and explosives from balloons or by other new methods of similar nature. The use of poison or poisoned weapons was prohibited by regulations annexed to conventions adopted at the 1899 and 1907 International Peace Conferences. Nevertheless, chemical weapons were used extensively during the First World War. It subsequently became evident that it was necessary to arrive at a global prohibition on chemical weapons.

The Protocol for the Prohibition of the Use in War of Asphyxiating, Poisonous or Other Gases, and of Bacteriological Methods of Warfare (The Geneva Protocol), which was signed at Geneva on 17 June 1925 and entered into force on 8 February 1928, was a step in this direction. A disarmament conference was held in Geneva in 1932-33 to discuss proposals to extend the Geneva Protocol in various ways, including a total prohibition on chemical weapons; however, the conference was not successful.

The importance of negotiating a comprehensive global prohibition against chemical weapons was stressed in the Biological and Toxin Weapons Convention. The preamble of the Convention states that it represents a first possible step towards the achievement of agreement on effective measures and also for the production of the development and stockpiling of chemical weapons and that the States Parties are determined to continue negotiations to that end. In Article IX of the Convention, each State Party affirms the recognized objective of effective prohibition of chemical weapons and, to this end, undertakes to continue negotiations in good faith with a view toward reaching early agreement on *inter alia* effective measures for the prohibition of their development, production and stockpiling and for their destruction.

In paragraph 75 of the Final Document of the First Special Session devoted to Disarmament in 1978, it was stated that the complete and effective prohibition of the development, production and stockpiling of all chemical weapons and their destruction represents one of the most urgent measures of disarmament. The document further stressed that the conclusion of a convention to this end (on which negotiations had been going on for several years) was one of the most urgent tasks of these multilateral negotiations.

Every year since the First Special Session devoted to Disarmament in 1978 and until 1991, the United Nations General Assembly adopted resolutions urging the Conference on Disarmament, as a matter of high priority, to finalize this task.

3.   The Importance Of The Chemical Weapons Convention

The Convention is so important both because it prohibits an entire category of weapons of mass destruction and because it contains novel and more comprehensive verification mechanisms than any previous multilateral disarmament treaty.

The Convention will therefore, without any doubt, enhance the prestige of the Conference on Disarmament. This is reflected in the fact that the CD will commence negotiations on a comprehensive nuclear test ban treaty in 1994. The decision on this was made on 10 August 1993 when the Conference's *ad hoc* Committee on a Nuclear Test Ban was given this mandate.

The Chemical Weapons Convention is also important because for the first time China took part in negotiations on a multilateral disarmament treaty. The First Special Session devoted to Disarmament decided that the Committee on Disarmament was to be open to the nuclear-weapon States and 32 to 35 other States to be chosen in consultation with the President of the 32nd Session of the UN General Assembly.[6] After that session, France, which had not participated in the Geneva negotiating forum for some eighteen years took its seat. In addition, China joined for the first time. Thus, all the five permanent members of the United Nations Security Council took part in the Conference on Disarmament from 1979 onwards.

4.   The Verification Dilemma

The negotiators in Geneva agreed that the CWC would require stringent verification provisions. However, it was generally assumed that it was impossible to elaborate a verification regime which was 100% foolproof.

An important first step was made in April 1984 when the Vice President of the United States, George Bush, introduced a comprehensive draft treaty which included the concept of short-notice mandatory challenge inspections, to be conducted by international inspectors at a State Party's request of another Party. Nevertheless, the negotiations on the challenge mechanism were stalled until August 1987 when the Soviets agreed in principle to such inspection. This change in the Soviet position came after the Soviet Union declared for the first time that it possessed stocks of chemical weapons.

The final result of the negotiations on challenge inspection was that such inspections would be conducted in the least intrusive manner possible, consistent with the effective and timely accomplishment of the inspectors' mission. The inspected State Party thus has the right to take the measures necessary to protect national security. This is known as managed access.

At the same time, the suspected party must undertake all reasonable efforts to satisfy the compliance concern and cooperate with the inspectors. Access to the requested site must be granted, but may be managed (i.e., restricted to some degree). The regime effectively balances the need for access with the need to protect national interests.

The concept of managed access was first launched in public by Ambassador Lynn M. Hansen of the United States at the Holmenkollen Symposium on the Chemical Weapons Convention, held in Oslo on 26-27 May 1987.[7] Challenge procedures of the type included in the CWC had never before formed part of a global disarmament treaty.

The finalization of the verification system was the most difficult issue in the negotiations of the CD. In fact, the problem of challenge inspections seemed at times to be insurmountable; however, it was essential to resolve the issue satisfactorily because challenge inspections were considered to be the ultimate safety net of the Convention.

5. The Effects On The Negotiations Of The Use And Proliferation Of Chemical Weapons

The identity of the chemically-armed states is not a matter of public record.[8] Nevertheless, R. James Woolsey, Director of the Central Intelligence Agency, stated in a testimony on 28 July 1993 before a subcommittee of the US House Foreign Affairs Committee that more than two dozen countries run research or development programs for chemical weapons, and a number, including Libya, Iran and Iraq, have stockpiled such weapons. The volatile political situation in the Middle East had also encouraged other countries in the region to acquire chemical weapons.[9]

The use of chemical weapons during the Iran-Iraq war in the 1980s made it clear that it was essential to include a prohibition on the use of such weapons in the Chemical Weapons Convention. This was necessary for at least two reasons: the 1925 Protocol contained no verification provisions, and 25 signatories of the Protocol reserved the right to use chemical weapons if others used them first. The scope of the Geneva Protocol is therefore limited. In fact, the Protocol is only binding between parties and only in wartime.

The fact that a number of chemical weapons states have sought to acquire ballistic missiles capable of carrying chemical weapons further underlined the necessity of concluding the Chemical Weapons Convention without delay. To counteract this development, the Partners of the Missile Technology Control Regime (MTCR) decided at their plenary meeting in Oslo in July 1992 to amend the Regime's Guidelines of Sensitive Missile-relevant Transfers so that the scope of this Regime was extended to include missiles capable of delivering all kinds of weapons of mass destruction (WMD).[10] The use of chemical weapons during the Iran - Iraq war also acted as an incentive to the negotiators to conclude the work on the new Convention as soon as possible.

In the Final Declaration of the Conference, the participating States solemnly affirmed their commitment not to use chemical weapons and condemned the use of such weapons. At the same time they called on the Conference on Disarmament to redouble its efforts, as a matter of urgency, to resolve expeditiously the remaining issues and to conclude the Convention at the earliest date.[11]

In July 1987 Canada and Norway tabled a document containing a proposal for an annex to Article IX concerning verification of the alleged use of chemical weapons. The annex described general procedures for such verification.[12] This proposal is reflected in the Convention's annex on implementation and verification, part XI of which concerns investigations of cases of alleged use of chemical weapons.

6. Adherence to the Convention

The Convention will enter into force 180 days after the date of the deposit of the 65th instrument of ratification, but in no case earlier than two years after it was opened for signature. However, complete elimination of chemical weapons from the world can only be achieved by universal adherence to and implementation of the CWC.

Preparations for the implementation of the Convention have started both in many of the countries which have signed or ratified the Convention and internationally in the Preparatory Commission for the Organization for the Prohibition of Chemical Weapons (OPCW) in The Hague.

At the Conference held in Paris on 13-14 January 1993, 130 states signed the CWC. As of the end of 1993, there were only 37 countries which had not signed or ratified the Convention. These included Libya and Sudan as well as Egypt, Iraq, Jordan and Syria in the Middle East. This reflects the linkage which several Arab countries perceive between chemical and nuclear disarmament; thus, the 98th session of the Council of the Arab League on 13 September 1992 agreed on a resolution regarding weapons of mass destruction. In the third operative paragraph of the resolution, the members of the Arab League were ready to deal with the Chemical Weapons Convention if it is considered in the context of efforts to establish a zone free of weapons of mass destruction in the Middle East, and depending on Israel's response to international demands to join the Non-Proliferation Treaty and to subject its nuclear facilities to the international safeguards system in accordance with Security Council Resolution No. 487 of 1981.

In their statements in the First Committee of the 47th session of the United Nations General Assembly, representatives of several Arab states referred to the linkage between chemical and nuclear disarmament. Thus, Abu Odeh of Jordan stated in the First Committee on 28 October 1992 that Jordan considered that "handling chemical weapons in isolation from all weapons of mass destruction, especially nuclear weapons, is insufficient."[13] Egypt's representative, Zahran, stated on the same day that Egypt does not believe in dealing with this Convention in isolation from other international efforts relating to other weapons of mass destruction, especially the Non-Proliferation Treaty, the safeguards and international inspections regime and the provision of credible international guarantees, in addition to the prohibition of biological weapons.[14]

7. The Chemical Industry

For the first time, a very large industrial sector will be involved in the implementation of a global disarmament treaty. In fact, many facilities in the chemical industry will be subject to monitoring in perpetuity through declarations and on-site inspections. This burden will not be as heavy as might be expected, because the industry is probably one of the most strictly regulated industries in the world.

In an article entitled "Economic Incidences of a Convention on the Elimination of Chemical Weapons," Herbert Beck argues:

> The costs for the chemical industry can be estimated to be rather low. The labour costs in an enterprise as large as BASF will not exceed two fully employed clerks plus staff. The effects on the profitability ... should be small if at all traceable. The cost factor should be inversely proportional with the size of the company, i.e., smaller factories will be charged relatively more than larger ones. On the other hand it seems plausible that in general a smaller-sized factory will have a smaller variety of products and will therefore be controlled less.[15]

The chemical industry's understanding of the necessity for such stringent verification resulted to a large extent from the Government-Industry Conference against Chemical Weapons, held in Canberra, Australia in September 1989. The conference brought together 375 delegates from 67 countries, including both government officials and industry and trade union representatives.[16] The conference provided the chemical industry with a better understanding of the negotiations then in progress in Geneva.

The provisions of the Convention ensure that an inspection is carried out without impairing production or processing, and without impeding the economic and technological development of the States Parties. Thousands of installations around the world will have to be monitored to ensure compliance with the global prohibition.

Chemicals are divided into three categories for monitoring purposes, according to the risk which they are perceived to pose within the objectives of the Convention: high risk chemicals are in schedule 1, significant risk chemicals in schedule 2, and risk chemicals in schedule 3. Other chemical facilities having the capability of producing scheduled chemicals will also be monitored.

The verification system includes routine inspections and challenge inspections, which are designed to prevent the clandestine production of chemical weapons. The international chemical industry will feel the effect of implementation of the verification activities. This is necessary because the chemicals used in the industry can also be used as chemical weapons precursors. Verification of non-production of chemical weapons by the civilian chemical industry is therefore an important aspect of the implementation of the CWC.

Special precautionary measures have been agreed upon to protect confidential business information. In accordance with the provisions of the Chemical Convention, every precaution shall be taken to protect the confidentiality of information on civilian and military activities and facilities which is obtained during the implementation of the Convention. Specific provisions are set out in the Convention's Annex on the Protection of Confidential Information ("The Confidentiality Annex").

7.1   Destruction Of Stocks Of Chemical Weapons

The US has eight stockpile sites in the continental United States and one on a Pacific atoll (Johnston Island). The storage sites in the continental US are located at

Tooele, Pine Bluff, Umatilla, Pueblo, Anniston, Aberdeen, Newport, and Lexington. The United States plans to have destruction facilities at each of these locations. More than 40 per cent of the US stockpile is located at the Tooele Army Depot and will be destroyed over a period of five years.[17]

At present, there is one destruction facility on Johnston Atoll and one at the Tooele Army Depot. The Johnston Atoll facility, which is designed for the incineration of mustard and nerve agents, was built at a cost of approximately $260 million.[18] The incineration process to be used at the Tooele facility costs about 10 times more to destroy chemical weapons than it did to produce them.[19] The Tooele Army Depot facilities is scheduled to begin normal operations in 1995.[20] The cost of destroying the US stock is estimated at $7.5 billion. There is, however, uncertainty attached to this figure.[21] Furthermore, the parties to the CWC have 10 years to destroy stocks of chemical weapons, but a party may be granted a five-year extension if that is essential for technical reasons. A number of states have chemical weapon stocks, but of those declared, only the United States has the financial and technological capability to undertake an effective destruction process.

Russia has declared about 40,000 tons of chemical weapons stockpiled at seven sites. In October 1987, the Soviet Union presented information on standard chemical munitions and the technology for the destruction of chemical weapons at a mobile unit at the Shikhany military facility.[22] In addition, a plan to build facilities to destroy up to 45 percent of the total Russian stockpile at three of the seven sites was submitted to Russia's parliament for approval. The three destruction facilities were proposed for Kambarka, Cheboksary and Gormy.[23] This plan is now being revised.

The destruction of existing stocks in a safe and environmentally sound manner is a major challenge. Various problems may arise in this context: for example, a destruction facility in Chapayevsk, near the Volga river, was to have been made operational, but these plans were canceled because of protests by the local population.

Both the destruction of chemical weapons production facilities and their conversion in accordance with the provisions of the Convention may cause environmental problems. The United States and the former Soviet Union signed an Agreement on Destruction and Non-Production of Chemical Weapons on 1 June 1990. According to this agreement, the two countries undertake to destroy most of their chemical weapons and to cooperate with regard to methods and technologies for the safe and efficient destruction of chemical weapons. Each party also will assign the highest priority to human safety and environmental protection during the destruction phase. One of the main features of this agreement is the development and use of safe and environmentally sound methods of destruction.

In a joint statement on chemical weapons on 17 June 1992, Presidents George Bush and Boris Yeltsin agreed that this agreement would be updated and entered into force promptly. They also signed the "agreement on the safe and secure transportation, storage and destruction of weapons and the prevention of weapons proliferation." According to Article 1 of this agreement, the Parties shall cooperate to assist the Russian Federation to achieve the following objectives:

-- the destruction of, *inter alia*, chemical weapons; and
-- the safe and secure transportation and storage of such weapons in connection with their destruction.

The United States has so far allocated $25 million under the terms of this agreement, which will be used towards planning for the overall Russian destruction program.[24] Additional assistance is under discussion.

This agreement has been followed up by an agreement signed in Washington, DC between the US Department of Defense and the Russian President's Committee on Conventional Problems of Chemical and Biological Weapons concerning the Safe, Secure and Ecologically Sound Destruction of Chemical Weapons. According to this agreement, the Department of Defense shall provide assistance in the destruction of chemical weapons at no cost to its Russian partner. This agreement must be seen in the light of the fact that Russia cannot destroy its chemical stocks without outside assistance.

All of these agreements are important because they provide for cooperation and sharing of practical experience in the transport and destruction of chemical weapons, between the two states with the largest stocks of chemical weapons and with other chemical weapons states. This will help to reduce the total costs of destruction and to make the process as safe as possible.

As well as chemical stocks, the CWC requires that the chemical weapons production facilities must also be destroyed. The United States has five such facilities, and the cost of their destruction will be considerable.

8. The Organization For The Prohibition Of Chemical Weapons (OPCW) And Its Preparatory Commission

The Provisional Technical Secretariat of the Preparatory Commission for the Organization for the Prohibition of Chemical Weapons (OPCW) started its work in February 1993. The OPCW will be established when the Convention enters into force, which can come about as early as January 1995.

The task of the OPCW will be to achieve the objectives and purpose of the CWC, to ensure the implementation of its provisions, including those concerning international verification of compliance, and to provide a forum for consultation and cooperation among States Parties. The headquarters of the OPCW is at The Hague.

The Organization consists of the Conference of the States Parties, the Executive Council, and the Technical Secretariat.

The Secretariat of the OPCW, which currently is being established in The Hague, will from the outset be a more global organization than the corresponding forum in the nuclear field, the International Atomic Energy Agency in Vienna. The latter was established in 1957 with 56 members. In 1968 its membership had increased to 96 and is now 113.[25]

By the end of 1993 the Provisional Technical Secretariat will already have about 60 staff members.[26] The nationalities of those occupying leading positions in the Provisional Technical Secretariat reflect the fact that most countries throughout the world have already signed the Chemical Weapons Convention: the Executive Secretary is from the United Kingdom, the Deputy Executive Secretary from China, the Head of the Verification Division from Australia, the Head of Technical Cooperation and Assistance from Zimbabwe, the Head of the Legal Affairs Division from Peru, the Head of the Administration Division from the United States, and the Head of the External Relations Divisions from the Russian Federation. The OPCW is also the first disarmament organization in which all five permanent members of the UN Security Council have participated from its establishment.

The operation of the OPCW will be expensive; thus the estimated cost of the Preparatory Commission for the calendar year 1993 is $8.8 million. The costs will rise substantially when the Convention enters into force and the appointment of inspectors begins, yet the Organization will require fewer inspectors than the IAEA, which currently employs about 200 persons. It has been estimated that its tasks with respect to verification of chemical weapons stockpiles, chemical weapons production facilities, monitory of chemical industry, and challenge inspection will require about 185 inspectors.

The Conference of States Parties is the highest body of the Organization. It will meet in regular annual sessions, but may also meet in special session. The special sessions may be convened by the Executive Council or a State Party supported by one third of the members of the Organization. The Chemical Weapons Convention also has provisions for such review conferences, which should be convened at regular five-year intervals to review the operation of the Convention. The work of the Conference of States Parties is based on consensus, but in the case of a vote each State has one vote. If consensus is not possible at the end of 24 hours, the Conference shall make a decision by a two-thirds majority of members present and voting.

The comprehensive provisions concerning the Conference of the States Parties ensure that all States Parties will have an opportunity to take an active role in all phases of the Convention's implementation. This is in contrast to the provisions of the Biological and Toxin Weapons Convention and the Non-Proliferation Treaty, according to which the States Parties only meet at review conferences at intervals of several years.

The Executive Council is responsible to the Conference of States Parties. Its primary functions will be to promote the effective implementation of the Convention and compliance with its provisions. The Council has 41 members. The representatives are elected for two-year terms on a geopolitical and industrial basis among the States Parties. These seats are allocated as follows: Africa 9, Asia 9, Latin America and the Caribbean 7, Eastern Europe 5, and Western Europe and other States 10. In addition, one seat will rotate between the Asian region and the Latin American and Caribbean region. This means that countries from the first three regions will have an absolute majority in the Executive Council, i.e., 26 of 41 members.

9. Export Controls

We can only be sure of ridding the world of chemical weapons by means of universal adherence to and effective implementation of the Chemical Weapons Convention. Before this can be achieved, export controls on dual-purpose chemicals and equipment are necessary to prevent further proliferation. This is why member countries of the Australia Group have imposed export controls on 54 chemical weapons precursors and dual-purpose chemical equipment and technology. The member countries of the Australia Group have agreed that there is a continuing and important role for the group in the harmonization of national non-proliferation controls over chemical and biological weapons materials, in a manner consistent with the Group's primary interest in an effectively operating Chemical Weapons Convention and Biological and Toxin Weapons Convention.

The Australian representative to the Conference on Disarmament, Ambassador Paul

O'Sullivan, stated in a plenary meeting of the Conference on 6 August 1992 that the members of the Australia Group "undertake to review in light of implementation of the Convention, the measures that they take to prevent the spread of chemical substances and equipment for purposes contrary to the objectives of the Convention, with the aim of removing such measures for the benefit of States Parties to the Convention acting in full compliance with their obligations under the Convention."[27] The Convention contains stringent rules concerning transfer of chemicals; thus, the States Parties must impose both import and export controls on, and bans in some cases of, the chemicals in the three schedules.

Schedule 1 chemicals may only be transferred to another State Party and only for research, medical, pharmaceutical, or protective purposes. For schedule 2 chemicals, an end-use certificate is required for transfers to non-States Parties during an interim period of three years after entry into force of the Convention. After this, such chemicals may no longer be transferred to or received from non-States Parties. When transferring schedule three chemicals to non-States Parties, each State Party shall adopt the necessary measures to ensure that the transferred chemicals are used only for purposes not prohibited by the Convention.

In this connection, it should be stressed that in the preamble of the Convention states that the States Parties desire to promote free trade in chemicals as well as international cooperation and exchange of scientific and technical information on chemicals for purposes not prohibited by the Convention. Furthermore, in Article VI it is stated that the provisions of this Article shall be implemented in a manner which avoids hampering the economic or technological development of States Parties and international cooperation in the field of chemical activities for purposes not prohibited under the Convention, including the international exchange of scientific and technical information and chemicals and equipment for the production, processing, or use of chemicals for purposes not prohibited under the Convention. Article XI makes it clear that the States Parties shall not maintain among themselves any restrictions incompatible with the obligations undertaken under the Convention, which would restrict or impede trade and the development and promotion of scientific and technological knowledge in the field of chemistry for industrial, agricultural, research, medical, pharmaceutical, or other peaceful purposes.

10.   Conclusions

The conclusion of the Chemical Weapons Convention represents a significant success for multilateral disarmament. Effective implementation of the CWC demonstrates that it is worthwhile to negotiate multilateral disarmament treaties with such comprehensive verification mechanisms. Future negotiators will be able to draw on the experience gained in both routine and challenge verification of a global prohibition on chemical weapons. In this way, the Convention will serve as a guideline for future global disarmament treaties, in particular for the negotiations on a comprehensive nuclear test ban treaty, which are to begin in the Conference on Disarmament in January 1994.

The costs of implementing the Chemical Weapons Convention will be substantial; however, know-how and intellectual resources which have been devoted to developing chemical weapons in a number of countries will be released for much more productive purposes.

Notes

1. United Nations document A/47/690.
2. Arms Control and Disarmament Agreements. Text and Histories of the Negotiations, United States Arms Control and Disarmament Agency, 1990 Edition, p. 131.
3. Conference of the Committee on Disarmament documents CD/48 of 7 August 1979 and CD/112 of 7 July 1980.
4. Sten Lundbo, statement included in the UNIDIR Report on Interrelationship of Bilateral and Multilateral Negotiations, Proceedings of the Baku Conference, 2- 4 June 1987, United Nations, New York, 1988, p. 191.
5. Paragraph 120 of the Final Document of the First Special Session devoted to Disarmament, United Nations document A/S-10/23.
6. Paragraph 120 of the Final Document of the First Special Session.
7. The Holmenkollen Report on the Chemical Weapons Convention, Royal Norwegian Ministry of Foreign Affairs, 1987, p. 121.
8. Brad Roberts, "Chemical Disarmament and International Security," *Adelphi Papers 267*, International Institute for Strategic Studies, Spring 1992.
9. Wireless File, United States Embassy in Oslo, 28 July 1993.
10. Press release dated 2 July 1992 from the Royal Norwegian Ministry of Foreign Affairs.
11. Conference on Disarmament document CD/880 of 30 January 1989.
12. Conference on Disarmament document CD/766 of 2 July 1987.
13. United Nations document A/C.1/47/PV.21 of 28 October 1992.
14. Ibid.
15. United Nations Institute for Disarmament Research (UNIDIR), *Disarmament Agreements and Negotiations. The Economic Dimension.* (London : Dartmouth Publishers, 1991), p. 180.
16. Final Record of the Government Industry Conference against Chemical Weapons, Canberra, Australia, 18-22 September 1989, Department of Foreign Affairs and Trade, Canberra.
17. Robert Mikulak, "Destruction of Chemical Weapons", *UNIDIR Newsletter*, No. 20, 1992, p. 13.
18. Robert Mikulak, *op. cit*, p. 13.
19. Sten Lundbo, "The Economic Implication of a Chemical Weapons Convention", *UNIDIR Report on Disarmament Agreements and Negotiations*, 1991, p. 214.
20. Robert Mikulak, *op.cit.*, p. 13.
21. A. Wenschenk, "Price of CW Destruction Jumps by $1 Billion", *Defense Week*, 10 February 1993.
22. Conference on Disarmament document CD/789 of 16 December 1987.
23. Lois Ember, "Russia Seeks US Expertise, Money to Destroy Its Chemical Arms," *Industrial and Engineering Chemistry, News Edition*, November 1992.
24. Robert Mikulak, *op. cit.*, p. 14.
25. IAEA document INFCIRC/2/Rev.42, 25 January 1993.
26. Statement by Ian R. Kenyon at the First Moscow Conference on Chemical and Biological Disarmament, Demilitarization and Conversion, 19-21 May 1993.
27. Australian Group document AG/June 93/Press/Chair/10 of 10 June 1993.

Chapter 18

THE EVOLUTION AND RAMIFICATIONS OF THE US DECISION TO ADVOCATE THE CWC CHALLENGE INSPECTION REGIME

R. Nicholas Palarino

The negotiation of the Chemical Weapons Convention has been described by General Bill Burns, former director of the Arms Control and Disarmament Agency (ACDA), as a "political ballet"[1] while another ACDA official characterized the talks as not really having been designed from the perspective of the United States o go anywhere, just to talk. A third official noted that the US must now be prepared to implement it.[2]

1. An Historical Perspective

The Chemical Weapons Convention had been under negotiation for 25 years when it was finally signed in January 1993. The United States and 129 other nations (now over 160 signatories) agreed to ban the development, production, and stockpiling of chemical weapons. To verify this agreement is quite complex and costly and includes data exchanges, on-site inspections of declared facilities, and challenge inspections of declared and undeclared facilities anytime, anywhere.

It was President Reagan's administration that breathed new life back into the CW negotiations that had been faltering for years. The Reagan administration's plan for conducting arms control negotiations was called the "dual-track approach" whereby the United States continued to produce chemical weapons while simultaneously negotiating their reduction or elimination with the Soviet Union. The Reagan administration's fundamental assumption was that the former USSR (FUSSR) could be dealt with only from a position of strength applied no less to chemical weapons than heretofore to nuclear or conventional weapons. It was in 1981 that the United States renounced its unilateral moratorium of chemical weapons production, which had been in place since 1969, and proceeded to produce these weapons to reach the stockpile levels of the Soviet Union.

The administration for three years sought unsuccessfully to obtain funds from the US Congress to produce binary chemical weapons. On two separate occasions, then-Vice President Bush cast the tie-breaking vote in the Senate, only to see the proposal die in the House of Representatives. Finally, in December of 1985, Congress appropriated $130 million to begin production of chemical weapons (CW). Other States Parties, and especially Moscow, viewed the resurgence of American CW production as a signal that the United States was not serious about negotiating a ban.

1.1 Coincidental Arms Control Initiatives

The dual-track approach and on-site inspection were equally significant in negotiating arms control agreements during the Reagan administration. In fact, one ACDA official stated that many in the United States believed in order to have effective verification there must be on-site inspection.[3] As early as August 21, 1981, the director of ACDA indicated to the Soviet Union's chargé d'affaires in Washington that on-site inspection and data exchanges were necessary ingredients of future arms control accords. Contrary to past experiences, the Soviets did not balk at this statement.

On-site inspection and challenge on-site inspection had been proposed in negotiations for other arms control treaties, in addition to the CWC. The first major arms control announcement under General Secretary Chernenko's regime in 1984 was that the Soviets would agree to the principle of permanent on-site inspection for the destruction of chemical stocks. In late 1984 the Soviets offered limited on-site inspection at nuclear test sites as a means of enticing the United States to agree to ratify the 10 year old Threshold Test Ban Treaty (TTBT). Challenge inspections were proposed in the INF negotiations but were not pursued because of concerns from the Department of Defense and the Intelligence Community. None of these discussions prepared the administration for the announcement by General Secretary Gorbachev in 1987 that Moscow was prepared to accept the provisions of the US draft CWC Treaty that included a challenge inspection regime with no right of refusal.

1.2 Domestic Arms Control Environment

It is important to examine the views of the domestic arms control environment before determining what the US draft CWC Treaty said and why it was presented in the manner it was. The Reagan cabinet underwent some momentous personnel changes after 1983. Though some officials, especially in the Department of Defense, warned that pursuing the CWC Treaty was not in the best interests of the United States, largely because it would be virtually impossible to verify, other officials felt differently. Then-Vice President George Bush and Secretary of State George Schultz argued that the United States had a moral imperative to provide leadership in the negotiations for a ban on CW. Richard Pipes, the former National Security Council advisor on Soviet Affairs stated, "The shift of the Reagan administration toward making arms control the dominant focus of US-Soviet relations can be traced to the bureaucratic ascendancy of Mr. Schultz."[4]

1.3 The 1984 Bush Proposal

In 1983 Vice President Bush before the Conference on Disarmament (CD) in Geneva presented a set of principles for the world-wide elimination of chemical weapons. This speech laid out the bases for a CWC Treaty.

In January 1984 then-Secretary of State George Schultz made a speech at the Conference on Security and Cooperation in Europe (CSCE) in Stockholm. Schultz declared it was the US intention to table a draft CWC Treaty in the forthcoming months. Secretary Schultz, believing that the White House had formally cleared the speech, delivered it, and received front-page coverage. It was now incumbent upon Washington to put forth a draft CWC Treaty.

The White House interpreted "in coming months" as meaning before the conclusion in April 1984 of the current round of discussions of the Conference on Disarmament (CD) in New York. The administration had less than three months to come up with a draft treaty to table at the CD. The decision was made to use a draft CWC Treaty that had been developed by the State Department. With very little time to coordinate this proposal, Douglas Feith, former Deputy Assistant Secretary of Defense for Negotiations Policy and the key author of the original "anytime, anywhere, no right of refusal" challenge inspection provision, described the urgency of the situation as follows: "We only had time to focus on the most glaring flaw of the State Department draft, and that was determined to be the absence of a mandatory challenge inspection regime."[5] Because elements in the Department of Defense firmly believed that the CWC would be unverifiable without it, Article 10 was included as a means of providing an objective way of assessing treaty violations. As former Ambassador Ronald Lehman stated, "You don't table it if you can't live with it."[6]

Vice President George Bush did table the US draft CWC Treaty at the CD on April 18, 1984. The rationalizations -- both pro and con -- among elements in the US government regarding this draft proposal were extremely diverse. Some components felt that the State Department and ACDA were interested in pursuing the treaty for political reasons; others felt that members of the Department of Defense questioned the issue of verification as a means to continue to produce and deploy chemical weapons. Still others felt that the Intelligence Community was in favor of the proposal for the challenge inspections because they saw it as an opportunity to collect intelligence. On the other hand, the Chemical Manufacturers Association (CMA) was not only interested in seeing a verification regime that actually worked but wanted a way to prove its disassociation with chemical weapons. General Burns stated recently, "The degree of support for the challenge inspection regime initially might have been predicated in part on the fact that it would be unacceptable to the Russians so it's a fairly safe thing to advocate. Go along with it because it isn't going to happen."[7] The thaw in the Cold War saw Gorbachev formally accept the relevant and previously unacceptable provisions of the draft US CWC Treaty in 1987. Once this occurred, compromises needed to be made. Describing the dynamics of the time, General Burns said, "The fundamental problem was that in the late 80's we had no idea of the breadth and depth of change in the Soviet Union."[8]

2. Ramifications Of The Original Bush Proposal

The Reagan administration's requirement to ensure that the CWC be a verifiable agreement was in contrast with the fact that this agreement had to be verified in the United States as well as on other States Parties territories. This truth was not universally understood at that time. As former Ambassador Ronald Lehman stated, "As in the INF experience, the left hand didn't always know what the right hand was doing. You had a lot of programs in defense that did not understand what was being negotiated, and you had a lot of people involved in negotiations that did not understand what the implications were for specific defense programs."[9] Sensitive national security assets would now be subject to inspection by China, France, Iran, or any other State Party which might be on a challenge inspection team. The Departments of Defense and Energy and the Intelligence Community that had sites susceptible to inspection were also very concerned when they realized President Bush was firmly committed to this treaty.

The Bush administration ordered a review of the "anytime, anywhere, no right of refusal" provision to the challenge inspection regime when it became clear that the ramifications of this provision were unacceptable to the departments and agencies. The compromise which was reached was to embrace the British concept of "managed access." What exactly was meant by the phrase "managed access" was not initially apparent. The United States incorporated the managed access provisions into the challenge inspection regime in July 1991 and presented the new proposal to the CD.

3. Implementing The CWC

3.1 Government Agencies

The US government must now proceed with preparations for implementation, though many questions about how to implement the CWC remain unanswered. No agreement has been reached regarding what constitutes responsible provocation for denial of access. No formal US government position for decision-making has been established, as evidenced by the unwieldy size of the US delegation to the Preparatory Commission. This uncertainty of roles and the requirements for implementation are compounded by the addition of a non-traditional arms control interagency player, the Department of Commerce. Under the CWC, the Commerce Department is expected to be part of the arms control community because of its responsibilities and relationship with the chemical industry where heretofore its responsibilities were to encourage international trade.

3.2 Private Industry

The Chemical Manufacturers' Association (CMA) has been involved in the CWC negotiations for some 14 years. Its position is that if a chemical weapons treaty is to have a chance of working, chemical plants must be subject to inspections anywhere without going through challenge inspections. In June 1991 the CMA and chemical industry associations from Europe, Japan, Canada, and Australia issued a booklet which stated that every chemical plant ought to be open and eligible for inspection. Leo Zeftel, an industry member of the CMA working group, which serves as an industry advocate for CWC implementation, captured the position of the chemical industry as follows: "While industry is not overjoyed with having an international inspection team come into US industry, the only way to make this treaty work is to say, 'I'll suffer a little bit -- maybe a lot -- in order to deter some of those who are really going to violate this treaty.'"[10]

Unfortunately, not all of private industry has taken the same approach as the CMA. Industries such as those producing pharmaceuticals and synthetic organic materials are also equally accountable under the CWC Treaty provisions. Furthermore, because industries like aerospace companies have facility signatures which are similar to those of chemical plants, their likelihood of challenge inspections also increases. These and other chemical industry associations have for various reasons abstained from joining the CWC working group. Some felt that short-term, largely economic problems were more pressing and preferred to worry about CWC implementation once the treaty entered into force. Others simply were not aware of this treaty and the possible ramifications that the challenge inspection provisions posed for them. In the spring of 1993, ACDA initiated an outreach program to US industry to mitigate this problem. Through regional seminars ACDA hopes to acquaint industry with their rights and obligations under the CWC.

3.3 Protection Of Equities

The protection of equities is the rationale used in preparing for challenge inspections. Once managed access became accepted as the US position, many agencies were forced to change their position from "this treaty is not verifiable" to "how do we protect our facilities?" This is the fundamental question. The US government must determine what assets must be absolutely protected, and facilities must be surveyed ahead of time to know exactly where compartmented programs exist. It would be impossible to wait until the day of an inspection and expect to protect the proper things. Some agencies have taken a pro-active role and have made a conscious decision to prepare ahead of time. For instance, Tony Czajkowski of the Office of Arms Control at the Department of Energy (DOE) described DOE's assessment that it could not wait until entry into force of the treaty resulted in the initiation of National Trial Inspections and the formation of a CWC Treaty implementation working group.[11] Clearly actions such as these will better prepare agency facilities for the eventuality of a challenge inspection.

The protection of the equities of private industry is not as directly assignable as it is for government facilities. Concern regarding the potential loss of proprietary business information during the course of a CWC challenge inspection is precisely the reason why the CMA has been involved in the CWC negotiations. However, the recourse that private industry may have should valuable proprietary information be lost is not as yet determined. Thus far, the federal government has not offered to assume responsibility to make restitutions for the loss of proprietary information.

3.4 Legal Issues

Though the primary legal issue that has arisen from the CWC is the question of compensation for the loss of proprietary information, other constitutional questions linger. Facilities without government contracts are in a particularly difficult position because they lack direct government guidance on how to handle inspections and legal questions that may emerge. The Fourth and Fifth Amendments to the US Constitution, which deal with unlawful searches and seizures and the right to due process respectively, bear directly on the implementation of the challenge inspection regime of the CWC. Universally accepted legal determinations regarding the applicability of the Fourth and Fifth amendments to the CWC challenge inspection regime have yet to be made. Analysis has been conducted to determine what type of search warrant would be required for each type of facility if a private facility official should deny access to a challenge inspection team. These battles will ultimately be settled by the courts where lawyers will wrangle for years. In the meantime, the challenge inspection team will have long finished the inspection of the facility in question with the aid of a search warrant, and for the facility manager involved, the constitutionality of the procedure will have become a moot point. The Justice Department is currently examining the CWC Treaty to provide some authoritative guidance on such legal questions. Though it is true that international measures cannot be effective without national laws and regulations the question remains of how to ensure that constitutional rights are not damaged in the process.

3.5 Cost(s)

People in the legal profession may view the promulgation of the CWC as a welcome source of new business; however, others in the US government and in private industry do not hold the same sentiment. The preparation and eventual implementation of the CWC will be costly, with cost estimates varying widely. For instance, one estimate from ACDA places the burden between $100 and $150 million dollars a year to operate, while CMA has estimated that it might be closer to $300 to $500 million a year. Expenses range from dues to support the Organization for the Prohibition of Chemical Weapons (OPCW) to educational programs by the US government to private industry support for an inspection in the United States. Other costs are even less tangible. For instance, it is impossible to put a price tag on the loss of proprietary or national security information. Tony Czajkowski has said, "The overall cost to implement the verification regime will be unbelievable -- and definitely unforeseen -- when the United States proposed the regime."[12] What would be the result if an economic impact statement on the CWC were to be requested at the ratification hearings of this treaty?

4. Conclusion

The negotiation of the CWC Treaty has taught the United States an important lesson. The Reagan administration broke the stalemate that had long characterized the CWC negotiations, and the continued advocacy of the Bush administration got the treat -- but at what price? The safety of US national security assets and the rights of US citizens and industry were not then considered but must be dealt with now. The United States must accept the ramifications of this decision and prepare for implementation.

Notes

1.   Telephone interview on August 23, 1993, with General William Burns, Carlisle Barracks, Carlisle, PA.
2.   Interview on September 2, 1993, with two key personnel in the State Department with expertise on CWC and who were involved in the process in the 1980s.
3.   Ibid.
4.   Albert L. Weeks. "The Reagan Detente," *Global Affairs*, Spring 1998.
5.   Interview on October 11, 1993, with Douglas Feith, former Deputy Assistant Secretary of Defense for Negotiations Policy 1984-1986.

6. Telephone interview on August 23, 1993, with Ambassador Ronald F. Lehman, former Director of the Arms Control and Disarmament Agency (ACDA).
7. Burns Interview, *op. cit.,* August 23, 1993.
8. Ibid.
9. Lehman Interview, *op. cit.,* August 23, 1993.
10. Telephone interview on September 28, 1993, with Leo Zeftel, an industry member of the CMA working group.
11. Interview on September 1, 1993, with Tony Czajkowski, Office of Arms Control of the Department of Energy.
12. Ibid.

PART V

INSPECTIONS AND INSPECTORS: PERSPECTIVES ON VARIOUS TREATIES

Chapter 19
NEW TRENDS IN ARMS CONTROL INSPECTIONS

Sean McCormack and John W. Mentz[1]

Beginning with the Intermediate Nuclear Forces (INF) Treaty, inspections have become an important, integral part of arms control agreements.[2] As part of verification regimes, inspections have fulfilled a variety of roles, from domestic political tools to means of compliance monitoring. Regardless of their use, they have been driven by, and may be characterized by, the domestic arms control agenda. The authors believe that the arms control agenda is shifting in reaction to recent global events. The shift is from a bilateral/Euro-centric focus to a multilateral and regional focus on means to stem the proliferation of weapons of mass destruction (WMD).[3]

Just as the arms control agenda is moving away from its Cold War past, so are arms control inspections. In recent years US and Russian inspections have become mostly perfunctory because the items limited by the INF Treaty have been eliminated. Furthermore, the Iraqi experience has demonstrated that International Atomic Energy Agency (IAEA) inspections urgently require modification. Based on policy goals of major international actors in the arms control community, such as the United States, the post-Cold War era of inspections shows signs of being dramatically different from the recent past. From this viewpoint, this paper identifies three general trends for inspections in this new era:
-- the dominant role of multinational inspectorates;
-- the leveling of the current trend toward increasingly greater intrusiveness in inspections; and
-- the increased use of inspections as international political tools.

For the purposes of this paper, the term "inspection" includes on-site inspection, aerial and ground observation, and long-term monitoring. Additionally, the term "arms control" is used here in a broad sense that encompasses traditional Cold War arms control, nonproliferation regimes, and confidence-building measures at both the regional and global levels.

1. The Recipe For Change

As relations warmed between East and West from 1987 to 1992, the arms control community witnessed a flurry of activity unprecedented in the previous forty years, both in the number of agreements signed and the scope of verification measures agreed upon. The inspection measures demonstrated an escalating trend of intrusiveness that originated with the signing of the Conference on Disarmament (CD) Stockholm accords, whose implementing agreements allowed on-site observation of military exercises. The next step, the INF Treaty, marked a milestone in arms control inspections when it incorporated intrusive, short-notice on-site inspections as part of a verification scheme. The Conventional Forces in Europe (CFE) Treaty was built on the INF precedent and incorporated elements of short-notice "challenge" inspections. The START Treaty continued the trend towards greater intrusiveness with reentry vehicle inspections and challenge inspections of undeclared facilities.[4] The Open Skies Treaty allows unimpeded aerial access to signatory states' territory by intelligence-quality collection sensors. Figure 1 depicts this steady progression of inspection intrusiveness.[5]

Figure 1 Trend of Increasing Inspection Intrusiveness

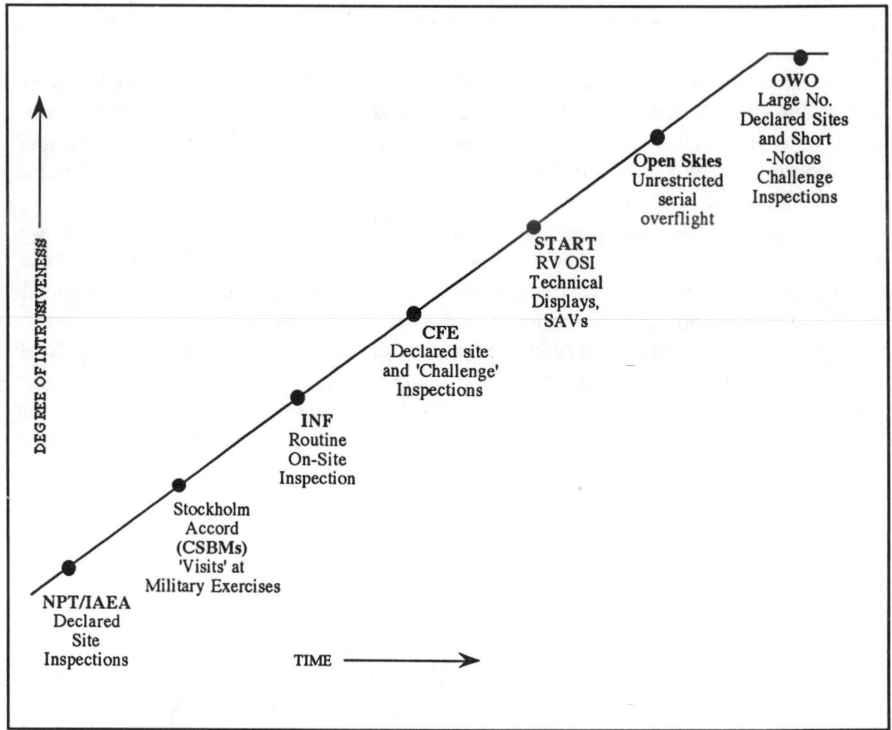

Just as warmer relations between East and West made the string of arms control agreements possible, the dissolution of the Soviet Union and end of the Cold War set the stage for the beginning of a new chapter in arms control. It opened new possibilities that previously "seemed no more than rhetorical or idle dreams."[6] In general, the possibility of greater political cooperation and elimination of the threat of general war in Europe allowed East and West to address new challenges on a global arms control agenda. Additionally, US-Soviet, later US-Russian, cooperation muted some old ideological aspects of competition in other regions, such as the Korean Peninsula, the Middle East, and South Asia. The cooperation between the two superpowers led to improved conditions for initiating regional arms control proposals.

Iraq had a similarly influential effect on the direction of the international arms control agenda. The Iraqi government's alleged use in 1984 of chemical weapons against the Kurds in northern Iraq had already influenced the arms control agenda.[7] The lingering memory of this incident and additional reports of Iraqi chemical weapons (CW) capability pervaded allied preparations during the Gulf War and later heightened international awareness about the dangers of CW proliferation in particular and of weapons of mass destruction in general.

Physical evidence gathered by IAEA and United Nations Special Commission (UNSCOM) inspectors in Iraq confirmed the worst nightmare of the international non-proliferation community. Inspection teams from the IAEA found evidence of a massive Iraqi effort to develop nuclear weapons despite the country's signature of the Non-Proliferation Treaty (NPT) and IAEA safeguard agreements. UNSCOM inspectors found large stocks of artillery munitions and ballistic missile warheads filled with chemical agents.[8] Questions were also raised about the Iraqi biological weapons capability. Although no "smoking gun" was found, some believed that the Iraqis were concealing a biological weapons (BW) program, which served to widen concerns about WMDs in general.[9]

The accumulated evidence in Iraq led directly to important arms control inspection events that will directly shape future inspection trends. First, the IAEA Board of Governors affirmed the right of the IAEA to conduct "special inspections" at non-declared facilities. Although some felt this was a reaffirmation of IAEA rights[10], the Board of Governors' vote marked a dramatic shift in IAEA operating policy to a more aggressive role in seeking out violations of the NPT.

Second, world opinion on the Iraqi chemical weapon threat helped accelerate progress in Chemical Weapons Convention (CWC) talks to their initial signing in January 1993, little less than two years after the end of the Persian Gulf War.[11] CWC signature culminated over two decades of discussion in the UN Conference on Disarmament (CD) on the issue and codifies the most intrusive arms control inspection regime to date. The convention contains provisions for short-notice, very intrusive challenge inspections at government and non-government undeclared facilities. Additionally, it provides for review of facility records and the conduct of personnel interviews that set a new standard in inspection intrusiveness that have a potential impact on a nation's international economic competitiveness. The CWC's focus on chemical weapons proliferation signaled the beginning of a new direction for arms control.

2. The New Agenda

The end of the Cold War and events surrounding the Persian Gulf War produced a fundamental change in the direction of the arms control agenda. At its core, the agenda is a search for ways to address WMD proliferation. The evolution of the search will be influenced by a number of competing interests, but United States policy will, to a great extent, "determine the nonproliferation agenda for the post-Cold War era."[12] The US agenda currently includes initiation of multilateral comprehensive test ban (CTB) talks;[13] proposals for fissile material production controls and monitoring; backing for enhanced IAEA safeguards monitoring; early implementation of the CWC; and discussions on Biological Weapons Convention (BWC) proposals for confidence-building measures.[14] However, the US will not be the sole voice in the international arms control community, and there is international interest in a number of other areas, such as expansion of the Open Skies Treaty to allow for environmental monitoring.

In addition to a global agenda, there are a variety of other proposals at the regional level that signify a new direction for arms control. Like previous talks in Europe, the new proposals reflect the particular concerns of countries in their respective region, and associated inspection regimes will be tailored to meet those needs. Some proposals at the regional level include provisions for inspections. The primary example of regional inspection regimes is the recently signed Brazil-Argentina agreement on full-scope nuclear material safeguards. The agreement includes an inspection regime and provides for establishment of the Argentine-Brazil Agency for Accounting and Control of Nuclear Materials to carry out inspections of facilities in both countries. In addition to developments in South America, proposals involving inspection regimes are under consideration in South Asia and on the Korean Peninsula.

The result of the dramatic change in the arms control environment is a two-tier arms control agenda. One level consists of a global agenda focusing on WMD proliferation and the other includes diverse regional agenda reflecting immediate national concerns, most of which are WMD related.

3. New Trends For Inspections

The nature and direction of the new global arms control agenda dictate that arms control inspections trends will be different from those of the immediate Cold War past. Inspection trends will reflect the global nature and expansiveness of the new agenda, as well as the difficulty of overcoming norms established by Cold War politics. The transformation of inspections in the new era of arms control will be characterized by significant differences in the way inspection regimes are implemented and used. The process will not be without growing pains. One example of the adjustment to new realities is the way a country goes about planning and executing an inspection. Rather than planning and executing inspections with their national resources, countries will conduct many inspections by proxy through international inspectorates.

To date, the frame of reference for arms control inspections is limited largely to periodic inspections conducted by the IAEA at civilian nuclear facilities, CFE inspections, and inspections under the INF Treaty. Inspections under these agreements are implemented on a bilateral basis and, generally, are characterized by outward cooperation between inspector and inspected. IAEA inspections have been limited to cordial visits to declared facilities in member countries. CFE inspections are most notable for the spectacle of former Warsaw Pact countries inspecting facilities occupied by their one-time Russian allies. INF inspections have developed into routine exchanges between professionals who know each other on sight. One apocryphal anecdote notes that short-notice INF inspections by the Russians always begin on the weekends so as to conform to Aeroflot flight schedules. The point is that these inspection regimes have served their intended purpose, and their modalities have formed the basis for trends in inspections over recent history.

In the years to come, these existing patterns will change. New international political goals for arms control and subsequent agreements or discussions will accelerate this process. These changes form the basis for a new era in inspections that reflects new global realities and that is distinguishable from the previous Cold War era in three general respects:
-- the dominant role of multinational inspectorates;
-- the leveling of the current trend toward increasingly greater inspection intrusiveness; and

-- the increased use of inspections as international political tools.

Each of the differences brings with it new issues for the US and other countries, and each identifies a new trend in inspections. It is likely that each country will formulate solutions unique to its own needs, but in doing so, all must address some basic conflicts arising from the goals of the arms control agenda.

For example, the recent historic trend toward increasingly intrusive inspection regimes carried over from the US-Russian agreements to the global level with the CWC. This trend is also influenced by larger global forces like spreading democratization and the global information explosion. On the other hand, the level of intrusiveness that is part of the CWC inspection regime raises for the first time the specter of a basic conflict between the goals of arms control and a nation's international economic competitiveness. Calculations regarding the effectiveness and costs of inspections are not new. These were part of the debate during the CWC negotiation. The very success of negotiating a CWC inspection regime[15], however, has brought to the forefront issues of direct implementation cost, impact on economic competitiveness, and deterrent value. For instance, as nations consider difficult issues like those related to BWC verification or possible extension of the Open Skies Treaty to include environmental monitoring, the overall future path of inspection intrusiveness is toward less intrusive inspections.

The following sections elaborate on three trends that distinguish the new era of inspections from the immediate past. It is important to keep in mind that the ultimate force driving trends in inspections is politics, and the trends are therefore subject to change. Each will reflect, over time, changes in global politics, and the relative predominance of each trend will mirror new developments in the arms control agenda.

3.1   International Inspectorates

The first distinguishing trend of the new period in arms control inspections will be the central role of international inspectorates in monitoring compliance with arms control agreements. These inspectorates will derive their original legitimacy and take their operational cues from member states. The norms and modalities developed by the inspectorate under the influence of member states will have a tremendous influence on how an agreement is implemented. In this role, the IAEA and the Organization for the Prohibition of Chemical Weapons (OPCW) will assume center stage in the world of arms control inspections as much for the importance of their mission to the international arms control agenda as for the sheer number of inspections they will perform.

The shift in focus from bilateral to multilateral and international inspections constitutes a major change for the US and Russia. It also mirrors the existing struggle in the new world order between national goals and multilateral action. Both countries are accustomed to having vertically integrated domestic inspection operations, from inspection planning to compliance assessment for implementation of agreements, like INF and START. Multilateral agreements, such as the NPT and CWC, however, require a different approach.

The Cold War experience of dealing with an international inspectorate is limited mainly to dealings with the IAEA, which from time to time has had its ability to carry out even periodic inspections of facilities with declared nuclear materials called into question. Until 1992, the IAEA operated on a cooperative basis with member states in monitoring compliance with safeguard agreements, but the discovery of presence of a covert Iraqi nuclear weapons program pointed to the need to reassess this operating premise. Its defenders argued that in order to have had the opportunity to detect Iraqi cheating, the IAEA would have needed the ability to conduct challenge-type inspections of undeclared facilities, which requires Board of Governor approval based on substantiating proof. In response to the apparent systemic breakdown in monitoring the NPT, the IAEA Board of Governors, with prodding from the international arms control community, affirmed (some would say reaffirmed) the right. Now, with a new inspection mandate, the IAEA will be able to actively seek out violations of the NPT. In 1992, the IAEA exercised this new right and it "obtained access to undeclared sites in several countries."[16] This interest on the part of the international community in reinvigorating the IAEA is an important indicator of the future importance of the organization to arms control inspections.

As the IAEA began to consider new standards set by the international community, negotiators at the Conference on Disarmament put the finishing touches on a CWC that included provisions for short-notice, challenge inspections of undeclared facilities. Similar to IAEA responsibilities with the NPT, the OPCW will be responsible for monitoring compliance with the CWC and will be charged with carrying out routine inspections and challenge inspections as requested by member states. The prominent new role of the international inspectorates, in the form of the IAEA and OPCW, raise a host of questions for countries like the United States, including issues related to sharing intelligence information with both the IAEA and OPCW.[17]

Having invested political capital to get the CWC signed and to reinvigorate the IAEA, countries like the United States will seek to use these new assets. This can be deduced from the stated foreign policy goals of many states seeking to stem the spread of WMDs and the proven utility of challenge inspections demonstrated by the Iraqi experience. To meet the goals set for international regimes such as the NPT and CWC, it will be important for members states to share intelligence information with international inspectorates.

In implementing the INF and CFE agreements, each participant could rely exclusively on its own intelligence resources and did not have to share information beyond a comfortable circle of allies. In the future, countries will have to be willing to provide a significant volume of sensitive information to the IAEA and OPCW, which may prove difficult for the normally reticent US intelligence community. Demand for intelligence information is underlined by the fact that both the IAEA and OPCW have positive controls for initiating challenge inspections. In the case of the IAEA, the Board of Governors must approve special inspections based on information from the IAEA bureaucracy and outside sources, such as the United States.[18] Although specific procedures for the OPCW have not yet been established, the CWC calls for a two-pronged request for a challenge inspection. The requesting country must simultaneously submit requests and supporting information to the OPCW Director General and the Executive Secretariat. The 41-member Executive Secretariat reviews the supporting information and decides on the request. If member countries wish to use challenge inspection provisions aggressively, they will need to share intelligence with information that, either in quantity or quality, is significant.

To an extent, the United States is preparing itself for this eventuality, and the preparations outwardly manifest themselves in the establishment of the Nonproliferation Center at the Central Intelligence Agency (CIA). James Woolsey, Director of the CIA, acknowledged US efforts to improve the exchange of "actionable intelligence" within the confines of its longstanding allies and the UNSCOM.[19] But the issue of sharing intelligence with international organizations, such as the OPCW, is a different matter, and Woolsey cautioned that, although the US is making progress toward the goal of broader sharing of information, it is a "complex issue" that requires a long-term commitment, patience and perseverance.[20] For example, the more diverse membership of the OPCW Executive Secretariat and lack of historical safeguards (as developed for UN, UNSCOM and IAEA) will pose unique sanitization problems for the US intelligence community.

The ability of states to adapt to the real need for sharing intelligence information will play a significant part in determining the utility of international inspection regimes. The need for adaptation is particularly true for the challenge inspection regime of the CWC and special inspection powers of the IAEA. Ultimately, the credibility of the inspectorate will depend on its ability to use information provided by member countries to detect potential violations of the agreement. Without a means and will to share information with an international inspectorate, the effectiveness of the agreements and associated inspection regimes as part of an effort to change the norms of behavior regarding WMD proliferation will fail.

3.2 Intrusiveness

The end of the Bush administration signaled the end of the last of four discernible periods in Cold War arms control inspections.[21] The motivations in making arms control inspection proposals during these periods varied according to political climate. At the height of the East-West conflict, inspection proposals often were used as political tools to highlight the secretive nature of the Soviet bloc. As relations changed, inspection proposals were also motivated by a mixture of interest in compliance monitoring and political confidence-building, with the latter dominating during the final years of the Cold War.[22] In addition to those explicit uses, inspections also provided countries opportunities outside the letter of the agreements, such as for collection of collateral intelligence.[23] As shown in Figure 1, the inspection regimes associated with the agreements during the latter part of the Cold War form a continuum of increasingly intrusive inspections. With the end of the Cold War, the question for those considering new inspection regimes is whether this trend will continue.

As new inspection proposals aimed at countering the spread of WMD, it appears poised for a repeat of the domestic debate over how much verification is enough. During the 1980s, debate over the theology of arms control verification focused mainly on the need for on-site inspections of military facilities related to the nuclear weapons systems infrastructure. Three general schools of thought emerged from the debate: the assurance, deterrence, and detection schools.[24] In the final analysis, the deterrence school carried the day.

Even as the resulting trend toward intrusive inspections reaches a new peak with the CWC and new IAEA powers, the pertinent question is whether we have "come too far, too fast." A new twist in considering a response is the important role economics and competitiveness will play in policy making. For some, particularly in the US, the CWC tests the acceptable limits of the balance between arms control goals, constitutional guarantees, and economics. A related precedent is the clash of economic and nonproliferation interests that arises almost daily in the longstanding debate between commercial industry and those in government responsible for export controls.[25] As the first arms control treaty that significantly affects private industry[26] (Table 1), the CWC inspection regime reflects the same type of free market versus national security concern questions.In spite of subdued rumblings from the chemical and pharmaceutical industries, however, the CWC likely will enter into force because of the persuasiveness of arguments of the convention's deterrent affect on chemical weapon proliferation.[27] Yet conflict between economics of the marketplace and arms control inspections, symbolized by export controls and the CWC, will be revisited in the future as proposals for a BWC verification regime and environmental monitoring in connection with the Open Skies Treaty[28] are considered.

Table 1 Private Industry Affected by Arms Control Inspections

Treaty	Affected Facilities
INF	Hercules, Inc. Magna, UT Martin Marietta Middle River, MD General Dynamics San Diego, CA
START	Hercules, Inc. Magna, UT Thiokol Corp. Promontory, UT Aerojet, Inc. Sacraments, CA
CWC	Thousands of facilities, including commercial facilities, may be inspected.*

* US Congress, Office of Technology Assessment, "The Chemical Weapons Convention: Effects on the US Chemical Industry,", p. 15

It is fair to say that future inspection regimes with the intrusiveness of the CWC will raise serious concern in many countries. As verification regimes move beyond inspections at government-owned or government contractor facilities, issues of economic competitiveness and loss of key technologies could quickly surface. Concern will not be limited to challenge inspections. In industries that rely on unique processes or techniques for their competitive advantage, such as the chemical, pharmaceutical, and bio-technology industries, compromise of information through inspection is a threat. Historically, such issues have not been a concern because inspections were limited to military facilities or defense contractors where a government assumes liability for inspection costs. In the future, as verification regimes are driven by nonproliferation goals toward inspection of non-nuclear WMD infrastructure, cost calculations in the cost versus deterrent value equation will be increasingly driven by economic competitiveness considerations. Economic self-interest will drive the leveling-off of the scope and degree of intrusiveness in future inspection regimes.

Further complicating the issue of intrusiveness is the phenomenon of cross-treaty synergy. When a particular facility is subject to the inspection regimes of more than one treaty, information gathered under one regime may be used to cue, cross-check, and confirm data from other treaties and other sources. Furthermore, under these circumstances the totality of the information available on that particular facility is greater than the mere sum of information gathered under the individual inspection regimes. This is true because some information would be made available only as a result of unique cueing from preceding inspections. For example, evaluation of Open Skies photography may reveal signatures unique to an undeclared facility inspectable under START. The START visit with the right of special access may provide the "ground truth" for further inspection under the CWC. In this example, a complete description of the facility, its operations, processes, and methodologies would be accomplished. If the facility was commercial, the phenomenon is problematic because proprietary information or key technologies may be compromised.

As regional arms control initiatives involving inspections become more commonplace, material decisions regarding inspection intrusiveness will be based on national or regional factors. Although there may be some interplay between activities at the global and regional levels, regional inspection trends will not necessarily follow the international trend.[29] For example, the extensive confidence-building measures put in place between Egypt and Israel after the Camp David Accords were far ahead of budding discussions in Europe.[30] Another, hypothetical, example would be that inspections under a potential North-South Korean nuclear inspection accord could be substantially more intrusive than those acceptable internationally. Thus, in considering future trends for intrusiveness, it is important to consider that regional and global initiatives will follow the pertinent arms control agenda and may take different paths.

3.3 Political Use of Inspections

Arms control inspection proposals and inspections have been used as political instruments in the past and will be used likewise in the future. At the height of the Cold War, US inspection proposals to the Soviets were often made "with no expectation that the Soviets would actually agree, reflecting again the narrower political purposes of on-site inspection."[31] In short, the US used inspection proposals to establish the expectation of a behavioral norm by applying the international spotlight to the Soviets and their rejection of the inspection proposals. In later years, the highly politicized nature of arms control in general continued, but began to wane with the Soviet acceptance of US INF proposals. This atmosphere gave way to the trend of inspections being increasingly important as compliance monitoring and then political confidence-building tools. The new era of political cooperation in inspections, however, will give way to a period in which the old confrontational politics of the type surrounding inspection proposals early in the Cold War will return.

Although it is defensible to argue that the spread of nuclear weapons around the world was slowed by Cold War nonproliferation regimes, examples such as Pakistan, India, Israel, and South Africa demonstrate the previously porous nature of the regime. It is debatable whether any regime could prevent a state determined to acquire nuclear weapons from acquiring them.[32] As the arms control agenda shifts to nonproliferation concerns, perceptions based on past experience about the willingness to enforce nonproliferation regimes must be overcome if the new and reinvigorated regimes are to be effective. Part of the effort to overcome perceptions will likely involve the use of inspections as political or diplomatic tools.[33]

Inspections are one element of an international effort directed at stemming the spread of WMDs, and they have unique value for countries that may want to draw "lines in the sand" with regard to WMDs. Inspections can serve the purpose of sending a clear, public message to a country involved in WMD development that the country's behavior is no longer acceptable by international standards of behavior. Moreover, in contrast with unilateral policy statements from an individual country, the message sent in form of an inspection may have greater international "legitimacy" because it carries weight as a legitimate action under an internationally recognized agreement.

Use of inspections alone, however, is always susceptible to the "what next" question. The response to the question might include both "carrots," like security guarantees, and "sticks," such as economic sanctions or military force. The Clinton administration is working on policy proposals and ways to approach implementation of these carrots and sticks. The overall framework for the new implementation approach is referred to as "counterproliferation," and it is intended to provide policymakers with a range of options to neutralize the threat from future or actual WMD use. Inspections have a place in this spectrum of responses to WMD proliferation or use, which runs the gamut from diplomatic protest, to economic sanctions, to the use of military force. Elements of this policy have existed for years, but they have not been put together as a coherent whole toward the specific goal of countering the spread of WMDs. In the counterproliferation framework, inspections are useful because they may serve as a potential starting point. As the US attempts to reshape the norms of behavior with regard to WMD, inspections may occasionally take center stage (as they have in Iraq).

The norms that the US will have to lead in reshaping were learned during the four decades of the Cold War and will not be easily changed. The challenge now facing the US and world community is how to learn norms of behavior, on the part of both proliferator and proliferant, that emphasize inhibiting or preventing proliferation of WMDs, as well as related materials, technology, and expertise. One existing tool that may play a part in reshaping global norms are arms control inspections. US backing for recent actions, such as the request for IAEA inspections directed at suspected North Korean nuclear weapons fuel reprocessing facilities, is an example of the way inspections may be used in the future. If the inspection is refused or the gathered evidence rejected by the inspected party, a country is left with a set of accusatory compliance assessment reports. As the North Korean experience points out, this may still be a liability of arms control verification. However, the effort to use inspections as a political tool in North Korea represents an effort to reshape the international norms concerning WMD proliferation. This trend, although unfamiliar in recent times, conjures memories of an earlier role as the US and Soviet Union debated the role of inspections in arms control verification.

There is one important caveat regarding the use of inspections as political instruments. Because inspections are an operational extension of policy, use of inspections is and will be often dependent on ephemeral variables such as the political will of major international actors. Predicting the winds of international politics is tricky business but there are some useful indicators. First among these indicators will be experience with implementing the CWC and its challenge inspections -- both how they are used and how they are accepted. Another measure will be how the IAEA uses its "special inspection" powers. Both these inspection regimes can be useful political tools for the United States and other countries as they seek to establish a new norm of behavior with respect to WMD proliferation; however, the ultimate utility of the policy goals and inspection effectiveness will depend on the political will of these countries.

4. Observations

The role of arms control inspections is at a crossroads. As the international arms control agenda takes shape and new agreements like the CWC are implemented, trends in inspections will conform to changing international political agenda. New inspection trends are beginning, and indications are that they will differ in significant ways from those at the close of the Cold War.

The first and most obvious change will be in the emergence of international inspectorates as major players in arms control inspections. As the arms control agenda shifts to global treaties aimed at limiting the spread of WMDs, international inspection organizations like the IAEA and OPCW will be key to building and maintaining the legitimacy of the multilateral regimes they monitor. The power of these organizations to monitor regimes, however, will be derived from the willingness of major countries like the US to use inspection regimes aggressively and to provide the inspectorate quality intelligence information on which to act. The demand for distribution of intelligence information to international inspectorates will require new ways for countries with significant intelligence assets to interact with international inspectorates.

The second major trend, which will affect the other trends identified in this paper, is a reversal of the previously steady trend toward increasing intrusiveness. In some cases there will continue to be a willingness to negotiate and participate in highly intrusive inspection regimes comparable to the CWC. In areas such as monitoring of fissile material storage or monitoring an international nuclear test ban, intrusive inspection may be needed and implemented. The trend toward decreasing inspection intrusiveness will occur in other areas of the arms control agenda. This trend derives largely from the increasing conflict between economic competitiveness and the goals of arms control.

The final major defining trend for inspections will be the use of inspections as political instruments. Recent history shows that politics drive inspections and inspections serve political purposes. The INF inspection regime was one of the first indicators of a new Soviet attitude in warmer relations with the West. By 1991, INF inspections had become largely confidence-building measures adding to the growing political goodwill between East and West. And, once again, inspections are at the forefront of a shift in international politics. The stated determination of the United States and its allies to counter the spread and use of WMDs will require a summoning of political will to reverse years of expediency in dealing with proliferation threats as a consequence of Cold War politics. In the United States, the determination is manifested in the evolving counterproliferation policy of which arms control and associated inspections play an important role. US backing of IAEA inspection efforts in North Korea represents the way in which the US and other countries will seek to use inspections in reshaping norms of behavior concerning WMD proliferation.

The three trends identified in this paper are alternately complementary and antagonistic. The effectiveness of international inspectorates will be determined in large part by political support from major international arms control players like the United States. In turn, support from the US and like-minded countries will be predicated on judgments about the utility of inspections in shaping norms of international behavior in WMD proliferation. Trends discussed in this paper will be dynamic as various influences predominate over time. For example, the desire to use inspections as political tools and as means of verification by policy makers will be tempered to an extent by calculations about the costs of inspections. Regardless of which trend dominates at a given moment, it is clear that inspections have entered a new era distinct from the recent Cold War past.

Notes

1. The views and opinions reflected in this paper are those of the authors, and they do not necessarily reflect those of Meridian Corporation or its clients.
2. The authors wish to thank Lou Nosenzo and John Hardenbergh for their support in writing this paper and Andy Burns for his invaluable research assistance. The authors also wish to acknowledge the contribution of Allan Cameron, Jill Jermano, and Cindy Warren Mentz in providing their comments. All responsibility for the content of the paper, however, is the authors' alone.
3. Weapons of mass destruction include nuclear, biological, and chemical weapons, as well as the means to deliver them.
4. Under the START Treaty, visits with right of special access may be negotiated between the US and Russia during a special session of the Joint Consultative Commission (JCC). These visits, referred to in the US Government as SAVs, represent the functional remnants of an actual suspect site inspection regime. START does have "Suspect Site Inspection" (SSI) at *declared* facilities. Neither constitutes a "no right of refusal" on-site inspection at any undeclared site.
5. The term "intrusiveness" encompasses a number of different inspection variables: number of inspections, length of inspection time, inspection preparation time, right to refuse inspections, sensitivity of potential "inspectable" areas, allowance for challenge inspections, and inspection equipment allowed. In each of the cases cited above, there was a general trend toward increasing intrusiveness. During this time, negotiators agreed to successive inspection regimes that built upon intrusiveness "gains" from previous agreements and then added new elements of intrusiveness.
6. James F. Leonard and Adam M. Scheinman, "Denuclearizing South Asia: Global Approaches to a Regional Problem," *Arms Control Today,* June 1993, p. 17.
7. "Iraq's behavior has long given impetus to arms control initiatives. Its use of chemical weapons against Iran inspired the creation of the Australia Group in 1984." Ronald F. Lehman, "Arms Control: Passing the Torch as Time Runs Out," *The Washington Quarterly,* Summer 1993, p. 44.
8. According to one congressional report, UNSCOM inspectors found about 1,000 tons of chemical agents, which included 46,000 filled munitions, 30 warheads for ballistic missiles, and 6,400 artillery projectiles. US Congress, House of Representatives, Committee on Armed Services, Special Inquiry into the Chemical and Biological Threat, *Countering the Chemical and Biological Weapons Threat in the Post-Soviet World,* 102nd Cong. (2d sess.) 1993, Committee Print, p. 20.
9. Ibid. p. 22.
10. Leonard Spector, "Repentant Nuclear Proliferants," *Foreign Policy,* Fall 1992, p. 23.
11. Lehman, *op. cit.,* pp. 44-45. Lehman points out that the Gulf War "helped alter ... the CW proliferation equation as the negotiation of a multilateral Chemical Weapons Convention in the Conference on Disarmament accelerated to a conclusion."
12. US Congress, House of Representatives, Committee on Foreign Affairs, *Nonprolif-

eration Regimes: Policies to Control the Spread of Nuclear, Chemical, and Biological Weapons and Missiles, report prepared by the Congress Congressional Research Service Library of Congress (102nd Cong.), (1st sess.), 1993, Committee Print, p. 6.

13. President, Speech, "Remarks at the United States Military Academy Commencement Ceremony in West Point, New York," *Federal Register* (29 May 1993), Vol. 29, No. 22, p. 997.

14. White House Press Release, *Nonproliferation and Export Control Policy,* 27 September 1993.

15. It is important to note that discussions are ongoing in the OPCW on developing means and modalities for CWC implementation. For example, issues such as "managed access" have to be clarified in these talks.

16. US Department of State, *Report to Congress Pursuant to Section 601 of the Nuclear Non-Proliferation Act of 1978 for the Year Ending December 31, 1992* (Washington, DC: US Department of State, January 1993), p. 26.

17. It should be noted, however, that information sharing is not a one-way street. One author writes: "There is an important synergistic interaction between national intelligence efforts and the international inspection system. National intelligence can both verify the effectiveness of international inspections and alert international inspectors to problem areas." Joseph S. Nye Jr., "New Approaches to Nuclear Proliferation Policy," *Science,* Vol. 256, 29 May 1992, p. 1297.

18. Spector, "Repentant Nuclear Proliferants," *op. cit.,* p. 22.

19. Amb. Woolsey defines actionable intelligence by stating that it is "intelligence which would lead the United States or its allies actually to action in the short run to stop something that is underway." James Woolsey, *Testimony of Director James Woolsey before the US House of Representatives Subcommittee on International Security, International Organizations, and Human Rights,* 28 July 1993, p. 12.

20. Ibid., p. 11.

21. Timothy J. Pounds, "Proposals for On-Site Inspection Over the Years: From the Baruch Plan to the Reagan Initiatives," in Lewis A. Dunn (ed.), *Arms Control Verification and the New Role of On-Site Inspection: Challenges, Issues, and Realities* (Lexington, MA: Lexington Books, 1990), pp. 69-81.

22. Ibid.

23. United States Congress Office of Technology Assessment, *Verification Technologies: Cooperative Aerial Surveillance in International Agreements* (Washington, DC: US Government Printing Office, July 1991), p. 6.

24. Charles A. Appleby and John C. Baker, "Verification and Mobile Missiles: Deterrence, Detection, or Assurance?" in John G. Tower, James Brown, and William K. Cheek (eds.), *Verification: The Key to Arms Control in the 1990s,* (Washington, DC: Brassey's (US), Inc., 1992, pp. 60-75.

25. As one analyst put it, "bluntly stated, current US practice is to abstain from enforcing nuclear export controls wherever competing interests are deemed to take precedence -- which is almost always. To date, almost any political, industrial, or diplomatic interest takes precedence over nuclear nonproliferation." Paul L. Levanthal, "Plugging the Leaks in Nuclear Export Controls: Why Bother?" *Orbis* Spring 1992, p. 169.

26. Additionally, under the NPT, US civilian nuclear facilities are subject to safeguard inspections by the IAEA.
27. A recent congressional study found "if the chemical companies perceive the treaty's provisions as too onerous, they could trigger a political backlash that would make it difficult for the United States and other countries to implement the treaty regime." It went on to state, however, "because of strong public support for banning chemical weapons, US chemical producers are unlikely to go on record opposing Senate ratification of the CWC. Instead they will try to ensure that their interests are protected in the implementing legislation and during deliberations of the PrepCom." United States Congress Office of Technology Assessment, *The Chemical Weapons Convention: Effects on the US Chemical Industry,* (Washington, DC: US Government Printing Office, August 1993), pp. 11-12.
28. The Senate report on ratification of the Open Skies Treaty when it states:
    "new or improved sensors could transform Open Skies into a more valuable information-gathering regime for the United States, but could also cause security or legal problems ... They [environmental sensors] could also raise Fourth Amendment questions if used in legal investigations or proceedings, however, and their potential security implications have not been analyzed. Improved optical, infrared, or synthetic aperture radar sensors could raise security concerns, and perhaps Fourth Amendment concerns as well."
    US Congress, Senate, *Report [To accompany Treaty Doc. 102-37],* 103d Cong. (1st sess.), 1993, pp. 137-138.
29. Although there are individual examples of at the regional level, the most widely varied and voluminous precedent for arms control inspections is in the US-European-Soviet experience.
30. The measures focus on activity in the Sinai, and call for:
    -- aerial reconnaissance;
    -- manned and unmanned observation posts;
    -- early warning posts in sensitive areas; and
    -- routine and challenge on-site inspections.
    Some of these services like aerial overflight are provided by the United States. Itshak Lederman, "The Arab-Israeli Experience in Verification and its Relevance to Conventional Arms Control in Europe," *Occasional Paper 2,* Center for International Security Studies at Maryland, College Park, MD, 1989; quoted in James E. Goodby, "Transparency in the Middle East," *Arms Control Today* May 1992, p. 8.
31. Pounds, "Proposals for On-Site Inspection Over the Years," *op. cit.,* p. 75.
32. George W. Rathjens and Marvin Miller, "Nuclear Proliferation After the Cold War," *Technology Review* August/September 1991, p. 26; and Seymour M. Hersh, *The Sampson Option: Israel's Nuclear Arsenal and American Foreign Policy* (New York: Random House, 1991.)
33. This approach to inspections was hinted at by Walter Slocombe, Principal Deputy Under Secretary of Defense (Policy): "... arms control verification, Nunn-Lugar Funds, and counterproliferation. These represent three very important tools for us to shape the future -- to secure the advantages of this new era, while hedging against the dangers and conflict still endemic to it." Walter B. Slocombe, *Remarks Before the Senate Armed Services Committee,* June 23, 1993, p. 27.

Chapter 20
ARMS CONTROL AND ANTARCTICA:
ON-SITE INSPECTIONS ON THE FROZEN CONTINENT

Edward J. Lacey

It is commonly thought that on-site inspection rights are a recent development in arms control. In fact, it was the 1959 Antarctic Treaty that pioneered such on-site inspection concepts as routine inspections, "anytime, anywhere" inspections, and aerial overflight to verify compliance with arms control commitments. Since December 1987 with the signing of the Intermediate Nuclear Forces (INF) Treaty, on-site inspection has become the centerpiece of arms control agreements between the United States and the former Soviet Union. The inspection provisions incorporated in that agreement were universally hailed as unprecedented in scope and application. Inspectors from each side were granted access to declared INF missile operating bases and support units, as well as to selected production facilities in order to confirm compliance with the treaty's prohibitions.

Every major arms control agreement since that time -- whether bilateral, multilateral, or international -- has included on-site inspection provisions. The Threshold Test Ban (TTBT) and Peaceful Nuclear Explosions (PNET) Treaties that went into effect between the United States and the former Soviet Union in 1990 permit on-site inspection and technical measurements of nuclear test activities. The 1990 multilateral Treaty on Conventional Forces in Europe (CFE) created an elaborate inspection regime on the continent of Europe to verify compliance with limitations on conventional armaments.

The 1991 Strategic Arms Reduction Treaty (START) provides for 12 types of inspections on the territories of the United States and Russia to monitor strategic offensive nuclear forces -- intercontinental range and submarine launched ballistic missiles, and heavy bomber aircraft. The much-heralded Chemical Weapons Convention (CWC) that was signed in January 1993 and has over 160 signatories worldwide will, when it enters into force, include the right of "challenge inspections" virtually anywhere on the territories of the States Parties to investigate suspected violations of the Convention's prohibitions on the production, stockpiling, and use of chemical weapons.

Somewhat before this explosion of on-site inspection provisions in arms control agreements, the international Nuclear Non-Proliferation Treaty (NPT) of 1970 provided for the establishment of Safeguards Agreements between the International Atomic Energy Agency (IAEA) and individual States Parties. Under the terms of these agreements, inspectors from the IAEA could undertake inspections at more than 600 nuclear facilities globally. These inspections are intended to determine whether nuclear material is being diverted from peaceful uses. A major breakthrough in the operation of this regime occurred in 1985 when the former Soviet Union, a steadfast opponent of on-site inspection, announced that for the first time it would open some of its civilian nuclear facilities to inspection by the IAEA.

While this rush to embrace and expand the concept and practice of on-site inspection for verification of arms control commitments was transpiring in the 1980s and 1990s, the world's first arms control on-site inspection regime was operating efficiently and without fanfare -- as it had been since the early 1960s and as it continues to do -- at the bottom of the world, on the frozen continent of Antarctica.

1. Antarctica

The Antarctic continent constitutes an area of approximately 5,598,000 square miles -- roughly the size of the United States and Europe combined (see Figure 1). All but a very small portion of the continent (2.4 percent) is covered by a thick sheet of ice known as the "ice cap." At its thickest point, the ice cap is over two miles high. Along the coastline, the ice cap stretches into the sea and floats upon it, while remaining permanently attached to the continental landmass. These extensions are called "ice shelves." The most significant of these is the Ross Sea ice shelf that is some 403 miles wide. In addition to the ice shelves, Antarctica is surrounded by a belt of floating ice and icebergs known as pack ice. Until the twentieth century, these ice barriers in the sea kept Antarctica largely isolated.

This continent is divided by a chain of mountains (the Transantarctic Mountains) into what is known as East Antarctica and West Antarctica. The ice cap is studded with lesser mountains, plains, valleys, glaciers, and permanently frozen lakes. There are very few ice-free areas on the continent.

Clearly, the Antarctic continent is one of the least hospitable areas in the world (see Figure 2). With recorded temperatures as low as -87 C, it is the coldest place on Earth. It also is one of the windiest. Surface winds sweep across the ice cap at speeds of 120-180 miles per hour from time to time and blow at a steady 20 miles per hour at the South Pole. There is virtually no surface vegetation in Antarctica, and the principal life forms are birds (most notably penguins), crustaceans, and sea mammals.

2. Territorial Claims

Exploration of Antarctica began in the sixteenth century. Although seamen from a number of countries may have reached some of the islands off the coast of Antarctica, it was not until 1599 that a Dutch expedition, led by Dirk Gherritsz, conclusively reached the frozen continent. Explorations continued throughout the seventeenth, eighteenth, and nineteenth centuries and involved explorers from many countries, including Norway, Belgium, Portugal, France, Russia, Germany, the United Kingdom, and the United States. Many of these explorers claimed the lands they visited on behalf of their governments, however, these claims were never acted upon.

It was not until the twentieth century that nations began seriously to assert territorial claims to Antarctica. The United Kingdom was the first to put forward a territorial claim in 1908. New Zealand followed suit in 1923, and Australia in 1933. France thereafter asserted a claim to a small section of the continent on the basis of the 1838 explorations of Frenchman Dumont d'Urville. In the 1930s, the United States carried out extensive aerial surveys of Antarctica, depositing claims markers over vast portions of the continent. Germany likewise used aircraft to drop claims markers throughout Antarctica. During the Second World War, Argentina and Chile joined the fray, laying claims to areas previously claimed by the United Kingdom.

In the post-World War II era, several nations began actively to establish military and scientific stations in Antarctica to solidify their territorial claims. Argentina, Chile, the United Kingdom, and the United States all sent naval forces to the continent. At the same time, the then Soviet Union began to assert its interest in Antarctica, declaring in June

Figure 1 Antarctica: selected stations and physical features
(Source: National Science Foundation)

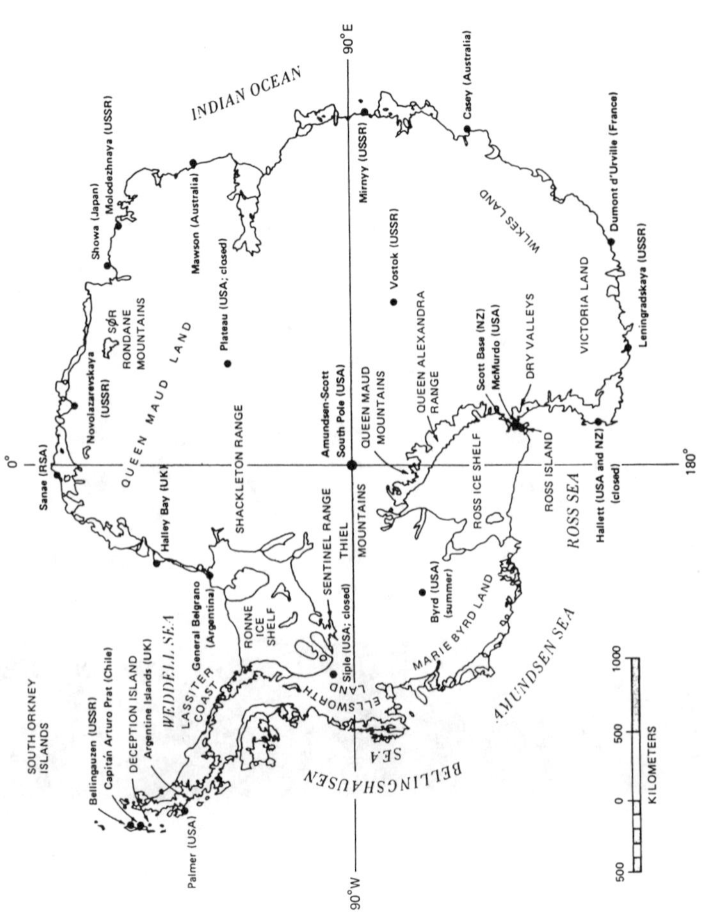

Figure 2 The Antarctic Continent
(Source: Author)

1950 that it would not recognize as lawful any claims to the continent and any international arrangements that excluded the USSR.

In mid-1957, the International Geophysical Year (IGY) was launched to, among other things, carry out intensive geographical and geophysics studies in Antarctica. The Soviets were a very active participant in this effort, exploring the continent and establishing scientific research stations throughout. Both the USSR and the United States opened up previously unexplored and uncharted areas of the continent, but both refused to assert territorial claims, declaring rather that they would reserve the right to do so in the future.

3. The Antarctic Treaty

During the course of the IGY (July 1, 1957 to December 31, 1958), all of the countries actively involved on the continent tacitly agreed to hold their territorial claims in abeyance. It was largely agreed by all that the scientific effort called forth by the IGY should be paramount and that questions of territorial sovereignty should not be allowed to impede scientific progress. This "precedent" ultimately led to the establishment of an international regime for the continent embodied in the Antarctic Treaty.

In 1958, US President Dwight D. Eisenhower invited the 11 other parties that had participated in Antarctica during the IGY to a conference intended to consider the future of the continent. In his invitation, Eisenhower asserted the United States view that, as was the case during the IGY, territorial claims in Antarctica should be "frozen" for the duration of a regime to be negotiated. Such a freeze would not require states to relinquish their territorial claims to Antarctica, but only to agree to maintain the legal *status quo*.

The Conference was convened in Washington, DC in June 1958, with representatives from all 12 of the countries then active in Antarctica -- Argentina, Australia, Belgium, Chile, France, Japan, New Zealand, Norway, South Africa, the Soviet Union, the United Kingdom, and the United States. The negotiations lasted 15 months and resulted in the signing on December 1, 1959, of the Antarctic Treaty. The treaty specifies that:
-- Nothing in the treaty shall in any way be interpreted as constituting a renunciation of previously asserted territorial claims in Antarctica. Likewise, for the duration of the treaty, no new claims to territorial sovereignty in Antarctica will be asserted;
-- Antarctica shall be used for peaceful purposes only;
-- The establishment of military bases and fortifications, the carrying out of military maneuvers, and the testing of any type of weapon are prohibited;
-- Nuclear detonations and the disposal of radioactive waste are likewise prohibited in Antarctica; and
-- National representatives of States Parties have the right to conduct on-site inspections anywhere on the Antarctic continent to ensure compliance with the terms of the treaty.
The Antarctic Treaty entered into force on June 23, 1961. There are currently 37 States Parties to this Treaty.

4.   Inspection Provisions

During the negotiation of the treaty, New Zealand first made the case that in order to ensure the continent is used only for peaceful purposes, provision should be made for "observers." The United States supported this view, and argued for a regime of unlimited, unilateral on-site inspections. Although originally opposed to such a regime, the Soviet Union ultimately agreed to the inclusion in the treaty of an Antarctic inspection system that included unlimited on-site inspections by any number of national observers.

This system of "anytime, anywhere" inspections is articulated in Article VII of the treaty. Article VII states that each State Party "shall have the right to designate observers to carry out any inspection ..." It further states that observers (i.e., inspectors) "shall have complete freedom of access at any time to any or all areas of Antarctica." These areas include "all stations, installations and equipment ..., and all ships and aircraft at points of discharging or embarking cargoes or personnel in Antarctica ..." In addition to hands-on, on-site inspection, Article VII provides, "Aerial observation may be carried out at any time over any or all areas of Antarctica ..." (the first Open Skies regime!).

Article VII of the Antarctic Treaty also stipulates that inspection personnel shall be "nationals" of the inspecting State Party, and that they shall be "designated." "The names of observers shall be communicated to every other Contracting Party ... and like notice shall be given of the termination of their appointment."

5. On-Site Inspections In Antarctica

The first on-site inspection in Antarctica was conducted by two observers from New Zealand in November 1963. They inspected the United States base at McMurdo Sound (see Figure 3), as well as the US installations at the South Pole and Byrd Station. They reported that all facilities and activities inspected were found to be in compliance with the treaty. Later the same month, a joint Australia/United Kingdom observer team carried out the second inspection on the continent. The joint team inspected the same three US installations as had the New Zealand team, as well as several US scientific research field camps in the Dry Valleys near McMurdo. While conducting their inspection of McMurdo, the observers examined aircraft at the adjacent airfield and ships unloading cargo. Once again, the observers reported that no violations of the Antarctic Treaty had been uncovered.

The success of these two inspections did much to dispel concerns that the on-site inspection process might become confrontational. Indeed, it was these very concerns that delayed implementation of the on-site inspection provisions for over two years after the treaty had entered into force. Now, however, States Parties felt they had a "green light" to go forward.

The United States carried out its first inspection of New Zealand's Scott Base on January 9, 1964. The following day, the US conducted an aerial inspection of the French Dumont d'Urville Station. On January 12, US observers inspected the Soviet Mirnyy research facility -- the first on-site inspection of a Soviet facility anywhere. Three days later, the US inspected another Soviet Antarctic research station, Vostok. All of these inspections were executed without incident, and the United States reported that it had uncovered no violations of the Antarctic Treaty.

Since then, on-site inspection has become a routine but infrequent activity in Antarctica. The United States has been the most active state in this regard, carrying out subsequent inspections in 1967, 1971, 1975, 1977, 1980, 1983, 1985, and 1989. The next most active inspecting state has been Australia. The Soviet Union did not conduct an

Figure 3 US Base at McMurdo Bay
(Source: Author)

inspection under the Antarctic Treaty until 1989. However, in that year Soviet observers inspected 15 installations of 13 States Parties. Other treaty parties that have exercised their on-site inspection rights include Argentina, Brazil, Chile, the People's Republic of China, France, and Norway. In all, some 170 inspections of individual national installations in Antarctica have taken place. Additionally, certain historical monuments and protected areas have been inspected as well.

No violations of the Antarctic Treaty by any party have been reported as a result of these inspections.

6. The United States Inspection Process

Due to the precedent-setting and potentially controversial nature of the first inspections, direct authorization from the President of the United States was required before the first US inspection in Antarctica could be undertaken. This authorization was given by President John F. Kennedy on September 4, 1963. Since then, as the inspections have become "routine," the planning and approval process has been carried out by an interdepartmental body presently known as the Antarctic Policy Group. This group is chaired by the US Department of State and includes all of the Executive Branch departments and agencies with a direct interest in Antarctica. The principal members of this group are the Department of State, the Arms Control and Disarmament Agency (ACDA), the National Science Foundation (NSF), the United States Coast Guard, the Office of the Secretary of Defense, the Department of Commerce, the Environmental Protection Agency, and the Department of the Interior.

From the beginning, ACDA has been responsible for the formulation of the Antarctic Treaty inspection plans. Working closely with the State Department, ACDA recommends the timing of inspections and the facilities to be inspected. This is approved at the Assistant Secretary level in both agencies. Thereafter, these agencies work with NSF, which is responsible for overall management of the United States Antarctic Program, and the Coast Guard to allocate the necessary logistical resources to support the inspection.

After an inspection team is selected, the Department of State provides the required notifications to the other States Parties "designating" the United States "observers." The inspection can take place anytime thereafter. Due to the severe weather conditions in Antarctica, inspection activities almost invariably take place during the Antarctic summer months (December-March). Advance notice of inspections is not required by the treaty, but for logistical reasons usually this is provided 24 hours before the team's arrival at the base or station to be inspected.

A "typical" United States inspection team would consist of five to seven designated observers. These would include a team leader, one or more translators, and a variety of arms control and Antarctic experts from the State Department, ACDA, the NSF, and other relevant agencies. The team would be ferried to Antarctica either by aircraft -- ski-equipped LC-130 Hercules transports (see Figure 4) or the larger C-141s -- or by ship, depending upon the location of the facilities to be inspected. Most of the national scientific research stations in Antarctica are located near the coasts.

Once in Antarctica, in most cases the team would be transported to the sites to be inspected by UH-1 Huey helicopters (see Figure 5). These helicopters can carry about six inspectors, in addition to a three-man crew. In some cases where the inspected site is

Figure 4 LC-130 Hercules at the South Pole
(Source: Author)

Figure 5   UH-1 Huey Helicopter in the Dry Valleys
(Source: Author)

close to a US base (such as New Zealand's Scott Base), the inspection team would travel overland by motor transport. In other cases, where the site to be inspected is beyond the range of helicopters (such as Russia's Vostok station), the team would be flown in by ski-equipped, fixed-wing aircraft.

Figure 6   US Antarctic Inspection List

Physical Description	**Equipment Facilities**
Number of buildings	Generators
Landing or dock facilities	Incinerators
History of site	Fuel storage
Age of buildings	Notable scientific equipment
New or recent construction	Radioisotope handling equipment
Future plans	Medical facilities
Sketch or map of buildings	Water system: type, capacity
Personnel	**Vehicles**
Personnel list	Boats
Total number	Aircraft
Winter-over staff	Motor vehicles
Responsible agency or ministry	Cargo handling or earth-moving equipment
Length of tour of personnel	Other
Number of military	
Primary Mission	**Re-Supply**
Commander's view of primary mission	Frequency
Other staff's views	How accomplished
Scientific Program	**Arms**
Main type of study	Weapons
Types of scientists	Ammunition/explosives
How is research published	Military activities
How is program determined, or approved	Military officers/personnel
Foreign scientists	
	Communications
	Radio transmission frequency
	Times frequencies are monitored
	Stations time zone
	Satellite communications

A typical US inspection activity might last two to four weeks and involve inspection visits to a dozen or so foreign facilities. In 1983, the US inspected 14 foreign installations in Antarctica, the most ever inspected in one year. In 1989, six sites were inspected. It is rare for an inspection team to spend more than a day at any given facility. The bulk of the time involved in carrying out an inspection activity is spent in traveling to and from the continent and between stations. When flying to an inspection site by helicopter, the US inspection team usually first overflys the installation, carrying out an aerial inspection as permitted by the treaty.

Unlike more recent arms control inspection regimes, there are no agreed lists of inspection equipment. US inspection teams generally rely on visual observation and notetaking. To assist them in their treaty-related observations, the inspectors employ a standard checklist (see Figure 6). The only "technical" equipment regularly employed by US observers are cameras. These need to be protected when not in use to prevent the lens cap and shutter from freezing over. The only equipment specifically provided to inspection team members is cold-weather survival clothing. This equipment is not peculiar to inspection team members. Rather, it is the same survival gear issued to all participants in the US Antarctic program.

United States observers inspect first and foremost to ensure compliance with the Antarctic Treaty's prohibitions on military and nuclear activities. However, they are also afforded an opportunity to inspect for compliance with the panoply of environmental regulations for the preservation of the Antarctic environment that have been adopted by the States Parties to the treaty. The inspections historically have been conducted in a businesslike but cordial atmosphere. Indeed, isolated stations readily welcome their foreign guests, and genuinely seem to enjoy the visits.

In addition to inspecting foreign installations in Antarctica, United States observers inspect various historical sites and structures, monuments, protected areas (such as penguin rookeries), and sites of special scientific interest. Following an inspection, the US observers prepare a report of their observations and findings. Copies of these reports are made available to the other treaty parties soon after they are completed.

To date, the United States has detected no violations of the arms control provisions of the Antarctic Treaty during the course of its on-site inspection activities.

7.   Conclusion

The on-site inspection regime embodied in the Antarctic Treaty of 1959 has proven to be of great significance both in itself and as a precedent. The regime plays a major role in assuring the community of nations that the Antarctic continent remains at all times demilitarized and reserved solely for peaceful pursuits. The confidence that these inspections have engendered has led to over three decades of international cooperative effort in the peaceful scientific exploration of the frozen continent. At the same time, the success of the Antarctic on-site inspection system provides an important precedent for the elaboration of inspection regimes in subsequent arms control agreements such as the INF, START, and the CWC. Indeed, as we approach the dawn of the twentieth century and the new era of global cooperation developing in the wake of the cold war, the Antarctic Treaty inspection regime may well become the model for future cooperative efforts in arms control verification and confidence-building.

Chapter 21

IRAQ AND UN SECURITY COUNCIL RESOLUTION 687:
THE ROLE OF THE IAEA AND LESSONS TO BE LEARNED

Maurizio Zifferero

Two and one half years have elapsed since the United Nations Security Council adopted Resolution 687, the cease-fire arrangement that mandated the destruction, removal, or rendering harmless of Iraq's unconventional weapons capabilities (nuclear, chemical and biological weapons and ballistic missiles with ranges over 150 kilometers). To fulfill this mandate, the Vienna-based International Atomic Energy Agency (IAEA), developed a detailed picture of the vast and previously undiscovered scope of Iraq's nuclear weapon program. In the process, the IAEA and the global community learned valuable lessons which will help in the future to detect similar threats.

UN Security Council Resolution 687 charged two bodies, the IAEA and the newly formed UN Special Commission (UNSCOM), with mapping and neutralizing Iraq's weapons of mass destruction programs. The IAEA was tasked with neutralizing the nuclear component of Baghdad's programs, with the assistance of UNSCOM. On the other hand, UNSCOM was given specific responsibility for dismantling Iraq's biological, chemical, and ballistic missile programs.

IAEA's mandate spelled out under the Security Council resolution has two phases: first, full investigation and the destruction, removal, or rendering harmless of those items relevant to the Iraqi nuclear weapons program; and second, establishing and implementing a longer-term monitoring and verification plan to prevent any future revival of this program. The first phase involved highly intrusive on-site inspections at more than 70 sites, and the collection of information regarding the equipment and technical advice supplied to Iraq. In the course of the past two and half years, the IAEA has succeeded in identifying and removing or destroying most of Iraq's nuclear weapons potential.

IAEA activities in Iraq have also established a sound basis for long-term monitoring of Iraq. This involves routine procedures and techniques as well as a number of imaginative ones, including the use of sophisticated sensors, the periodic monitoring of Iraq's principal bodies of water to examine signatures of prohibited activities, and unannounced visits of resident inspectors to plants, factories, and research centers.

Immediately after Resolution 687 was adopted on April 3, 1991, the IAEA set about its initial task of establishing an "action team." The team drew on the IAEA's own expertise and that of its laboratories, as well as on its network of international contacts, thus making use of experts with additional special skills. This blend proved very successful despite the difficult environment in which the teams were forced to operate.

The first on-site inspection by the IAEA action team took place from May 15 to 20, 1991. During the earliest stages of the inspection process, several disquieting discoveries came to light. None was more sobering than the growing realization of the true dimensions of Iraq's secret nuclear weapons program. By the end of September 1991, the main components of Iraq's clandestine nuclear program were uncovered: a program that involved over 10,000 scientist, engineers, and technicians working on projects with an estimated cost (by Western standards) of several billion dollars. It is estimated that Iraq may have been within three to five years of producing its first nuclear weapon when the

Gulf War began and was pursuing no less than three different paths toward acquiring the key materials for such a nuclear weapon.

Unquestionably, this was a serious intelligence failure. In particular, until the passage of Resolution 687, the IAEA possessed no intelligence unit of its own or had any access to the intelligence information of other nations. All IAEA pre-war inspections had been directed only at declared facilities.

Iraq's clandestine nuclear program was initiated in earnest after the 1981 Israeli bombing of the French-supplied *Osiraq* research reactor under construction at the Al Tuwaitha complex south of Baghdad. The program escaped largely undetected by Western intelligence agencies and indeed by the IAEA's own safeguards system. Iraq's secrecy was successful even though part of the program depended for its progress and success on the supply of substantial technical know-how, materials, and equipment from abroad. Iraqi success in keeping the program secret was achieved by conducting its large-scale activities almost solely at secret and undeclared sites not visited by the IAEA in the pre-war period.

No one guessed that, in its quest for nuclear weapons, Iraq had revived and updated a 1940s-vintage uranium enrichment method developed at Oak Ridge to produce the highly-enriched uranium used in the Hiroshima bomb. This process is known as electromagnetic isotope separation (EMIS).

Iraq had two EMIS uranium enrichment industrial sites located at Al-Sharqat and Tarmiya. The Tarmiya site was under commissioning at the time it was hit by allied bombing raids during the Gulf War; Al-Sharqat at that time was under construction. Both sites were extensively destroyed during the war. The plant at which Iraq was preparing to begin large-scale production of centrifuges was code named "Al Furat" (Euphrates). Al-Furat and the large facility at Al-Atheer escaped almost entirely unscathed during the war. Both of these nuclear weapons development facilities were destroyed under IAEA supervision in April 1992.

Why were these massive portions of Iraq's program not detected earlier? In addition to previously mentioned intelligence failures, Iraq's closed society and extensive financial resources played a part. Another key factor that existed prior to the Gulf War was that the IAEA safeguards inspections were limited in Iraq (as they were elsewhere) to inspections and accounting for nuclear materials and activities at declared facilities. The IAEA inspected the highly-enriched uranium fuel elements from Iraq's reactors twice a year and checked to see that the declared facilities were not used for unapproved purposes. These operations were limited, in part, by the desire of the IAEA member states to control the financial cost of safeguards inspections measures. Moreover, prior to the Gulf War, no intelligence information was ever provided to the IAEA regarding illegal activities which were taking place at the undeclared facilities in Iraq. If such information had been made available, it might have been used to uncover Iraq's clandestine programs before the war, providing that Iraq had submitted to inspections. By denying access to the IAEA, this would have focused attention on this problem.

The nuclear materials which Iraq obtained from abroad, totaling over 12 kilograms of fresh weapons-grade uranium and over 35 kilograms of irradiated, but potentially usable, weapons-grade uranium, remained under IAEA safeguards through the IAEA's pre-war relationship with Iraq. Iraq perhaps was tempted to divert this weapons-grade material to this clandestine program. By doing so it would have saved Baghdad many millions of dollars and several years of effort to produce a nuclear weapon. All of the unirradiated materials have now been removed from Iraq and the removal of the remaining irradiated fuel elements began in the summer of 1993; the process should be completed by February 1994.

As indicted earlier, full-scope inspections on an unprecedented scale began in May 1991. Presently, the IAEA has conducted over 21 on-site nuclear inspections in Iraq. Altogether over 3,000 inspector days have been spent in Iraq. Despite early efforts by Iraq to disregard its obligations under the nuclear Non-Proliferation Treaty (NPT) and its continuing intransigence regarding the submission of procurement data, an internally consistent picture, both in scope and technical detail, has emerged. This program consisted of nine major research and development, production and support facilities, including uranium enrichment plants; a complex and highly successful procurement network; a number of technical advisors who were hired from abroad; an unlimited access to services from the Iraq State Industrial Establishments; and a large, well-trained technical work force. It is also worth nothing that this picture is further validated by the analyses of thousands of samples taken in Iraq by the inspection teams, by the content of hundreds of secret Iraqi documents confiscated by the inspectors, and by intelligence information.

It is clear that Iraq was pursuing at least three different routes to uranium enrichment: EMIS, ultracentrifuge, and chemical enrichment processes. In addition, laboratory experimentation had begun in 1989 to produce and separate about 6 grams of plutonium from fuel irradiated in Iraq's research reactor. The EMIS option was the closest to fruition. Both of the EMIS plants at Al-Tarmiya and Al Sharqat were severely damaged during the war. Iraq, however, made a major effort to disguise the true nature of these installations before the IAEA inspection teams arrived. For example, all the EMIS equipment was removed from both sites and a new concrete floor was installed. Despite these efforts and through a combination of chemical and isotopic analyses of samples, defector-generated information, and the assistance of experts who were familiar with EMIS technology, the IAEA identified the real purpose of both sites and rendered them harmless.

Iraq's efforts in the use of ultracentrifuges had not progressed as far as the EMIS program. Iraq had in its possession enough information to begin to purchase all the material required to mass-produce centrifuges and had also conducted a series of single centrifuge tests. Baghdad declared that it planned to produce a test assembly, or cascade, of 100 centrifuges by 1993 and a 500-unit assembly by 1996. This appeared to be a credible goal and the IAEA teams uncovered no evidence that Iraq had produced a significant number of centrifuges. Iraqi scientists made comparatively smaller efforts in enriching uranium by chemical means although they were successful in preliminary laboratory-scale experiments. To complete the picture it should be noted that Iraqi scientists spent several years studying enrichment by gaseous diffusion with no useful results.

Currently, all the plants and associated equipment identified as being related directly to the production and use of fissionable materials (hundreds of millions of dollars worth of facilities and material) have been destroyed either by coalition bombing in the Gulf War or subsequently at the behest of the IAEA inspection teams. Industrial buildings at Al Atheer, Tarmiya and Al Sharqat covering a floor area in excess of half a million square feet have been demolished under the IAEA's supervision. Specialized equipment, instrumentation, and components relevant to enrichment and weaponization activities (over 1900 items in total) have also been destroyed. Six hundred and six tons of special metal alloys intended for use in centrifuge manufacturing have been converted to unusable scrap.

Further, all known stocks of uranium have been identified, verified, and placed under IAEA seal. In the process, the IAEA has identified and inventoried more than 1,000 computer numerically controlled (CNC) machine tools and selected those which will be monitored in the future. Most of the suppliers and manufacturers of this equipment and materials have been identified by the IAEA. Recently, Baghdad provided the IAEA with a list of suppliers of prohibited materials and the sources for technical advice. Subject to the verification of this information for accuracy and completeness, Iraq now has complied with all disclosure requirements concerning its nuclear activities as required in Resolutions 687 and 707; however, before the IAEA is ready to report that, in its view, Iraq has complied with the relevant paragraphs of Resolution 687, Baghdad must formally acknowledge its acceptance of Resolution 715 and of the ongoing monitoring and verification plan required by the Security Council of the United Nations.

While the picture which has been drawn of Iraq's nuclear program is reasonably consistent, a compelling question is whether it is a complete picture. Most experts believe this is the case, although a few still harbor doubts. Because there are still some lingering doubts, the IAEA is now embarked on the second phase of its effort by establishing an ongoing monitoring program for the long term.

One of the elements of this long-term monitoring and verification effort is a countrywide periodic radiometric survey of Iraqi's main bodies of water. This process is designed to pick up any telltale radioactive traces that would betray any large-scale nuclear-related activity. This plan also includes the identification and regular monitoring of facilities and equipment, the continuation of short-notice inspections, and the extensive use of surveillance equipment and sophisticated sensors. All of these efforts could be used to reconstitute Iraq's nuclear program.

The IAEA received information from the intelligence resources of several member states which indicated the possible existence of an underground plutonium production facility comprising of a nuclear reactor and an associated chemical separation (reprocessing) plant. No evidence has been found as yet that such a facility exists. On the contrary, the analysis of environmental samples taken in Iraq suggests that facilities of this nature, if they exist at all, have not operated in the recent years.

Further, concerns have also been voiced over the existence of a centrifuge cascade facility. Experts in centrifuge enrichment who have assisted the IAEA in the inspection process and in the overall assessment of the Iraqi centrifuge efforts do not believe that there is any evidence to support this view.

The IAEA is nevertheless continuing its inspection activities ever mindful of the possibility of uncovering additional Iraqi violations of its obligation to the United Nations. It is the general consensus among experts and team members and shared by the United States government that the IAEA effort has terminated Iraq's nuclear program. While it is true that blueprints and computer codes may be hidden from the inspectors, it is also equally true that Iraq's coherent, industrial-scale support infrastructure has been devastated. It cannot be re-established as long as there is effective monitoring by the United Nations.

The large amount of information arising from the IAEA's activities in Iraq is fully documented. This includes detailed inspections reports, thousand of photographs, video tapes, sample analysis results, verbatim recorded interviews with Iraqi technicians, translations of hundreds of Iraqi secret documents confiscated during these inspections, and detailed correspondence with IAEA member governments and private companies regarding Iraq's procurement efforts. This information has been shared continually as a matter of course with the Special Commission, the IAEA's Board of Governors, and the Security Council.

The lessons of Iraq for the IAEA safeguards regime have certainly not gone unheeded. The events in Iraq have not only highlighted the need to strengthen the IAEA safeguards system - and, in fact, the non-proliferation regime as a whole - but also have heightened the readiness of nations to contribute to these improvements. During 1992 and 1993, the IAEA Board of Governors supported measures for strengthening the safeguards and increasing the ability of the safeguards system to detect the existence of, and gain access to, undeclared nuclear activities. These measures are intended to improve and broaden the scope of the existing safeguards system. The system has worked well in verifying the non-diversion of declared nuclear material at declared nuclear installations. The system was not designed to provide assurance that no undeclared nuclear installations exist. Although the safeguards system, as originally conceived, provided the legal authority to undertake inspections, the Secretariat lacked the information needed to implement this authority. Therefore, it was not timidity but the lack of information which prevented the discovery of Iraq's clandestine program.

The IAEA, with substantial support from many countries, has embarked on an aggressive program to remedy the shortcomings revealed by the Iraqi experience by creating new accounting procedures and establishing universal reporting programs. These include reports on nuclear and nuclear-relevant exports and imports; information on nuclear facility designs; verification of equipment procurement data; environmental sampling analysis; and strengthening the regime so that the IAEA can initiate if any new information concerning clandestine activity is suspected.

On the other hand, the IAEA has been criticized on a number of fronts. One such criticism is that the IAEA inspectors in Iraq should have destroyed all machine tools and other "dual-use" items that might conceivably be connected to Baghdad's nuclear weapons effort. Many of these "dual use" items, in fact, have been destroyed. It is important, however, to note that the IAEA must avoid acting in a manner that might conflict with the carefully crafted mandate of the United Nations Security Council. This mandate does not include preventing Iraq from rebuilding its industrial base, including the manufacturing of conventional weapons. If the IAEA were to undertake a general destruction of Iraq's industrial base, this action might undermine the broadly based support that the Security Council and the United Nations have enjoyed on this issue and which might undermine the long-term investigative and monitoring operation inside Iraq.

Another point of criticism has to be with Iraq's secret and undiscovered attempts at plutonium separation. This was a violation of Iraq's safeguards agreement with the IAEA, and Baghdad was roundly condemned for it. The amount of separated plutonium that was involved was only about six grams. This discovery was far less important in terms of proliferation than the vast Iraqi uranium enrichment effort which was uncovered.

Finally, there are the critics who are concerned that Iraq is hiding major components of its nuclear program. To this date, the IAEA, with the assistance of many governments, has found no evidence to support this. In fact, the evidence found is totally consistent with documentation. However, the IAEA will continue to monitor Iraq in the long-term so that a revival of Iraqi's nuclear ambitions is thwarted.

One of the major lessons learned from the Iraq experience is the importance of intelligence information. Such information increased the effectiveness of the IAEA although it is important to note that the IAEA is not an intelligence organization nor should it attempt to be one. Consequently, in order to be effective the IAEA requires the full support of the international community, especially if new threats of nuclear proliferation are to be averted in the future.

Chapter 22
MONITORING UNITED NATIONS PEACE OPERATIONS:
A NEW APPROACH TO VERIFICATION

H. J. van der Graaf

For some time now, the focus of verification has been on verifying formally negotiated and legally binding treaties and agreements dealing with arms control, arms limitation, and disarmament, but international attention is now focusing on verification in a variety of other contexts going beyond such formal treaties.

Cambodia, one of the greatest undertakings in verification in the history of the United Nations, is a point in case. The concept of monitoring and verifying in this case goes far beyond treaty specific verification requirements. In the Cambodian case, verification has been used as an instrument in the process of peacekeeping and peacemaking. In fact, the whole peace process has been monitored, ranging from monitoring and controlling the state machinery to issues of human rights and the holding of free and democratic elections. It can be argued that in the case of Cambodia, new roles for verification and monitoring have been clearly established.

On 23 October 1991, after 10 years of diplomatic efforts, the Agreements on a Comprehensive Political Settlement of the Cambodian Conflict[1] were signed by Cambodia and eighteen other nations. These agreements should lead to the establishment of an independent, neutral, and non-aligned Cambodian state. The agreements provided for a cease-fire and the withdrawal of all foreign forces; the disposition of the Cambodian armed elements; free and fair general elections; the formation of a national reconciliation administration; the repatriation and re-integration of refugees and the restoration of human rights, all with international supervision and verification. The agreement also specifies that an international control mechanism should play a role in supervising and controlling the implementation of these measures. During the negotiations leading to the signing of the Paris Peace Accords, the Secretary General of the United Nations was mandated to gather the necessary technical information through several fact-finding missions to Cambodia. These missions gathered a vast range of information on communications and the transportation infrastructure, as well as on the administrative apparatus, water supply, sanitation, repatriation of refugees, etc.

As a result of the Paris Conference on Cambodia, a United Nations Transitional Authority in Cambodia (UNTAC) was established with civilian and military components directly responsible to the Secretary General of the United Nations.

All administrative agencies and offices acting in the field of foreign affairs, defense, finance, public security, and information were placed under direct control of UNTAC. UNTAC personnel was comprised of 20,000 peacekeeping troops, 5,000 civilians and 3,500 international police officers.This effort was an unprecedented expansion in peacekeeping and has been enlarged to an extent without precedence. Thus peacekeepers were used in the traditional way not only to investigate and verify compliance with the agreements and to establish and monitor buffer zones between hostile factions but also to help create the conditions for the implementation of a political settlement and to provide humanitarian support to the local population and the returning refugees; consequently, the military verification and monitoring functions of UNTAC have been substantially increased to include:

-- supervising, monitoring, and verifying the withdrawal of foreign forces and their non-return to Cambodia;
-- monitoring the cessation of outside military assistance to all Cambodian parties;
-- locating and confiscating weapons and military supplies throughout the country;
-- supervising the regrouping and relocation of all military forces to designated areas;
-- verifying the process of arms control and arms reduction;
-- assisting in and verifying the clearing of mines;
-- monitoring and safeguarding the electoral process; and
-- monitoring and protecting the return of refugees.

Not all of these tasks have been accomplished. Monitoring the frontiers in order to prevent the return of foreign troops has only been partly successful; no foreign troops have entered the country but an enormous smuggling effort continues unabated. The safe return of the 370,000 refugees can be recorded as a success. The disarmament of the 200,000[2] soldiers of the four factions (the Khmer Rouge, the "Government" army, the troops under the command of Son Sann and the troops loyal to Prince Ranarith, son of Norodom Sihanouk) was unsuccessful. From the beginning, this was attributable to the Party of Democratic Kampuchea (Khmer Rouge), which was unwilling to cooperate. They refused to allow UNTAC forces to deploy in the areas under Khmer Rouge control and refused also to provide information on the number of troops and equipment as required under the Paris Treaty. Consequently, the Khmer Rouge was unwilling to commit its forces to cantonment. As a result, the cantonment, disarmament, and demobilization processes in the other areas, which had already been initiated, were suspended and a series of cease-fire violations followed during the course of 1992 and increased substantially in 1993 immediately prior to the elections. In fact, the majority of the forces in Cambodia continued to remain under arms; however, this situation did not prevent UNTAC from establishing a network of checkpoints in the border areas and in other parts of the country.

The military component of UNTAC was able to establish 31 checkpoints on the borders of Cambodia as well as at the airports and on major routes within the country. Moreover, UNTAC battalions were regularly patrolling and monitoring these areas in order to check for alleged non-compliance and to discourage unauthorized movements of armed personnel and weapons. It should be noted, however, that these activities by UNTAC varied depending on the professional training of the personnel. A number of UNTAC battalions were not sufficiently trained nor equipped for their monitoring and verification missions. Using military units for peacekeeping purposes requires that these forces have a common understanding of the political principles involved and be given the necessary tools for peacekeeping. It is also important that they develop common criteria and operational principles for this process. Common operational, training, and logistical standards need to be established in order for these forces to be able to operate together in one theater. Besides their military operational skills, they require extensive additional training in monitoring and verification techniques and procedures.

It is not my intention to dwell in detail on the Cambodian experience, but it does serve as an example of how monitoring and verification techniques have become part and parcel of conflict prevention and conflict resolution including peace operations such as this.

Contrary to the verification and monitoring of concluded treaties and agreements, monitoring in the context of peace operations must often be conducted in hostile environments, most especially when monitoring takes place in a so-called gray area between peacekeeping and peace-enforcing as was the case in Cambodia. A case-in-point has to do with the sanctions imposed by the Security Council against any party which did not abide by the military provisions of the Paris Agreements. These sanctions were not at all effective. The monitoring of the ban on the export of logs, minerals, and gems to Thailand and the import of oil from that country was unsuccessful primarily because the UN monitors were denied access to a number of border regions. Although Thailand pledged to abide by the decisions taken by the Security Council, it can be assumed that a vast number of goods were transported to and from Thailand through unofficial channels.[3]

Examining verification processes beyond the limited constraints of treaty specific arrangements is not a completely new phenomenon. If we assume that the process of verification establishes the truth, then we can also note that monitoring and fact-finding have always been a part of the process of settling international disputes and conflicts. In the past five years, the Secretary General of the UN has verified the withdrawal of Soviet forces from Afghanistan and Cuban forces from Angola; supervised the cease fire in the Iran/Iraq war; monitored Namibian transition to democracy; observed the disarmament and demobilization of the Contras in Nicaragua; verified the destruction of Iraq's weapons of mass destruction; supervised elections in several countries; and monitored human rights violations in other countries, such as El Salvador. Fact-finding by the Secretary General is strongly supported by the UN General Assembly. In 1991 the Declaration on Fact-Finding, undertaken by the General Assembly, encouraged the Secretary General to carry out continuous monitoring for the purposes of maintaining peace.

Within the context of crisis management, peacekeeping, monitoring, and fact-finding are playing important, ever-expanding roles. No doubt peacekeepers are well versed in the mechanics of conducting weapons inspections, monitoring troop withdrawals, and surveying disengagement zones. Verification and inspection procedures are crucial to the implementation of these resolutions of the Security Council. This was especially noted when the United Nations Special Commission (UNSCOM) conducted inspections in Iraq under Security Council Resolutions 687, 707 and 715. Regional organizations, notably in Europe, are also taking part in monitoring and verifying events, for example in former Yugoslavia and in a number of the republics of the former Soviet Union. At present, in Europe the European Economic Community, the Conference for Security and Cooperation in Europe, the Western European Union, the North Atlantic Treaty Organization, and the United Nations are all involved in conducting monitoring, surveillance, fact finding, and verification missions.

In Africa, the Organization of African Unity (OAU) is increasingly playing a more dynamic role in monitoring and verifying events in a number of African States. The Charter of the OAU makes no specific reference to peacekeeping operations or security arrangements, but the OAU is assuming more responsibility in these areas while in Central America, the Organization of American States (OAS) is playing a dominant role in monitoring and verifying Central American peace processes.[4] Furthermore, the newly established Asian Security Forum in Southeast Asia may become a mechanism for monitoring and verifying events in that part of the world.

There is no doubt of a growing awareness that arms control, arms limitation, disarmament, and verification can be seen in the more general context of international peace and security. Arms control and disarmament are also playing an increasingly important role in peace operations; consequently, verification should be included as part of this broader agenda.

Traditional arms control and disarmament schema, accompanied by intrusive verification arrangements and marked by prolonged negotiations between states or groups of states, do not provide solutions for a growing number of conflicts *within* states. Here, arms limitation and disarmament steps accompanied by monitoring and verification are part of conflict prevention and conflict management. All of these contrivances may infringe upon the sovereignty of a state. To what extent is the sovereignty of a nation violated for the purpose of restoring peace and security? No doubt future arms control and verifications procedures may violate state sovereignty.

At present, there is uncoordinated growth in treaty-related verification procedures. The present treaties require several thousand inspections annually; for example, under the Treaty on Conventional Forces in Europe (CFE) almost 1,000 inspections have already been conducted. Furthermore, the IAEA is conducting about 2,000 inspections a year, of which 70 percent take place in countries which are not suspected of treaty violations, namely Japan, Germany, and Canada.[5] The Chemical Weapons Convention is expected to launch several thousand inspections annually, and under the Vienna agreement on Confidence and Security-Building Measures several hundred inspections are foreseen.

This will most likely be the case for the START Treaties. No doubt there is an urgent need for harmonization and coordination of inspections. Estimates for these inspections have been put at about $100 million dollars for the CFE Treaty to $3 billion dollars for the Chemical Weapons Convention with perhaps a total of more than $4.5 billion dollars for all inspections required by treaties. (Estimated costs are those of the US government only.) These costs are not exorbitant when compared to total world-wide defense expenditures, which are estimated at $1 trillion dollars a year. Unfortunately, governments are not measuring the costs of verification against their total defense budgets!

It is evident that the total verification costs are probably less than one percent of the world's annual defense expenditures; however, the need to economize in these methods is necessary and can take several measures. First, a shift in emphasis is necessary from routine to challenge inspections. Routine inspections should continue to play a role; however, challenge inspections are more cost-effective, in particular when conducted on an "any time, any where" basis. Such inspections will have a much greater overall deterrence value; furthermore, there should be a shift in emphasis from treaty-specific-verification to verification and monitoring missions in troubled areas. Finally, more research is required toward an efficient harmonization or integration of various overlapping verification agreements.

In my opinion, the primary function of verification is to verify compliance and deter violations. Confidence-building measures should never be the primary purpose of verification; however, when a verification system is changing its function towards confidence-building, as is now the case with the relations between Western and Eastern European countries, then the establishment of specific confidence-building measures seems to be a more appropriate and cost-effective approach. However, it should be noted that verification procedures cannot contribute to building more confidence between parties. One should not operate a costly verification system whose primary purpose is that of confidence-building. Finally, verification should not be seen exclusively in the context of formally negotiated and legally or politically binding treaties but should be envisioned in the broader context of furthering international peace and security.

Proliferation of weapons of mass destruction and the excessive spread of conventional weapons is now considered by the UN Security Council as constituting a threat to international peace and security. The earlier-mentioned Declaration on UN Fact-Finding, endorsed by the UN General Assembly, provides a whole range of fact-finding and monitoring activities which may be undertaken by the Secretary General in the field of international peace and security. Formal fact-finding can be mandated by the Security Council or the General Assembly of the United Nations. In his *Agenda for Peace* the Secretary General Boutros Boutros Ghali stressed the importance of fact-finding as a necessity in meeting his responsibilities under Article 99 of the Charter, which states that the Secretary General may bring to the attention of the Security Council any matter which in his opinion threatens the maintenance of international peace and security.[6] In fact, the Secretary General is pleading with the United Nations members to enable him to acquire timely and accurate knowledge of the facts.

Triggered by the *Agenda for Peace*, international attention is now being focused on verification in a variety of contexts which go far beyond the traditional focus of verification as found in arms control and arms limitation treaties.[7] Verification and monitoring are now increasingly being viewed as ways of monitoring the proliferation of weapons of mass destruction, their delivery systems, and related technology; the excessive spread of conventional weapons; unilateral arms limitations proposals; the enforcement of disarmament under Security Council resolutions on disarmament; and arms control, arms limitation, and disarmament treaties which include conflict prevention and conflict management.

In October 1992 the Secretary General of the United Nations issued a report *New Dimensions of Arms Regulation and Disarmament in the Post-Cold War Era* in which he expressed the view that the time had come for the practical integration of disarmament and arms regulation issues and these should be placed in the broader context of the international peace and security agenda. He further noted that the end of bipolarity has increased the need for disarmament and that it was an inherent part of preventive diplomacy, peacemaking, peacekeeping, and peacebuilding, while the proliferation of weapons and related technologies required responsible proliferation controls.[8]

The shift of emphasis from treaty-specific verification to verification in a broader context of international peace and security does not mean that the era of formally negotiated arms limitation and disarmament treaties has become obsolete. Verifying the recently concluded treaties such as the CWC, START, and the CFE will be an ongoing requirement. In addition, there will be a growing need for formally negotiated arms limitation and disarmament treaties in regions where arms control is still a rather unknown and even unpopular phenomenon. As a participant on Asia-Pacific security remarked, "As for weapon proliferation, to halt this process in Asia as an end in itself is neither desirable nor feasible. The [Asian] countries are increasingly wealthy countries, which feel that their economic riches should be defended by a requisite level of military strength."[9]

These new dimensions to arms control and disarmament may now require more comprehensive international monitoring and verification capabilities than presently available. If the international community does not want to rely completely on individual country's national technical means for verification, re-evaluation in enhancing the role of the United Nations in verification and monitoring should be considered. The UN Cambodian experience is clearly telling here in highlighting the importance of monitoring and verification when placed in the broader context of international peace and security.

Additionally, international monitoring and verification of global and regional anti-proliferation efforts is needed, especially for the Missile Technology Control Regime (MTCR),[10] the Australia Group,[11] and other export control regimes.

Such internationalizing of verification and monitoring efforts can only be realized if global or regional organizations are properly equipped and financed for such undertakings. The United Nations does not have the resources for such efforts. Of the 182 members of the UN, some 150 are not paying their delegations. Both the United States and Russia, two of the principal contributors, are in arrears. Without adequate funding no new initiatives are possible and time is ever-fleeting.

Two years ago a group of governmental experts concluded that the time was not ripe for the United Nations to be substantially involved in verification, but the situation has changed dramatically over the past two years. Now the role of the Security Council in containing proliferation and resolving regional conflicts has been enhanced because of the new international environment. Expanding the UN machinery for monitoring and fact-finding is therefore a *conditio sine qua non*.[12] The dramatic changes which have taken place in the international political arena and the recent monitoring activities undertaken by the United Nations, especially its successful performance in Iraq by UNSCOM in inspecting and monitoring Iraq's nuclear, biological, and chemical (NBC) capabilities, provides ample reasons to explore and update the need for a greater United Nations involvement in monitoring and verification.

Consideration should also be given to the idea of a United Nations Special Commission becoming a permanent international inspectorate at the disposal of the Secretary General. The primary function of a United Nations verification body could be the performance of monitoring, fact-finding, and verification of missions in the context of Security Council resolutions against member states which the Security Council considers threats to international peace and security of the community. Such an agency could also render technical support and offer its good offices to bilateral and regional negotiations.

The time is ripe and the political climate propitious for the United Nations to explore the lessons learned from the past few years regarding monitoring and verification as applying to new political realities found in the international arena. It is time to revitalize the group of experts who conducted the 1990 study on the role of the United Nations in the field of verification. A follow-up study should also embrace a review of recent experiences as well as an analysis of the trends in monitoring and verification which have taken place recently in light of the new-found role of the United Nations and the Security Council in furthering peace and security.

Notes

1. Agreements on a Comprehensive Political Settlement of the Cambodian Conflict, Paris, 23 October 1991, United Nations, New York.
2. The regular military forces of the four factions totaled over 200,000, deployed in some 650 locations. In addition, militias, totaling some 250,000, operated throughout the country. Those forces were armed with over 300,000 weapons of all types and some 80 million rounds of ammunition. United Nations report prepared by the

Field Personnel Section, Field Operations Division, Department of Administration and Management, 93-23525, 23 April 1993.
3. Ramses Amer, "The United Nations' Peacekeeping Operation in Cambodia: Overview and Assessment," in *Contemporary Southeast Asia,* Vol. 15, No. 2, September 1993.
4. H. P. Klepak, *Security Considerations and Verification of a Central American Arms Control Regime,* Occasional paper Nr. 5, External Affairs and International Trade Canada, Ottawa, 1990.
5. David Fischer, "The Nuclear Non-Proliferation Regime: Template for the Future?" in James Brown (ed.), *Challenges in Arms Control for the 1990s* (Amsterdam: VU University Press, 1992).
6. *An Agenda for Peace, Preventive Diplomacy, Peacemaking and Peacekeeping,* Report of the UN Secretary-General, 17 June 1992, United Nations, New York.
7. Letter from the Permanent Mission of Canada to the United Nations Secretary General, 14 June 1993 on the Canadian Government's views on verification.
8. Boutros Boutros Ghali, *New Dimensions of Arms Regulation and Disarmament in the Post-Cold War Era,* 27 October 1992, United Nations A/C.1/47/7, New York.
9. Derek da Cunha, presentation on "Conventional Arms and Security in the Southeast Asia," at a seminar on the UN and Asia-Pacific Security, Beijing, 2-4 November 1993.
10. The 1987 MTCR is a set of guidelines which member states agree to follow in their national export controls. It is neither a treaty nor a formal agreement and has no institutional secretariat or verification mechanism. It focuses on limiting proliferation of missiles (and related technology) carrying a payload of 500 kg for a distance of over 300 km. At present the MTCR has 24 members, while China, Russia, Israel, South Africa , Argentina, and Brazil have agreed to abide by the guidelines.
11. The 1985 Australia Group is a group of mainly Western countries which coordinate their export controls on about 50 dual-use chemical precursors as well as so-called "warning guidelines" for the export of plants and equipment. The group is not only covering chemicals and related equipment but also biological and toxin agents and equipment. The group has no verification mechanisms. Its future usefulness is questionable because of the Chemical Weapons Convention as well as the imminent ratification of the Biological Weapons Convention.
12. The US was the only one casting a negative vote against the 1988 General Assembly resolution regarding a study to be conducted by the Secretary General on the UN's role in verification.

Chapter 23

MIXING AND MATCHING INITIATIVES IN ARMS CONTROL IN SOUTH AMERICA: THE RELATIONSHIP BETWEEN THREAT PERCEPTION AND INTERNATIONAL INSPECTIONS IN THE NUCLEAR FIELD FOR BRAZIL

Thomaz G. Costa

This analysis addresses the question of why Brazil adopted a "dual-use" model for its nuclear program up until the mid-1980s and since the early 1990s has striven for the creation of a new non-proliferation model in South America.

The primary argument of this study is that Brazil's relation with Argentina was the predominant factor in defining Brazil's national nuclear policy, which in turn affected the country's global relations in the nuclear arena. As the incentives for cooperation with Argentina became greater, the perceptions of regional threats were reduced significantly, creating a proper environment for mutual verification. A system of mutual inspection arrangements was organized, in opposition to the mechanism of the global regime which was structured around the Non-Proliferation Treaty (NPT), resulting in more effective confidence-building measures between the two countries, reducing the notions of threats, eliminating mistrust, introducing greater transparency, and providing international assurance regarding the peaceful purposes of both Brazil's and Argentina's nuclear programs.

As Lamazière and Jaguaribe have argued, the regional model by-passed the global prescriptions for non-proliferation. The sequential approach was from cooperation to verification, and not verification to cooperation.[1] As Brazil finds confidence at the regional level, mistrust still remains for the International Atomic Energy Agency's (IAEA) prescriptions to comprehensive safeguards in order to attain non-proliferation. In the eyes of Brazilians, such safeguards threaten their own nuclear technological development.

1. "Dual Use" Nuclear Program?

In March of 1987, General Haroldo Erichsen, Brazil's Army Chief for Science and Technology, stated, "... to manufacture atomic bombs is not our objective, but, if necessary, we will. With the knowledge we are gaining, obviously, we will be in a position to manufacture them. If we have the resources, we can do it in two years time."[2] This declaration may sound out of context if one considers the importance of the Joint Declaration on Nuclear Policy of Foz de Iguaçú, signed by the presidents of Argentina and Brazil on 30 November 1985. This joint declaration set forth the bases for active cooperation in the nuclear field between the two countries, functioning as the first practical guide for a common nuclear policy, with mutual aspirations for international inspection, technological exchange, and joint-ventures in industrial development.

The contradiction between the interpretation that could have been made by foreign decision-makers regarding General Erichsen's warning and the concrete steps for regional nuclear cooperation undertaken by Brazil at that time reveals the strategic complexity and ambiguities present in a nuclear program such as the one developed by Brazil. For its program, Brazil eventually established goals to build research and power-generating nuclear facilities, to enrich fuel, and to control the technology for nuclear propulsion. Although Brazil has had many economic and financial difficulties that have greatly reduced the pace of many projects since the late 1980s, it is known that achievements in the field of nuclear technologies have been significant, especially in the areas of civilian (energy generation) and military use (submarine propulsion). Because of the government's secrecy policy, the general international communities apprehension was that Brazil was on its way to build nuclear weapons.

Many states, such as Australia, Canada, Nigeria, South Korea, Japan, Mexico, and Sweden have agreed and signed the Non-Proliferation Treaty (NPT) relinquishing the goal of acquiring nuclear weapons. But other countries still reject the NPT regime. Among its non-member countries, India has exploded an atomic bomb in 1974 and Israel and the Republic of South Africa have long been considered countries that possess nuclear weapons. Pakistan, Iraq, Taiwan, Argentina, and Brazil have been of concern to the international community because it is suspected that they have developed indigenous nuclear programs capable of building nuclear weapons.

In order to frame Brazil's nuclear decisions, this study suggests that Brazil played two simultaneous strategic "games" in the past three decades: one was played with Argentina at the regional level; in game two, Brazil faced the alliance of the United States and the IAEA in their efforts to contain proliferation. In the regional game, one can suggest that Brazil's threat perception was guided by attributing to Argentina a mirror-image drive for regional hegemony. In the global game, Brazil pursued a national policy that could have resulted in the acquisition of nuclear weapons "know-how", driven by a perceived need, especially within the military, to break-up the technological oligopoly of the major powers that contained Brazil's drive to become a major power.[3] In general, Brazil's nuclear policy has been built upon the official view that it should not accept a discriminatory international status, in which it relinquishes its nuclear capabilities while other nations remain nuclear powers, allowing them to use the leverage of their weapons for national interests, thus harvesting both military and commercial benefits.[4]

2.   The Elusive Notion Of Threat

The notion of threat perception is one of the most important variables in the conduct of international politics; it is also an elusive concept, difficult to analyze systematically.[5] It arises from the interpretation of capabilities and intentions of other actors that result in the decision-makers creating images of threat, thus believing that harmful actions can happen either at a particular time or in a diffuse and uncertain future.[6]

Since the end of World War II, Brazilian society and governments have retained a very diffuse notion of threat perception to their national security. In the 1960s and 1970s, many social segments, led by the armed forces, developed a sharp notion of threat because of internal guerrilla warfare, an subversion that was based on ideological confrontation.[7] The main arguments for the increase of national power was a result of the diffuse perceptions that carried with it the notion of future risks. The relationship of this increase in national power with nuclear technology came about because of Brazil's vulnerability to the fluctuation of oil prices and the recurring negative effects of the Middle East crises, thus supporting the argument that Brazil needed to be self-sufficient in energy sources.

As one surveys Brazil's strategic rhetoric since the mid-1950s, its aim has been to become a major power in the international arena. There is a general belief among Brazilians that the country must not just eliminate its vulnerabilities but must also become an important international actor. It must take advantage of its potential due to abundant natural resources, large population and markets, and its repeated favorable results of national growth that was achieved up until the early 1980s. Still, for many analysts, it is quite difficult to identify the reasons why Brazil would have taken the initiative to achieve nuclear technological competence and atomic weapons' capability during these past decades. Although the country has striven to advance both socially and economically, becoming one of the largest economies of the world, Brazil still retains many characteristics of an under-developed nation, with chronic triple-digit inflation, large internal and external debts, and one-fifth of its population living in total poverty. However, there are still large concentrations of national wealth in the hands of few, inefficient public administration, and political instability, even now within the democratic framework of the 1988 Constitution.

On the other hand, Brazil has enjoyed a very favorable political and geographical environment, without any clear disputes with its neighbors nor having a national agenda of debates that gives importance to national defense issues or to questions of foreign threats to its territorial integrity. Historically, the country has been marginally affected by international conflicts. Only recently, led by some military officers and local politicians, the question of sovereignty over the Amazon region has entered the debates nationally. Some envision a potential foreign threat to Brazil's control over this region due to national environmental policies protecting the tropical forest.

If one turns to the national debate regarding nuclear policy, one notes concerns about environmental safety, the cost-benefits of energy production, the operational-bureaucratic structure, and the budget constraints in the Brazilian program.[8] But there is no debate over its military strategic affect, either in terms of nuclear weapons or in terms of the nuclear-powered submarine program. There have been, however, discussions regarding the secrecy and high costs of the projects, but not a public discussion of their strategic benefits.[9] The official attitude in justifying the nuclear program is only done in terms of the technological autonomy and international equality Brazil attains. Because of the secrecy that surrounds this program, it is difficult to evaluate its management, budgetary process, and strategic reasoning for integrating nuclear weapons as part of Brazil's national defense policy. This lack of access to official records has created impediments to revealing its actual nuclear capabilities and intentions before the 1990s.

3. International Inspection As Source Of Mistrust

International inspections are a key factor for political conflict in the non-proliferation agenda. Since it is the prime mechanism for assuring non-proliferation, it has become a source of sour relations between Brazil, on one hand, and the United States and IAEA, on the other.

In the United States and among its allies, it is generally accepted that proliferation is undesirable; that is, nuclear proliferation is essentially harmful to regional peace and stability because it threatens the stability of international security and the safety of humankind. This view has produced policy decisions that are rejected by the non-members of the NPT.[10] For the leaders of non-proliferation policy, the effort toward nuclear non-proliferation has been based on decisions in controlling the transfer of nuclear technologies and delivery systems' technologies. The argument is made that if sensitive technology is denied or if pressures can be imposed to halt national programs, then non-proliferation can be sustained.[11] Thus, little effort has been directed toward understanding alternative international mechanisms or actions that could be used to neutralize the incentives to acquire such weapons.

4. Incentive To Go Nuclear

The general objectives of the Brazilian nuclear program have been to provide technological development and industrial capability for both civilian and military use.[12] Nuclear technology was perceived during the 1964-1986 period as an important element of national power, a technological force capable of assisting in national development and security. Since then, the country has made large investments of approximately \$13 billion in training personnel and in building facilities to manufacture, purify, and enrich nuclear fuel, made to reprocess the fuel spent, in generating energy for the manufacture of equipment for new nuclear facilities, and for the export of fuel, products, and technology for the international markets.

Regarding the use of nuclear technology in the military arena, evidence indicates that Brazil has had explicit, long-range plans to build nuclear-powered ships, especially submarines. As to the manufacturing and testing of nuclear weapons, there is no official confirmation of such objectives, although, at one time, efforts perhaps were made in acquiring such capability.[13] If, on one hand, Brazil's drive to use nuclear technology for civilian purposes was not a concern, the potential use for military purposes, on the other hand, was of central concern at two levels.

4.1   Game One: Rivalry With Argentina

The first context is to analyze Brazil's potential dispute with Argentina for regional hegemony. One can suggest that Brazil's strategic interaction was a situation analogous to the Prisoner's Dilemma (PD). The Prisoner's Dilemma, a concept generated by game theory, offers a scenario of a non-zero sum game that aims to explain the selection of payoffs (decisions) by the players involved. The utility of this analogy in international relations is powerful because it portrays interactions where the success of player A's strategy depends on B's choice of movement, with both being subject to the consequences of the interdependence of individual decisions. The uncertainty that exists with its unclear promises of punishments and rewards, the difficulties of distinguishing cooperative movement from defection in simultaneous decisions, and the complexity that is introduced by mixed strategies and interaction provide a rich theoretical model to frame data and produce alternative explanation to behavior and unintended consequences in such interactions.[14]

As this game is brought to the regional arena, involving Brazil and Argentina, three possible results were eminent: both countries deciding to acquire the nuclear weapons' technology, neither country acquiring it, or one country acquiring it while the other does not. One can say that if only one country had decided to acquire the nuclear capability, it would be possible to assume that some strategic advantage would be harvested by the new nuclear power in this regional context, while avoiding the potential cost of being viewed as the "sucker." The mutual non-cooperation equilibrium had the costs of risking the effects of a nuclear weapons' race at the lower margin and of the risk of an atomic war at the upper end of the scale if both were to go to war. The only attractiveness for the nuclear option was to sustain an equilibrium based on deterrence.

Cooperation with the NPT regime has been the satisfactory solution achieved thus far. But it only happened as each country was able to break down the PD's perceived structure, modifying perceptions and values that dominated the regional foreign policy of both countries during these past decades. The potential for conflict between Brazil and Argentina comes quickly to the minds of many. It is either based on the rhetoric of the geopolitical thinking that developed between the 1930s and the 1970s, or the sustained dispute on how to explore and use the rivers in the Plata Basin for hydroelectric power. This was before the settlement between Brasilia and Buenos Aires in late 1970s.[15]

Thus, one can suggest that Brazil's initiatives in the late 1940s would "fit" a reaction to Argentina's decision to advance a nuclear program for military ends. It was in 1945 that Buenos Aires decided to undertake an independent program "plowing ahead, disregarding adversity and outside pressures."[16]

4.2   *Game Two: Responding To The Global Control*

Like any other leadership following world events, the Brazilian government quickly understood the effect of the nuclear revolution and began to organize its national resources and developed technologies and to participate in the world nuclear market in the late 1940s. Between 1945 and 1947, Brazil's nuclear policy had the objective of exporting fissile material, from its rich mineral reserves to the United States and to any other countries in exchange for training, equipment, and scientific information.

If Brazil had at that period the objective of acquiring "know-how" to build an atomic bomb, the results to achieve such goal were constrained up until 1953 by the "secrecy policy" that prevailed among the nuclear powers.[17] This policy was a modification of the wartime non-proliferation stand adopted by Canada, Great Britain, and the United States, under the Quebec Agreement of 1943. It prohibited scientific and technological disclosure of applications of nuclear energy. Other measures imposed by the US government, such as the MacMahon Act, prevented exchange and commerce in this field aiming also to control proliferation. The primary lesson for the "secrecy policy" period was the American proposal of the Baruch Plan (1946), which called for a world supranational authority to manage nuclear activities.

Brazil was not just dissatisfied with the pattern of "international cooperation" in the nuclear field during this period but also was subject to pressures from the United States. In 1953, the US intervened to stop the shipment from Germany of an ultracentrifuge developed by scientist Otto Hahn, a former member of Hitler's atomic power project.[18]

Another period of international structuring of nuclear technological transfer was known as the "liberal policy." This phase basically began in 1953 with President Eisenhower's "Atoms for Peace" proposal and ended around 1965 with the negotiations for a Comprehensive Nuclear Test Ban Treaty. The British had exploded their atomic bomb early in 1952, and by 1953 the Soviet Union had acquired full capacity to manufacture and to deploy nuclear weapons. At that time, the United States began to fear that the Soviet Union could now use the transfer of nuclear technology to others to exercise political influence. Thus, the United States' reaction was to facilitate the transfer of scientific knowledge and establish close monitoring of the supply and flow of nuclear materials and equipment for technological development. For Brazil, this liberal policy envisioned cooperation and exchange in nuclear research for peaceful means, by providing that facilities would be open to international inspections.[19]

For Brazil, its major effort in the nuclear field, up until 1967, was to install research reactors. Brazil purchased two from the United States and one was locally built. Interests regarding the basics of nuclear science and industrial applications were the primary incentive for cooperation between Brazil and the proponents of non-proliferation, thus avoiding the implementation of a secret program for weapons' development. During this period there was no need for Brazil to disclose any decision about keeping open the option of producing a nuclear device in the future because Buenos Aires did not possess even the basic scientific knowledge necessary to do so.

4.3   *Interdependence Of The Games*

By 1965, Brazil had no desire or reason to demonstrate non-cooperative behavior either in its relations with Argentina or with the advanced nuclear power states. There was also no need to have a clear commitment either for a sole "peaceful" program or for a "dual-use" one. But in 1965, the first research reactor without international inspections began to operate in Argentina. Simultaneously, several tracks of international negotiations were begun, especially with a proposal for the Latin American countries to establish a nuclear-weapons- free zone in the hemisphere. Thus, it became inevitable that a decision would have to be made, affecting both Brazil's interaction with Argentina and her relations with the global effort of non-proliferation.

The 1967 Treaty for the Prohibition of Nuclear Weapons in Latin America (Tlatelolco) and the Non-Proliferation Treaty of 1968 began a new round of diplomacy between Brazil and Argentina. The decision was occasioned by Brazil's deciding to sign both treaties. If cooperation meant that Brazil had to abide by the newly-set non-proliferation regimes, then Brazil abjured its actions. But again, ambiguity existed. The parties to the Treaty of Tlatelolco agreed not to manufacture, test, or acquire nuclear weapons nor to accept weapons which were deployed by nuclear powers into their countries. They agreed to account for and allow inspection of all their nuclear activities. Furthermore, they created a regional agency known as the Organization for the Prohibition of Nuclear Weapons (OPANAL) to investigate, at the request of treaty members, whether another party was engaging in prohibited activities and was establishing full-scope safeguard procedures. A protocol requiring that outside nations respect the denuclearization of the area was added and was signed by the United States, United Kingdom, France, and The Netherlands, but not by the Soviet Union. A second protocol, that eventually was ratified by all nuclear powers, prohibits these countries from using or threatening to use their nuclear arms against treaty members. Until the early 1990s, Brazil and Chile retained the entry into force provision until all states ratified it. If Brazil had as its official policy the intention to acquire atomic weapons' technology, it did not feel constrained by the

Tlatelolco Treaty since that treaty permits States to "carry out explosions of nuclear devices for peaceful purposes -- including explosions which involve similar devices to those used in nuclear weapons."[20] The main constraint was the treaty's determination to its own verification agency and member-states to establish agreements with the IAEA, allowing full IAEA's inspections to all national facilities.[21]

From the States belonging to the NPT, it is possible to identify three different groups. First, there is the so-called "nuclear weapons club" made up of States that had actually integrated nuclear weapons into their arsenals before the treaty (United States, Soviet Union, United Kingdom, and China). Second, there is a large number of States which subscribed to the NPT and relinquished their rights to the acquisition of nuclear weapons. There remains a third "club" consisting of States that, by word and deed, retained the option to develop their nuclear program without foreign safeguards to their national installations. It is assumed that this group plans to possess nuclear arms capability. They have neither signed nor ratified the Treaty. Among these countries, India was the first to explode an experimental atomic device (1974) and the Republic of South Africa, which was a member of this latter group, declared (1992) that it had nuclear weapons but was dismantling its program and destroying these weapons.

Since 1968, the official view of Brazil remains that the NPT regime discriminates between nuclear and non-nuclear States. To Brazil, the resulting distribution of power and potential use of force were unacceptable.[22] Thus, in 1975, Brazil decided to increase its nuclear scientific and industrial programs with an extensive plan for technology transfer negotiated with Germany. The view of then President Ernesto Geisel of Brazil was that the nuclear powers were not negotiating to disarm and that nuclear cooperation was limited and dictated by the interests of those countries that could export nuclear technology. "There are only restrictions for the non-nuclear States, while the nuclear powers have the 'obligation' not to transfer nuclear weapons to non-nuclear countries."[23] The inability of the major powers to disarm and the imposed controls to secure access to critical technologies became an issue in Brazil's decision to expand its own nuclear research efforts. After the agreement with Germany, new pressures began to appear from the United States, especially in providing fuel supply for Brazil's nuclear power plants.

Outside analysts may misinterpret the decisions taken and the real intentions proffered by the decisionmakers since these actions were taken in secret. It is possible to assume that in the period prior to the NPT there were no significant demands from the non-proliferation leaders upon Brazil (and Argentina) to restrain their nuclear goals. The creation of national programs in the 1950s by Brazil can be simply explained that she required a minimum competence in nuclear technology so that she could absorb the economic developments derived from it. We could also hypothesize that the military authorities had no military objectives in mind; therefore, many decisions or signals given at that time about this issue could have been interpreted as tactical moves to enhance nuclear cooperation bargaining, assure greater access to technologies at the lowest costs, and use deception to develop national programs without revealing the acquired technological "know-how."

Brazil's decision to sign and ratify the Tlatelolco Treaty, but not to waive the entry into force requirement, could also have been understood as a signal or desire to cooperate if the other partners were willing to do so. Until the mid-1980s, Brazil had no incentives to cooperate, that is to abdicate unilaterally its nuclear weapons' technology. But something caused Brazil to change its national perceptions regarding its nuclear program. It started to provide international assurances that its national program was going to shift from an ambiguous "dual use" track to one clearly aimed at "peaceful means."

5.   Mixing Strategies, Matching For Cooperation

There is no evidence that suggests how Brazilian governmental officials analyzed the way in which to integrate into its weapons' arsenal nuclear weapons. One does not find public statements that shed light on how Brazil's decisionmakers considered these implications at the regional level, especially on how it would affect relations with Buenos Aires. At the global level, the logic of breaking up the "nuclear power freeze" and the drive to make Brazil a key world player seemed to be enough to justify for most government official the "dual track" program.

Nevertheless, in the mid-1980s a confluence of factors changed the prospects of Brazil's nuclear program. First, it is important to recall that in 1979 Argentina and Brazil settled their differences over the exploration of the water resources in the Plata Basin.[24] Henceforth, these two countries were able to establish mechanisms for joint construction of hydroelectric power plants, coordinate long-range plans for viable river navigation, and agree upon complementary electric power grids. In addition, the military failure of Argentina during the Falklands War in 1982 and the consequent demobilization of its military reduced Brazil's fears of Argentine military intentions.

Second, as the military government came to its demise on the Brazilian political scene, the popular demands for greater transparency and accountability of the nuclear program were transformed into greater constitutional and congressional controls. In the 1988 Constitution, an article banned the building of nuclear weapons, and by the time of President Fernando Collor's administration, there was the imposition of controls in the undertaking of nuclear research for military uses. It now required that it be under civilian supervision. At the same time the secret "parallel program" nuclear program came to a halt.

Further, Brazil and Argentina in 1988 celebrated a treaty aiming to establish regional economic integration. This treaty was later supplemented by the Treaty of Asuncion (1991) that set forth a vast network of political commitments to coordinate trade policies and market access for a economically integrated regional unit.

Finally, by the late 1980s Brazil's official nuclear program under the agreement with Germany almost came to an end because of Brazil's economic and fiscal difficulties that started in 1982. The program for construction of nuclear power-plants was paralyzed, and the agreement with Germany was interrupted.[25]

The ever-quickening political shifts in Brazil in its regional relations and the remarkable changes in world politics provided strong incentives for concrete steps to be taken in nuclear cooperation between Brazil and Argentina. This necessitated the revision of the Tlatelolco Treaty and the surge of accommodating proposals that were instituted between Brazil and the NPT regime.

6.   Concrete Steps For Nuclear Cooperation

It is recognized that the agreement for nuclear cooperation signed between Brazil and Argentina in 1980 was within an environment of mutual mistrust that would last for years to come as long as military authoritarian governments were in power in both countries. These governments, in search of technological developments and the sharing of world markets, were strongly pursuing to establish local arms industries and to acquire advanced military manufacturing capabilities, either through national means or importing projects from overseas. In their secrecy, an agreement for bilateral cooperation was seen as a mere piece of diplomatic rhetoric and good will, without extending credibility among the non-proliferation advocates.

By 1985, in an era of democratization, Brazil and Argentina signed the Declaration of Iguaçú. Both countries committed themselves to develop nuclear energy for peaceful means, cooperate in technological nuclear development, and to extend this collaboration to other countries in the region. The Declaration established a working group, made up of members of the respective national nuclear commissions and companies in order to implement the measures agreed upon. As an immediate consequence of this protocol and as part of the overall process of regional integration, both countries in 1986 agreed to organize notification procedures for nuclear accidents and emergencies and to undertake joint nuclear research and development efforts.

From 1986 to 1990, several joint declarations were signed. Technical visits became routine, and political leaders began to visit each other's nuclear facilities as symbols of joint cooperation. In 1990, the countries agreed in the Declaration on a Common Nuclear Policy to establish mutual inspection procedures for all nuclear installations, joint technical accounting of nuclear materials, the beginning of joint negotiations with the IAEA for a comprehensive safeguard agreement, and a joint effort to adjust the Tlatelolco Treaty for purposes of regional enforcement.

Nevertheless, the most important decision of the bilateral non-proliferation regime was the creation of the Argentina-Brazil Agency for Accounting and Control of Nuclear Materials (ABACC), with the Declaration of Guadalajara, in July of 1991. In addition, a "Quadripartite Agreement", among Brazil, Argentina, ABACC, and the IAEA was drafted that provided for comprehensive safeguards of all nuclear installations in both countries.

The strategic relevance of ABACC is that this is the agency that implements the political decision of mutual inspection between the two countries. It operates with a team of 50 inspectors that are verifying systematically the operations of facilities and are accounting for fissile materials in both nations. The benefits of these procedures are not just at the political level. Total transparency can reveal capacity and intent of the individual national programs. These verification procedures are establishing technical norms for operational safety and in optimizing the results of nuclear technology for commercial civilian use; nevertheless, evidence of mistrust remains.

This agreement between Brazil and Argentina came about in 1987, a time when Brazil was able to enrich nuclear fuel, through the ultracentrifuge process. At present Brazilian authorities are quite skeptical about the IAEA's inspections since Brazil was able to develop this process without the assistance of the nuclear powers. Brazilian authorities are reluctant to ratify the Quadripartite Agreement without clear assurances from the IAEA on how the subsidiary arrangements will be handled when it comes to comprehensive inspections. They mistrust the IAEA, believing that this agency and most of its officials serve the best interests of the nuclear powers. These officials argue that these inspections by the IAEA could serve to disclose commercial secrets of Brazil's remarkable achievments in nuclear development.[26] By Buenos Aires subscribing to the agreement with the IAEA, it cannot deny access to its nuclear installations; otherwise it risks the imposition of sanctions by the UN Security Council.

7.   Conclusion

Brazil's nuclear program was seen by members of the international community as one aimed at developing both military and civilian uses, since this was an explicit policy for Brazil to become a world power. For many decades, Brazil kept this option open on the regional arena and attempted to accommodate and control an atomic arms race with rival Argentina. The developments of cooperation and joint nuclear policy with Argentina has also eliminated the general mistrust that existed for years between the two countries. The proponents of non-proliferation have achieved their goals.

Brazil and Argentina are now on the non-nuclear weapons track, but whether both stay on this track will depend upon developments in the international arena. Even with legal agreements and political promises by Argentina and Brazil of not pursuing nuclear weapons development, this picture may someday change and either or both countries could decide to develop nuclear weapons. This joint development is made possible with the current bilateral instruments; thereby, neither Brazil nor Argentina has to abide by the wisdom of the nuclear powers.

Notes

1.   George Lamazière and Roberto Jaguaribe, "Beyond Confidence-Building: Brazilian-Argentine Nuclear Cooperation," *Disarmament* , Vol. XV, No. 3, 1992, pp. 104-105.
2.   *Foreign Broadcast Information Service (FBIS)/Latin America*, 25 March 1987, p. D1.
3.   On the subject of Brazil's desire to become a major power and its international politics, see Peter Bell, "Brazilian-American Relations" in Riordan Roett (ed.) *Brazil in the Sixties* (Nashville: Vanderbilt University Press, 1972), pp. 77-102; Frank D. McCann, "Brazilian Foreign Relations in the Twentieth Century" in Wayne A. Selcher (ed.) *Brazil in the International System* (Boulder: Westview Press, 1981), pp. 1-23; William Perry, *Contemporary Brazilian Foreign Policy: The International Strategy of an Emerging Power* (Beverly Hills: Sage Publications, 1976) and "Brazil: A Local Leviathan" in W. Rodney and Steven A. Hildreth (eds.) *Emerging Powers* (New York: Praeger Co., 1986), pp. 307-342.
4.   For a most complete survey of Brazil's position on disarmament, see Marcos Castrioto de Azambuja, "Desarmamento -- Posiçoes Brasileiras," in Gelson Fonseca Júnior e Valdemar Carneiro Leao (eds.), *Temas de Política Externa Brasileira* (Brasília: IPRI/MRE, 1989), pp. 177-193.
5.   Robert Jervis, "Cooperation Under the Security Dilemma," *World Politics* XXV (Jan 1978), p. 175; David A. Baldwin, "Thinking About Threat," *Journal of Conflict Resolution* Vol. XV (Mar 1971), p. 72.
6.   Thomas C. Schelling, *The Strategy of Conflict* (Cambridge: Harvard University

Press, 1960,) pp. 37-43.

7. Thomaz G. Costa, "La Percepcion de amenazas desde el punto de vista de los militares brasileros en las decadas del 70 y 80", in Rigoberto Cruz Johnson and Augusto Varas (eds.) *Percepciones de Amenaza y Politicas de Defensa en America Latina* (Santiago, Chile: FLACSO, 1993,) pp. 193-210.

8. Luís Pinguelli Rosa, "A Segurança de Angra I" *Ciência Hoje* Vol. 9, No. 53, 1990, pp. 24-32.

9. About Brazil's naval strategy, one of the few authoritative accounts is Admiral Mario Cesar Flores (Secretary for Strategic Affairs and former Navy Minister) "O preparo da Marinha nos anos 90" *Revista Marítima Brasileira* Vol. 110, Nos. 1/3 (Jan 1990), pp. 13-42.

10. For perhaps the classic contrary view see Kenneth N. Waltz, "Toward Nuclear Peace," in Dagobert L. Brito, Michael D. Intriligator, and Adele E. Wick, (eds.), *Strategies for Managing Nuclear Proliferation*, (Lexington: Lexington Books, 1983); for an optimistic view about the permanence of current trends see George Quester, "Preventing Proliferation: The Impact on International Politics," *International Organization* Vol. 35, No. 1 (Winter 1981), pp. 213-240; for a traditional pessimistic argument, see Leonard S. Spector, "Nuclear Proliferation: The Pace Quickens." *The Bulleting of the Atomic Scientists* Vol. 41, No. 1 (January 1985), pp. 11-14.

11. Leonard S. Spector and Virgina Foran, "Preventing Weapons Proliferation; Should the Regimes be Combined?" *A Report to the Thirty-Third Strategy for Peace*, US Foreign Policy Conference, Oct 22-24, 1992, Warrenton, Virginia (Muscatine: The Stanley Foundation, 1992); Patricia Bliss *et. al., Containing Proliferation: The Contribution of Verification Synergies, Arms Control Verification Studies* No. 5 (Ottawa: The Non-Proliferation, Arms Control and Disarmament Division, Department of External Affairs, 1993).

12. About official positions and records of Brazil's nuclear program, see Rex Nazare Alves, "O Programa Nuclear Brasileiro" 6 Mai 1987 (mimeo.), a presentation to the national Constitutional Commission; and Brazil's Presidência da República, Assessoria de Imprensa, "Brazil Prepara seu Futuro," in *Ministério das Relaçoes Exteriores, Resenha da Política Exterior do Brazil* Vol. II, No. 5, pp. 8-14.

13. The most explicit confirmation that Brazil had a nuclear weapons program comes from former Navy Minister Admiral Maximiano da Fonseca (1981-1986) that stated in an interview that the motivation for the program was "to strengthen de country's independence, demonstrating that it had the capability to manufacture the bomb and thus breaking away the technological apartheid imposed by the countries that already had the nuclear technology capability ... and aiming to retain a colonial control over the countries that did not have such stage of development." *Interview*, (Julho 1993), p. 105. For a series of systematic denials of Brazilian authorities that the country had plans to built nuclear weapons, see FBIS/LA, 28 March 1980, p. D1; 10 August 1982, p. D1; 29 April 1983, p. D4; 10 September 1985, p. D1; 23 October 1986, p. D1.

14. For the theoretical importance of the Prisoner Dilemma game, see R. Ducan Luce and Howard Raiffa, *Games and Decisions* (New York: Wiley Publisher, 1957). For application in international politics, see Kenneth A. Oye, "The Conditions for Cooperation in World Politics" in Robert J. Art and Robert Jervis, (eds.) *International*

Politics, Enduring Concepts and Contemporary Issues (New York: Harper Collins, 1992), pp. 36-50.

15. Christian G. Caubet, "Diplomacia, Geopolítica e Direito na Bacia do Prata" *Política e Estratégia* Vol. II, No. 2 (April-June 1984), pp.337-346. About the relations of the two countries at the time see also R. Saraiva Guerreiro (former Minister of Foreign Relations) *Lembranças de um empregado do Itamaraty* (Sao Paulo: Siciliano, 1992).

16. Daniel Poneman and David J. Myers, "Nuclear Proliferation Prospect for Argentina," *Orbis* (Winter 1984), p. 865.

17. Bertrand Goldschmidt, "A Historical Survey of Nonproliferation Policies," *International Security* Vol. 2, No. 5 (Summer 1977), pp. 69-87.

18. "A Aventura das Centrifugas no Brazil de 1953," *Veja*, 9 September 1987, pp. 24-25.

19. Goldschmidt, *op. cit.* pp. 71-73.

20. Treaty for the Prohibition of Nuclear Weapons in Latin America (Treaty of Tlatelolco), Article 18.

21. Ibid., Article 16.

22. Azambuja, *op. cit.*

23. Ernesto Geisel, :Discurso do President" in *Resenha da Politica Exterior do Brazil,* Vol. XI, No. 42 (Brazilia: Ministerio das Relazoes Exteriores, 1983) p. 14. See also Azambuja, *op. cit.*

24. Interpretation about competition and cooperation between the two countries at the time, see Hélio Jaguaribe, "Brazil-Argentina: breve analisis de las relaciones de conflicto e cooperación." *Estudios Internacionales* Vol. XV, No. 57 (January-March 1982), pp. 9-27; and Wayne A. Selcher. "Brazilian-Argentine Relations in the 1980s; From Wary Rivalry to Friendly Competition." *Journal of Inter-American Studies and World Affairs* Vol. 27, No. 2 (Summer 1985), pp. 25-53. For the analysis of foreign policy and the nuclear cooperation between the two countries, see Monica Hirst and Hector Eduardo Bocco, "Cooperaçao Nuclear e Integraçao Brazil-Argentina" *Contexto International* Vol. 9 (January/July 1989), pp. 63-67.

25. For a critical evaluation of the program and its status, see Paulo Nogueira Batista, "O Acordo Nuclear Brazil-Alemanha", paper presented in the fourth national seminar "60 Anos da Política Externa", Brasília, 8 March 1993.

26. "Técnicos temem inspeção a instalação," *Gazeta Mercantil*, 27 Ago 1993, p. 16.

PART VI

DISARMAMENT, VERIFICATION, AND ECONOMIC CHOICES

Chapter 24
ECONOMIC ADJUSTMENT TO DISARMAMENT: RECENT US EXPERIENCES

Rachel Schmidt[1]

As a result of the collapse of the Soviet Union, many believe that the United States can protect its interests with lower levels of defense spending. Initially, the promise of a "peace dividend" led US policymakers to devise lists of alternative uses for the resources that would have been spent on defense, such as education or crime prevention. But as some of the more difficult consequences of disarmament became apparent (namely lay-offs), there has been some reluctance to cut military spending too quickly and a growing consensus that the federal government should "do something" to ease the restructuring of the economy toward less defense production.

Disarmament is an economic paradox; something so seemingly beneficial for a nation can, in the short run, have very hurtful effects on its economy. If military resources are redirected to reduce the federal deficit or to fund public investments that increase productivity, they will ultimately lead to higher economic growth and a higher standard of living. In the near term, however, the transition to a less defense-oriented economy is painful for many workers, communities, and businesses.

This paper describes the effects of the current defense drawdown on the US economy as well as the debate over the role the federal government might play in easing the transition to lower levels of military production.

1. This Drawdown is Less Severe Than Previous Ones

To those affected by it, the magnitude of today's decline in defense spending seems quite large. Real outlays for defense have been falling since they peaked at $355 billion (in 1994 dollars) over the 1987 to 1989 period. Under levels proposed in early 1993 by the Clinton Administration, annual defense outlays will fall from $277 billion in fiscal year 1994 to $233 billion (in 1994 dollars) by fiscal year 1998—about 34 percent lower than in peak years (see Fig. 1). This decline will bring the ratio of national defense spending to gross domestic product (GDP) to 3.2 percent—its lowest share since before World War II. More cuts in national defense spending would lower this ratio further.

But how does the magnitude of this drawdown compare with earlier eras? In the three-year period just after World War II, defense outlays dropped by nearly seven times what the United States is likely to experience now. During this decade, real defense outlays will fall by more than that after the Korean War and roughly the same as after the Viet Nam War. But relative to all previous drawdowns since World War II, this one is taking place at a slower rate (see Table 1).

The current drawdown is different from previous ones in several ways. On the heels of the 1990-1991 recession, today's defense downturn has been occurring during a period of slow economic growth and job creation. It is coinciding with other structural changes in the economy -- due to foreign competition, technological innovation, and increasing productivity in manufacturing industries -- that are also associated with near term job losses. Pent-up demand for consumer goods that eased reconversion after World War

II is absent today, and unlike previous drawdowns that followed "hot" conflicts, the end of the Cold War may mark permanently lower levels of US defense spending.

Figure 1 National Defense Outlays

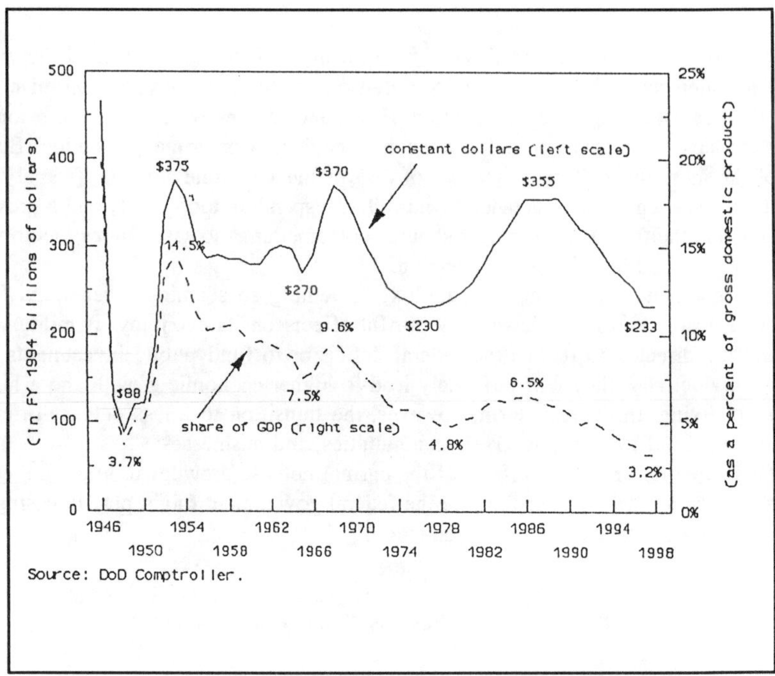

Table 1. Comparison of Defense Drawdowns
(outlays in fiscal year 1994 billions of dollars)

Era	Peak		Trough		Difference		Average Annual % Change
	Year	Outlays	Year	Outlays	Years	Outlays	
World War II	1945	903.8	1948	82.0	3	821.7	-55.1%
Korea	1953	375.3	1956	286.9	3	88.4	-8.6%
Vietnam	1968	370.0	1976	230.3	8	139.7	-5.8%
Current	1989	355.2	1997	232.4	8	122.7	-5.2%

Source: World War II era figures from *Adjusting to the Drawdown* (Defense Conversion Commission, December 1992), p. 11, adjusted to fiscal year 1994 dollars. All other outlay numbers and deflators from *National Defense Budget Estimates for FY 1994* (Office of the Comptroller of the Department of Defense, May 1993).
Note: Includes all national defense spending, including Department of Energy defense activities.

2.   Short-Term Disruptions, Long-Term Growth

What are the economic repercussions of declining defense budgets? Most studies on the issue have had similar qualitative results: the US economy continues to grow, but in the near-term, the drawdown restrains that growth because workers and capital released from defense production may not be put to use immediately. For example, the Congressional Budget Office (CBO) estimated that cuts in 1998 budget authority of $25 billion to $50 billion below what the Bush Administration planned would temper annual GDP growth rates by 0.1 to 0.4 percentage points. CBO also estimated that budget cuts proposed by the Clinton Administration will result in eliminating about 1.4 million defense-related public and private sector jobs between 1992 and 1998.[2] In a study for the Defense Conversion Commission, the Institute for Defense Analysis (IDA) found that the defense downturn is slowing economic growth by less than 0.5 percentage points per year and adding less than 0.4 percentage points to the unemployment rate.[3] IDA concluded that these effects will be a less significant shock to the economy than the oil price increases that the United States experienced during the mid- and late-1970s.

Over the longer term, defense cutbacks could benefit the economy, depending upon how those resources are used. The CBO and IDA studies both argue that when the "peace dividend" is used to reduce the federal deficit, this effectively increases the pool of savings available for investment in productive physical or human capital such as equipment or training. These investments, in turn, are often associated with economic growth. Some alternative types of government spending, such as in carefully chosen research and development projects, may also raise productivity and lead to a higher standard of living. However, government spending that takes the form of transfer payments or tax reductions that simply raise personal consumption are unlikely to have much effect on the economy's long-term growth rate.[4]

Studies such as IDA's note that short-term disruptive effects on the economy are smaller if the "peace dividend" is used for alternative types of government spending or to reduce taxes. In this sense, defense conversion programs (particularly those that support the incomes of laid-off workers) may help mitigate the downturn's effects. There is a long-term, short-term tradeoff; however, if policies that emphasize consumption are used to offset near-term repercussions of military cutbacks, the US economy would miss the longer term economic growth associated with investment.

As the Defense Conversion Commission has argued, overall growth in the economy is key to a successful transition.[5] Because the US economy is so large (with GDP currently on the order of $6.3 trillion), overall economic growth creates far more jobs than could government spending for defense conversion programs.[6] CBO has estimated in its long-term projections that if, over the mid-1990s, the US economy gradually returns to full employment, it would gain approximately 2 million jobs per year. This would more than offset the estimated 200,000 to 300,000 job losses per year over the same period associated with the defense build-down.[7]

3.   Short-Term Economic Effects Are Concentrated

But if the short-term effects of the defense downturn are small relative to the overall economy, why has there been such a clamor for federally-sponsored defense conversion programs? One reason is that estimates of the disruption to the aggregate economy mask the more serious economic effects that are concentrated within certain industries and regions of the country.

Compared with funding for military personnel and defense operations and support, cutbacks historically have tended to hit spending for military equipment the hardest.[8] Over the fiscal year 1989 to 1994 period, outlays for procurement are expected to fall by 35 percent relative to 25 percent for military personnel, 14 percent each for operations and maintenance and military construction, and 12 percent for research, development, test and evaluation programs.

Although defense cutbacks will have little effect on most industries, disproportionate reductions in spending on military hardware will, in turn, affect industries that depend heavily on military contracts. These industries include guided missiles, ordnance, ammunition, shipbuilding, tanks and tank components, search and navigation (communication) equipment, aircraft and missile engines, aircraft and missile equipment, explosives, and complete aircraft.[9] The tank, shipbuilding, and explosives industries are likely to be among the hardest hit.[10] Other than the federal government, industries that are likely to suffer the most job losses as a result of the downturn include wholesale trade, complete aircraft, search and navigation (communication) equipment, guided missiles, and aircraft and missile engines.[11]

Defense-related layoffs are also geographically concentrated. Although businesses in most states receive some military contracts, the bulk of hardware production has taken place in what one analyst refers to as the "gunbelt": the perimeter of states from Seattle and the Silicon Valley down through Southern California, Texas, and Florida and up to Long Island and New England (noticeably omitting the Midwest).[12] These communities benefited from higher defense spending during the 1980s and are now experiencing most of the downturn's effect.

In which states will the effects be most pronounced? Alaska, Hawaii, and Virginia are affected heavily because defense spending accounts for a high percentage (nearly 12 percent) of each of these states' total economic output.[13] California, New York, and Texas are expected to lose the most jobs as a result of the drawdown, but, relative to the size of each state's work force, Connecticut, Virginia, and Massachusetts will be hardest hit.[14]

4.   Role of the Federal Government in Defense Conversion

What role should the federal government play to ease the transition toward less defense production? There are several aspects of this question to consider. Federal programs already exist to ease the effects of economic dislocation, whether due to the decline in defense spending, foreign competition, natural disaster, or other causes. For example, Unemployment Insurance and training programs under the Job Training Partnership Act (JTPA) help workers who have lost their jobs for any reason. Programs that target the defense sector in particular may not be necessary. But if policymakers decide that special defense conversion programs are warranted, should most funding go to workers who have lost their jobs, to communities affected by base closures and layoffs, or to businesses that have, in the past, relied heavily on defense production?

Currently, the Clinton Administration and the Congress are supporting all three varieties of programs, but are especially emphasizing research and development (R&D) to help businesses diversify. In March 1993, President Clinton announced a $19.3 billion defense conversion initiative for the 1993 to 1997 period (see Table 2).

Table 2   Clinton Administration Defense Conversion Initiative
(budget authority in millions of dollars)

	1993	1994	1995	1996	1997	1993-1997
Assistance to defense workers, personnel, and communities	718	1,126	1,148	1,148	1,148	5,288
DoD personnel assistance and community support	693	693	693[a]	693[a]	693[a]	3,465
Department of Energy personnel assistance	25	100	-	-	-	125
Department of Labor displaced worker training	-[b]	300[c]	400[c]	400[c]	400[c]	1,500
Department of Commerce community diversification assistance	-	33	55	55	55	198
DoD dual-use technology reinvestment (incl. TRP)[d]	927	890	890[a]	890[a]	890[a]	4,487
New federal high technology investments[e]	47	1,206	2,329	2,758	3,175	9,515
Grand Total	1,692	3,22	4,367	4,796	5,213	19,290

Source: CBO Paper, *The Technology Reinvestment Project: Integrating Military and Civilian Industries* (July 1993), p. 3

Notes: a.   1994 level—estimates for 1995, 1996, and 1997 will not be available until the DoD completes a comprehensive review of defense programs.
 b. $75 million will be transferred in 1993 from the DoD.
 c.   Portion of larger increase in job training that is expected to be used for displaced defense workers.
 d.   Includes the Technology Reinvestment Project, agile manufacturing, advanced materials partnerships, US-Japan management training, electronics and materials initiative, and small business innovative research refocused to dual-use technologies. Excludes broadened Independent Research and Development reimbursement.
 e.   Includes programs that the Clinton Administration claims will provide "direct conversion opportunities" (for example, Department of Energy industry partnerships and National Aeronautics and Space Administration civil aviation research) and 50 percent of programs that provide "some conversion opportunities" (for example, Department of Commerce programs for information highways, manufacturing and advanced technology). Not included are increases for Enterprise Zones, Community Development Banks, National Science Foundation, highway programs, and the R&D tax credit.

Nearly 50 percent of this funding would finance high-technology R&D projects managed by agencies other than the Department of Defense (DoD). Another 23 percent would support DoD R&D programs that orient contractors toward dual-use technologies -- those with both civil and military applications. The remainder -- just 27 percent of the total -- is directed toward communities and workers through programs in the Defense, Energy, Labor, and Commerce Departments.

Even with $19 billion in new federal spending, the initiative is small relative to the magnitude of military cutbacks that will take place over the same period. In real terms, national defense outlays in fiscal year 1997 will be $64 billion lower than those in fiscal year 1993. Therefore it is unlikely that the initiative will offset many of the resulting near-term job losses.

The programs may, however, promote longer term economic growth. By funding R&D, the conversion initiative appears to emphasize investment over consumption. But implicit in the Administration's plan is a premise that the federal government can select and promote effectively technologies that increase productivity and thereby spur growth.

5. Programs for Workers and Communities

There are a number of programs that assist military personnel, civilian employees of the Departments of Defense and Energy, and private sector workers affected by the drawdown. In some cases the Congress has appropriated funds to DoD that help expand existing programs at other agencies. For example, in fiscal year 1993, DoD transferred $75 million from its budget to the Department of Labor to extend training and employment services provided under the JTPA to former defense workers.

Special programs have been created as well. For example, the Congress established a program to encourage former defense workers to become teachers or to work for local police departments and health care agencies. Similarly, legislation in 1993 created a program that provides scholarships to individuals affected by the drawdown who choose to study waste management and environmental restoration.

Are special programs that target defense workers warranted? In a survey of JTPA Centers in nine states that serve laid-off defense workers, CBO found that they tended to be better educated and had higher average hourly earnings in their last job relative to all JTPA participants.[15] One could argue that because traditional JTPA training programs are oriented toward teaching basic skills, they may be unsuitable for better educated defense workers. Moreover, the nature of some defense work is highly specialized, and skills developed for the military sector may not be easily transferable to the commercial sector.[16]

However, CBO also found that workers at large military contractors tend to have some characteristics that are associated with finding new jobs more quickly. It may be more appropriate for programs like those under JTPA to focus their attention on those individuals who have difficulty finding new jobs. And some analysts argue that, while men and women in the armed forces may deserve some special consideration, private sector defense workers have no greater claim to public assistance than do workers who have lost their jobs in other industries.[17]

Conversion funding for communities is provided largely through two programs. Since it was created in 1961, the DoD's Office of Economic Adjustment (OEA), has been providing grants to communities in which a military facility is being closed. This assistance is not automatic (the affected community must submit a proposal to OEA) and the grants are relatively small in value, but they are intended to help communities make long-range plans for economic development and to reuse base property once military personnel have left.

Funds through the Department of Commerce's Economic Development Administration (EDA) are also distributed to state and local governments affected by "sudden and severe economic dislocations," such as those that can result when defense contractors lose business. EDA grants may be used to help communities develop economic plans, establish revolving loan funds for local businesses, finance employee buyouts of companies, or support other services that otherwise encourage business development.

Policymakers have targeted some conversion aid to communities because the local effects of declining military spending can be so devastating. When a base is closed, for example, local retailers suffer as military personnel leave the community and civilian workers on that base lose their jobs. Finding a new job is especially difficult when local businesses are at higher risk of going under. The base's physical property may not be reused immediately either; some sites are contaminated with hazardous wastes that take time to clean up.[18] But in addition, local governments lose tax revenue just when there is greater demand for support services. Areas with high concentrations of defense contractors face similar obstacles.

As regrettable as these circumstances are, do communities affected by the defense build-down have greater claim to federal assistance than do, say, communities in the Northeast and Midwest that lost manufacturing jobs in the early 1980s?[19] Rather than creating special programs for defense communities, a more even-handed approach would be to provide grants to those localities that face the most severe economic dislocations, whether due to the closing of a tank plant or of a steel mill. The EDA has authority to award grants broadly to any community suffering from dislocations, but in recent years, some have questioned the agency's effectiveness in this role.[20]

6. Assisting the Defense Industrial Base

Perhaps more contentious than support for workers and communities is the debate over whether the federal government should help military contractors adjust to lower defense budgets, and if so, what policies it should use.[21]

During the Cold War, the United States relied on the superior capability of its military equipment to counter overwhelming numbers of weapons held by its chief opponent, the Soviet Union. Although the Cold War has ended, US national security planners continue to place a high priority on building technologically advanced weapons. Because of this strategy, the United States will need some capability to design and build this equipment, but, at the same time, declining US defense budgets raise questions about how many contractors will be needed for the future.

Most companies that manufacture products for DoD are diversified in at least one of two ways: either they produce several types of military goods (e.g., military aircraft parts and defense avionics) or they produce both military and civilian goods (e.g., military trainer aircraft and corporate jets). All firms involved in defense production are feeling the effects of smaller military budgets -- many are laying off employees and trying to sell excess capacity, but those companies that are not well-diversified (in either sense) and face falling government contractual demand will be among those most affected.

Firms are using several different strategies to weather the current industry shake-out. Martin Marietta, for example, has chosen to stick with defense production. It is purchasing what it believes are "top performing" companies that complement its military portfolio and then consolidating the combined assets. Other companies are reducing their defense work and focusing more of their attention on existing or new civilian technologies.

The Clinton Administration hopes to ease the transition for contractors by using three approaches. First, it will try to provide clear signals about the military hardware it intends to procure so that contractors do not hold on to idle workers and capacity out of hope that business will pick up in a year or two.[22] The Administration's recent intensive study of military requirements, known as the Bottom-Up Review, is an effort in that direction. Another example is former Deputy Secretary of Defense William Perry's public pronouncements that by the mid- to late-1990s, most defense market segments will only be about one-third of the size they were during the mid-1980s.[23]

Second, for certain industries that are unique to defense, the Administration plans to consider future industrial production capabilities explicitly in its acquisition decisions today. For example, the Administration would like to buy a third *Seawolf* -- not because the United States needs more nuclear submarines today to protect its interests but because it wants to keep General Dynamic's Electric Boat Division as a viable producer for the future. Armored vehicles and fighter aircraft are other types of military-unique equipment to which this policy will apply.

This form of insurance can be costly. The case of tank production provides one example: the United States is currently upgrading its M1 Abrams tank to the more capable M1A2 model because policymakers want to keep the industrial base active and maintain the ability to modernize tanks. CBO estimated that, depending on the pace of the conversion program, upgrading the M1 could cost in a given year from two to more than ten times as much as laying away the tank production line. If the United States were to "mothball" its assembly lines, it would take more time (72 months) to build up to a surge tank production rate than the likely length of a military contingency operation. But according to CBO estimates, it would even require 56 months to build up a tank line dedicated to an upgrade program to surge rates.[24]

Presumably, the Administration believes that for some defense equipment this policy is less expensive than the cost of reconstituting a design and production capability in the future. Maintaining certain defense-unique industrial capability also provides a hedge against the uncertainties of reconstitution -- how much it would cost and how long it would take. But one risk of this policy is that, in the political arena of budget-making, it may become difficult to agree on which defense sectors are most deserving of support. If DoD maintains more than a few sectors, the costs of this insurance could become excessive.

Third, the Administration wants the military and civilian sectors of the economy to become better integrated. Many of the technologies needed for military equipment such as electronics, computer software, and semiconductors have equivalents in the commercial market; they are often referred to as dual-use technologies. In some cases, defense equipment could benefit from using components available in the civilian sector because they are more capable and less expensive than their military counterparts.

How might the federal government promote civil-military integration? As one means, the Administration and some members of Congress are actively working to reform acquisition laws. Current procurement law is a morass of regulations -- some originally intended to avoid waste, fraud, and abuse, while others were designed to protect secrecy. For example, contractors are required to use unique cost accounting standards, special methods for handling classified information, and build equipment according to detailed military specifications. By waiving regulations for technologies with commercial counterparts, officials hope to broaden the industrial base from which DoD makes its purchases so that it can buy more or better quality goods with its limited budget.[25]

Another strategy adopted by the Administration is to encourage defense contractors to diversify into the commercial sector by procuring civilian high-technology products. Several contractors failed when they tried to enter commercial markets during past defense downturns. Some analysts have attributed this failure to lack of skill in commercial marketing, low capitalization, and inexperience at emphasizing low unit costs in production.[26] These characteristics of defense firms may be less of a competitive weakness in the civilian federal procurement market.

In addition to acquisition reform and civilian procurement, the Congress and the Administration have also created special defense conversion programs in which DoD directly funds R&D projects in dual-use technologies. The programs were created to encourage defense firms to enter commercial markets, to identify fields in which military and civilian R&D can benefit from each another, and to disseminate technology more widely.

Perhaps the best known initiative of this type is the Technology Reinvestment Project (TRP), led by DoD's Advanced Research Projects Agency (ARPA). TRP is a relatively small program that aims to develop and disseminate dual-use technologies by awarding matching funds to groups of firms, nonprofit organizations, national laboratories, and educational institutions that propose collaborative R&D projects.

ARPA received over 2,800 proposals in July 1993 for a total of $472 million in 1993 program funding. Since award recipients must at least match federal funding, the total size of R&D projects under TRP will be on the order of $1 billion. Proposals were reviewed and selected on a competitive basis by technical experts at ARPA, the Departments of Energy, Commerce, and Transportation, the National Aeronautics and Space Administration, and the National Science Foundation. As of early December 1993, 162 projects had been selected to receive $415 million in federal funds. Organizations from all but six states will participate in the projects selected so far, and a final set of awards will be announced by the end of 1993. TRP has strong support in the Congress, which recently appropriated $474 million for the program in fiscal year 1994.

TRP marks a shift in policy because the federal government is choosing and funding applied R&D projects partly on the basis of their commercial potential. Historically, agencies such as NSF have supported basic research, and DoD has funded both basic and applied R&D so long as it has had military application. But previous administrations have largely left the financing of applied civilian R&D projects to the private sector. Programs like TRP make up part of the Administration's technology policy, which is aimed at encouraging organizations to develop their research into commercial products or manufacturing processes. Administration officials believe that by funding and selectively promoting applied generic R&D (the development of technologies useful among several industries), the federal government can improve the productivity and competitive position of US businesses.[27]

But while promoting economic growth through investment in R&D may be an admirable goal, it is important to consider whether programs in which the federal government selects R&D projects are the most effective way to achieve economic growth. It is difficult to establish and maintain methods for the government to select among research projects based on technical and commercial merit rather than other motives. And, once funds are provided, it is even more difficult to evaluate the effectiveness of that assistance, particularly when organizations might have pursued the R&D on their own. Given these difficulties, it is not surprising that funding for certain projects can become entrenched politically and hard to discontinue.

Even in the case of TRP, there are pressures to politicize the awards process. For example, the Congress earmarked about $123 million (24 percent) of total funding for TRP in the 1993 defense appropriations conference report.[28] Authorizing legislation requires that ARPA award TRP funds competitively, and this instruction was even reiterated explicitly for 1994 appropriations when the Congress adopted an amendment introduced by Representative George Brown of California. Nevertheless, nearly $104 million out of $474 million for the dual-use programs was earmarked in 1994 conference report.[29] The Administration and ARPA have devoted much attention to running the program in a careful manner and they appear to be selecting projects based on their technical merit. Nonetheless, there is pressure to politicize this process and executive branch agencies may still choose to fund earmarked projects in programs other than TRP.

7. Summary

Studies on the effects of the decline in military spending suggest that the US economy will continue to grow in the 1990s, but its rate of growth will be impeded slightly by the drawdown. Industries that are heavily reliant on defense contracts, such as shipbuilding and tank production, will face more severe effects, however. These industries tend to be geographically concentrated, and the negative effects from lower levels of defense spending are particularly magnified in the communities in which they are situated. Near-term disruptive effects of the drawdown can be mitigated somewhat by alternative government spending programs or reductions in taxes, but the economy would then miss the benefits of longer-term growth associated with investment.

The Clinton Administration has chosen a combination of short-term assistance programs and public investment in worker training and R&D projects for longer-term growth. Its five-year conversion initiative will provide more than $5 billion for training and reemployment services to former defense workers and planning grants to communities affected by the drawdown. But clearly it has chosen to emphasize assistance to the industrial base most heavily; nearly three-fourths of the funding (some $14 billion) focuses on civilian and dual-use R&D projects like those sponsored by TRP.

Some of this funding is being used to create new programs that target the defense sector. But it is difficult to argue that workers, communities, and firms that have relied on defense production are more deserving of federal support than those in other industries which have suffered from economic dislocations. If policymakers want to provide assistance, it would be more even-handed to expand funding for and improve the administration of programs that are available to all workers, communities, and businesses, such as retraining provided under the Job Training Partnership Act or community assistance provided by the Economic Development Administration.

Alternative policies to new spending for defense conversion programs do exist. The federal government could, for example, institute R&D tax credits for certain categories of technology, such as those with dual-use. Tax incentives are attractive to some analysts because the private sector would initiate projects and would bear the risks of R&D. Alternatively, the Administration could emphasize deficit reduction rather than new spending on conversion programs, which in turn would expand savings and might promote broad investment in physical and human capital.

The size and structure of US defense conversion programs will be contentious issues throughout the remainder of the decade. But it is important to note that, within the current range of debate on federal conversion policy, the magnitude of spending will not offset many near-term job losses associated with the drawdown. Nor should it; by using the peace dividend for deficit reduction or carefully choosing public investments that increase productivity, the United States could obtain a higher standard of living.

Notes

1. The views expressed here are solely the author's.
2. Congressional Budget Office Paper, *Effects of Alternative Defense Budgets on Employment* (April 1993).
3. David R. Graham, An-Jen Tai, and Barbara A. Bicksler, *Defense and the Economy* (Institute for Defense Analysis Paper P-2810, January 1993).
4. CBO, *The Economic Effects of Reduced Defense Spending* (February 1992), pp. 5-7, and David Graham et al., *op. cit.*
5. *Adjusting to the Drawdown* (Report of the Defense Conversion Commission, December 31, 1992), pp. 13-14.
6. By the same token, one might argue that when defense spending is kept at a level higher than that needed to protect US national security interests, it is unlikely to "save" as many jobs as the number that would have been created if that spending had been invested.
7. CBO Paper, *Reemploying Defense Workers: Current Experiences and Policy Alternatives* (August 1993).
8. Because military production now accounts for a smaller share of US GDP, today's declines in procurement spending will have smaller repercussions than did those in previous downturns. Nonetheless, if historical patterns continue, procurement will face a steeper fall than other categories of defense spending.
9. For estimates of the defense share of these and other industries, see Edward Knight, "The Economy and the Shrinking Defense Budget," *Congressional Research Service Review* (April-May 1992), pp. 9-12.
10. CBO, *Effects of Alternative Defense Budgets on Employment, op. cit,* p. 18.
11. Norman Saunders, "Employment Effects of the Rise and Fall in Defense Spending," *Monthly Labor Review* (April 1993), pp. 3-10.
12. Ann Markusen, et al., *The Rise of the Gunbelt* (New York: Oxford University Press, 1991).

13. CBO, *Effects of Alternative Defense Budgets on Employment, op. cit,* pp. 20-21.
14. *Adjusting to the Drawdown, op. cit.,* pp. 41-42.
15. CBO, *Reemploying Defense Workers: Current Experiences and Policy Alternatives, op. cit,* p. 10. Note that CBO's survey was not based on a random sample.
16. Ibid. pp. 19-22.
17. C.R. Neu and Michael Kennedy, *Do We Need Special Federal Programs to Aid Defense Conversion?* (RAND Issue Paper, February 1993).
18. CBO Paper, *Environmental Cleanup Issues Associated with Closing Military Bases* (August 1992).
19. Neu and Kennedy, *op. cit.*
20. For example, the Defense Conversion Commission noted that, prior to fiscal year 1994, recent Administration budgets proposed to eliminate EDA entirely. Uncertainty over its future may have hampered the agency's effectiveness. See *Adjusting to the Drawdown, op. cit,* p. 48.
21. For an earlier discussion of these issues, see CBO Special Study, *Economic Conversion: What Should Be the Government's Role?* (January 1980).
22. Anthony Velocci, Jr., "Perry Forges New Shape for Industry," *Aviation Week and Space Technology* (November 15, 1993), pp. 52-57.
23. Velocci, p. 53.
24. CBO Paper, *Alternatives for the US Tank Industrial Base* (February 1993).
25. "Meet Mr. Procurement Reform," *Washington Technology* (May 6, 1993), pp. 5, 10.
26. Murray Weidenbaum, "A New Battle Plan for Defense Contractors," *The American Enterprise* (July/August 1991), pp. 10-13.
27. President William J. Clinton and Vice President Albert Gore, Jr., *Technology for America's Economic Growth, A New Direction to Build Economic Strength* (February 22, 1993).
28. CBO Paper, *The Technology Reinvestment Project: Integrating Military and Civilian Industries* (July 1993), p. 33.
29. "Brown Likens Appropriations Process to Game of Musical Chairs," *FYI,* electronic news service published by the American Institute of Physics (December 10, 1993).

Chapter 25

THE TRADE IN MISSILES AND THE FUTURE OF DISARMAMENT: LESSONS FOR CONTROLLING ADVANCED WEAPONS SYSTEMS

Michael O. Wheeler

The trade in missiles and missile technology provides a productive subject for anyone interested in studying future trends in arms control and the economic consequences of arms control activities. This is true for at least three reasons. First, when President Clinton spoke to the United Nations General Assembly in the fall of 1993, he said *inter alia*:

> I am proposing ... new steps to thwart the proliferation of ballistic missiles. Recently, working with Russia, Argentina, Hungary and South Africa, we have made significant progress toward that goal. *Now we will seek to strengthen the principles of the Missile Technology Control Regime [MTCR] by transforming it from an agreement on technology transfer among just 23 nations to a set of rules that can command universal adherence.*[1] (emphasis added)

These remarks suggest that the MTCR is about to move more into the mainstream of arms control policy. They also invite a renewed examination of what kind of regime (rules, principles, practices, institutions) for missile trade can reasonably be expected to elicit universal support. That is one of the themes which will be discussed in this paper.

A second reason for studying the missile trade is that missiles have become one of the most ubiquitous features of late twentieth century high-technology warfare. The 1991 Persian Gulf War demonstrates this phenomenon. Thousands of missiles of some two dozen or more types were fired during the two-month battle in early 1991. In fact, the very first weapons of the allied counteroffensive were missiles: Hellfire missiles fired from helicopters and Tomahawk cruise missiles launched against Baghdad. Missiles were used by the belligerents to attack urban population centers, hardened military facilities, aircraft, armored vehicles, ships, other missiles, and so forth. America (for the first time in combat) used conventional versions of the advanced air-launched and sea-launched cruise missiles which it had acquired as part of its Cold War strategic inventory. Iraqi ballistic missiles, although used with conventional warheads, were capable of carrying weapons of mass destruction. In addition to using high-explosive warheads, the allies employed missiles which relied on so-called 'non-lethal' weapons effects. Drones (a type of unmanned aerodynamic missile) were employed for reconnaissance and to confuse enemy radar. It is also instructive to recall that the satellites which provided critical support to the coalition effort had been placed in orbit by space launch vehicles whose boosters were functionally equivalent to (in some cases had been) long-range strategic weapon delivery systems produced for different missions during the Cold War.

The MTCR has tended in the past to focus mainly on ballistic missiles with ranges over 300 kilometers capable of carrying nuclear weapons, on the assumption that those are the most destabilizing weapons whose use (or threat of use) could expand the scope of (and in other ways complicate) an otherwise limited confrontation.[2] Although the desire to control these longer-range missiles has been linked with their potential to deliver weapons of mass destruction, most experts agree that missiles can be a significantly destabilizing factor in major regional conflicts, even when employed in so-called 'conventional' roles.

Egypt's acquisition of the self-propelled SA-6 and the man-portable SA-7 missiles, for instance, contributed significantly to Egypt's success in seizing the initiative in the early phases of the 1973 Middle East War.[3] Exocet missiles in the Argentine inventory in 1982 almost tipped the balance in the Falklands/Malvinas Islands fighting.[4] The Reagan administration worried a great deal about Chinese Silkworm missiles supplied to Iran, not because of their nuclear potential but because of the threat they posed to commercial and naval vessels in the Persian Gulf.[5] Saddam Hussein came close to achieving his strategic goal of dividing the allied coalition, simply by attacking Israel with conventionally armed ballistic missiles.

The strategic impact of ballistic missiles capable of carrying weapons of mass destruction and targeted against urban centers at a great distance is demonstrably important as a destabilizing factor. This, however, should not lead us to ignore the other ways in which missiles can (and do) affect regional conflicts. The firepower, ability to penetrate defenses, and symbolic qualities of missiles influence the milieu for regional conflict in numerous ways. Modern missile systems have been optimized over the past 50 years to allow delivery of an enormous variety of weapons against a wide range of targets at, near, or far removed from the immediate battlefield, day and night, in virtually all weather conditions. Missiles are extremely flexible instruments of war.

Thus, virtually any category of missile can, given the right circumstances, be a major factor in regional affairs. The examples discussed in this paper hint at the difficulty of distinguishing offensive from defensive missiles, strategic from tactical missiles, or missiles which are designed to deliver weapons from other kinds of missiles.[6]

This context is important because it helps highlight one of the reasons why trade in missiles and missile technology is such an enormously complex subject to attempt to control. One question of interest to this discussion is whether the technologies associated with missiles characterized in terms of such a specific mission (e.g., those acquired to deliver weapons of mass destruction) can be isolated and controlled without, in effect, seeking to control virtually all aspects of missile trade. Even a casual perusal of the MTCR Equipment and Technology Annex shows the lengths to which one must go in order to try to plug loopholes and prevent circumvention of a seemingly straightforward restriction on missiles capable of delivering weapons of mass destruction.

Finally, studying the missile trade is important because of the economic questions associated with attempts to restrict that trade. Here, the opportunities for detailed inquiry are endless. This paper will focus on four broad economic issues and their implications: (a) the conversion of missile-related defense industries to civilian missions; (b) the civilian-military mix in research and development on missile technologies; (c) the relationship between missile technologies and national economic competitiveness; and (d) the contribution of missile technologies and industries to long-term economic growth.

1. Missile Technologies

The MTCR aims at controlling trade in missile *technology,* not simply trade in missiles. Technology is a broad topic which includes the tools, materials, and techniques needed to carry out engineering plans and designs.[7] Modern missile technologies often are divided into six general categories: (a) structures and materials; (b) propulsion systems; (c) guidance and control systems; (d) payloads; (e) testing and development; and (f) infrastructure. This last category includes the intricate process and production activities which are associated with missile industries, and the specialized equipment and procedures to maintain and operate missile systems.

In 1984 Aaron Karp published one of the earliest pieces calling for the United States "to initiate discussions aimed at establishing a missile suppliers' regime." At the time, unpublicized talks already were underway on the MTCR, which makes Karp's article all the more worth citing because it appears to record the major premise behind MTCR policymaking in the early 1980s, i.e., that a suppliers' consortium led by the United States could have a major and lasting impact on Third World missile programs.

Karp's arguments were sophisticated and well-documented, but employed arguable assumptions about (a) the status of missile programs already underway in the Third World; (b) the progress which determined nations could make even if denied access to most Western missile technology; and (c) the prospects of circumventing export controls. Overall, the article communicated the theme that missile technology was beyond the capabilities of most Third World nations.[8] Events of the 1980s have proved otherwise.

Guided missiles may be viewed as extraordinarily complex technical systems, and although it is true for many missiles, this can also be misleading. What makes a guided missile a "canonical complex system" is not so much the technologies it incorporates as the care and precision needed to assemble a number of technologies into a finished product, and to translate that process from simply producing hand-crafted prototypes to a high-volume production line.[9] Acquiring experience in producing complex systems other than missiles is, of course, one of the roads to developing an indigenous capability for missile production.

David Kay has pointed out a feature of the Iraqi nuclear program. This is also relevant to other nations' missile programs, as Kay explains:

> The Iraqis defeated the export control regimes [for nuclear weapons] not because of the ineptness of the regime or because of corruption, but because they learned that they did not have to buy a final assembled instrument with everything they wanted. If they could buy it in parts from three different countries and had the proper project management skills, they could put it together themselves.[10]

Nations like Iraq can legally, and largely above board, assemble an array of engineering and management talent for modern high-tech programs. General Motors was about to build a large truck self-assembly plant in Iraq prior to the Kuwait invasion. GM's senior management wanted to sell a technology enhancement program to the Iraqis as part of the deal, but backed off after a GM team of experts visited Iraq and found the state of Iraqi process engineering to be exceptionally advanced. "The Iraqis were making three-axis computer numerically controlled machine tools of their own," David Kay points out, "and doing electron beam welding."[11] Iraq did not need GM's aid.

One way to break out of the corrosive mindset that only the most state-of-the-art industrial nations can master advanced technologies is to recall some salient themes in modern studies of how technologies have been pursued in the past by different cultures, using early missile technology as the model. Technically, a missile is any "object that is, or is designed to be, thrown, dropped, projected, or propelled, for the purpose of making it strike a target."[12] The earliest missiles were rocks or sticks that prehistoric man picked up and hurled at animals (or at other prehistoric men).[13] Missiles developed relatively slowly during the first several hundred millennia, primarily through advances in materials and propulsion. Until the discovery and application of gunpowder, missiles were limited to ranges of less than half a kilometer, something like the following:

<u>Missiles Propelled By</u>	<u>Range</u>
Unassisted arm (stone, spear)	50 meters
Sling	100-200 meters
Simple or Composite bow	200-250 meters
Handheld crossbow	200-250 meters
Longbow	250-400 meters
Catapult	300-450 meters

The discovery of gunpowder in the early eighth century A.D. (and its application by the twelfth century to military purposes) led to successive increases in missile range.[14] Early artillery pieces (bombards) could propel objects at targets up to two kilometers, and unguided rockets had achieved ranges on the order of three kilometers by the early nineteenth century, in the form of so-called Congreve rockets.[15] Of course, the quantum leaps in range came in the twentieth century. The massive artillery piece used by the Germans in the siege of Paris in World War I (the so-called Paris Gun) could fire projectiles to a range of 130 kilometers.[16] The V-1 (cruise missile) of World War II typically operated at ranges of 200-300 kilometers, while the V-2 (ballistic missile) operated at distances of about 300 kilometers.[17] Within two decades of the V-2, modern Intercontinental Ballistic Missiles (ICBMs) with ranges exceeding 5500 kilometers were a reality.

By the early 1990s, missiles and missile technologies have proliferated widely throughout the world. China and North Korea today have the most active production lines for longer-range surface-to-surface missiles, and relatively advanced missile systems have been (and in some cases, still are being) pursued by Argentina, Brazil, India, Israel, Pakistan, South Africa, South Korea, and Taiwan. Leonard Sullivan points out the wider phenomena encountered by American policymakers:

> The United States is discovering to its dismay that technological superiority ... is not an American birthright. The spread of technology is uncontrollable, and technological leadership migrates toward the best educated, most motivated, and most industrious people.[18]

Contemporary missile proliferation reflects this tension. So does the long history of evolving missile technology in the vastly different cultures around the world.

There are numerous instances in military history where governments seek to keep innovative weapons out of the hands of enemies. As one might expect, this approach to policy proves to be the rule in international relations, not the exception. It is difficult to identify clearcut cases where a nation over a long period of time has been denied a technology which it seeks with determination, skill, and persistence.[19] It appears that while embargoes, blockades, sanctions, and less dramatic means of intervening in weapons trade (like export controls) can slow the pace of technology transfer and affect near-term military balances, they cannot prevent technology diffusion over the longer term.

Technology transfer is itself a misleading phrase. The deficiency of the concept "is that it implies a process in which the recipients of a new technique passively adopt it without modification. The reality is that transfers of technology nearly always involve modifications to suit new conditions, and often stimulate fresh innovations."[20] Or as Walter G. Vincenti writes: "Artifactual design is a social activity directed at a practical set of goals intended to serve human beings in some direct way. As such, it is intimately bound up with economic, military, social, personal, and environmental needs and constraints."[21]

This later observation is relevant because of the importance of missiles to so many aspects of modern combat. This suggests that any nation today wanting to field a competent military force will place a high premium on acquiring missile systems and may adapt or modify those systems in unexpected ways. In fact, it is difficult to find an organized military today that does not have at least some types of missiles in its inventory, no matter how poor the country.[22] One also finds a trend in the Third World to diversify sources of arms and military technology in order to reduce external dependence.[23] This is associated with wider agendas, including the dynamics of domestic civil-military relations, the creation of industries to generate near-term export profits, and a concern for developing technical bases which contribute to long-term growth. More will be said of this last factor later in this paper.

2.   Aerospace Industries And Missile Trade

The story of modern missiles cannot be separated from the more complex story of the evolution of the aerospace industry in the twentieth century. 'Aerospace' is emphasized because any advanced aircraft company can put together a cruise missile sector, and commercial missile companies also have the capacity to develop and produce ballistic missiles.

The contemporary American aerospace industry is one of the premier technical institutions of the twentieth century.[24] It evolved over the course of some eighty years, led partly by inspired entrepreneurship in the changing marketplace, sometimes with heavy doses of technology and technical assistance from abroad, and always (at least until the early 1990s) was within the wider national security demands generated by two World Wars and a Cold War.[25] The American Government provided much of the high-risk venture capital for this industry at critical junctures, was its largest market, and sponsored much of the research and development which nurtured its growth.

There is a broad consensus among economists that America's economic strength this century has, in complicated and sometimes subtle ways, been associated with investment in technology. Nowhere is this better seen than in the aerospace industry which today accounts for almost 10% of all American exports of manufactured goods.[26] The aerospace industry also has played an especially important role with respect to the advances in technology that are most relevant to industrial productivity. Jacques S. Gansler points out:

> Those who investigate the issue of productivity tend to look in detail at three specific areas: manufacturing technology, research and development, and management innovation. For example, the economist Joseph Schumpeter stated that a nation's long-term economic growth is driven primarily by technological innovation in three major categories: process innovation (advanced manufacturing tools and techniques), product innovation (through research and development), and management innovation (through the development and application of new management techniques).[27]

Western aerospace sectors (especially in the United States) played a dominating role with respect to all three categories of technological innovation in the 1950s and 1960s, as well as providing a market for other high-tech products (e.g., electronics, information systems) and stimulating the development of other major multi-use technologies (e.g., radar).

Like all industries heavily dependent on the defense sector, the American aerospace sector today is going through a mass transition marked by high levels of uncertainty and confusion. Some of the forces behind the transition represent the natural reallocation of resources in the aftermath of the Cold War, but others appear to reflect ongoing structural changes in the global economy. There is an emerging consensus that American industries must adjust or be left behind. A dominant theme in the last presidential campaign was that America's continued economic competitiveness requires a fundamental restructuring of the government-industry relation. This theme coincides with the view that more investment is needed in civilian or dual-use technologies and less in specifically military technologies; that the defense industrial base must somehow be integrated into the nation's commercial base; that a leaner Defense Department must use more commercially-available technologies and components; and that a significant portion of the defense technology base should contribute more directly to civilian applications.[28]

The American aerospace industry today faces shrinking markets at home and abroad. Military sales have been declining, and there is no government policy yet on how much excess capacity is needed to maintain for mobilization in an emergency, nor is there any clear indication of the outcome of the industrial policy debate. Restructuring major American aerospace companies already was underway prior to the end of the Cold War. From 1987 to 1989, the sector of the US economy selling aerospace goods and services to the federal government saw its sales decline by 25% and began adjusting accordingly. A review of the contemporary trade literature on the US aerospace industry suggests the following major trends for the immediate future:

-- continued cuts in workforces;[29]

-- more mergers and acquisitions;[30]

-- more efforts to diversify;[31]

-- more multifirm and multinational teaming arrangements;

-- purchase of an increasing number of components abroad (so-called 'global sourcing');

-- looking for expanded opportunities to co-develop civilian and military products and to reduce the existing restrictions on commercialization of defense-related technologies;[32] and
-- seeking expanded exports.

These trends coincide with emerging emphasis in the Defense Department on a defense technology base and acquisition system which: (a) make do with lower budgets; (b) have fewer major program starts; (c) seek high-payoff modifications to existing systems; (d) develop fieldable prototypes which can be tested and then put on the shelf until needed; (e) explore more single-product systems to satisfy multiple mission requirements; and (f) invest in leveraging technologies, especially those associated with command, control, communications, computers, and intelligence (C^4I).

These factors have been discussed at such length because they affect the aerospace industries in all the major industrialized countries today. They suggest a future in which commercial and military sectors are significantly less distinct from one another and in which multinational arrangements multiply. It is not impossible to enforce export controls in that kind of milieu, but it will be much more difficult than it has been in the past or is today.[33] These changes are taking place at a time when the aerospace industry in Russia also is more active than ever in seeking foreign markets for its products and services.[34] The vast expertise of the former Soviet aerospace establishment already is diffusing into Third World settings. These changes also take place against the backdrop of a changing global economy in which the aerospace industries of at least three of the larger industrializing countries (China, India, and Brazil) are emerging as significant factors in international political affairs.[35]

Not surprisingly, the goal of expanding Western aerospace exports contributes to suspicions on the part of less developed countries that the thus-far largely Western-led effort to control the trade in missiles reflects market as well as arms control forces, and may be no more than a thinly-veiled attempt to protect comparative strengths and dominant markets during a time of disruptive transition. The Chinese argue, for instance, that the West is hypocritical in seeking to control missile exports tightly while promoting the export of advanced fighter/strike aircraft. India argues the case for an indigenous space launch capability.[36] Others make similar arguments across the wider range of aerospace products, commercial and military.[37]

Theories of long-term economic growth increasingly stress the role of investment in technology and education as major factors in productivity growth, and therefore in the growth of the income and wealth of nations.[38] The United Nations Conference on Trade and Development (UNCTAD) and similar forums are likely to see the theme of technology transfer moving more to the front of Third World agendas in the 1990s, as the international community seeks a new, post-Cold-War consensus on the norms, principles, and institutional practices that should govern international trade.[39]

Taken by itself, the trade in missiles today is a relatively insignificant amount of overall world trade. In the 1980s, for instance, world trade averaged about \$2 trillion a year. The entire trade in military systems and services amounted to something on the order of 2% of global trade, while trade in missiles was no more than a small fraction of the global and military accounts.[40] As has been suggested, however, the economic and political questions raised by restricting transfer of the sorts of technologies controlled by the MTCR are broader than simply the issue of current trade balances. They get to the heart of the role of technology in the late twentieth and early twenty-first centuries. These economic and political questions drive economic growth and emphasize the importance of the aerospace industry in providing a framework for the evolution of advanced technologies.

3.   Universal Rules For Missile Trade?

The argument can be made that it is in America's security interest to try to prevent countries like Libya or Iran from acquiring the most advanced missile systems today or to intensify efforts to calm down the arms races in the Middle East and South Asia. It makes a great deal of difference for arms control policy, however, how these goals are conceived. Thus far, American policymakers have tended to treat the MTCR less like the Cold War institution of COCOM (the Co-ordinating Committee on Multilateral Export Controls) and more like the supplier consortiums for nuclear exports (the London Group) or for chemical exports (the Australian Group). Independent of the issue of difficulty in restricting trade in missile technology, this approach is not sustainable because of the norms involved.

The concept of a chemical (or biological) weapons control regime has been universalized, i.e., the norm is to ban the development, possession, and use of those weapons. The concept of a nuclear weapon control regime is not as clear, since there is no clearcut mandate for nuclear-weapon states party to the Nuclear Nonproliferation Treaty (NPT) to eliminate their nuclear weapons.[41] The dual-use technologies associated with chemical, biological, and nuclear weapons, moreover, do not lend themselves to as many applications as those associated with missiles.

What is the arms control goal for missile weapons? Seeking to ban all types of missiles clearly is impractical and utopian, on a par probably with attempts earlier this century to ban aircraft or submarines. This paper has just scratched the surface of the extent to which modern militaries rely upon missiles and the technologies they embody.

Some suggest a ban on certain types of weapons, e.g., banning all "ballistic" missiles, or banning all ground-launched ballistic and cruise missiles whose range is over 500 kilometers (the latter being a sort of global INF). These schemes raise enormous problems of circumvention and verification. Air defense missiles -- which presumably would not be banned -- can (and have been) converted to ground-attack modes. Microelectronics and advances in propulsion and structures are rendering moot the distinction between unguided tactical rockets and longer-range ground attack systems, and with nanoengineering breakthroughs on the horizon, this distinction will be even less relevant in the future. The Multiple Launch Rocket System (MLRS), which is becoming the artillery component of choice in many modern militaries, can be used to launch a variety of the sorts of missiles which probably would be prohibited under a universal INF regime. Unmanned aerial vehicles are appearing in increasing numbers across the globe. The difficulties experienced by American and Soviet negotiators in INF and START pale in comparison to the difficulties facing negotiators trying to cope with circumvention of a wider sort of ban on missiles.

All that might be surmountable, however, or at least acceptable politically as part of a long and involved negotiation, were it not for the background question of space launch activities. Possessing a space industry is the obvious and likely easiest way to circumvent any universal arms control regime for ballistic missiles. As recognized in the MTCR, space launch is a universal right.[42] Unless the United States and other major nations are willing to place their space launch activities under an IAEA-like safeguard system or to pursue plans to otherwise internationalize and control space launch activities, it is difficult to envision achieving for missiles the sort of norms that are pursued for weapons of mass destruction.

It will be difficult, if not impossible, to achieve a new set of rules that can command universal adherence if those rules are based upon clearcut double standards or if they protect the important equities of only one set of adherents. No regime to control missiles can be justified or sustained if it begins with the premise that some nations are allowed national space programs, while others are denied the right to such programs. Nor can the regime be based upon arguments by Western nations that it is economically unsound over the long run for larger industrializing nations to pursue indigenous aerospace industries.[43]

4.   Conclusions

The first conclusion drawn from this analysis is that American policy is best served by viewing the MTCR as: (a) a consortium of major suppliers (not a normative regime); (b) a deterrent and delaying barrier against some nations' easily acquiring the most advanced missile programs; (c) part of an overall plan to cope with more fundamental regional instabilities driven by complicated (and sometimes seemingly intractable) political factors; and (d) an element of foreign policy decisions on important bilateral questions.[44] Viewed in this light, the politics of MTCR will be more like the politics of negotiating terms in the General Agreement on Trade and Tariffs (GATT), and less like the politics of a global INF. Each nation will seek to protect comparative advantages, but most nations are likely to agree to some degree of MTCR restrictions because overall interests are served by not allowing unrestricted and accelerating proliferation of advanced missiles globally.

Second, the future of attempts to control the proliferation of advanced conventional weapons from the militaries of the major industrial powers to the militaries of the Third World cannot, for the most part, build directly upon the MTCR experience. The association of longer-range missile delivery systems with weapons of mass destruction provides a minimum rationale for sustaining an MTCR-like system, even though that system also affects the much wider military equation of missile systems delivering advanced conventional weapons, non-lethal weapons, and payloads performing other military missions. If this association with weapons of mass destruction were removed, it would be far more difficult to cut the political deals and defend the MTCR in public debate than has been the case. This does not preclude regional arms control arrangements for conventional weapons.[45] Such arrangements will depend, however, on forces other than those involved in the genesis and evolution of the MTCR.

Notes

1. President Bill Clinton, Address to the United Nations General Assembly, *New York Times*, September 28, 1993, p. A16.
2. The MTCR began as an agreement among the G-7 trading partners (the United States, Japan, Great Britain, France, Germany, Italy, and Canada) to coordinate and reconcile their national systems for regulating export of missile technologies. There is considerable confusion in public discussion as to what it means to "belong" to the MTCR. The 23 nations cited by President Clinton are known, in MTCR parlance, as "partners". An MTCR partner has the right to participate in MTCR plenary meetings, six of which have taken place since 1987 (next plenary: Interlaken, Switzerland, November 30-December 2, 1993). The current 23 MTCR partners include all members of the Organization of Economic Cooperation and Development (OECD) except for Turkey. Argentina and Hungary are the two nations most likely to next attain "partner" status.

    Although the MTCR from its inception in 1987 has covered cruise as well as ballistic missiles, most attention has been paid to the latter. The parameters in the original April 1987 guidelines were designed against limiting the risk of nuclear proliferation by controlling transfers that could make a contribution to nuclear weapons delivery systems other than manned aircraft. For a Category I ballistic missile (against which the most   stringent reviews would be applied, with a strong presumption of denying such transfers), the operational criterion was capability of delivering at least a 500 kilogram payload to a range of at least 300 kilometers. In January 1993 the criterion was revised to extend the strong presumption of denial to the transfer of missiles intended for delivering chemical or biological weapons as well as nuclear weapons. Biological payloads can be much smaller and lighter than nuclear payloads. Thus, while the 500 kilogram/300 kilometer was not explicitly eliminated from the guidelines, the change allows for more restrictive assessment of whether a technology transfer will be approved, even if it involves a missile below the former quantitative guidelines, since lighter payload weight can be traded for greater range.
3. Early post-war analyses probably attributed too much to the SA-6 and SA-7. It appears now that it was the combination of those weapons with the emergence of a massive, integrated surface-to-air missile (SAM) and anti-air artillery (AAA) defense network that forced the Israeli air force to switch its attack priorities to concentrate on SAM-suppression tasks during the crucial early phases of the war. See Anthony H. Cordesman and Abraham R. Wagner, *The Arab-Israeli Conflicts, 1973-1989, The Lessons of Modern War*, Vol. I (Boulder: Westview Press, 1990), pp. 82-85.
4. At the start of the war, Argentina had about half a dozen AM-39 air-launched Exocet missiles and a slightly larger stockpile of MM-38 ship and land-launched Exocets. An Exocet struck and sank the frigate *Sheffield*, while another sank the large container ship *Atlantic Conveyor*. The destroyer *Glamorgan* was hit by a shore-fired Exocet but survived the attack.

    It is misleading to conclude that Argentina would have won the war if only it had more air-launched Exocets in its inventory. However, even given the weaknesses in Argentine strategy and execution (especially the arguments between the Argentine Air Force and Naval Aviation elements on where to concentrate attacks), more air-launched Exocets and a deliberate Argentine campaign against British logistics could have changed the war's outcome dramatically. See Anthony H. Cordesman and Abraham R. Wagner, *The Afghan and Falklands Conflicts, The Lessons of Modern War,* Vol. III (Boulder: Westview Press, 1991), pp. 319-323 and Lawrence Freedman and Virginia Gamba-Stonehouse, *Signals of War: The Falklands Conflict of 1982* (Princeton: Princeton University Press, 1991), pp. 288-290, 358-361, and 379-380.

5.   Caspar Weinberger discusses Iranian acquisition of Silkworm missiles and the threat they pose to tankers in the Persian Gulf, at length in his memoirs, *Fighting for Peace: Seven Critical Years in the Pentagon* (New York: Charles Scribner's Sons, 1993). It is interesting to note that Weinberger does not discuss the MTCR (not even in a footnote) in his memoirs, nor do any of his senior colleagues from the Reagan administration, despite the fact that the MTCR was negotiated in diplomatic circles from 1983 to 1987. See Ronald Reagan, *An American Life* (New York: Simon and Schuster, 1990); and George P. Shultz, *Turmoil and Triumph: My Years as Secretary of State* (New York: Charles Scribner's Sons, 1993).

6.   Defining "weapon" for arms control purposes is notoriously difficult. Questions raised by Congress during ratification of INF required follow-on negotiations, after initial signature of the treaty, on what was meant by "weapon" in the phrase "any ground-launched ballistic missile or cruise missile in the 500-kilometer to 5500-kilometer range that has been flight-tested or deployed to carry or be used as a weapon." Weapon was agreed to mean "any warhead, mechanism or device which, when directed against any target, is designed to damage or destroy it" -- a definition applied to current and future technologies. See the May 1988 exchange of notes between the United States and the Soviet Union, reprinted in US Arms Control and Disarmament Agency, *Arms Control and Disarmament Agreements: Texts and Histories of the Negotiations* (Washington, DC: US Government Printing Office, 1990), pp. 449-452. This definition was carried over into the START treaty.

7.   Robert S. Sherwood and Harold B. Maynard, "Technology," in Sybil P. Parker, (ed.), *McGraw Hill Encyclopedia of Engineering,* 2d ed. (New York: McGraw Hill, 1993), p. 1224. I add the concept of "materials" to their definition.

8.   See Aaron Karp, "Ballistic Missiles in the Third World," *International Security* (Winter 1984-85), pp. 166-195.

9.   Richard B. Nelson of Columbia University points out: "In some [industries], the products take the form of complex systems. Our respondents [to a study of 'commercial' technologies] from industries producing aircraft and guided missiles, canonical complex systems, reported that it would cost a competent imitator three-fourths or more of what the innovator invested to come up with something comparable, that considerable time would be involved as well, and that it did not matter much whether or not there were patents. Producing complex systems effectively requires that many components and details be got right, and this is difficult to learn to do even if one has a model to take apart, or a blueprint to follow. These industries, and others like semiconductors, also involve complex production processes with tooling and equipment often finely tuned to product design. Simply getting the production line in place and running right can yield the inventor a substantial lead over potential followers." This passage is taken from Professor Nelson's article,

"What is 'Commercial' and What is 'Public'," in Nathan Rosenberg, Ralph Landau, and David C. Mowery, *Technology and the Wealth of Nations* (Stanford: Stanford University Press, 1992), p. 63.

10. David Kay, "Iraqi Inspections: Lessons Learned." Talk given for the Program of Nonproliferation Studies, Monterey Institute of International Studies, Februar, 10, 1993.

11. Ibid.

12. Sybil P. Parker, (ed.), *McGraw Hill Dictionary of Scientific and Technical Terms,* 4th ed. (New York: McGraw Hill, 1989), p. 1211.

13. There is evidence from the Lower Paleolithic era (circa 500,000 BC) of a Neanderthal skeleton clearly marked by the impress of a spearpoint. See Chester G. Starr, *A History   of the Ancient World,* 4th ed. (New York: Oxford University Press, 1991), p. 10.

14. The earliest gunpowder (called at the time "black powder") appears to have been invented in China sometime around AD. 700. Black powder is a mixture of sulfur, charcoal, and saltpeter (potassium nitrate). Sulfur occurred naturally in volcanic regions, charcoal was produced from by heating wood, and saltpeter results from the decay of animal or vegetable material *in situ,* under appropriate conditions. The composition of the mixture determines its use (and was the 'secret' that early societies tried to protect). The relatively low detonation velocity of some gunpowder mixtures was what made it suitable for propelling projectiles. Much of the investment in perfecting black powder mixtures from the 16th to 19th century was driven by its commercial as well as military uses, i.e., its use as a blasting powder for mining and for excavating waterways and in ceremonial firework displays. See A. Bailey and S.G. Murray, Explosives, *Propellants and Pyrotechnics* (London: Brassey's, 1989); Wernher von Braun and Frederick I. Ordway III, T*he Rocket's Red Glare* (Garden City: Anchor Press, 1976); and "Gunpowder," *The Way Things Work: An Illustrated Encyclopedia of Technology,* Vol. I (New York: Simon and Schuster, 1967), pp. 448-449.

15. During a three-day siege of Copenhagen in 1807, the British navy fired 40,000 Congreve rockets at the city. The resulting fire destroyed three-quarters of the buildings in Copenhagen and led the Danish authorities to capitulate on British terms.

16. It is interesting to note that twice the range of the Paris Gun was one of the design parameters adopted by the German military as a requirement for the V-2 program. For a comprehensive discussion of the V-2 program, see Frederick I. Ordway III and Mitchell R. Sharpe, T*he Rocket Team: From the V-2 to the Saturn Moon Rocket* (Cambridge: The MIT Press, 1982).

17. The V-1 was a cheap, simple, rugged cruise missile, constructed out of thin sheet metal and powered by a very simple motor using standard 75 octane aviation fuel. The V-2 was a more expensive, demanding system. Both achieved results that far outweighed their so-called "military value", in terms of impact on British morale, disruption of British activities (including shutting down factories while workers went to cover), and reallocation of allied air power from other missions to deal with the V-weapon threat. This "lesson" was relearned by allied forces in the Persian Gulf

War of 1991, when an Iraqi campaign using modified Scuds (whose basic design essentially was that of the V-2) achieved very similar results.

18. Leonard Sullivan, Jr., "The Defense Budget in Transition," in Joseph Kruzel, (ed.),*1993 American Defense Annual*, Mershon Center, Ohio State University (New York: Lexington Books, 1993), p. 26.

19. Works consulted in reaching this conclusion include Bernard and Fawn M. Brodie, *From Crossbow to H-Bomb: The Evolution of the Weapons and Tactics of Warfare*, revised ed. (Bloomington: Indiana University Press, 1973); Martin van Crevald, *Technology and War from 2000 BC to the Present* (New York: The Free Press, 1989); R. Ernest Dupuy and Trevor N. Dupuy, *The Encyclopedia of Military History from 3500 BC to the Present*, 2d ed. (New York: Harper & Row, Publishers, 1986); and Lynn Montross, *War Through the Ages*, 3d ed. (New York: Harper & Row, Publishers, 1960).

20. Arnold Pacey, *Technology in World Civilization* (Cambridge: The MIT Press, 1990), pp. 50-51.

21. Walter G. Vincenti, *What Engineers Know and How They Know It: Analytical Studies from Aeronautical History* (Baltimore: The John Hopkins University Press, 1990). p. 11.

22. According to the IISS *The Military Balance, 1992-1993*, even Bangladesh has a frigate and four smaller patrol craft armed with the Chinese *Hai Ying*-2 missile.

23. For instance, see Kwang-Il Baek, Ronald D. McLaurin, and Chung-in Moon, (eds.), *The Dilemma of Third World Defense Industries: Supplier Control or Regional Autonomy?* (Boulder: Westview Press, 1989).

24. There is no totally satisfactory way of distinguishing the American "aerospace industry" from other closely related industries. In the May 31, 1993, "Industry Scorecard" issue of *Aviation Week & Space Technology*, 29 US companies are listed under the heading "aerospace"; however, another 173 US companies also are listed in three categories closely related to "aerospace": "electronics and computers," "airline leasing & related," and "diversified & others." And this listing leaves out hundreds of other US companies (large and small) that have sectors highly involved in aerospace activities, e.g., providing engineering services to NASA.

25. For the history of the American aerospace industry, I rely heavily on three works: Wayne Biddle, *Barons of the Sky: From Early Flight to Strategic Warfare: The Story of the American Aerospace Industry* (New York: Henry Holt and Co., 1991); Walter A.McDougall, ... *The Heavens and the Earth: A Political History of the Space Age* (New York: Basic Books Inc., 1985); and Harry Wulforst, *The Rocketmakers: The Dreamers Who Made Space Flight a Reality* (New York: Orion Books, 1990).

26. The US Department of Commerce compiles statistics on US trade. In 1992 the United States exported $448.2 billion of merchandise, $368.5 billion of which was represented by manufactured goods. Of those manufactured goods, $33.9 billion (almost 10% of America's exports in manufactured goods) came from the US aerospace industry. These figures come from US Department of Commerce, *US Foreign Trade Highlights, 1992* (Washington, DC: US Government Printing Office, June 1993).

27. Jacques S. Gansler, *Affording Defense* (Cambridge: The MIT Press, 1989), p. 88.

28. In preparing this discussion, I drew upon a number of sources, including: US Congress, Office of Technology Assessment, *Holding the Edge: Maintaining the Defense Technology Base* (Washington, DC: US Government Printing Office, April 1989); US Congress, Office of Technology Assessment, *Arming Our Allies: Cooperation and Competition in Defense Technology* (Washington, DC: US Government Printing Office, May 1990); Ashton Carter and Gerald Epstein, "Defense Research and International Competitiveness," in Eric H. Arnett, (ed.), *New Perspectives for a Changing World Order* (Washington, DC: American Association for the Advancement of Science, 1991), pp. 207-219; John A. Alic *et al.*, (eds.), *Beyond Spinoff: Military and Commercial Technologies in a Changing World* (Boston: Harvard Business School Press, 1992); US Congress, Office of Technology Assessment, *Building Future Security: Strategies for Restructuring the Defense Technology and Industrial Base* (Washington, DC: US Government Printing Office, June 1992); US Congress, Office of Technology Assessment, *Defense Conversion: Redirecting R&D* (Washington, DC: US Government Printing Office, May 1993); and the standard trade journals that cover the Pentagon.

29. An estimated 34,000 workers were laid off in the defense sector of the American aerospace industry from 1987 to 1989 alone, before the major restructuring of the 1990s began. The numbers now are much higher.

30. For instance, Lockheed acquired Sanders Associates in 1986; Loral acquired Ford Aerospace in 1989; GE acquired RCA's Astro Space Division in 1986, which was subsequently acquired by Martin Marietta in 1993 for $3 billion. *The Economist of London* points out in its October 2, 1993, issue: "Faced with shrinking demand and one main customer, defense companies deserve some relief from anti-trust rules that stand in the way of needed mergers." p. 17.

31. Efforts to diversify by large aerospace companies have mixed records. Grumman tried unsuccessfully to build buses in the 1970s, for instance, and Boeing failed in its attempt to build hydrofoils. These and other examples are cited in an article on defense conversion in *The Economist of London*, October 2, 1993, p. 17.

32. The highest priority critical technologies receiving the bulk of DoD funding in the early 1990s have near-term commercial applications, e.g., fiber optics, simulation and modeling, and composite materials.

33. Robert B. Reich, formerly on the faculty of Harvard's John F. Kennedy School of Government and currently US Secretary of Labor, published a provocative book in 1991 entitled *The Wealth of Nations*. Reich argued that corporate alliances and mergers across borders, combined with a world shrunk through efficiencies in telecommunications and transportation, are making it increasingly futile to try to inhibit the flow of knowledge, much less finished or semifinished products. Reich concludes: "By the last decade of the twentieth century, governments could successfully block at their national borders few things other than tangible objects weighing more than three hundred pounds."

34. One of the most recent MTCR decisions for American policymakers involved blocking the $350 million deal between the Indian Space Research Organization (ISRO) and the Moscow-based commercial arm of the Russian space organization (Glaskosnos), in which Russia had agreed to sell two cryogenic rocket engines and supporting technology to India. Washington began discussing the issue with

Moscow in late 1990 and applied increasing pressure in 1992 and 1993. Moscow finally agreed in July 1993 not to sell the manufacturing technology, at which time India indicated it was not interested in only acquiring the engines. This complicated transaction adversely influences US-Indian relations, probably cost the Russians millions of dollars more in business opportunities in India, catalyzed additional efforts in India for self-reliance, and involved (as a *quid pro quo*) expanded cooperation between America and Russia in space projects. For a good overview of the scope of the Russian space industry, see Gregory H. Canavan, *Former Soviet Republic Capabilities in Space and Science* (Los Alamos: Los Alamos National Laboratory, February 1993).

35. American policymakers have focused a great deal of energy and attention on China as a supplier of advanced missile technologies (especially the M-9 and M-11) to the Middle East and South Asia. In August 1993 Washington announced sanctions against China because of Chinese missile sales to Pakistan. China expressed indignation at this action. For context on the scope and complicated politics of Chinese missile sales, see Richard A. Bitzinger, *Chinese Arms Production and Sales to the Third World*, RAND Note N-3334-USDP (Santa Monica: RAND, 1991); R. Bates Gill, *Chinese Arms Transfers: Purposes, Practices, and Prospects in the New World Order* (Westport: Praeger, 1992); Gordon Jacobs and Tim McCarthy, "China's Missile Sales -- Few Changes for the Future," *Jane's Intelligence Review* (December 1992), pp. 559-563; John W. Lewis, Hua Di, and Xue Litai, "Beijing's Defense Establishment: Solving the Arms-Export Enigma," *International Security* (Spring 1991), pp. 87-109; and John W. Lewis and Hua Di, "Chinese Ballistic Missile Programs: Technologies, Strategies, Goals, *International Security* (Fall 1992), pp. 5-40.

36. For instance, Indian Prime Minister P. V. Rao, in protesting the American move to block Russian missile-technology sales to India, said in August 1993 that India would not give up its "right" to acquire missile and space technology, adding that companies in the United States, France, Russia, and China are competing to launch future Indian communications satellites, and asserting that the United States was attempting to protect market share. India already has developed lower-thrust cyrogenic engines and was seeking through the deal with Moscow to acquire the capability to produce 12-ton upper stage engines powered by liquid oxygen (LOX) and liquid hydrogen. This, added to its solid-fuel lower stages, would give it the capability to launch INSAT-type satellites into geosynchronous orbit, thus not having to pay for services abroad in the $3.2 billion annual market for commercial satellite launches. This is a case where both sides are correct. Washington is correct in claiming that the Indians have used their space launch program to help develop military missiles and that an improved Indian cyrogenic capability could (probably would) contribute directly to longer-range ballistic missiles. India is correct in claiming that it has a legitimate commercial/civilian use for the cyrogenic technology.

37. More recently, the theme of a renewed American thrust to penetrate foreign markets appears in reactions to airline routes abroad. On September 17, 1993, the *Bangkok Post* reported that a meeting in Bangkok of chief executives of the 15 Asia-Pacific airlines that are members of the Orient Airlines Association (OAA) had been advised by their Australian aviation consultant that emerging US policy supporting the efforts

of US airlines to penetrate Asian markets formed the prelude to "'a declaration of war' by the US aviation and aeronautical industry, which is said to be determined to resist anyone standing in its way of global domination."

38. See, for instance, "Explaining the Mystery," in *The Economist Yearbook: 1992 in Review* (London: The Economist Books Ltd., 1993), pp. 248-250; and Rosenberg, Landau, and Mowery, (eds.) *Technology and the Wealth of Nations.* The *Economist* article provides a brief, non-technical discussion of the more prominent theories of long-term economic growth. The Stanford volume, which is an outgrowth of the Technology and Economic Growth Program at Stanford's Center for Economic Policy Research, provides more technical discussion of the theme.

39. See the chapter on "Technology and International Relations," in Robert S. Walters and David H. Blake, *The Politics of Global Economic Relations*, 4th ed. (Englewood Cliffs: Prentice Hall, 1992).

40. These figures are extrapolated from the discussion in Congress of the United States, Office of Technology Assessment, *Global Arms Trade: Commerce in Advanced Military Technology and Weapons* (Washington, DC: US Government Printing Office, June 1991). I do not attempt to quantify the overall trade in missiles or missile technologies and services because of (a) definitional ambiquities of the sorts discussed earlier in the paper on what to include in missile trade; and (b) the fact that many nations do not publicize the details of such trade, making attempts by third parties to characterize it (even in broad terms) highly problematic.

As for the costs associated with missile programs (whether pursued domestically or abroad), the following examples provide some context. During World War II, Germany spent about $3 billion (in then-year dollars) on its V-missile programs. This was about $1 billion more than the United States spent at roughly the same time on the Manhattan Project. The 1988 Chinese sale of CSS-2 (DF-3) missiles to Saudi Arabia was worth an estimated $2 billion. Reports in the South Korean press in the summer of 1993 cited Israeli officials estimating that North Korea would lose about $1 billion if it suspended its military sales (mainly missiles) to the Middle East. Russia's total space budget in 1991 was an estimated $3.4 billion.

41. Article VI of the NPT establishes the goal of complete disarmament for all Parties to the NPT. There is no requirement for nuclear abolition apart from that goal.

42. The most recent fact sheet on the MTCR issued by the US Arms Control and Disarmament Agency states: "The MTCR Partners recognize that the technology used in ballistic missiles is virtually identical to that used in space launch vehicles and that there are several countries whose missile or space launch vehicle projects would enable them to export missile technology. The MTCR Guidelines have been designed not to impede national space programs or international cooperation in such programs as long as such programs could not contribute to delivery systems for weapons of mass destruction."

43. It is difficult to support that argument if national goals are long-term development and growth, given the Western experience in what an aerospace industry does in stimulating and contributing to the overall technology base of a country.

44. The recent American decisions with respect to applying sanctions because of Russian-Indian and Chinese-Pakistani missile trade (discussed in earlier footnotes) reflect a continuing tension in executive-congressional relations in the United States,

totally independent of the merits of the cases. Title XVII of the National Defense Authorization Act for Fiscal Year 1991 (P.L. 101-510, November 5, 1990) amended the Arms Export Control Act (AECA) and the Export Administration Act (EAA) to require imposition of sanctions against US and foreign "persons" for specific missile proliferation activities. Section 323 of the Foreign Relations Authorization Act for Fiscal Years 1992 and 1993 (the Helms amendment) amended the AECA sanctions enacted in 1990 with the main effect of broadening the sanctions triggered by proliferation activities. In these and related instances, Congress has moved to restrict the president's room for maneuver in dealing with a nation involved in questionable missile trade activities. For the MTCR to be a more effective policy tool in the complicated world of missile trade, the American President needs considerably more flexibility than now is allowed by the law.

45. Nations in many regions reject the European models (CFE and CSCE) as not appropriate to their specific needs.